THE COLLECTED WORKS OF W. B. YEATS

George Bornstein, George Mills Harper, and Richard J. Finneran,
General Editors

VOLUME I THE POEMS
ed. Richard J. Finneran

VOLUME II THE PLAYS
ed. David R. Clark and Rosalind E. Clark

VOLUME III AUTOBIOGRAPHIES
ed. William H. O'Donnell and Douglas N. Archibald

VOLUME IV EARLY ESSAYS
ed. Richard J. Finneran and George Bornstein

VOLUME V LATER ESSAYS
ed. William H. O'Donnell with Elizabeth Bergmann Loizeaux

VOLUME VI PREFACES AND INTRODUCTIONS
ed. William H. O'Donnell

VOLUME VII LETTERS TO THE NEW ISLAND
ed. George Bornstein and Hugh Witemeyer

VOLUME VIII THE IRISH DRAMATIC MOVEMENT
ed. Mary FitzGerald and Richard J. Finneran

VOLUME IX EARLY ARTICLES AND REVIEWS
ed. John P. Frayne and Madeleine Marchaterre

VOLUME X LATER ARTICLES AND REVIEWS
ed. Colton Johnson

VOLUME XI MYTHOLOGIES
ed. Jonathan Allison

VOLUME XII JOHN SHERMAN AND DHOYA
ed. Richard J. Finneran

VOLUME XIII A VISION (1925)
ed. Catherine E. Paul and Margaret Mills Harper

VOLUME XIV A VISION (1937)
ed. Margaret Mills Harper and Catherine E. Paul

THE COLLECTED WORKS
OF W. B. YEATS

VOLUME XIII

W. B. YEATS

A Vision (1925)

EDITED BY
Catherine E. Paul
and Margaret Mills Harper

Scribner
NEW YORK   LONDON   TORONTO   SYDNEY

SCRIBNER
A Division of Simon & Schuster, Inc.
1230 Avenue of the Americas
New York, NY 10020

First Scribner hardcover edition March 2008

SCRIBNER and design are trademarks of Macmillan Library Reference USA, Inc.,
used under license by Simon & Schuster, the publisher of this work.

For information about special discounts for bulk purchases,
please contact Simon & Schuster Special Sales:
1-800-456-6798 or business@simonandschuster.com

Text set in Sabon

Manufactured in the United States of America

1   3   5   7   9   10   8   6   4   2

Library of Congress Control Number: 88027365

ISBN-13: 978-0-684-80733-1
ISBN-10: 0-684-80733-5

In memory of
George Mills Harper
and
Richard J. Finneran

CONTENTS

Editors' Preface and Acknowledgments   *xi*

Abbreviations   *xiii*

Illustrations   *xix*

Editors' Introduction   *xxi*

A Vision

Dedication   *liii*

Introduction   *lvii*

Book I—What the Caliph Partly Learned   1

Book II—What the Caliph Refused to Learn   95

Book III—Dove or Swan   145

Book IV—The Gates of Pluto   179

Textual Matters and Notes

Notes   213

Corrections to the Yeatses' Copies of A Vision *(1925)*   339

Emendations to the Copy-Text   353

End-of-Line Word Division in the Copy-Text   365

Index   367

EDITORS' PREFACE
AND ACKNOWLEDGMENTS

This edition, like all scholarly work on W. B. and George Yeats, would not be possible without the generosity of the Yeats family, especially the late Senator Michael B. Yeats and the late Anne Yeats. For many years, they have given of their family's resources as well as their own time and energy to provide unparalleled assistance to scholars. In particular, their gift of W. B. and George Yeats's library and occult papers to the National Library of Ireland has made possible new levels of scholarly investigation of *A Vision*. We are grateful to Michael B. and Gráinne Yeats for their great and ongoing kindness.

The editors gratefully acknowledge the assistance of Walter Kelly Hood and Connie Hood, former designated editors of *AVA* and *AVB* in this series, who shared with us the results of many years of labor as they passed the project on to us. We are grateful to Jonathan Allison, Alan Baragona, George Bornstein, Terence Brown, Wayne K. Chapman, Elizabeth Butler Cullingford, Michael de Nie, Stephen B. Dobranski, the late Richard J. Finneran, R. F. Foster, Christine Gallant, Warwick Gould, Eloise Grathwohl, Mary Jane Harper, James Hirsh, Nancy Kojima, Scott Lightsey, George Maalouf, Elizabeth Muller, Claire Nally, William H. O'Donnell, Ann Saddlemyer, Ronald Schuchard, James Shimkus, Malinda Snow, Maria Thanassa, Deirdre Toomey, Michael Vickers, and the Yeats Society of Sligo. Thanks are due to Rebecca Drummond at the Georgia State University Library; Dr. Stephen Ennis at Woodruff Special Collections, Emory University; Peter Kenny, Tom Desmond, Ciara McDonnell, and Nicola Ralston at the National Library of Ireland; Charles McNamara at the Walter Royal Davis Library at the University of North Carolina at Chapel Hill; Kristen Nyitray and F. Jason Torres at the William Butler Yeats Microfilmed Manuscripts Collection,

Special Collections Department, Frank Melville, Jr., Memorial Library at the State University of New York at Stony Brook; and staff at the British Library and the Robert Muldrow Cooper Library at Clemson University. Emily Benthall Weathers, Charis Chapman, and Stefanie Peters, research assistants to Professor Paul, gave invaluable assistance. Richard W. Stoops provided unparalleled technical support. We thank the Department of English and College of Architecture, Arts and Humanities at Clemson University and the Department of English at Georgia State University for support of this project. Samantha Martin, our editor at Scribner, has been of immense help, and we are more than grateful for her management and expertise.

We wish especially to acknowledge the work of George Mills Harper. In addition to invaluable published work and personal assistance, he left extensive files that have helped us immeasurably in understanding WBY's methods of composition and the ordering of many manuscripts and typescripts, not to mention drawing our attention to significant aspects of the genesis of *AVA* and helping with transcriptions of WBY's nearly illegible handwriting. We have also drawn on notes he made to himself in his copy of *CVA* after its publication, as he continued his work on the Yeatses' occultiana. This edition is deeply indebted to Harper's immense knowledge and scholarly precision.

ABBREVIATIONS

AS   Automatic Script (see *YVP* 1–2)

Au   *Autobiographies.* Edited by William H. O'Donnell and Douglas N. Archibald. *The Collected Works of W. B. Yeats 3.* New York: Scribner, 1999.

AVA   W. B. Yeats. *A Vision.* London: T. Werner Laurie, 1926.

AVB   W. B. Yeats. *A Vision.* 1937. London: Macmillan, 1962.

Burnet   John Burnet. *Early Greek Philosophy.* London: Adam and Charles Black, 1892. (O'Shea 308)

CF   Card File (see *YVP* 3)

CVA   *A Critical Edition of Yeats's* A Vision *(1925).* Edited by George Mills Harper and Walter Kelly Hood. London: Macmillan, 1978.

DMR-MS   "The Discoveries of Michael Robartes" manuscript (see *YVP* 4)

DMR-TS   "The Discoveries of Michael Robartes" typescript (see *YVP* 4)

DMR-UMS   "The Discoveries of Michael Robartes" untitled manuscript (see *YVP* 4)

Duhem   Pierre Duhem. *Le système du monde: Histoire des doctrines cosmologiques de Platon à Copernic.* 10 vols. Paris: Librairie Scientifique A. Hermann et Fils, 1913–59.

EAR   *Early Articles and Reviews.* Edited by John P. Frayne and Madeleine Marchaterre. *The Collected Works of W. B. Yeats 9.* New York: Scribner, 2004.

EE   *Early Essays.* Edited by Richard J. Finneran and George Bornstein. *The Collected Works of W. B. Yeats 4.* New York: Scribner, 2007.

Enc Rel Eth   *Encyclopaedia of Religion and Ethics.* Edited by

James Hastings. 13 vols. Edinburgh: T. & T. Clark, 1908–26. (O'Shea 855)

Erdman   *The Complete Poetry and Prose of William Blake.* Revised edition. Edited by David V. Erdman. New York: Random House (Anchor Books), 1988.

Ex   *Explorations.* Selected by Mrs. W. B. Yeats. London: Macmillan, 1962.

Foster   R. F. Foster. *W. B. Yeats: A Life.* 2 vols. Oxford and New York: Oxford University Press, 1997, 2003.

FPS   *Frank Pearce Sturm: His Life, Letters, and Collected Work.* Edited by Richard Taylor. Urbana: University of Illinois Press, 1969.

Gibbon   Edward Gibbon. *The History of the Decline and Fall of the Roman Empire.* Edited by J. B. Bury. 7 vols. London: Methuen, 1909–14. (O'Shea 746)

GY   George Yeats

Hobby   Diana Poteat Hobby. "William Butler Yeats and Edmund Dulac: A Correspondence, 1916–1938." PhD diss., Rice University, 1981.

IDM   *The Irish Dramatic Movement.* Edited by Mary FitzGerald and Richard J. Finneran. *The Collected Works of W. B. Yeats 8.* New York and London: Scribner, 2003.

JSD   *John Sherman* and *Dhoya.* Edited by Richard J. Finneran. *The Collected Works of W. B. Yeats 12.* New York: Macmillan, 1991.

L   *The Letters of W. B. Yeats.* Edited by Allan Wade. London: Rupert Hart-Davis, 1954.

LE   *Later Essays.* Edited by William H. O'Donnell with Elizabeth Bergmann Loizeaux. *The Collected Works of W. B. Yeats 5.* New York and London: Charles Scribner's Sons, 1994.

LNI   *Letters to the New Island.* Edited by George Bornstein and Hugh Witemeyer. *The Collected Works of W. B. Yeats 7.* New York: Macmillan, 1989.

LWBY   *Letters to W. B. Yeats.* Edited by Richard J. Finneran, George Mills Harper, and William M. Murphy.

2 vols. (continuous pagination). New York: Columbia University Press, 1977.

Mem   *Memoirs: Autobiography—First Draft, Journal.* Transcribed and edited by Denis Donoghue. London: Macmillan, 1972.

Milton   John Milton. *Complete Poems and Major Prose.* Edited by Merritt Y. Hughes. New York: Odyssey Press, 1957.

Myth1   *Mythologies.* New York: Macmillan, 1959.

Myth2   *Mythologies.* Edited by Warwick Gould and Deirdre Toomey. London: Palgrave Macmillan, 2005.

MYV   George Mills Harper. *The Making of Yeats's A Vision: A Study of the Automatic Script.* 2 vols. Carbondale and Edwardsville: Southern Illinois University Press, 1987.

NLI   National Library of Ireland / Leabharlann Náisiúnta na hÉireann. Holdings cited by manuscript number.

OED   Oxford English Dictionary

O'Shea   Edward O'Shea. *A Descriptive Catalog of W. B. Yeats's Library.* New York and London: Garland, 1985. Cited by item number.

P&I   *Prefaces and Introductions.* Edited by William H. O'Donnell. *The Collected Works of W. B. Yeats 6.* New York: Macmillan, 1989.

Plays   *The Plays.* Edited by David R. Clark and Rosalind E. Clark. *The Collected Works of W. B. Yeats 2.* New York and London: Scribner, 2001.

Poems   *The Poems.* Edited by Richard J. Finneran. 2nd edition. *The Collected Works of W. B. Yeats 1.* New York: Scribner, 1997.

Saddlemyer   Ann Saddlemyer. *Becoming George: The Life of Mrs W. B. Yeats.* Oxford: Oxford University Press, 2002.

SB   *The Speckled Bird.* Edited by William H. O'Donnell. 2 vols. Dublin: The Cuala Press, 1973–74.

SDNB#   Sleep and Dream Notebook (see *YVP 3*)

Shelley   Percy Bysshe Shelley. *Poetical Works.* Edited by Thomas Hutchinson, corrected by G. M. Matthews.

	Oxford and New York: Oxford University Press, 1970.
Synge	J. M. Synge. *Collected Works.* 4 vols. London: Oxford University Press, 1962–68.
UP#	*Uncollected Prose by W. B. Yeats.* Edited by John P. Frayne and Colton Johnson (vol. 2 only). 2 vols. New York: Columbia University Press, 1970, 1976.
VersB	Version B manuscript (see *YVP* 4)
VNB#	*Vision* Notebooks (see *YVP* 3)
VP	*The Variorum Edition of the Poems of W. B. Yeats.* Edited by Peter Allt and Russell K. Alspach. Sixth printing. New York: Macmillan, 1973.
VPl	*The Variorum Edition of the Plays of W. B. Yeats.* Edited by Russell K. Alspach with Catharine C. Alspach. New York: Macmillan, 1966.
Wade	Allan Wade. *A Bibliography of the Writings of W. B. Yeats.* 3rd edition. Revised and edited by Russell K. Alspach. London: Rupert Hart-Davis, 1968. Cited by item number.
WBY	William Butler Yeats
WWB	*The Works of William Blake.* Edited by Edwin John Ellis and William Butler Yeats. 3 vols. London: Bernard Quaritch, 1893. (O'Shea 220); New York: AMS Press, 1979.
YA	*Yeats Annual.* Edited by Warwick Gould.
YAACTS	*Yeats: An Annual of Critical and Textual Studies.* Edited by Richard Finneran.
YGD	George Mills Harper. *Yeats's Golden Dawn.* London: Macmillan, 1974.
YO	*Yeats and the Occult.* Edited by George Mills Harper. Yeats Studies Series. Toronto: Macmillan, 1975.
YVP	*Yeats's Vision Papers.* 4 vols. George Mills Harper, general editor, assisted by Mary Jane Harper. Vol. 1, *The Automatic Script: 5 November 1917–18 June 1918*, edited by Steve L. Adams, Barbara J. Frieling, and Sandra L. Sprayberry. Vol. 2, *The Automatic Script: 25 June 1918–29 March 1920*, edited by Steve L. Adams, Barbara J. Frieling, and Sandra L. Spray-

berry. Vol. 3, *Sleep and Dream Notebooks,* Vision *Notebooks 1 and 2, Card File,* edited by Robert Anthony Martinich and Margaret Mills Harper. Vol. 4, *"The Discoveries of Michael Robartes,"* Version B (*"The Great Wheel"* and *"The Twenty-Eight Embodiments"*), edited by George Mills Harper and Margaret Mills Harper. London: Macmillan, 1992; Palgrave, 2001.

ILLUSTRATIONS

1. [Frontispiece of *A Vision*]   *l*
2. [Title page of *A Vision*]   *li*
3. [Copyright page of *A Vision*]   *lii*
4. The Great Wheel   *lviii*
5. [Unicorn]   9
6. [Lunar Phases]   14
7. [Gyres as Lines]   104
8. [Gyres as Cones]   105
9. [Gyres of Destiny and Will, Fate, and Mind]   109
10. [Approaching and Separating Gyres]   110
11. [Contracting and Expanding Gyres]   110
12. [Gyres "placed one within the other"]   111
13. [Gyres of the Four Faculties]   112
14. [Solar and Lunar Circles]   113
15. [Solar and Lunar Months]   115
16. [Solar and Lunar Year]   116
17. [Solar and Lunar Gyres]   118
18. [Gyres of Principles and Faculties]   119
19. ["simplest form" of "History Cone"]   134
20. [Cones of "entire Era"]   135
21. The Historical Cones   147

EDITORS' INTRODUCTION

I

A Vision appeared in the dead of winter. On 15 January 1926, the London publisher T. Werner Laurie distributed to subscribers six hundred signed copies of W. B. Yeats's occult mythography.[1] As recently as the previous July, WBY had indulged in high-flown hope for it, telling Laurie, "I dare say I delude myself in thinking this book my book of books."[2] However, Laurie and WBY had long known that, as WBY mentioned understatedly in March 1923, "the book is entirely unlike any other work of mine and will not appeal to the same public."[3] They estimated correctly that a limited print run would be best. *A Vision* was a handsome volume, with light blue paper boards, parchment half-binding, woodcuts by Edmund Dulac printed on brown paper, and untrimmed pages, with one striking diagram of "historical cones" in both red and black ink. It was appropriately expensive, selling for £3.6s.[4] It was reviewed by WBY's old friend and fellow mystic Æ and seemed to disappear soon afterward.

By spring, WBY wrote to Olivia Shakespear that the book's reception "reminds me of the stones I used to drop as a child into a certain very deep well. The splash is very far off and very faint" (*L, 712*). The lack of response does not seem to have disturbed him, however: WBY ends the letter to Shakespear fantasizing whimsically about founding "an Irish heresy" with his few readers on his side of the Irish Sea. Interestingly, a tone approaching levity pervades much of his correspondence about the book, both before and after publication. To some degree, such a tone is attributable to simple relief: WBY had been compiling and composing the book for years, struggling to get the philosophy right, the structure intelligible, the prose understandable, the details consistent. It had taken nearly ten years to receive, sort through, and present the "system" outlined in the book. That system had brought with it extraordinary changes in his life and work, and it had been no easy task to come to terms with it all. By 1925, upward of ten thousand manuscript and typed pages of queries, replies, notes, outlines, charts, diagrams, drafts, revisions, and corrected proofs—including nearly four thousand pages of automatic script (AS), four hundred pages in journals, six hundred alphabetized index cards, and over two thousand sheets of handwritten as well as scribally typed drafts—stand testament to the difficulty of arriving at 256 published pages.[5] As WBY put it to Laurie, "getting a book of this sort into print is a reverse of the Christian miracle for one has to turn twelve basketfuls of fragments into—is it not?—two loaves and two little fishes—a greater miracle than the other."[6] Neither WBY nor others was sure if *A Vision* contained profound truths and creative genius or if it had been a ridiculous exercise in obsession. As it was being delivered to booksellers, WBY wrote to Laurie that he was waiting for the book "with some excitement as I don't know whether I am a goose that has hatched a swan or a swan that has hatched a goose."[7]

It might be answered that WBY was neither a goose nor a swan but a heron—Aherne or A Herne, as WBY sometimes spelled it in the drafts, one of the figures of the "phantasmagoria" of characters, authors, redactors, and players in the drama that swirls around the philosophical matter of the book. Owen Aherne and his associate, Michael Robartes, fictional characters revived from the trio of occult stories, "Rosa Alchemica," "The Tables of the Law," and "The Adoration of the Magi," written over two decades earlier for inclusion in *The Secret Rose* (1897), were at one stage meant to speak the philosophy, in a dialogue that WBY worked on for several years before finally abandoning it in favor of the discursive form of the published book.[8] This form retained the dynamism of the system, which depended upon its dialogic arrival. In fact, the story of *A Vision* is riddled with dialogues and doubles, beginning with the collaboration between WBY and GY, which took place in spiritualistic sessions of automatic writing (and other methods, which will be explained below) during which he asked questions and she wrote the answers that came to her from regions beyond the grave and outside material existence. The spiritualist nature of the automatic script also presumes a second kind of dialogue, between the human partners and a host of "instructors" and "communicators" of various supernatural kinds who wrote or spoke through GY's hand or voice as she acted as a medium for their revelations. Writing the book was another exercise in dialogism, as WBY strained to find adequate ways to explain material of which he was frequently in less than perfect command. He found, as readers of *A Vision* also find, that the relationship between writer and text that is authorship itself is more than usually unstable in this book. The author is not a unified entity: there is both explanation and instruction, argument and agreement, a sense of monologue or even diatribe, as well as a sense of conversation or even just several voices speaking all at once. Finally, the book called *A Vision* is two books: the 1925 book here presented was followed, after over a decade of revision, by a second book of the same title. Published by Macmillan in 1937, it is so different from the earlier text that it may effectively be regarded as a separate work. Some sections were kept intact, but others were added, dropped, or radically changed, and a new and large body of introductory material changes the feel of the book as a whole. The general editors of the *Collected Works of W. B. Yeats* have wisely decided to present *A Vision* (1937), here abbreviated as *AVB*, in a separate volume from this one, here abbreviated as *AVA*.

The later *Vision* is less deceptive than this earlier one. It is more philosophical and smoother in presentation. *AVA* is more personal and eccentric, again like the phantasmagoria of such characters as Robartes and Aherne who play major roles in the hoax that surrounds the explication of the system. A session of automatic script from January 1918, soon after the experiments began and at roughly the time that WBY began to write the first drafts of the dialogue between these two characters, explained why the poet was warned against studying philosophy as he started to compose: "I warn you against the philosophy that is bred in stagnation—it is a bitter philosophy a philosophy which destroys—I give you one which leads—I give you one which is from outside—a light which you follow not one which will burn you."[9] The Robartes-Aherne dialogues had another purpose: to deflect the outside reader from intuiting the most sensitive of the dialogues at work. They allowed GY to remain in the background, with her role in the project a secret, as she and the instructors insisted (on 4 March 1918, for example, the injunction came that they "do not *wish* the spirit source revealed" and that

WBY when writing should "only speak of those actual machineries of the philosophy that may be in the book" [*YVP* 1:369]).

Although dramatized speakers were finally unworkable, a number of distancing devices remain, in layers of personae, stories, and thinly veiled hoaxes, from frontispiece to final poem. Edmund Dulac created the frontispiece of Giraldus, the supposed author of a book outlining the system, entitled, in bad (and misspelled) Latin, "Speculum Angelorum et Homenorum."[10] Dulac's woodcut of a sly-looking visage in a turban, which bears a strong resemblance to WBY as well as a slight one to GY, faces the title page of *A Vision*, where textual convention places a portrait of the author. WBY was very pleased with the image, writing to Dulac that he even doubted "if Laurie would have taken the book but for the amusing deceit that your designs make possible" (*L*, 700). Others enjoyed the "deceit" as well: Frank Pearce Sturm, one of very few serious readers of *AVA*, wrote admiringly to WBY that "Every book I pick up seems to speak with the voice of W. B. Giraldus, of cones & gyres" (*FPS*, 92).

A tongue-in-cheek tone punctuates the book, ironically revealing in his most occult work an aspect of WBY that is most often hidden: an inclination toward humor, even in the spiritual system that is at the same time a dreadfully serious matter. In "All Souls' Night," the poem appended as a coda to the book, the poet declares,

> I have mummy truths to tell
> Whereat the living mock;
> Though not for sober ear
> For maybe all that hear
> Should weep and laugh an hour upon the clock.

A Vision has certainly caused some readers to laugh and others (or maybe the same ones) to weep. It is comedy and tragedy: a grave and playful, poetic and geometric, concrete and abstract, earnest and slippery work, aiming to be all at once a work of theoretical history, an esoteric philosophy, an aesthetic symbology, a psychological schema, and a sacred book. It is as difficult as it is essential reading for any student of WBY. George Mills Harper, one of the early scholarly proponents of WBY's occult interests and general editor of the four-volume edition of the automatic script and related materials, declared the unwieldy work "the most maligned and misunderstood *tour de force* in the history of modern literature" (*MYV* 1:xiv). Richard Ellmann, one of the few critics whom GY allowed to examine the *Vision* materials after her husband's death, called it "The strangest work written by a great poet in English since Blake's Prophetic Books."[11] R. F. Foster remarks in his authoritative biography that *A Vision* not only "provides necessary illumination for a key section of [WBY's] oeuvre" but that "the book's real value is to students of WBY's mind, and of his aspirations" (Foster 2:285).

Many of WBY's literary texts are indeed enmeshed in the net cast by *A Vision,* from well-known poems such as "Leda and the Swan" and "The Second Coming," to the volumes *Michael Robartes and the Dancer* and *The Tower,* to plays like *The Only Jealousy of Emer* and *Calvary,* to sections of the autobiography including *The Trembling of the Veil,* and even to WBY's published version of his Nobel acceptance speech. *A Vision* is also a work that provides a distillation as well as exploded elaboration of ideas that had been gestating for many years. It is more difficult to track the maturation of GY's thought than her husband's, but with the aid of Ann Saddlemyer's authoritative biography, we can recognize her intellectual contributions as well as her genius for organization and synthesis of the complicated data that flowed into their lives.[12] For its editors, *AVA* provides opportunities to present formally the "reverse miracle" that WBY saw: the published text is not finally separable from the multitudinous papers that represent its genesis. The 1925 book represents WBY's final intentions even less than do many modern texts and is inexplicable without many details from stages of composition outside its pages. The challenge of this edition is to document its multiple sources, for *AVA* is both the culmination of WBY's many years of occult study as well as the most collaborative of his many esoteric works.

II

Crucially, *A Vision* is the product of two Yeatses: the poet and the young Englishwoman who took his surname when she married him in the autumn of 1917. GY is responsible for much of the system and its exposition, although it is not possible to untangle the intertwined threads of authority for any of the material. It is nonetheless certain that the philosophy that made its way into the pages as well as its many ambiguities have their source in the collaboration that was its raison d'être. That collaboration began within days of the Yeatses' marriage in October 1917, when GY emptied her mind as she held her pen over a sheet of paper to see whether her hand would write without her conscious guidance. She was trying to salvage a near disaster: the honeymoon had been riddled with unhappiness as WBY made himself ill with anxiety over his choice of bride, and GY certainly hoped and intended for mediumistic communication to occur if it were possible. The pen moved, setting off the immediate genesis of *A Vision* and the numerous texts associated with it. Although the experience was, as WBY would later describe it, "incredible" (*AVB*, 8), it did not arrive in a vacuum: both WBY and GY were seasoned occultists, with considerable knowledge of such areas of inquiry as astrology, Western esotericism, folk beliefs, and spiritualism. The AS that began so abruptly was prepared for by years of study, raising the question of the degree to which it is explained by its sources in the Yeatses' reading, magical practices, and other knowledge and experience. This question, of course, begs another: What levels of automaticity and volition are represented by the writing that began to flow from GY's hand in response to her husband's questions?

In fact, the earliest scripts do not record those questions; they are lists of answers, sometimes just "yes" or "no," to unrecorded questions or topics. Gradually, it became obvious that the revelations that were arriving would need to be kept and structured, so in order to improve efficiency and also to assist themselves in shaping the mass of AS into the order of a book, the Yeatses developed organized methods for their great experiment. They sat at table, usually in the evenings, and, perhaps after some conversation about provisional topics and some ritual such as the lighting of incense, would begin each session. GY recorded the location and time and the name of the instructor or instructors for the session. Usually, an evening of AS would begin with a stream of writing that is not governed by the precise logic that applied to the question-and-answer sequences, by which, as WBY explained later, "I had always to question, and every question to rise out of a previous answer and to deal with their chosen topic" (*AVB*, 10). After free-form writing, the numbered queries and responses would begin. Sometimes WBY wrote his questions on one sheet of paper and GY her answers on another; later, she wrote down both question and answer, switching psychic gears from secretary to medium with each succeeding statement. Sometimes she would act as questioner, indicating that she was doing so by initialing her query, and sometimes the communicators gave answers to both members of the couple, or to GY alone, as well as WBY. At extremes of her conscious participation in the receiving of information, sometimes answers appear in "mirror writing," with the letters formed in reverse, so that she would presumably be prevented from knowing what she was writing, and sometimes responses to awkward questions by WBY (some about Maud Gonne, for example) are answered by strongly drawn straight horizontal lines, indicating refusal to reply. Frequently, GY drew diagrams or made lists. She was doing what contemporary spiritualists would call "channeling," relaxing her conscious mind in order to be receptive to messages from outside her ordinary consciousness, and also actively participating in the joint enterprise of discovery, clarification, organization, and application of the system. In subject matter as well as method, many sessions focus on the issues of the degree to which the system is external to either of its principal investigators and how intrinsically it is associated with their conscious wills as well as subconscious desires. Much of this information was not translated from AS to the published book.

The instructors are a part of this complicated issue; they, to some degree, mirror the levels of active control over or passive reception of the information that flowed onto the pages of the AS. They are of several types: controls, who are usually named, have more or less human personalities and engage with the Yeatses as if they are third members of a conversation. Thomas of Dorlowicz, for example, stayed with them for an extended period and helped them to develop many of the system's fundamental concepts. Such later controls as Ameritus and Dionertes had distinctively different voices and areas of expertise. In addition to controls, guides are often present; these entities are more shadowy, perhaps on a more distant plane, as if levels of spiritual existence operate like links in a vast metaphysical network, and they usually have nonhuman names like Fish or Apple. The system is also guided by daimons, personal genii or otherworldly counterparts, who are enactments of concepts about which WBY had thought and written for some time. Reincarnation is assumed, and at times ancestral or historical personages appear— sometimes wrongly, as verifiable information might confirm. The probability of error or mischief is also personified in "frustrators" or spirits whose purpose, like some of the fairy people of Ireland in stories with which WBY was familiar, was to deceive or cause trouble in whatever ways they could.

The Yeatses worked together on the philosophy almost daily for more than two years, in a number of different locations, through events including the Great War and the Irish war of independence, as well as the births of their two children. The web of messages also gave instruction about the Yeatses' personal lives, often in intertwined strings of dialogic text in which cosmically abstract topics also speak to deeply intimate matters. The intense sessions continued until the spring of 1920, when, on an American lecture tour, the Yeatses were informed by Dionertes that he preferred "other methods—sleeps" (*YVP* 2:539). The labor-intensive automatic writing yielded accordingly to a method that allowed for greater discursivity and direct comment, in which, according to an entry in a notebook, "George speaks while asleep" (*YVP* 3:9). Some of these sleeps were accompanied by nightmares as well as inconvenient and sometimes unsettling phenomena during the day, such as the smells of flowers, burnt wax, or incense, or the sounds of whistles, animals, or human voices.

By April 1921, WBY recorded in a notebook that "All communication by external means—sleaps—whistles—voices—renounced, as too exhausting for George," then pregnant with their second child. "Philosophy is now coming in a new way," WBY wrote. "I am getting it in sleap & when half awake, & George has correspondential dreams or visions" (*YVP* 3:85–86). They also recorded "talks" or "conversations," so that, as a late "Record," typed probably by GY, notes, "Since we gave up the sleeps we have worked at the system by discussion, each bringing to these their discoveries" (*YVP* 3:120). The revelations gradually grew from stray words written in awkwardly large, rounded handwriting by a pen not lifted from the page except at the ends of lines, to information recorded in automatic answers to recorded questions, to a barrage of material invading the Yeatses' waking and sleeping lives, an experience that encompassed much of their time and creative energy. As readers of this edition will see from the notes to the text, the Yeatses' system has a number of precursors and influences. Both WBY and GY were adepts in the Hermetic Order of the Golden Dawn, "the crowning glory of the occult revival in the nineteenth century,"[13] a magical society that stressed the mastery of a body of knowledge that has been called the *philosophia perennis*.[14] They read widely in Neoplatonic, kabbalist, alchemical, Rosicrucian, hermetic, theosophic, and wisdom literature, from Agrippa through A. E. Waite, through such writers as Blavatsky, Boehme, Dante's *Convito*, Hermes Trismegistus, Eliphas Lévi, G. R. S. Mead, S. L. MacGregor Mathers, Ptolemy, Pico della Mirandola, Plato, Plotinus, and Swedenborg. Blake is a particularly important literary precursor, not only for ideas but also for the concrete example Blake presented of another poet who created his own mythographic system that joined imaginative and spiritual truth, working in concert with his wife. In some respects, *A Vision* takes its place among other Romantic fragments and literary hoaxes, participating in the popularity of antiquity and Orientalized Otherness in English poetry as well as literary Celticism, from MacPherson to Fiona MacLeod, whose alter ego, the writer William Sharp, was a friend of WBY's. Nor are texts, whether philosophical or belletristic, the only underpinnings for the system. Both WBY and GY were active astrologers; they also read tarot cards, practiced divination, and studied numerology. WBY in particular had attended a number of seances and studied psychic occurrences from ghost stories to religious miracles. Automatic writing itself was far from new to them. A number of nineteenth- and early twentieth-century spiritualists used the technique, notable among them William Stainton Moses, one of the founders of the Society for Psychical Research, to which organization WBY belonged from 1913 to 1928.[15] As recently as 1912 and 1913, WBY had studied the automatic writing of a young medium named Elizabeth Radcliffe and written an essay about her.[16]

WBY's oeuvre is perhaps the best preparation for a reader of the 1925 *A Vision*, as it was for its authors. His occult essays like the well-known "Magic" (1901); the magical stories written for *The Secret Rose*; the Cuchulain plays, especially *The Hawk's Well*; and the two essays and notes composed for inclusion in Lady Gregory's *Visions and Beliefs in the West of Ireland,* particularly "Sweden-borg, Mediums, and the Desolate Places," are all essential reading. Two essays that remained unpublished during the Yeatses' lifetimes are thematically and formally related to *A Vision*: an experiment with assuming the voice of the "anti-self" Leo Africanus, in the form of letters to and from a historical character and writer re-created as a mythic opposite; and an essay written in 1916, in dia-logue form, between two personae on the topic of masks, entitled "The Poet and the Actress."[17] All of these sources pale in compari-son with the two essays that comprise *Per Amica Silentia Lunae,* a slim monograph published in 1916 that represents the furthest development of WBY's thought prior to his marriage and the advent of the automatic experiments.[18] *Per Amica* is mentioned frequently in the AS, notes, and drafts, and it also blends the personal and the abstract in its context as well as its form. WBY admits in the intro-duction to the utterly transformed 1937 edition of *A Vision,* in which he tells the story of the automatic script openly, that "The unknown writer took his theme at first from my just published *Per Amica Silentia Lunae*" (*AVB,* 8). In fact, the themes of the auto-matic script in the first scripts that the Yeatses preserved include the idea of opposites (found in Plato's *Phaedrus*), given to WBY on a "scrap of paper" from his friend W. T. Horton and also in an auto-matic script produced by Lady Edith Lyttelton in 1914.[19] Leo Africanus, now not an anti-self but a frustrator, also appears. Antitheses characterize the script, and it was perhaps to be expected that they dominate the form as well as the content of the book in its early states of composition.

III

WBY had begun to compose the dialogues between Aherne and Robartes that comprise the first drafts of the book very early in the reception of the automatic messages (perhaps, indeed, as early as 21 November 1917, when he asks for corroboration of system-related ideas "in my essay"). GY had suggested, and WBY had accepted, the fictional author Giraldus for his essay or book, probably in Decem-ber 1917. He wrote to Lady Gregory in early January 1918 of the "very profound, very exciting mystical philosophy . . . coming in strange ways to George and myself." He continued,

It is coming into my work a great deal and makes me feel that for the first time I understand human life. I am writing it all out in a series of dialogues about a supposed medieval book, the *Speculum Angelorum et Hominum* by Giraldus, and a sect of Arabs called the Judwalis (diagrammatists). Ross has helped me with the Arabic. I live with a strange sense of revelation and never know what the day will bring. You will be astonished at the change in my work, at its intricate passion.[20]

Three days after posting the letter to Lady Gregory, WBY wrote to Edmund Dulac, who was in on the joke, to say that "Every evening the speculum of Giraldus becomes more engrossing. I am more and more astonished at the profundity of that learned author and at the neglect into which he has fallen, a neglect only comparable to that which has covered with the moss of oblivion the even more profound work of Kusta ibm [*sic*] Luka of Bagdad whose honor remains alone in the obscure sect of the Judwalis" (Hobby, 107). The first mention of Giraldus in the automatic script occurs on 12 January 1918, in a session that contains a reference to "the two books we invented" and a warning, one of many, against "deliberate reading" (*YVP* 1:250), presumably to buttress the ideas of the system. It was not until the first *A Vision* was being drastically revised for its second version that WBY was encouraged to fit the wisdom of this myth into larger intellectual currents. As was perhaps inevitable given that he was writing while information was still being received (and engaging in many other activities, whether personal, literary, theatrical, or political), the next years saw WBY working and often reworking as new information arrived or as he was able to synthesize or understand details received earlier, and being sure at many points that he was nearly finished. He announced to Dulac in October 1923 that he was within "I hope another month" of completion (Hobby, 158; *L*, 699); in February 1924, he revised his schedule: "Certain new editions of my work which I have had to correct the proofs for have delayed the philosophy, but I expect that another month will finish the manuscript" (Hobby, 163). Finally, a year later, on 23 April 1925, he sent

Dulac a definitive announcement: "Yesterday I finished the book" (Hobby, 173).

In order to give a sense of the complexity of WBY's work during these years, we offer the following list, which contains a provisional chronology of the less fragmentary and more significant of the often undatable manuscripts and typescripts that represent stages of composition of *A Vision,* along with dates of composition and publication of relevant literary volumes from this period.[21]

November 1917:

Robartes-Aherne dialogues begin. WBY starts writing in dialogue, a form in which he was to continue probably all during the latter months of 1919. On 29 November, he writes to John Quinn that he is writing "a fourth Cuchulain play . . . and a dialogue in the manner of Landor" (unpublished letter, cited in *YVP* 1:15).

December 1917:

"Appendix by Michael Robartes," perhaps finished earlier than the text it was designed to append, describes the Great Diagram and its aesthetic and moral applications.[22] The spelling of the title of the *Speculum* suggests this early date, before Ross corrected the Latin phrase. It is also possible to date this manuscript much later than 1917, using as evidence a citation of an appendix in Version B, dated June 1920 (*YVP* 4:213).

January 1918:

Beginning at this time, the "Discoveries of Michael Robartes" is expanded from one to several dialogues. WBY writes to Lady Gregory on 4 January that he is "writing it all out in a series of dialogues. . . ."

14 January 1918:

WBY finishes the system-related play *The Only Jealousy of Emer.*

8 April 1918:

The control Aymor mentions that the Yeatses should "code and question" or "Codify" the materials they have been receiving (*YVP* 1:420). They begin to organize, using methods such as chronological notes (one notebook summarizes sessions from 9 November 1917 through 1 February 1918; *YVP* 3:143–82), a card file (*YVP* 3:222–430), and a notebook with entries arranged according to topic using alphabetical tabs (NLI, 36,259/2).

15 July 1918:

WBY writes to Pound that he is "now at the 30th page of my prose dialogue expounding this symbol & there will be 3 dialogues of some 40 pages each, full of my sort of violence and passion" (unpublished letter, cited in *YVP* 1:23). The first dialogue, or "conversation," includes an introduction and the material which appears in *A Vision* in "The Great Wheel" (book 1, part 3). The second conversation covers "The Twenty-Eight Embodiments" (book 1, part 4), although it breaks off at Phase 21.

3 October 1918:

WBY mentions in a letter to GY, who is away for a fortnight, that he will "finish dictation of dialogue before lunch" (*YVP* 4:4). The "Discoveries of Michael Robartes," in other words, may at this point have been sent out for typing. WBY then makes corrections to the typescript.²³

October 1918:

The small volume *Nine Poems* is published in a private printing of twenty-five copies by Clement Shorter (Wade, 122). The volume includes "Solomon to Sheba," "Tom O'Roughley," "The Cat and the Moon," and "Under the Round Tower"; seven of these poems are also published in *The Little Review*.

Late 1918–1920:

As automatic script continues to be generated, WBY begins to try to cope with the challenge of new data by dating sections of manuscript. A rejected typescript notes "P.S. I have dated the various sections of this book because my knowledge grew as I wrote, and there are slight changes of emphasis, and blank spaces that need explanation."

At some point, the dialogue form is abandoned.

January 1919:

The fine press volume *Two Plays for Dancers,* containing *The Dreaming of the Bones* and *The Only Jealousy of Emer,* is published by Cuala Press (Wade, 123). Separately, also in January 1919, *The Dreaming of the Bones* appears in *The Little Review* and *The Only Jealousy of Emer* in *Poetry.* Near the end of the script on 21 January 1919, the control Thomas of Dorlowicz reiterates that in the published version, the system's "Supernormal origin [will be] received through a person we will call Gyraldus" (*YVP* 2:183). WBY writes to Dulac, sending him "remainder of Speculum" (Hobby, 129), possibly indicating that a text in essay instead of dialogue form was finished enough to provide to Dulac as context for his illustrations.

February 1919:

The Wild Swans at Coole appears in a volume expanded from its original small press version by Cuala Press in 1917 (Wade, 118). In its new Macmillan incarnation (Wade, 124), it includes new material, including the poems from *Nine Poems,* and others, including "The Phases of the Moon," "The Saint and the Hunchback," "Two Songs of a Fool," "Another Song of a Fool," and "The Double Vision of Michael Robartes."

21 March 1920:

Dionertes, the control for the session conducted in Portland, Oregon, urges, "You have got to begin to write soon" (*YVP* 2:535). WBY has begun to write in expository prose, perhaps producing a draft that would in retrospect be regarded as "Version A."

June, July, August 1920:

The first version of "Four Years," book 1 of the autobiography to be entitled *The Trembling of the Veil* (*Au,* 113–68), is published in three installments in *The London Mercury.*

June 1920:

"Version B," perhaps partly reworked from drafts begun the previous spring, is finished. Although the phantasmagoria is fictional, the dates offered at the beginning of the manuscript are probably correct:

In the spring of nineteen nineteen immediately after Michael Robartes['] return to Mesopotamia I received from his friend John Aherne the following fragments, partly extracts from letters written by Robartes to John Aherne, & partly records of conversations. I offer these now to the few friends & diciples [*sic*] of a singular philosophy & visionary. WBY. June. 1920 (*YVP* 4:141).

Autumn 1920:
The poem "All Souls' Night," as it appears in *A Vision,* is dated "Oxford, *Autumn, 1920.*"

February 1921:
Four hundred copies of the volume of poems entitled *Michael Robartes and the Dancer* appear in a fine press edition from Cuala Press (Wade, 127). The phantasmagoria is here offered to the public for the first time. The preface mentions that WBY "came into possession of Michael Robartes' exposition of the *Speculum Angelorum et Hominum* of Geraldus" and that WBY's forthcoming "selection from the great mass of his letters and table talk, which I owe to his friend John Aherne, may be published before, or at any rate but soon after this little book." Ten pages of notes at the back, beginning "Robartes writes to Aherne," expound ideas based, writes WBY, on

> mathematical diagrams from the *Speculum,* squares and spheres, cones made up of revolving gyres intersecting each other at various angles, figures sometimes of great complexity. [Robartes'] explanation of these . . . is founded upon a single fundamental thought. The mind, whether expressed in history or in the individual life, has a precise movement, which can be quickened or slackened but cannot be fundamentally altered, and this movement can be expressed by a mathematical form.[24]

June, July, August 1921:
"Four Years," book 1 of *The Trembling of the Veil,* is published in *The London Mercury* and *The Dial.*

October 1921:
The book *Four Plays for Dancers* is issued by Macmillan (Wade,

129). The four plays are *At the Hawk's Well, The Only Jealousy of Emer, The Dreaming of the Bones,* and *Calvary.*

December 1921:
    Four Years, an autobiographical account, is published by Cuala Press (Wade, 131).

May, June, July 1922:
    "More Memories," versions of materials from "Ireland after Parnell," "Hodos Chameliontos," and "The Tragic Generation" (books 2, 3, and 4 of *The Trembling of the Veil* [*Au,* 169–266]), is published in *The London Mercury* and *The Dial.*

June 1922:
    The slim volume *Seven Poems and a Fragment* is published by Cuala Press (Wade, 132); one poem is "All Souls' Night."

October 1922:
    The Trembling of the Veil (*Au,* 109–286) is published in full book form: "1000 copies on hand-made papers, signed by the author, issued to subscribers by Werner Laurie" (Wade, 133). Three years later, its physical appearance will be echoed in that of *AVA.*

9 October 1922:
    In a letter to Olivia Shakespear, WBY writes that he is "busy writing out the system—getting a 'Book A' written that can be typed and shown to interested persons and talked over" (*L,* 690).

October–December 1922:
    Book A: The first two parts of a three-part typescript of some 130 pages are intended as preliminarily drafted sections of "Book A," according to the typescript, which is also titled "Version C" (NLI, 36,265/9/1–11).[25] In this typescript, the introduction by Aherne precedes parts 1 and 2 (which became Book I of *A Vision*), and the start of part 3. At the end of Book I of the published *Vision,* a date overstates in hindsight its state of completion by this time: "Finished at Thoor, Ballylee, 1922, in a time of Civil War." The Yeatses leave Ballylee at the end of September 1922; the Anglo-Irish Treaty of 1921,

narrowly ratified in January 1922, has sparked the civil war that will end in May 1923.

November 1922:

Later Poems, the first volume of the *Collected Edition of the Works*, is published by Macmillan (Wade, 134). The play *The Player Queen* is published in *The Dial*, then in *Plays in Prose and Verse*, published by Macmillan simultaneously and uniformly with *Later Poems* (Wade, 136).

1 December 1922:

WBY writes to Dulac, mentioning his membership in the Irish Senate but also that he is "working every morning on the philosophy which Werner Laurie is ready to accept with effusion. He would sign an agreement at once, if I would let him, but I am insisting on his reading a hundred or so pages first" (*L*, 694). The hundred or so pages are probably the typescript mentioned above; the book is planned to be a two-volume work, produced in uniform binding with *The Trembling of the Veil*.

December 1922:

A first version of the "Introduction by Owen Aherne" to *AVA* is dated "Dec 1922."[26]

18 December 1922:

WBY writes to Olivia Shakespear that "If Laurie does not repent, a year from now should see the first half published. It will need another volume to finish it" (*L*, 695).

January 1923:

The poem "Meditations in Time of Civil War," composed in the summer of 1922, is printed in *The Dial* and *The London Mercury*.

13 March 1923:

WBY writes in a letter marked "<u>Private</u>" to Laurie that "I promised you a hundred pages of my philosophical book by the end of January and I doubt if the end of March will see those hundred pages finished. They are all there, in a more or less completed state, but I have to dictate everything to a typist as my handwriting is illegible. I have been delayed in part by the inherent difficulty of work of this kind but partly by all kinds of distractions arising out of the condition of this country."[27]

26 July 1923:

WBY sends Dulac "my preface, in the rough, or rather Owen Aherne's. It will give you all the facts as I see them" (Hobby, 157). In the drafted introduction, Aherne and Robartes quarrel after Aherne "used these words: 'In the Introduction I will of course explain my own point of view; that I concede to this Arabian system exactly the same measure of belief that an intelligent reader concedes to a Platonic myth.' He [Robartes] flew up into a rage and said that I had lead [sic] him to believe that I was convinced; that I had indeed been convinced until my Catholicism gripped me by the throat; he even asked me if I had not taken the advice of some confessor and before the evening was out we had our old quarrel over again." The next day, they go to see "Mr. Yeats," whom Robartes asks "to undertake the editorship." Mr. Yeats surprises them by pulling out "a number of copy-books full of notes and diagrams" that are almost identical to those of Aherne and Robartes. He shows them "that our notes only differed from his because our examples and our general atmosphere were Arabian, whereas his were drawn from European history and literature." Mr. Yeats then explains that "I was looking at my canary, which was darting about the cage in rather brilliant light, when I found myself in a strangely still and silent state and in that state I saw with the mind's eye symbols streaming before me." Hobby discusses and reprints the differences between this preface and the published version (165–69).

7 September 1923:

WBY sends Laurie "the first big bundle of my new book,"[28] a typescript of "Book A" (NLI, 36,268). By this time, the section entitled "The Dance of the Four Royal Persons" has been removed from its original place and revised to become an introductory section, as in the published book. Likewise, part 1 is a version of "The Great Wheel" in *AVA*, and part 2, "Analysis of the 28 Phases," presents the essays entitled in *AVA* "The Twenty-Eight Embodiments." Two other sections have been combined to form the beginning of part 3 (which had earlier been intended for "Book B"), entitled in the typescript "The Geometrical Foundation."

Autumn 1923:
    The "big bundle" gone, WBY begins to write Book III of *AVA*, "Dove or Swan," originally entitled "History." A sixty-three-page manuscript probably dates from about this time (NLI, 36,269/1). "Dove or Swan" will be composed and extensively revised over a long and not precisely datable period of time. WBY reads a good deal of history in conjunction with the composition of this section, and he will keep it almost entirely intact for the 1937 revision of the book, although all of the material after page 210, line 26, will be omitted from the second edition. In the published book, this section is also dated: "Finished at Capri, February, 1925." The Yeatses, joined by the Pounds, have traveled in Italy from 4 January through about 24 February.

September 1923:
    WBY finishes a first draft of the poem "Leda and the Swan," originally entitled "Annunciation." Dulac sends WBY the illustration of Giraldus (Hobby, 170).

October 1923:
    Werner Laurie provides WBY with a contract for five hundred copies of a private printing of the book. The publisher also writes to WBY's agent, A. P. Watt, to ask if he might "coax WBY into writing a description of *A Vision* as no-one has the faintest idea what it is about."[29] On 14 October, WBY writes to Dulac,

> The portrait of Giraldus is admirable. I enclose the sketch for the diagram. the pencilled words all have to be in Latin and I will get the Latin I hope tomorrow. The man I count on for it was out yesterday. You can use any symbolism you like for the elements—nymphs, salamanders, air spirits, or Roman gods or more natural objects. . . . The book will be finished in I hope another month—it contains only a little of my system but the rest can follow. Werner Laurie is to publish it uniform with 'The Trembling of the Veil'. That introduction I sent you

has been greatly rewritten and is much more authentic looking. It keeps the 'modesty of Nature' in mind now and the canary is gone. I don't know when I shall get to London and at the moment can think of nothing but writing out the system. The Mss. sent off I shall give myself three months more writing and perhaps produce here a Noh play if Civil War does not start again with the long nights (Hobby, 157–58).

Book IV of *AVA*, "The Gates of Pluto," is also begun as early as the autumn of 1923. On 23 October, WBY writes to Dulac that "I am writing at a last highly technical chapter of my philosophy," and a sleep dated 26 October 1923 refers to the "chapter on covens in 'A Vision'" (*YVP* 4:185), the first reference in the AS and notebooks to the title of the book in its published form. The exposition of "Life After Death," as Book IV is at one time to be called, is at one stage to begin with a story called "Michael Robartes and the Judwali Doctor." Explanatory notes to this story refer to information that WBY mentions in an unpublished letter dated 5 April 1923. At one point this material is to be divided into two sections, "Death, the Soul, and the Life after Death" and "The Soul between Death and Birth." Much of the first section will eventually be moved to Book II, necessitating a revision of that part.

13 December 1923:
WBY, recipient of the Nobel Prize, delivers the lecture "The Irish Dramatic Movement" to the Royal Swedish Academy.

January 1924:
The veiled autobiographical narrative poem "The Gift of Harun Al-Raschid" is published in *English Life and The Illustrated Review*. WBY sees his old friend Moina Mathers (whose motto in the Golden Dawn is "Vestigia") after many years without contact.

28 January 1924:
WBY writes to Dulac that "I am very far from finished, so there is no hurry about your design. I work for days and then find I have muddled something, and have to do it all again, especially whenever I have to break new ground" (*L*, 703).

20 April 1924:

WBY writes to Laurie, "You have sent me your circular with announcement of 'A Vision' marked which is no doubt a hint that you are in a hurry, or at any rate a request for information. All I can say is that for the last year I have written nothing except two poems and an essay and this book for you. So far as absolute bulk is concerned it has been written many times, but it is not easy to break through into the other world, and that must be my excuse."[30]

Summer 1924:

Probably during the past six months, WBY has decided to restructure Book IV, revision that necessitates significant revision also to Book II. Moina Mathers writes to him that she is dismayed by the portrait of her late husband in *The Trembling of the Veil* (see *Au*, 159–63, 257–59; *LWBY*, 446–48). WBY decides to dedicate the book, now nearly complete, to her and composes a first draft of the dedication, as well as an unused epilogue, "To Vestigia" (NLI, 36,264/2–6).

July 1924:

Cuala Press publishes five hundred copies of the volume of poetry *The Cat and the Moon and Certain Poems* (Wade, 145). The poems include "Meditations in Time of Civil War" and "The Gift of Harun Al-Raschid," which is dated 1923.

12 August 1924:

WBY writes to Laurie that he is relieved to have the publication date postponed, "for I was dissatisfied with what I had written and started afresh. . . . I am now, however, arranging to disappear from the public eye for a couple of months, which should finish the work."[31]

January 1925:

The final section of the published book announces its final date: "Finished at Syracuse, January, 1925."

February 1925:

The final section of "Dove or Swan," the last section of the book

to be composed, is completed at Capri and so dated. The dedication
to "Vestigia" also bears this date. It was written the previous summer
and predicts that *A Vision* is not finished, even in its published state:
"Doubtless I must someday complete what I have begun" (*AVA*, xiii,
and the present edition, lvi).

April 1925:

WBY records in a notebook entry dated 23 April 1925, "Yesterday I finished 'A Vision,' I can write letters again & idle" (*CVA*, xlvii;
NLI, 13,576). He writes to Dulac that "now at last it is done and all
that remains is for George to see that the corrected type script is leg-
ible and so forth" and for Dulac to send his designs on to A. P. Watt,
WBY's agent, to forward to Laurie (Hobby, 173).

May 1925:

A Vision is sent to Laurie. WBY tells Dulac on 5 May that "The
designs are exactly right. 'The Wheel' would take in the whole
British Museum. George is at work on the material shape of my
typed copy of the book, making it all clean and neat and tomorrow
it goes to the publisher." The same letter announces that WBY is
beginning "a play in one act on the appearance of Christ to his dis-
ciples after his Crucifixion," i.e., *The Resurrection* (Hobby, 174).
The date for the introduction to the book is given as May 1925,
although it has been composed perhaps as much as two and a half
years before, in late 1922.

July 1925:

The Bounty of Sweden: A Meditation, and a Lecture, a small
book containing WBY's Nobel Prize speech, is published by Cuala
Press (Wade, 146).

15 January 1926:

A Vision is published by Werner Laurie (Wade, 149).

IV

The reader leafing through the stiff pages of *AVA* encountered a
book that attempts to explain all that exists or can be imagined (and

these two are the same, according to the system). The multiplicity may be expressed by means of "a single fundamental thought," as WBY asserts in a note to the poem "The Second Coming," from the notes at the back of the Cuala Press volume *Michael Robartes and the Dancer.*

> The mind, whether expressed in history or in the individual life, has a precise movement, which can be quickened or slackened but cannot be fundamentally altered, and this movement can be expressed by a mathematical form. . . . A supreme religious act of [the Judwalis'] faith is to fix the attention on the mathematical form of this movement until the whole past and future of humanity, or of an individual man, shall be present to the intellect as if it were accomplished in a single moment. The intensity of the Beatific Vision when it comes depends upon the intensity of this realization. (30–31; *VP,* 823–24)

A central symbol is expressed in two ways, as a wheel, in two dimensions, and as a double cone, in three. Both are always moving. Change and opposition in predetermined pattern is the theme. One phase yields to another; faculties and principles all have their opposites and corners; souls spin forward and backward through lives and afterlives; eras in history and movements in art and thought push toward and repel their own opposites. The whole is not fatalistic, as the note to "The Second Coming" continues, "because the mathematical figure is an expression of the mind's desire."

The Yeatses created and countercreated their evocative system out of their own "mind's desire" at the turbulent beginning of their personal relationship, the Irish Free State, and the conflicts between political movements that became larger markers of a century marked by change and violence. Both coauthors are immediately present, despite the text's air of mystery. GY's ideas can be traced from this book backward through the genetic material, upon which *AVA* relies heavily. Ironically, given that in this *Vision* she is not mentioned by name, she is more present in this text as a silent coauthor than in *AVB;* by the time *AVB* came to be written, WBY had been encouraged to add to the private system various philosophical contexts that additional reading and study made available to him. In *AVA,* too, and again ironically, given the rhetorical impression of uncertainty rather than authorial command of its material, this text expresses with immediacy WBY's views from one of his most important periods.

For example, the 1925 book shows WBY's attitudes toward international modernism during the welter of its most intense decade—and without the distance of the *Vision* from the 1930s. As he remarks in the pages at the end of "Dove or Swan" that were excised from the later edition, this phase is

> it is said the first where there is hatred of the abstract, where the intellect turns upon itself, Mr Ezra Pound, Mr Eliot, Mr Joyce, Signor Pirandello, who either eliminate from metaphor the poet's phantasy and substitute a strangeness discovered by historical or contemporary research or who break up the logical processes of thought by flooding them with associated ideas or words that seem to drift into the mind by chance. (the present edition, 174–75)

AVA also puts such aesthetics in close proximity with WBY's early interests in Italian fascism. In the same, later omitted passage, WBY writes that because myth and fact have fallen apart, decadence will ensue, and afterward a new era will arise, characterized by "organic groups, *covens* of physical or intellectual kin." "I imagine new races, as it were, seeking domination, a world resembling but for its immensity that of the Greek tribes—each with its own *Daimon* or ancestral hero—the brood of Leda, War and Love; history grown symbolic, the biography changed into a myth" (the present edition, 176). WBY had in common with Mussolini his desire to infuse actual world events with the power of myth, and it is significant that *A Vision* shares a publication date with the first English edition of Margherita Sarfatti's biography of Mussolini, a book with a much larger readership than *A Vision*, but which shares with it a conflation of fascism and myth.[32] (Sarfatti's book was largely responsible for cementing the myth of il Duce that would be so important to Mussolini's status in Italy.)

WBY's interest in fascism continued to develop after the first printing of *A Vision*, as his reading in fascist philosophy and awareness of international fascist movements expanded. *AVA* captures an idealistic moment in his investment in fascism, moderately shaped by the writings of fascist thinkers (and the thinking of Ezra Pound) but mostly based in myth. By 1937, when *AVB* was published, his sense of this relationship had shifted, so he removed many of these passages. While *AVB* still contains traces of his faith in many of the doctrines of fascism—its elitism, its antiliberalism, its corporativism—it also hints at uncertainty about whether the fascist experiment can succeed. In a new concluding section to "Dove or Swan," dated 1934–36, he refers to the central fascist figure of speech to ask, "What discords will drive Europe to that artificial unity—only dry or drying sticks can be tied into a bundle—which is the decadence of every civilization?" (*AVB*, 301–2). He fears the death that must attend the unity of fascism, the *fascio* or bundle of rods and an axe that had become the symbol of Italian fascism.

This idea of "organic groups, *covens* of physical or intellectual kin," is largely absent from *AVB* and is an example of how interpretation may not only move forward in time to see WBY's changing thought but also back in order to see that his political reading was not GY's. Covens were discussed at length in a number of sleeps as intersections between individual minds and imagined communities. The interests of the younger partner in the experiments may be inferred from discussions in which the spirits tried to limit covens to "an interaction between the places of self and C.G. [Creative Genius]," thus stressing a relationship between creativity and self that is more like the effort to "break up the logical processes of thought by flooding them with associated ideas or words that seem to drift into the mind by chance," which WBY deplores in his description of modernist writing quoted above, than like WBY's dismay at such effort. There is an echo of WBY's poem "Michael Robartes and the Dancer," a discussion between an older man, certain of his opinions about modernity, and a younger woman who does not share them, in a sleep from 29 November 1920: "If a covin is not in contact with the memory of the opposite covin through its dragon its thought is empty. It is because the spiritualist covin loses contact with the psychological memory of its opposite that it is so stupid. The covin is a mechanism & without the opposite memory that mechanism has nothing to work on. This process has nothing to do with Daimons or guides & is a condition of all fruitful thought" (*YVP* 3:58). *AVA* is a linchpin for informed readings of the developing thought of both WBY and GY. Their phantasmagoric contribution that is this book, insisting on instability and symbol, has an enduring interest, and it is to be hoped that readers of this edition may encounter, as WBY wrote, "Such thought, that in it bound / I need no other thing, / Wound in mind's wandering / As mummies in the mummy-cloth are wound" ([211]).

V

The creators of *AVA* knew that it was both finished and incomplete, like all books but to a considerably greater extent than most others. It announces the need for revision in its opening pages; its rhetoric throughout is characterized by hesitation as well as poses that claim certitude. The book is a beautiful artifact but hardly an accurate text, and it has never been reset or corrected. Instead, it was replaced, by the 1937 Macmillan trade publication (Wade, 191). The current edition presupposes integrity for the 1925 text rather than treating it as a quirky predecessor for the "improved" 1937 edition, as has often happened in the history of the two very different books entitled *A Vision* by W. B. Yeats. We agree with the notion of "versioning" as defined by Donald Reiman. He writes that "it is both more useful and more efficient to provide critics and students with complete texts of two or more different stages of a literary work, each of which can be read as an integral whole, than to chop all but one version into small pieces and then mix and sprinkle these dismembered fragments at the bottoms of pages, or shuffle them at the back of the book as tables of 'variants' or 'collations.' "33 On a theoretical level, producing these two versions allows us, in George Bornstein's words, "an interesting middle ground between stable, unitary notions of the text on the one hand and post-structuralist freeplay of endless deferral on the other."34

Given that the two printed versions were in WBY's mind part of a single process of composition, it is important to delineate where one volume stops and the other begins. Our *AVA* volume focuses on the book as it was published in 1925, reserving for *AVB* revisions made toward a later printing, as well as explanations of contextual material that relates primarily to the later book, such as the prominent role of Western philosophy buttressing its arguments. However, those changes intended as corrections—as opposed to revisions—of

AVA are treated in annotations and in an appendix to this volume, in which we present textual corrections made by GY and WBY after the publication of the 1925 text but not necessarily incorporated into the 1937 printing. As Richard J. Finneran has noted, three of the four copies of *AVA* in WBY's library contain markings by WBY and GY, many of which were not adopted in the 1937 printing.[35] Their appropriate place is in annotations and tables of variants. We have also drawn on the letters between WBY and Frank Pearce Sturm, a poet, scholar, and mystic, noting in annotations Sturm's corrections to WBY's Latin, his understanding of the movement of the moon, and his knowledge of the language in which Cicero wrote; where they were incorporated into *AVB*, they will be printed there as primary text. Thus our text of *AVA* freezes the moment of its publication, with annotations suggesting some links between it and *AVB*.

This volume differs significantly from others in the Collected Works series, which follow closely the principle of final and expressed authorial intentions. While this principle will determine the editorial choices made for *AVB*, *AVA* must be understood as a version rooted in the historical moment of 1925; to extend it into the future is to move it toward or into *AVB*. Our focus on the T. Werner Laurie printed text as copy-text, rather than attempting to posit authorial intention beyond its pages or synthesize an ideal text, also follows from instabilities in the concept of authorial intention. Although this idea has a distinguished history in the field of scholarly editing, it is less meaningful for *A Vision* than for many texts, if only because of the complex collaboration that was its genesis. For these reasons, we have made this volume a first-presentation edition, adhering closely to the text as printed by T. Werner Laurie in its limited edition. As a part of our endeavor to present this text as published in 1925, we have retained most of the front matter of that edition, including its frontispiece and title page, which contains references to texts by Giraldus and Kusta ben Luka—all of which combine to insinuate that the book is not truly authored, so much as compiled, by WBY.

This edition is not a facsimile edition, however, and as such it presents the opportunity for small corrections and standardizations—work for which the 1925 version seems to cry out. The copia of misprints, textual errors, and lack of standardization in *AVA* is well known to scholars familiar with that text. One need look no further than the descriptions of the phases in "The Twenty-Eight Embodiments" to see the kind of variations in capitalization, abbreviation, and italicization that riddle the 1925 text. Each phase has at the beginning of its description a summary of its characteristics, divided into *Will, Mask, Creative Mind,* and *Body of Fate.* When the summary notes relationships to other phases, the number of the phase is, over the course of the section, given as "*P. 14,*" "*Phase 14,*" "phase 14," and "Phase 14." In this case, we have regularized all phase references in this section to "Phase 14," as that is the predominant style. Similarly, we have regularized other formatting presented in tables, section headings, and phase headings, as these parts of the text seem to be designed with regularity in mind. Likewise, we have corrected the spelling of proper names. We have also corrected the misnumbering of section headings that begins on page 82 (page 68 in this edition). Similarly, and for ease of distinction between our endnotes and WBY's footnotes, we have regularized the reference mark for WBY's own notes to an asterisk (*), although in a couple of instances the copy-text uses a "1" instead. All of the changes above are listed in the table of emendations at the end of this volume, but two categories of changes to punctuation are made silently: we have standardized quotation marks and removed occasional italicization of semicolons.

Capitalization and italicization of terms is also wildly variable in *AVA.* For the most part, we have retained the capitalization and italicization found in the copy-text, in order to retain the impression that *AVA* would have given its original readers. The main exception is the body of terminology that is particular to *A Vision* and crucial to an understanding of the Yeatses' system. At a late stage of proofs, WBY himself attempted to standardize the capitalization and italicization of technical terms.[36] Throughout the text, readers are often reminded that these are precise technical terms, and we have honored that aim by standardizing the capitalization and italicization of the following terms: *Anima Hominis, Anima Mundi, antithetical, Daimon, Fall,* Great Wheel, Great Year, *Head, Heart, Loins,* Phase (when referring to a specifically numbered phase) and phase (when being used generally), *primary,* the *Four Principles* (*Celestial Body, Husk, Passionate Body, Spirit*), and True and False when they are used with respect to *Faculties*. *Will,* one of the *Four Faculties* (*Body of Fate, Creative Mind, Mask,* and *Will*), is not regularized with the others. Since WBY also uses the word *will* in its ordinary sense, and it is not always clear whether he refers to the common concept or the specialized term, we have yielded to the authority of the copy-text for this word.

All students of *A Vision* will continue to rely heavily on the important edition *CVA,* with its extensive introduction and notes. George Mills Harper and Walter Kelly Hood, its editors, presented the text in facsimile, a fact that left the text uncorrected but gives readers the opportunity now to examine both this reset text and also a photostat of the original Laurie edition. This edition does not hope to supplant so much as complement *CVA,* and we have used Harper and Hood extensively, often borrowing without major change from their notes. However, our notes can take advantage of scholarly advances since the publication of *CVA,* foremost among which is the four-volume edition of the *Vision Papers* (*YVP*), of which Harper was the general editor; when *AVA* refers directly to the AS or other documents, as it does with significant frequency, our notes direct readers when possible to *YVP*.

Among other editions of WBY, note should be made of the special case of *Mythologies,* whose collected occult texts are often relevant to *AVA.* Although the Collected Works edition of that text, to be edited by Jonathan Allison, has yet to be published, there are two existing editions. The first, published by Macmillan in 1959, is unannotated and has not been recently reedited, but it has the advantage of being widely available. Warwick Gould and Deirdre Toomey published in 2005 an impressive scholarly edition with Palgrave, an edition that is rich with annotations but not as common as the other. Wishing to present readers with as many possibilities for further reading as possible, we have presented references to both in our annotations.

Portrait of Giraldus
from the Speculum Angelorum et Homenorum [1]

A VISION

AN EXPLANATION OF LIFE
FOUNDED UPON THE WRITINGS
OF GIRALDUS AND UPON CER-
TAIN DOCTRINES ATTRIBUTED
TO KUSTA BEN LUKA

By
WILLIAM
BUTLER
YEATS

LONDON
PRIVATELY PRINTED FOR SUBSCRIBERS ONLY BY
T. WERNER LAURIE, LTD.
1925

[Figure 2]²

I thank Messrs Macmillan & Co., the publishers of my book " Later Poems," for permission to reprint from that work " The Phases of the Moon."

W. B. Y.

Printed in Great Britain by
The Dunedin Press, Limited, Edinburgh.

[Figure 3][3]

Dedication
TO VESTIGIA[4]

It is a constant thought of mine that what we write is often a com-
mendation of, or expostulation with the friends of our youth, and
that even if we survive all our friends we continue to prolong or to
amend conversations that took place before our five-and-twentieth
year. Perhaps this book has been written because a number of young
men and women, you and I among the number, met nearly forty
years ago in London and in Paris to discuss mystical philosophy. You
with your beauty and your learning and your mysterious gifts were
held by all in affection, and though, when the first draft of this dedication was written, I had not seen you for more than thirty years,[5]
nor knew where you were nor what you were doing, and though
much had happened since we copied the Jewish Schemahamphorasch[6] with its seventy-two Names of God in Hebrew characters,
it was plain that I must dedicate my book to you. All other students
who were once friends or friends' friends were dead or estranged.
Florence Farr[7] coming to her fiftieth year, dreading old age and fading beauty, had made a decision we all dreamt of at one time or
another, and accepted a position as English teacher in a native school
in Ceylon that she might study oriental thought, and had died there.
Another had become a Buddhist monk,[8] and some ten years ago a
traveller of my acquaintance found him in a Burmese monastery. A
third[9] lived through that strange adventure, perhaps the strangest of
all adventures—Platonic love. When he was a child his nurse said to
him—'An Angel bent over your bed last night', and in his seventeenth year he awoke to see the phantom of a beautiful woman at his
bedside. Presently he gave himself up to all kinds of amorous adventures, until at last, in I think his fiftieth year but when he had still all

his physical vigour, he thought 'I do not need women but God.' Then he and a very good, charming, young fellow-student[10] fell in love with one another and though he could only keep down his passion with the most bitter struggle, they lived together platonically, and this they did, not from prejudice, for I think they had none, but from a clear sense of something to be attained by what seemed a most needless trampling of the grapes of life. She died, and he survived her but a little time during which he saw her in apparition and attained through her certain of the traditional experiences of the saint. He was my close friend, and had he lived I would have asked him to accept the dedication of a book I could not expect him to approve, for in his later life he cared for little but what seemed to him a very simple piety. We all, so far as I can remember, differed from ordinary students of philosophy or religion through our belief that truth cannot be discovered[11] but may be revealed, and that if a man do not lose faith, and if he go through certain preparations, revelation will find him at the fitting moment. I remember a learned brassfounder[12] in the North of England who visited us occasionally, and was convinced that there was a certain moment in every year which, once known, brought with it 'The Summum Bonum, the Stone of the Wise'.[13] But others, for it was clear that there must be a vehicle or symbol of communication, were of opinion that some messenger would make himself known, in a railway train let us say,[14] or might be found after search in some distant land. I look back to it as a time when we were full of a phantasy that has been handed down for generations, and is now an interpretation, now an enlargement of the folk-lore of the villages. That phantasy did not explain the world to our intellects which were after all very modern, but it recalled certain forgotten methods of meditation and chiefly how so to suspend the will that the mind became automatic, a possible vehicle for spiritual beings. It carried us to what we had learned to call *Hodos Chameliontos*.[15]

II

Some were looking for spiritual happiness or for some form of unknown power, but I had a practical object. I wished for a system of thought that would leave my imagination free to create as it chose and yet make all that it created, or could create, part of the one history, and that the soul's. The Greeks certainly had such a system, and Dante—though Boccaccio thought him a bitter partisan and therefore a modern abstract man[16]—and I think no man since. Then when I had ceased all active search, yet had not ceased from desire, the documents upon which this book is founded were put into my hands,[17] and I had what I needed, though it may be too late. What I have found indeed is nothing new, for I will show presently that Swedenborg and Blake and many before them knew that all things had their gyres; but Swedenborg and Blake preferred to explain them figuratively,[18] and so I am the first to substitute for Biblical or mythological figures, historical movements and actual men and women.

III

I have moments of exaltation like that in which I wrote 'All Souls' Night',[19] but I have other moments when remembering my ignorance of philosophy[20] I doubt if I can make another share my excitement. As I most fear to disappoint those that come to this book through some interest in my poetry and in that alone,[21] I warn them from that part of the book called 'The Great Wheel' and from the whole of Book II, and beg them to dip here and there in the verse and into my comments upon life and history. Upon the other hand my old fellow students may confine themselves to what is most technical and explanatory; thought is nothing without action,[22] but if they will master what is most abstract there and make it the foundation of their visions, the curtain may ring up on a new drama.

I could I daresay make the book richer, perhaps immeasurably so, if I were to keep it by me for another year, and I have not even dealt with the whole of my subject,[23] perhaps not even with what is most important, writing nothing about the Beatific Vision, little of sexual love; but I am longing to put it out of reach that I may write the poetry it seems to have made possible.[24] I can now, if I have the energy, find the simplicity I have sought in vain. I need no longer write poems like 'The Phases of the Moon' nor 'Ego Dominus Tuus',[25] nor spend barren years, as I have done some three or four times, striving with abstractions that substituted themselves for the play that I had planned.[26]

IV

Doubtless I must someday complete what I have begun, but for the moment my imagination dwells upon a copy of Powys Mather's *Arabian Nights*[27] that awaits my return home. I would forget the wisdom of the East and remember its grossness and its romance. Yet when I wander upon the cliffs where Augustus and Tiberius wandered,[28] I know that the new intensity that seems to have come into all visible and tangible things is not a reaction from that wisdom but its very self. Yesterday when I saw the dry and leafless vineyards at the very edge of the motionless sea, or lifting their brown stems from almost inaccessible patches of earth high up on the cliff-side, or met at the turn of the path the orange and lemon trees in full fruit, or the crimson cactus flower, or felt the warm sunlight falling between blue and blue, I murmured, as I have countless times, 'I have been part of it always and there is maybe no escape, forgetting and returning life after life like an insect in the roots of the grass.'[29] But murmured it without terror, in exultation almost.

W.B.Y.

CAPRI, FEBRUARY, 1925.[30]

INTRODUCTION

By Owen Aherne[31]

In the spring of 1917 I met in the National Gallery[32] a man whom I had known in the late Eighties and early Nineties, and had never thought to see again. Michael Robartes[33] and I had been intimate friends and fellow-students for a time, and later, after matters of theological difference arose between us, I lost sight of him, but heard a vague rumour that he was wandering or settled somewhere in the Near East. At first I was not certain if this were indeed he, and passed him in hesitation several times, but his athletic body, and his skin that had seemed, even when I first met him, sundried and sundarkened, his hawk-like profile, could belong to no other man. I wish the thirty years had changed me as little, for I saw no change in that erect body except that the hair that had been some kind of red, was grey, and in places, fading into white. I had known him as an uncompromising Pre-Raphaelite,[34] and there he stood before the story of Griselda pictured in a number of episodes, the sort of thing he had admired thirty years ago.[35] Even when I had made him understand who I was I drew him from the picture with difficulty, because his indignation that the authorities of the gallery had not thought it was worth saving from the German bombs had heightened his admiration for all pictures of that type and his need for its expression. 'The old painters,' he said, 'painted women with whom they would if they could have spent the night or a life, battles they would if they could have fought in, and all manner of desirable houses and places, but now all is changed, and God knows why anybody paints anything. But why should we complain, things move by mathematical necessity, all changes can be dated by gyre and cone, and pricked beforehand upon the Calendar.' I brought him to a seat in the middle of the room, and I had begun to speak of the changed world we met in when he said: 'Where is Yeats? I want his address. I am lost in this town and I don't know where to find anybody or anything.' I felt a slight chill, for we had both quarrelled with Mr Yeats on what I considered good grounds. Mr Yeats had given the name of Michael Robartes and that of Owen Aherne to fictitious characters, and made those characters live through events that were a travesty of real events.[36] 'Remember,' I said, 'that he not only described your death but represented it as taking place amid associations which must, I should have thought, have been highly disagreeable to an honourable man.' 'I was fool enough to mind once,' he said, 'but I soon found that he had done me a service. His story started a rumour of my death that became more and more circumstantial as it grew. One by one my correspondents ceased to write. My name had

The Great Wheel[37]

become known to a large number of fellow-students, and but for that rumour I could not have lived in peace even in the desert. If I had left no address I could never have got it out of my head that there was a vast heap of their letters lying somewhere, or even crossing the desert upon camel back.' I did not know where Mr Yeats lived, but said that we could find out from Mr Watkins the bookseller in Cecil's Court[38]: and having so found out, he said we must call upon Mr Yeats, and we started, keeping as much as possible from the main streets that we might have silence for our talk. 'What have you to say to Yeats?' I said, and instead of answering he began to describe his own life since our last meeting. 'You will remember the village riot which Yeats exaggerated in "Rosa Alchemica".[39] A couple of old friends died of their injuries, and that, and certain evil results of another kind, turned me for a long time from my favourite studies. I had all through my early life periods of pleasure, or at least of excitement, that alternated with periods of asceticism. I went from Paris to Rome, and from Rome to Vienna, in pursuit of a ballet dancer, and in Vienna we quarrelled. I tried to forget my sorrow in wine, but in a few weeks I had tired of that, and then, with some faint stirring of the old interest I went to Cracow, partly because of its fame as a centre of printing, but more I think because Dr. Dee and his friend Edward Kelly had in Cracow practised alchemy and scrying.[40] There I took up with a fiery handsome girl of the poorer classes, and hired a couple of rooms in an old tumble-down house. One night I was thrown out of bed and when I lit my tallow candle found that the bed, which had fallen at one end, had been propped up by a joint stool and an old book bound in calf.[41] In the morning I found that the book was called *Speculum Angelorum et Hominorum*,[42] had been written by Giraldus[43] and printed at Cracow in 1594, a good many years before the celebrated Cracow publications,[44] and was of a very much earlier style both as to woodcut and type. It was very dilapidated and all the middle pages had been torn out; but at the end of the book were a number of curious allegorical pictures;[45] a woman with a stone in one hand and an arrow in the other; a man whipping his shadow; a man being torn in two by an eagle and some kind of wild beast; and so on to the number of eight and twenty; a portrait of Giraldus and a unicorn; and many diagrams where gyres and circles grew out of one another like strange vegetables; and there was a large diagram at the beginning where lunar phases and zodiacal signs were mixed with various unintelligible symbols—an apple, an acorn, a cup.[46] My beggar maid had found it, she told me, on the top shelf in a wall cupboard where it had been left by the last tenant, an unfrocked priest who had joined a troup of gypsies[47] and disappeared, and she had torn out the middle pages to light our fire. What little remained of the text was in Latin, and I was piecing the passages together and getting a little light on two or three of the diagrams when a quarrel with my beggar maid plunged me into wine and gloom once more. Then turning violently from all sensual pleasure I decided to say my prayers at the Holy Sepulchre, and from there I went to Damascus that I might learn Arabic for I had decided to continue my prayers at Mecca, and hoped to get there in disguise.[48] I had gone the greater portion of the way when I saw certain markings upon the sands which corresponded almost exactly to a diagram in the *Speculum*. Nobody could explain them or say who made them, but when I discovered that an unknown tribe of Arabs had camped near by a couple of nights before and that they had moved in a northerly direction, I took the first opportunity of plunging into the desert in pursuit. I went from tribe to tribe for several months, learnt nothing and found myself at last in a remote town where, thanks to a small medicine chest which I always carry, I became first doctor, and then a kind of steward to an Arab chief or petty king. I constantly spoke about those markings upon the sand but learnt nothing till our town or village was visited by a tribe of Judwalis.[49] There are several tribes of this strange sect, who are known among the Arabs for the violent contrasts of character amongst them, for their licentiousness and their sanctity. Fanatical in matters of doctrine, they seem tolerant of human frailty beyond any believing people I have met.[50] One of them, an old man well known for his piety, asked me to prescribe for some complaint of his. When he came into my house, the book lay open upon a table, the frontispiece spread out: he turned towards it because it was European, and everything European filled him with curiosity, and then, pointing to the lunar phases and the mythological emblems, declared that he saw the doctrines of his tribe. The Judwali had once possessed a learned book called *The Way of the Soul between the Sun and the Moon*[51] and attributed to a certain

Kusta ben Luka, Christian Philosopher at the Court of Harun Al-Raschid,[52] and though this, and a smaller book describing the personal life of the philosopher, had been lost or destroyed in desert fighting some generations before his time, its doctrines were remembered, for they had always constituted the beliefs of the Judwalis who look upon Kusta ben Luka as their founder. As my attempt to understand the diagrams of Giraldus, in the absence of other intellectual interests, had come to fill all my thoughts, I persuaded him to accept me into his tribe and for some years wandered with the Judwalis, though not always with the same tribe. I found that though their Sacred Book had been lost they had a vast doctrine which was constantly explained to their growing boys and girls by the aid of diagrams drawn by old religious men upon the sands, and that these diagrams were in many cases identical with those in the *Speculum Angelorum et Hominorum*. I am convinced, however, that this doctrine did not originate with Kusta ben Luka, for certain terms and forms of expression suggest some remote Syriac origin. I once told an old Judwali of my conviction upon this point but he merely said that Kusta ben Luka had doubtless been taught by the desert djinns[53] who lived to a great age and remembered ancient languages.'

We had come by this to the little Bloomsbury court where Mr Yeats had his lodging;[54] but when I told him so, he said, 'No, it will be better to write and make an appointment.[55] He is almost certain to be out.' The evening had begun to darken and I pointed to a gleam of light through a slit in the curtain of the room on the second floor, but he said 'No, no, I will write,' and then 'I have great gifts in my hands and I stand between two enemies; Yeats that I quarrelled with and have not forgiven; you that quarrelled with me and have not forgiven me.' He began to walk away and I followed, and presently we fell into talk about indifferent things. I dined with him at the hotel and after dinner he brought out diagrams and notes, and began explaining their general drift. The sheets of paper which were often soiled and torn were rolled up in a bit of old camel skin and tied in bundles with bits of cord and bits of an old shoe-lace. This bundle, he explained, described the mathematical law of history, that bundle the adventure of the soul after death, that other the interaction between the living and the dead and so on. He saw that I was interested and asked if I would arrange them for publication. Such things fascinate me and I consented and from then on for months we were travelling companions, and he explained notes and diagrams in words almost as obscure. Certainly no man had ever less gift of expression. He came with me to France and later on to Ireland because of his wish to see once more places that he had known. In Dublin we stayed for a time in my Dominick Street house, described so extravagantly in 'The Tables of the Law', which keeps its eighteenth century state, though slum children play upon its steps and the windows of the next house are patched with brown paper.[56] On a walking tour in Connaught we passed Thoor Ballylee[57] where Mr Yeats had settled for the summer, and words were spoken between us slightly resembling those in 'The Phases of the Moon',[58] and I noticed that as his friendship with me grew closer, his animosity against Mr Yeats revived.

Suddenly, however, our friendship was shattered by a violent scene like those of our youth. We had returned to London and I had there written eighty or ninety pages of exposition. He complained in exaggerated language that I interpreted the system as a form of Christianity, that only those aspects of character that were an expression of Christianity interested me—*primary* character to use the terms of the philosophy—and that I was neither informed nor interested when I came to the opposite type. I contended that there could be nothing incompatible between his system and Christianity. St Clement of Alexandria had taught the re-birth of the Soul and had remained a saint, and in our own time the Capuchin Archbishop Passavalli has taught it and keeps his mitre.[59] Through lack of it, I said, the mediæval Church got into a labyrinth of absurdity about Limbo and unbaptised children, but a certain number of modern Catholics have come to think that God may very well command a soul that has left its work unfinished to leave Purgatory and return to the world.[60] Nothing, however, would persuade him, and he declared that he would give all his material to Mr Yeats and let him do what he liked with it. Now it was my turn to get angry, for I had spent much toil upon his often confused and rambling notes. 'You will give them to a man', I said, 'who has thought more of the love of woman than of the love of God.' 'Yes,' he replied, 'I want a lyric poet, and if he cares for nothing but expression, so much the better, my desert geometry will take care of the truth.' I replied—I think it better to set my words down without disguise—'Mr Yeats has intellectual belief but he is entirely without moral faith, without that sense, which should come to a man with terror and joy,[61] of a Divine Presence, and though he may seek, and may have always sought it, I am certain that he will not find it in this life.' This increased Robartes' anger, for I had almost repeated words of his own, and he accused Christianity of destroying Greco-Roman art and science, because it thought nothing mattered but faith. I denied this but said that even barbarism had not been too great a price to pay for pity and a conscience, and I reminded him that the system itself made a realisation of God one half of life. He then used ungenerous words, revived a quarrel of thirty years before, said that I was always the same, that I was but a free man for a moment, and even asked if I had consulted my confessor.* He called next day with some kind of an apology but said I must come to see Mr Yeats and that he had made an appointment for us both. At Mr Yeats's Bloomsbury lodging he talked of his travels and his discovery, and as during the night I had thought the matter over and thought myself well out of a troublesome and thankless work, I helped his exposition. He had brought the Giraldus diagrams, and they seemed to interest Mr Yeats at first sight as much as they had Robartes himself. Mr Yeats consented to write the exposition on the condition that I wrote the introduction and any notes I pleased, and would have persuaded me to accept a portion of the profits but this I refused as later on I may publish my own commentary.

Two days later Robartes returned to Mesopotamia,[62] for the armistice[63] had made some spot, where he planned to spend his declining years, habitable once more, and from that day to this I have heard neither of him nor from him. This silence that has closed round him has made it natural to write, as I know he wished that I should, as if his conversation and his foibles were already a part of history. In all probability he will never read what Mr Yeats or I have written, and he has lived so long out of Europe that he has no friends to find offence in a too candid record.

Mr Yeats's completed manuscript now lies before me. The system

---

*I think Mr Aherne has remembered his own part in this conversation more accurately than that of his opponent.—W.B.Y.

itself has grown clearer for his concrete expression of it, but I notice that if I made too little of the *antithetical* phases he has done no better by the *primary*. I think too that Mr Yeats himself must feel that the abstract foundation needs some such exploration as I myself had attempted. The twelve rotations associated with the lunar and solar months of the Great Year first arose, as Mr Yeats understands, from the meeting and separation of certain spheres.[64] I consider that the form should be called elliptoid, and that rotation as we know it is not the movement that corresponds most closely to reality. At any rate I can remember Robartes saying in one of his paradoxical figurative moods that he pictured reality as a number of great eggs laid by the Phœnix and that these eggs turn inside out perpetually without breaking the shell.[65]

O. A.

LONDON, MAY, 1925.[66]

BOOK I

What the Caliph Partly Learned

1. *THE WHEEL AND THE PHASES OF THE MOON*[1]

An old man cocked his ear upon a bridge;
He and his friend, their faces to the South,
Had trod the uneven road. Their boots were soiled,
Their Connemara cloth[2] *worn out of shape;*
They had kept a steady pace as though their beds,
Despite a dwindling and late risen moon,
Were distant still. An old man cocked his ear.

AHERNE

What made that sound?

ROBARTES

                    A rat or water-hen
Splashed, or an otter slid into the stream.
We are on the bridge; that shadow is the tower,
And the light proves that he is reading still.[3]
He has found, after the manner of his kind,
Mere images; chosen this place to live in
Because, it may be, of the candle light
From the far tower where Milton's platonist[4]
Sat late, or Shelley's visionary prince:[5]
The lonely light that Samuel Palmer[6] engraved,
An image of mysterious wisdom won by toil;
And now he seeks in book or manuscript
What he shall never find.

AHERNE

Why should not you
Who know it all ring at his door, and speak
Just truth enough to show that his whole life
Will scarcely find for him a broken crust
Of all those truths that are your daily bread;
And when you have spoken take the roads again?

ROBARTES

He wrote of me in that extravagant style
He had learned from Pater,[7] and to round his tale
Said I was dead; and dead I choose to be.[8]

AHERNE

Sing me the changes of the moon once more;
True song, though speech: 'mine author sung it me.'[9]

ROBARTES

Twenty-and-eight the phases of the moon,
The full and the moon's dark and all the crescents,
Twenty-and-eight, and yet but six-and-twenty
The cradles that a man must needs be rocked in:
For there's no human life at the full or the dark.
From the first crescent to the half, the dream
But summons to adventure and the man
Is always happy like a bird or a beast;
But while the moon is rounding towards the full
He follows whatever whim's most difficult
Among whims not impossible, and though scarred,
As with the cat-o'-nine-tails of the mind,
His body moulded from within his body
Grows comelier.[10] Eleven pass, and then
Athena takes Achilles by the hair,[11]
Hector is in the dust,[12] Nietzsche is born,[13]

Because the hero's crescent is the twelfth.
And yet, twice born, twice buried, grow he must,
Before the full moon, helpless as a worm.
The thirteenth moon but sets the soul at war
In its own being, and when that war's begun
There is no muscle in the arm; and after
Under the frenzy of the fourteenth moon
The soul begins to tremble into stillness,
To die into the labyrinth of itself!

AHERNE

Sing out the song; sing to the end, and sing
The strange award of all that discipline.

ROBARTES

All thought becomes an image and the soul
Becomes a body: that body and that soul
Too perfect at the full to lie in a cradle,
Too lonely for the traffic of the world:
Body and soul cast out and cast away
Beyond the visible world.

AHERNE

All dreams of the soul
End in a beautiful man's or woman's body.

ROBARTES

Have you not always known it?

AHERNE

The song will have it
That those that we have loved got their long fingers
From death, and wounds, or on Sinai's top,[14]

Or from some bloody whip in their own hands.
They ran from cradle to cradle till at last
Their beauty dropped out of the loneliness
Of body and soul.

ROBARTES

The lover's heart knows that.

AHERNE

It must be that the terror in their eyes
Is memory or foreknowledge of the hour
When all is fed with light and heaven is bare.

ROBARTES

When the moon's full those creatures of the full
Are met on the waste hills by country men
Who shudder and hurry by: body and soul
Estranged amid the strangeness of themselves,
Caught up in contemplation, the mind's eye
Fixed upon images that once were thought,
For separate, perfect, and immovable
Images can break the solitude
Of lovely, satisfied, indifferent eyes.

And thereupon with aged, high-pitched voice
Aherne laughed, thinking of the man within,
His sleepless candle and laborious pen.

ROBARTES

And after that the crumbling of the moon:
The soul remembering its loneliness
Shudders in many cradles; all is changed,
It would be the world's servant, and as it serves,

Choosing whatever task's most difficult
Among tasks not impossible,[15] it takes
Upon the body and upon the soul
The coarseness of the drudge.

AHERNE

Before the full
It sought itself and afterwards the world.

ROBARTES

Because you are forgotten, half out of life,
And never wrote a book, your thought is clear.[16]
Reformer, merchant, statesman, learned man,
Dutiful husband, honest wife by turn,
Cradle upon cradle, and all in flight and all
Deformed because there is no deformity
But saves us from a dream.

AHERNE

And what of those
That the last servile crescent has set free?

ROBARTES

Because all dark, like those that are all light,
They are cast beyond the verge, and in a cloud,
Crying to one another like the bats;
And having no desire they cannot tell
What's good or bad, or what it is to triumph
At the perfection of one's own obedience;
And yet they speak what's blown into the mind;
Deformed beyond deformity, unformed,
Insipid as the dough before it is baked,
They change their bodies at a word.

AHERNE

And then?

ROBARTES

When all the dough has been so kneaded up
That it can take what form cook Nature fancy
The first thin crescent is wheeled round once more.

AHERNE

But the escape; the song's not finished yet.

ROBARTES

Hunchback and Saint and Fool are the last crescents.[17]
The burning bow that once could shoot an arrow
Out of the up and down, the wagon wheel
Of beauty's cruelty and wisdom's chatter—
Out of that raving tide—is drawn betwixt
Deformity of body and of mind.

AHERNE

Were not our beds far off I'd ring the bell,
Stand under the rough roof-timbers of the hall
Beside the castle door, where all is stark
Austerity, a place set out for wisdom
That he will never find; I'd play a part;
He would never know me after all these years
But take me for some drunken country man;
I'd stand and mutter there until he caught
'Hunchback and Saint and Fool', and that they came
Under the three last crescents of the moon,
And then I'd stagger out. He'd crack his wits
Day after day, yet never find the meaning.

And then he laughed to think that what seemed hard
Should be so simple—a bat rose from the hazels
And circled round him with its squeaky cry,
The light in the tower window was put out.

[Figure 5][18]

2. THE DANCE OF
THE FOUR ROYAL PERSONS[19]

BY OWEN AHERNE

Michael Robartes gives the following account of the diagram called 'The Great Wheel' in Giraldus.[20] A Caliph[21] who reigned after the death of Harun Al-Raschid discovered one of his companions climbing the wall that encircled the garden of his favourite slave, and because he had believed this companion entirely devoted to his interests, gave himself up to astonishment. After much consideration he offered a large sum of money to any man who could explain human nature so completely that he should never be astonished again. Kusta ben Luka, now a very old man, went to the palace with his book of geometrical figures, but the Caliph, after he had explained them for an hour, banished him from the palace, and declared that all unintelligible visitors were to be put to death. A few days later four black but splendidly dressed persons stood at the city gate and announced that they had come from a most distant country to explain human nature, but that the Caliph must meet them on the edge of the desert. He came attended by his Vizir,[22] and asked their country. 'We are,' said the eldest of the four, 'the King, the Queen, the Prince and the Princess of the Country of Wisdom. It has reached our ears that a certain man has pretended that wisdom is difficult, but it is our intention to reveal all in a dance.' After they had danced for several minutes the Caliph said: 'Their dance is dull, and they dance without accompaniment, and I consider that nobody has ever been more unintelligible.' The Vizir gave the order for their execution, and while waiting the tightening of the bow-strings, each dancer said to the executioner: 'In the Name of Allah, smooth out the mark of my footfall on the sand.' And the executioner replied, 'If the Caliph permit.' When the Caliph heard what the dancers had said, he thought, 'There is certainly some great secret in the marks of their feet.'[23] He went at once to the dancing place, and, having stood for a long time looking at the marks, he said: 'Send us Kusta ben Luka, and tell him that he shall not die.' Kusta ben Luka was sent for, and from sunrise to sunset of the day after, and for many days, he explained the markings of the sand. At last the Caliph said: 'I now understand human nature; I can never be surprised again: I will put the amount of the reward into a tomb for the four dancers.' Kusta ben Luka answered: 'No, Sire, for the reward belongs to me.' 'How can that be?' said the other, 'for you have but explained the marks upon the sand, and those marks were not made by your feet.' 'They were made by the feet of my pupils,' said ben Luka. 'When you banished me from the Palace they gathered in my house to console me, and the wisest amongst them said, "He that dies is the chief person in the story,"[24] and he and three others offered to dance what I chose.' 'The reward is yours,' said the Caliph, 'and henceforth let the figure marked by their feet be called the Dance of the Four Royal Persons, for it is right that your pupils be rewarded for dying.'

According to the Robartes MSS the Dance of the Four Royal Persons is one of the names for the first figure drawn by the Judwali elders for the instruction of youth and is identical with the 'Great Wheel' of Giraldus.

I am inclined to see in the story of its origin a later embodiment of a story that it was the first diagram drawn upon the sand by the wife of Kusta ben Luka, and that its connection with lunar phases, the movements and the nature of the *Four Faculties* and their general application to the facts of human life, were fully explained before its geometrical composition was touched upon. The Judwali doctor of Bagdad,[25] who is mentioned elsewhere in this book, said that the whole philosophy was so expounded in a series of fragments which only displayed their meaning, like one of those child's pictures which are made up out of separate cubes, when all were put together. The object of this was, it seems, to prevent the intellect from forming its own conclusions, and so thwarting the Djinn who could only speak to curiosity and passivity. I cannot, however, let this pass without saying that I doubt the authenticity of this story, which Mr Yeats has expanded into the poem 'Desert Geometry or The Gift of Harun

Al-Raschid',[26] at least in its present form, and that an almost similar
adventure is attributed in one of the Robartes documents to a
Mahometan grammarian of a much later date.[27] I will, however, discuss all these matters at length in my own book upon the philosophy
and its sources.

O. A.

MAY, 1925.[28]

PART I

3. THE GREAT WHEEL

I

ANTITHETICAL AND PRIMARY

The diagram of the Great Wheel shows a series of numbers and symbols which represent the Lunar phases; and all possible human types can be classified under one or other of these twenty-eight phases. Their number is that of the Arabic Mansions of the Moon[29] but they are used merely as a method of classification and for simplicity of classification their symbols are composed in an entirely arbitrary way. As the lunar circle narrows to a crescent and as the crescent narrows to a still narrower crescent, the Moon approaches the Sun, falls as it were under his influence; and for this reason the Sun and Moon in diagram 1 are considered to be imposed one upon another.

They may be coloured gold and silver[30] respectively. The first phase is therefore full Sun as it were, and the 15th Phase full Moon, while Phases 8 and 22 are half Sun and half Moon. In Book II is described the geometrical foundation of this symbolism and of the other characters of the wheel. When one uses the phases, in popular exposition or for certain symbolic purposes, one considers full Sun as merely the night when there is no moon, and in representing any phase visibly one makes the part which is not lunar dark. The Sun is objective man and the Moon subjective man, or more properly the Sun is *primary* man and the Moon *antithetical* man—terms that will be explained later. Objective and Subjective are not used in their metaphysical but in their colloquial sense. Murray's dictionary[31] describes the colloquial use of the word 'objective' thus. All that 'is presented to consciousness as opposed to consciousness of self, that is the object of perception or thought, the non-ego'. And again, objective when used in describing works of art means 'dealing with or laying stress upon that which is external to the mind, treating of outward things and events rather than inward thought', 'treating a subject so as to exhibit the actual facts, not coloured by the opinions or feelings of the writer'. The volume of Murray's dictionary containing letter S is not yet published,[32] but as 'subjective' is the contrary to 'objective' it needs no further definition. Under the Sun's light we see things as they are, and go about our day's work, while under that of the Moon, we see things dimly, mysteriously, all is sleep and dream. All men are characterised upon a first analysis by the proportion in which these two characters or *Tinctures*,[33] the objective or *primary,* the subjective or *antithetical,* are combined. Man is said to have a series of embodiments (any one of which may be repeated) that correspond to the twenty-eight fundamental types. The *First* and *Fif-*

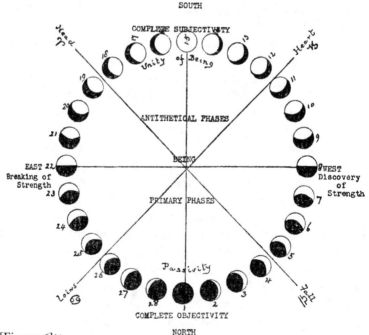

[Figure 6][34]

teenth, being wholly objective and subjective respectively, are not human embodiments, as human life is impossible without the strife between the *Tinctures*.[35]

II

THE FOUR FACULTIES[36]

Incarnate man has *Four Faculties* which constitute the *Tinctures*— the *Will*, the *Creative Mind*, the *Body of Fate*, and the *Mask*. The *Will* and *Mask* are predominately Lunar or *antithetical*, the *Creative Mind* and the *Body of Fate* predominately Solar or *primary*. When thought of in isolation, they take upon themselves the nature now of one phase, now of another. By *Will**[37] is understood feeling that has not become desire because there is no object to desire; a bias by which the soul is classified and its phase fixed but which as yet is without result in action; an energy as yet uninfluenced by thought, action, or emotion; the first matter of a certain personality—choice. If a man's *Will* is at say Phase 17 we say that he is a man of Phase 17, and so on. By *Mask* is understood the image of what we wish to become, or of that to which we give our reverence. Under certain circumstances it is called the *Image*.[38] By *Creative Mind* is meant intellect, as intellect was understood[39] before the close of the seventeenth century—all the mind that is consciously constructive. By *Body of Fate* is understood the physical and mental environment, the changing human body, the stream of Phenomena as this affects a particular individual, all that is forced upon us from without, Time as it affects sensation. The *Will* when represented in the diagram is always opposite the *Mask*, the *Creative Mind* always opposite the *Body of Fate*.

The *Will* looks into a painted picture. The *Creative Mind* looks into a photograph, but both look into something which is the oppo-

---

*I have changed the 'creative genius' of the Documents into *Creative Mind* to avoid confusion between 'genius' and *Daimon*; and 'Ego' into *Will* for 'Ego' suggests the total man who is all *Four Faculties*. *Will* or self-will was the only word I could find not for man but Man's root. If Blake had not given 'selfhood' a special meaning it might have served my turn.

September, 1925.

site of themselves. The picture is that which is chosen, while the photograph is heterogeneous. The photograph is fated, because by fate is understood that which comes from without, whereas the *Mask* is predestined, *Destiny* being that which comes to us from within.[40] We best express the heterogeneousness of the photograph if we call it a photograph of a crowded street, which the *Creative Mind*—when not under the influence of the *Mask*—contemplates coldly; while the picture contains but few objects and the contemplating *Will* is impassioned and solitary.

All *Four Faculties* influence each other and the object of the diagram of the Wheel is to show when and in what proportions. When the *Will* predominates, and there is strong desire, the *Mask* or *Image* is sensuous, but when *Creative Mind* predominates it is abstract. When the *Mask* predominates it is idealised, when *Body of Fate* predominates it is concrete, and so on. An object is sensuous if I relate it to myself, '*my* fire, *my* chair', etc., but it is concrete if I say '*a* chair, *a* fire', and abstract if I but speak of it as the representative of a class—'*the* chair, *the* fire', etc.[41]

III

THE PLACE OF THE FOUR FACULTIES ON THE WHEEL

A man whose *Will* is at Phase 17 will have his *Creative Mind* at Phase 13 and his *Mask* at Phase 3 and his *Body of Fate* at Phase 27; while a man whose *Will* is at Phase 3 would have all these positions exactly reversed. When *Will* is at Phase 15, *Creative Mind* is there also. On the other hand, when *Will* is at Phase 22, *Will* and *Body of Fate* are superimposed, while *Creative Mind* and *Mask* are superimposed at Phase 8. The points on diagram 1[42] marked *Head, Heart, Loins* and *Fall*[43] mark where the *Four Faculties* are at equal distances from one another and that in part is why they are also represented by cardinal signs. They have also another significance which will be explained later.[44]

Will and *Mask* are opposite in *Tincture, Creative Mind* and *Body of Fate* are opposite in *Tincture*. The one has the *primary* in the exact strength of the *antithetical* in the other, and vice versa. The *primary* and *antithetical* define the inclination of the *Will*, and through the

Will affect the other three; this may be called the difference in quality. A *Will* at Phase 18 would have the exact amount of *antithetical* inclination that a *Will* at Phase 4 would have of *primary*. On the other hand, a *Will* at Phase 18 and *Creative Mind* at Phase 12 are exactly the same in the proportions of their *Tinctures*, have exactly the same quality of *Tincture* but move in the opposite directions—one is going from Phase 1 to Phase 28 and the other from Phase 28 to Phase 1. It is therefore necessary to consider both direction and quality.

The relations between *Will* and *Mask*, *Creative Mind* and *Body of Fate* are called *oppositions*, and upon some occasions *contrasts*, while those between *Will* and *Creative Mind*, *Mask* and *Body of Fate* are called—for reasons which will appear later—*discords*.

Between Phase 12 and Phase 13, and between Phase 4 and Phase 5 in diagram 1 occurs what is called 'the *opening* of the *Tinctures*', and between Phase 18 and Phase 19, and between Phase 4 and Phase 5 what is called 'the *closing*'. This means that between Phase 12 and Phase 13 each *Tincture* divides into two, and closes up again between Phase 18 and Phase 19. Between Phase 26 and Phase 27 the *Tinctures* become one *Tincture*, and between Phase 4 and Phase 5 become two again. The *antithetical* before Phase 15 becomes the *primary* after Phase 15, and vice versa—that is to say, the thoughts and emotions that are in nature *antithetical* before Phase 15 are in nature *primary* after Phase 15; the man who before Phase 15 is harsh in his judgment of himself will turn that harshness to others after Phase 15.

The geometrical reasons both for this interchange and for the closing and opening of the *Tinctures* are discussed in Book II.

IV

DRAMA OF THE FACULTIES
AND OF THE TINCTURES, ETC.

One can describe *antithetical* man by comparing him to the *Commedia dell' Arte*[45] or improvised drama of Italy. The stage manager having chosen his actor, the *Will*, chooses for this actor, that he may display him the better, a scenario, *Body of Fate*, which offers to his *Creative Mind* the greatest possible difficulty that it can face without despair, and in which he must play a rôle and wear a *Mask* as unlike as possible to his natural character (or *Will*) and leaves him to improvise, through *Creative Mind,* the dialogue and details of the plot. He must discover a being which only exists with extreme effort, when his muscles are as it were all taut and all his energies active, and for that reason the *Mask* is described as 'A form created by passion to unite us to ourselves'. Much of what follows will be a definition or description of this deeper being, which may become the unity described by Dante in the *Convito*.[46]

For *primary* Man one must go to the Decline of the *Commedia dell' Arte* for an example. The *Will* is weak and cannot create a rôle, and so, if it transform itself, does so after an accepted pattern, some traditional clown or pantaloon. It has perhaps no object but to move the crowd, and if it 'gags' it is that there may be plenty of topical allusions. In the *primary* phases Man must cease to desire *Mask* and *Image* by ceasing from self-expression, and substitute a motive of service for that of self-expression. Instead of the created *Mask* he has an imitative *Mask*; and when he recognises this, his *Mask* may become an image of mankind. The author of *The Imitation of Christ*[47] was certainly a man of a late *primary* phase. It is said that the *antithetical Mask* is free, and the *primary Mask* enforced; and the free *Mask* is personality, a union of qualities, while the enforced *Mask* is character, a union of quantities, and of their limitations— that is to say, of those limitations which give strength precisely because they are enforced.[48] Personality, no matter how habitual, is a constantly renewed choice, and varies from an individual charm, in the more *antithetical* phases, to a hard objective dramatisation, which differs from character mainly because it is a dramatisation, in phases where the *antithetical Tincture* holds its predominance with difficulty.

Antithetical men are, like Landor,[49] violent in themselves because they hate all that impedes their personality, but are in their intellect (*Creative Mind*) gentle, but *primary* men whose hatreds are impersonal are violent in their intellect but gentle in themselves as doubtless Robespierre[50] was gentle.

The *Mask* before Phase 15 is described as 'a revelation' because through it the being obtains knowledge of itself, sees itself in personality; while after Phase 15 it is a 'concealment', for the being grows incoherent, vague and broken, as its intellect (*Creative Mind*) is more and more concerned with objects that have no relation to its unity but a relation to the unity of Society or of material things, known through the *Body of Fate,* and adopts a personality which it more and more casts outward, more and more dramatises. It is now a dissolving violent phantom which would grip itself and hold itself together. The being of *antithetical Man* is described as full of rage before Phase 12, against all in the world that hinders its expression, but after Phase 12 the rage is a knife turned against itself. After Phase 15, but before Phase 19, the being is full of phantasy, a continual escape from, and yet acknowledgment of all that allures in the world, a continual playing with all that must engulf it. The *primary* is that which serves, the *antithetical* is that which creates.

At Phase 8 is the 'Discovery of Strength', an embodiment in sensuality, for the imitation that held it to the norm of the race has ceased and the personality with its own norm has not begun. *Primary* and *antithetical* are equal and fight for mastery; and when this fight is ended through the conviction of weakness and the preparation for rage, the *Mask* becomes once more voluntary. At Phase 22 is the 'Breaking of Strength', for here the being makes its last attempt to impose its personality upon the world, before the *Mask* becomes enforced once more and Character is once more born.

To these two phases, perhaps to all phases, the being may return up to four times before it can pass on. It is claimed, however, that four times is the utmost possible.[51] By being is understood that which divides into *Four Faculties,* by individual the *Will* analysed in relation to itself, by personality the *Will* analysed in relation to the *Mask.* It is because of the antithesis between *Will* and *Mask* that subjective natures are called *antithetical,* while those in whom individuality and *Creative Mind* predominate, and who are content with things as they find them, are called *primary.* Personality is strongest near Phase 15, individuality near Phase 22 and Phase 8.

V

RULE FOR DISCOVERING TRUE AND FALSE MASKS[52]

When the Will is in antithetical phases the True Mask is the effect of Creative Mind of opposite phase upon that phase; and the False

Mask is the effect of Body of Fate of opposite phase upon that phase.

The True *Mask* of Phase 17 for instance is 'Simplification by intensity' and is derived from Phase 3 modified by the *Creative Mind* of that phase, which is described as 'Simplicity' and is from Phase 27 which is that of the Saint.

The False *Mask* of Phase 17 is 'Dispersal' and is derived from Phase 3, modified by the *Body of Fate* which is from Phase 13 and is described as 'Interest'. It will be found that this word describes with great accuracy the kind of 'Dispersal' which weakens men of Phase 17 when they try to live in the *primary Tincture.*

When the *Will* is in *primary* phases the True *Mask* is the effect of *Body of Fate* of opposite phase upon that phase; and the False *Mask* is the effect of *Creative Mind* of opposite phase upon that phase.

The True *Mask* of Phase 3, is 'Innocence' and it is derived from Phase 17 modified by its *Body of Fate* which is described as 'Loss' and derived from Phase 27, which is that of the Saint.

The False *Mask* of Phase 3 is 'Folly' and is derived from Phase 17 modified by *Creative Mind* of that phase which is described as 'Creative imagination through *antithetical* emotion'. The *primary* Phase 3 when it attempts to live *antithetically* gives itself up to inconsequence because it cannot be creative in the *Mask*. On the other hand, when it lives according to the *primary,* and is true to phase, it takes from its opposite phase delight in passing things, sees 'a world in a grain of sand, Heaven in a wild flower'[53] and becomes a child playing, knows nothing of consequence and purpose. 'Loss' effects Phase 17 itself as an enforced withdrawal of *primary* desire for the *Body of Fate* is inimical to *antithetical* natures.

Only long familiarity with the system can make the whole table of *Masks, Creative Minds,* etc.—see sec. xii—intelligible; it should be studied by the help of these two following rules:

In an antithetical phase the being seeks by the help of the Creative Mind to deliver the Mask from Body of Fate.

In a primary phase the being seeks by the help of the Body of Fate to deliver the Creative Mind from the Mask.

VI

RULE FOR FINDING THE TRUE
AND FALSE CREATIVE MIND[54]

When the Will is in antithetical phases the True Creative Mind is derived from the Creative Mind Phase modified by the Creative Mind of that phase; while the False Creative Mind is derived from the Creative Mind Phase, modified by the Body of Fate of that phase.

For instance the True *Creative Mind* of Phase 17 'Creative Imagination through *antithetical* Emotion' is derived from Phase 13 as that phase is modified by its *Creative Mind* which is described as 'Sincere expression of Self'.

The False *Creative Mind* of Phase 17 'Artificial self-realisation' is derived from Phase 13 as that phase is modified by its *Body of Fate* 'Enforced Love'.

Phase 17 has the same proportion of *Tinctures* as Phase 13 but a different direction, is growing more *primary* and so has intellectually what Phase 13 has emotionally, and is turning outward what Phase 13 turned inward.

Phase 13 stirred to creation by 'Sincere expression of self' stirs Phase 17 to creation of images; on the other hand Phase 13 stirred by 'Enforced love'—which had to Phase 13 itself been an influence forcing the being to seek what to it was an impossible *primary* activity and so to a morbid self-absorption—becomes in Phase 17 an 'artificial dramatisation of the Self'.

When the Will is in primary phases the True Creative Mind is derived from Creative Mind phase, modified by the Body of Fate of that phase; while the False Creative Mind is derived from the Creative Mind phase modified by the False Creative Mind of that phase.

For instance the True *Creative Mind* of Phase 27 is described as 'Spiritual Receptivity' and is derived from Phase 3 as that phase is modified by its *Body of Fate* derived from Phase 13, and is described as 'Interest'. While its False *Creative Mind* is described as 'Pride' and is derived from Phase 3, modified by the False *Creative Mind* of that phase which is derived from Phase 27 and described as 'Abstraction'. As will be seen later the phase of the Saint, Phase 27, has 'Abstraction' for its great sin and escapes from this sin by 'Humility'.

Again two mirrors face one another. Phase 3 and Phase 27 are alike in *Tincture* but different in direction. The meaning of the interchange between 'Pride' and 'Abstraction' will grow clear from the exposition of the phase.

VII

RULE FOR FINDING BODY OF FATE

The *Body of Fate* of any particular phase is the effect of the whole nature of its *Body of Fate* phase upon that particular phase. As, however, the *Body of Fate* is always *primary* it is in sympathy with the *primary* phase while it opposes the *antithetical* phase; in this it is the reverse of the *Mask* which is sympathetic to an *antithetical* phase but opposes a *primary*.

VIII

SUBDIVISIONS OF THE WHEEL

Excluding the four phases of crisis (Phases 8, 22, 15, 1) each quarter consists of six phases, or of two sets of three. In every case the first phase of each set can be described as a manifestation of power, the second of a code or arrangement of powers, and the third of a belief, the belief being an appreciation of, or submission to some quality which becomes power in the next phase. The reason of this is that each set of three is itself a wheel, and has the same character as the Great Wheel. The Phases 1 to 8 are associated with elemental earth, being phases of germination and sprouting; those between Phase 8 and Phase 15 with elemental *water,* because there the image-making power is at its height; those between Phase 15 and Phase 22 with elemental *air,* because through *air,* or space, things are divided from one another, and here intellect is at its height; those between Phase 22 and Phase 1 with elemental fire because here all things are made simple.[55] The *Will* is strongest in First Quarter, *Mask* in second, *Creative Mind* in third, and the *Body of Fate* in fourth.

There are other divisions and attributions to be considered later.

IX

DISCORDS, OPPOSITIONS AND CONTRASTS

The being becomes conscious of itself as a separate being, because of certain facts of *opposition* and *discord,* the emotional *opposition* of *Will* and *Mask,* the intellectual *opposition* of *Creative Mind* and *Body of Fate,* discords between *Will* and *Creative Mind, Creative Mind* and *Mask, Mask* and *Body of Fate, Body of Fate* and *Will.* A *discord* is always the enforced understanding of the unlikeness of *Will* and *Mask* or of *Creative Mind* and *Body of Fate.* There is an enforced attraction between *opposites,* for the *Will* has a natural desire for the *Mask* and the *Creative Mind* a natural perception of the *Body of Fate;* in one the dog bays the Moon,[56] in the other the eagle stares on the Sun[57] by natural right. When, however, the *Creative Mind* deceives the *Will,* by offering it some *primary* image of the *Mask,* or when the *Will* offers to the *Creative Mind* an emotion that should be turned towards the *Mask* alone, the *opposition* emerges again in its simplicity because of the jarring of the emotion, the grinding out of the *Image.* On the other hand it may be the *Mask* that slips on to the *Body of Fate* till we confuse what we would be with what we must be. As the *discords* through the circling of the *Four Faculties* approach *opposition,* when as at Phase 15 (say) the *Creative Mind* comes to be opposite the *Mask,* they share the qualities of *Opposition.* As the *Faculties* approach to one another, on the other hand, *Discord* gradually becomes identity, and one or other, according to whether it takes place at Phase 1 or Phase 15, is weakened and finally absorbed, *Creative Mind* in *Will* at Phase 15, *Will* in *Creative Mind* at Phase 1 and so on. While if it be at Phase 8 or Phase 22 first one predominates and then the other and there is instability.

Without this continual *discord* through *deception* there would be no conscience, no activity; and it will be seen later that *deception* is used as a technical term and may be substituted for 'desire'. Life is an endeavour, made vain by the Four Sails of its Mill,[58] to come to a double contemplation, that of the chosen *Image,* that of the Fated *Image.*

There are also *harmonies* but these which are geometrically connected with the centre of the figure can be best considered in relation to another part of the System.[59]

X

THE FOUR PERFECTIONS AND THE FOUR AUTOMATONISMS

The *Four Perfections* can only be understood when their phases come to be considered; it will be obvious for instance that self-sacrifice must be the typical virtue of phases where instinct or race is predominant, and especially in those three phases that come before reflection. *Automatonism* in *antithetical* phases arises from the *Mask* and *Creative Mind*, when separated from the *Body of Fate* and *Will*, through refusal of, or rest from conflict; and in *primary* phases from the *Body of Fate* and *Will*, when weary of the struggle for complete *primary* existence or when they refuse that struggle. It does not necessarily mean that the man is not true to phase or, as it is said, out of phase; the most powerful natures are precisely those who most often need *automatonism* as a rest. It is perhaps an element in our enjoyment of art and literature, being awakened in our minds by rhythm and by pattern. He is, however, out of phase, if he refuse for anything but need of rest the conflict with the *Body of Fate* which is the source of *antithetical* energy and so falls under *imitative* or *creative automatonism,* or if in *primary* phases he refuse conflict with the *Mask* and so falls under *obedient* or *instinctive automatonism.*

XI

THE DAIMON, THE SEXES, UNITY OF BEING, NATURAL AND SUPERNATURAL UNITY[60]

The *Will* and the *Creative Mind* are in the light, but the *Body of Fate* working through accident, in dark, while *Mask,* or *Image,* is a form selected instinctively for those emotional associations which come out of the dark, and this form is itself set before us by accident, or swims up from the dark portion of the mind. But there is another mind, or another part of our mind in this darkness, that is yet to its own perceptions in the light; and we in our turn are dark to that mind. These two minds (one always light*[61] and one always dark, when considered by one mind alone), make up man and *Daimon,* the *Will* of the man being the *Mask* of the *Daimon,* the *Creative Mind* of the man being the *Body of Fate* of the *Daimon* and so on.[62] The Wheel is in this way reversed, as St Peter at his crucifixion reversed by the position of his body the position of the crucified Christ:[63] 'Demon est Deus Inversus'.[64] Man's *Daimon* has therefore her energy and bias, in man's *Mask,* and her constructive power in man's fate, and man and *Daimon* face each other in a perpetual conflict or embrace. This relation (the *Daimon* being of the opposite sex to that of man) may create a passion like that of sexual love. The relation of man and woman, in so far as it is passionate, reproduces the relation of man and *Daimon,* and becomes an element where man and *Daimon* sport, pursue one another, and do one another good or evil. This does not mean, however, that the men and women of opposite phases love one another, for a man generally chooses a woman whose *Mask* falls between his *Mask* and his *Body of Fate,* or just outside one or other; but that every man is, in the right of his sex, a wheel, or group of *Four Faculties,* and that every woman is, in the right of her sex, a wheel which reverses the masculine wheel. In so far as man and woman are swayed by their sex they interact as man and *Daimon* interact, though at other moments their phases may be side by side. The *Daimon* carries on her conflict, or friendship with a man, not only through the events of life, but in the mind itself, for she is in possession of the entire dark of the mind. The things we dream, or that come suddenly into our heads, are therefore her *Creative Mind* (our *Creative Mind* is her *Body of Fate*) through which her energy, or bias, finds expression; one can therefore, if one will, think of man as *Will* and *Creative Mind* alone, perpetually face to face with another being who is also but *Will* and *Creative Mind,* though these appear to man as the object of desire, or beauty, and as fate in all its forms. If man seeks to live wholly in the light, the *Daimon* will seek to quench that light in what is to man

*Light and dark are not used in this section as in the description of the phases, but as it were cross that light and dark at right angles. See diagrams in Sec. XVII, Book II.
September, 1925.

wholly darkness, and there is conflict and *Mask* and *Body of Fate* become evil; when however in *antithetical* man the *Daimonic* mind is permitted to flow through the events of his life (the *Daimonic Creative Mind*) and so to animate his *Creative Mind*, without putting out its light, there is Unity of Being. A man becomes passionate and this passion makes the *Daimonic* thought luminous with its peculiar light—this is the object of the *Daimon*—and she so creates a very personal form of heroism or of poetry. The *Daimon* herself is now passionless and has a form of thought, which has no need of premise and deduction, nor of any language, for it apprehends the truth by a faculty which is analogous to sight, and hearing, and taste, and touch, and smell, though without organs. He who attains Unity of Being is some man, who, while struggling with his fate and his destiny until every energy of his being has been roused, is content that he should so struggle with no final conquest. For him fate and freedom are not to be distinguished; he is no longer bitter, he may even love tragedy like those 'who love the gods and withstand them'[65]; such men are able to bring all that happens, as well as all that they desire, into an emotional or intellectual synthesis and so to possess not the Vision of Good only but that of Evil. They are described as coming after death into dark and into light, whereas *primary* men, who do not receive revelation by conflict, are in dark or in light. In the *Convito* Dante speaks of his exile,[66] and the gregariousness it thrust upon him, as a great misfortune for such as he; and yet as poet he must have accepted, not only that exile, but his grief for the death of Beatrice[67] as that which made him *Daimonic*, not a writer of poetry alone like Guido Cavalcanti.[68] Intellectual creation accompanies or follows in *antithetical* man, the struggle of the being to overthrow its fate and this is symbolised by placing the *Creative Mind* in the phase opposite to that of the *Body of Fate*. Unity of Being[69] becomes possible at Phase 12, and ceases to be possible at Phase 18, but is rare before Phase 13 and after Phase 17, and is most common at Phase 17. When man is in his most *antithetical* phases the *Daimon* is most *primary*; man pursues, loves, or hates, or both loves and hates—a form of passion, an *antithetical* image is imposed upon the *Daimonic* thought—but in man's most *primary* phases the *Daimon* is at her most *antithetical*. Man is now pursued with hatred, or with love; must receive an alien terror or joy; and it is to this final acceptance of the *Image* that we apply the phrases 'Unity with God', 'Unity with Nature'. Unity with God is possible after Phase 26, though almost impossible before Phase 27 which is called 'The Saint', while Unity with Nature may take place after Phase 1, and in its turn becomes impossible after Phase 4. But for the possibility of this union man in his *primary* phases would sink into a mechanical objectivity, become wholly automatic. At Phase 26, however, he can escape from that which he apprehends through the organs of sense, by submission to that which he can apprehend by the mind's eye and ear, its palate and its touch. When he is content to be pursued, to be ignored, to be hated even by that he so apprehends, he becomes the object not of hatred but of love, for the *Daimonic* mind, being now *antithetical,* has passed from thought to passion. *Antithetical* man pursuing, or hungry, with a passion like that of the beasts, may be exalted with a passion first discovered and expressed by finer minds than his; and the *Daimon* so pursuing, so hungry, is also so exalted, and we have therefore the right to describe our union with it, as union with Nature, or with God. When Phase 1 has been passed, the union is with nature.

According to the Solar symbolism, which is explained in Book II, two are not in light and two in dark, but all four in light as contrasted to *Four Principles* that are solar and entirely dark.

XII

TABLE OF THE FOUR FACULTIES[70]

Each *Faculty* is placed after the number of the phase where it is formed, not after the phase which it affects.

Will.	Mask.	Creative Mind.	Body of Fate.
1.	No description except entire plasticity.		
2. Beginning of Energy.	*True.* Illusion. *False.* Delusion.	*True.* Physical activity. *False.* Cunning.	Enforced love of the world.
3. Beginning of Ambition.	*True.* Simplification through intensity. *False.* Dispersal.	*True.* Supersensitive receptivity. *False.* Pride.	Enforced love of another.

Will.	Mask.	Creative Mind.	Body of Fate.
4. Desire for Primary objects.	*True*. Intensity through emotions. *False*. Curiosity.	*True*. Abstract supersensitive thought. *False*. Fascination of sin.	Enforced intellectual action.
5. Separation from innocence.	*True*. Conviction. *False*. Domination.	*True*. Rhetoric. *False*. Spiritual arrogance.	Enforced belief.
6. Artificial Individuality.	*True*. Fatalism. *False*. Superstition.	*True*. Constructive emotion. *False*. Authority.	Enforced emotion.
7. Assertion of Individuality.	*True*. Self-analysis. *False*. Self-adaptation.	*True*. Creation through pity. *False*. Self-driven desire.	Enforced sensuality.
8. War between individuality and race.	*True*. Self-immolation. *False*. Self-assurance.	*True*. Amalgamation. *False*. Despair.	The beginning of true strength.
9. Belief takes place of individuality.	*True*. Wisdom. *False*. Self-pity.	*True*. Intellectual domination. *False*. Distortion.	Adventure that excites individuality.
10. The image-breaker.	*True*. Self-reliance. *False*. Isolation.	*True*. Dramatization of Mask. *False*. Self-desecration.	Humanity.
11. The consumer. The pyre-builder.	*True*. Consciousness of self. *False*. Self-consciousness.	*True*. Emotional intellect. *False*. The Unfaithful.	Natural law.
12. The Forerunner.	*True*. Self-realization. *False*. Self-abandonment.	*True*. Emotional philosophy. *False*. Enforced law.[71]	Search.
13. The sensuous man.	*True*. Renunciation. *False*. Emulation.	*True*. Creative imagination through antithetical emotion. *False*. Enforced self-realization.	Interest.
14. The obsessed man.	*True*. Oblivion. *False*. Malignity.	*True*. Vehemence. *False*. Opinionated will.	None except monotony.

Will.	Mask.	Creative Mind.	Body of Fate.
15.	No description except entire beauty.		
16. The positive man.	*True.* Player on Pan's Pipes. *False.* Fury.	*True.* Emotional will. *False.* Terror.	Fool is his own Body of Fate.
17. The Daimonic man.	*True.* Innocence. *False.* Folly.	*True.* Subjective Truth. *False.* Morbidity.	None except impersonal action.
18. The emotional man.	*True.* Passion. *False.* Will.	*True.* Subjective philosophy. *False.* War between two forms of expression.	Hunchback is his own Body of Fate.
19. The assertive man.	*True.* Excess. *False.* Limitation.	*True.* Moral iconoclasm. *False.* Self-assertion.	Persecution.
20. The concrete man.	*True.* Justice. *False.* Tyranny.	*True.* Domina-tion through emotional constriction. *False.* Reforma-tion.	Objective action.
21. The acquisitive man.	*True.* Altruism. *False.* Efficiency.	*True.* Self-dramatization. *False.* Anarchy.	Success.
22. Balance between ambition and contemplation.	*True.* Courage. *False.* Fear.	*True.* Versatility. *False.* Impotence.	Temptation versus strength.
23. The Receptive Man.	*True.* Facility. *False.* Obscurity.	*True.* Heroic sentiment. *False.* Dogmatic sentimentality.	Enforced triumph of achievement.
24. The end of ambition.	*True.* Organiza-tion. *False.* Inertia.	*True.* Ideality. *False.* Derision.	Enforced success in action.
25. The condi-tional man.	*True.* Rejection. *False.* Moral reformation.	*True.* Social intellect. *False.* Limitation.	Enforced failure of action.
26. The Multiple Man also called The Hunchback.	*True.* Self-exaggeration. *False.* Self-abandonment.	*True.* First perception of character. *False.* Mutilation.	Enforced disillusion.

Will.	Mask.	Creative Mind.	Body of Fate.
27. The Saint.	*True*. Self-expression. *False*. Self-absorption.	*True*. Simplicity. *False*. Abstraction.	Enforced cost.
28. The Fool.	*True*. Serenity. *False*. Self-distrust.	*True*. Hope. *False*. Moroseness.	Enforced illusion.

XIII

CHARACTERS OF CERTAIN PHASES[72]

FOUR PERFECTIONS

At P. 2, P. 3, P. 4	...	...	Self-sacrifice
At P. 13	...	...	Self-knowledge
At P. 16, P. 17, P. 18	...	...	Unity of Being
At P. 27	...	...	Sanctity

FOUR TYPES OF WISDOM[73]

At P. 4	...	...	Wisdom of Desire
At P. 12	...	...	Wisdom of Intellect
At P. 18	...	...	Wisdom of Heart
At P. 26	...	...	Wisdom of Knowledge

FOUR CONTESTS

At P. 1	...	...	Moral
At P. 8	...	...	Emotional
At P. 15	...	...	Physical
At P. 22	...	...	Spiritual or supersensual

RAGE, PHANTASY, ETC.

From P. 8 to P. 12	Rage
From P. 12 to P. 15	Spiritual or supersensual Rage
From P. 15 to P. 19	Phantasy
From P. 19 to P. 22	Power

XIV

*GENERAL CHARACTER OF CREATIVE MIND
AFFECTING CERTAIN PHASES[74]

(1) Affecting 28, 1, 2 from 2, 1, 28. Controlled.
(2)   "   3, 4, 5, 6 from 27, 26, 25, 24. Transformatory.
(3)   "   7, 8, 9 from 23, 22, 21. Mathematical.
(4)   "   10, 11, 12 from 20, 19, 18. Intellectually passionate.
(5)   "   13 from 17. Stillness.
(6) Affecting 14, 15, 16 from 16, 15, 14. Emotional.
(7)   "   17, 18, 19, 20 from 13, 12, 11, 10. Emotionally
             passionate.
(8)   "   21, 22, 23 from 9, 8, 7. Rational.
(9)   "   24 from 6. Obedient.
(10)   "   25, 26, 27 from 3, 4, 5.[75] Serenity.

XV

GENERAL CHARACTER OF BODY OF FATE[76]

(1) Affecting 28, 1, 2 from 16, 15, 14. Joy.
(2)   "   3, 4, 5, 6 from 13, 12, 11, 10. Breathing.
(3)   "   7, 8, 9 from 9, 8, 7. Tumult.
(4)   "   10, 11, 12 from 6, 5, 4. Tension.
(5)   "   13 from 3. Disease.
(6)   "   14, 15, 16 from 2, 1, 28. The world.
(7)   "   17, 18, 19, 20 from 27, 26, 25, 24. Sorrow.
(8)   "   21, 22, 23 from 23, 22, 21. Ambition.
(9)   "   24 from 20. Success.
(10)   "   25, 26, 27 from 19, 18, 17. Absorption.[77]

---

*This and the following Table are divided into ten divisions because they were given me in this form, and I have not sufficient confidence in my knowledge to turn them into the more convenient twelve-fold divisions. The relation of the Great Wheel and the Year is explained in Book II, and the makers of these tables may have had the old tenfold year in their minds.—W.B.Y.

XVI

TABLE OF THE QUARTERS

THE FOUR CONTESTS OF THE ANTITHETICAL WITHIN ITSELF

First quarter.	With body.	In the first quarter body should win, in the second heart, etc.
Second "	With heart.	
Third "	With mind.	
Fourth "	With soul.	

FOUR AUTOMATONISMS

First quarter. Instinctive.
Second " Imitative.
Third " Creative.
Fourth " Obedient.

FOUR CONDITIONS OF THE WILL

First quarter. Instinctive.
Second " Emotional.
Third " Intellectual.
Fourth " Moral.

FOUR CONDITIONS OF THE MASK

First quarter. Intensity (affecting Third Quarter).
Second " Tolerance (affecting Fourth Quarter).
Third " Convention or systematization (affecting First Quarter).
Fourth " Self-analysis (affecting Second Quarter).

DEFECTS OF FALSE CREATIVE MIND WHICH BRING THE FALSE MASK

First quarter.   Sentimentality.
Second   "   Brutality (desire for root facts of life).
Third   "   Hatred.
Fourth   "   Insensitiveness.

Note.—In *primary* phases these defects separate *Mask* from *Body of Fate*, in *antithetical*, *Creative Mind* from *Body of Fate*.

ELEMENTAL ATTRIBUTIONS

Earth   . . .   First quarter   . . .
Water   . . .   Second quarter   . . .
Air   . . .   Third quarter   . . .
Fire   . . .   Fourth quarter   . . .

XVII

UNCLASSIFIED ATTRIBUTES

Mask worn—moral and emotional.
Mask carried—emotional.

ABSTRACTION

Strong at 6, 7, 8.
Strongest at 22, 23, 24, 25.
Begins at 19, less at 20, increase again at 21.

THREE ENERGIES

Images from self give emotion.
Images from world give passion.
Images from the supersensual give will.

4. THE TWENTY-EIGHT EMBODIMENTS[78]

I

PHASE ONE AND THE INTERCHANGE OF THE TINCTURES

As will be seen, when late phases are described, every achievement of a being, after Phase 22, is an elimination of the individual intellect and a discovery of the moral life. When the individual intellect lingers on, it is arrogance, self-assertion, a sterile abstraction, for the being is forced by the growing *primary Tincture* to accept first the service of, and later on absorption in, the *primary* whole, a sensual or supersensual objectivity.

When the old *antithetical* becomes the new *primary,* moral feeling is changed into an organisation of experience which must in its turn seek a unity, the whole of experience. When the old *primary* becomes the new *antithetical,* the old realisation of an objective moral law is changed into a subconscious turbulent instinct. The world of rigid custom and law is broken up by 'the uncontrollable mystery upon the bestial floor'.[79]

Phase 1 not being human can better be described after Phase 28.

II

PHASE TWO

Will—Beginning of Energy.
Mask (from Phase 16). *True*—Player on Pan's Pipes. *False*—
   Fury.

Creative Mind (from Phase 28). *True*—Hope. *False*—Morose-
ness.
Body of Fate (from Phase 14)—'None except monotony'.

When the man lives out of phase and desires the *Mask,* and so
permits it to dominate the *Creative Mind,* he copies the emotional
explosion of Phase 16 in so far as difference of phase permits. He
gives himself to a violent animal assertion and can only destroy,
strike right and left as in the rage of a child, seek satisfaction of bodily need full of ignorance and gloom.

> But when they find the frowning Babe,
> Terror strikes through the region wide:
> They cry 'The babe! The babe is born!'
> And flee away on every side.[80]

But if he live according to phase, he uses the *Body of Fate* to clear the
intellect of the influence of the *Mask.* He frees himself from emotion;
and the *Body of Fate,* derived from Phase 14, pulls back the mind
into the supersensual, so changes it that it grows obedient to all that
recurs; and the *Mask,* now entirely enforced, is a rhythmical impulse.
He gives himself up to the function of the moment, the hope of the
moment, and yet is neither immoral nor violent but innocent; he is as
it were the breath stirring on the face of the deep[81]; the smile on the
face of a but half-awakened child. Nobody of our age has, it may be,
met him, certainly no record of such meeting exists, but, were such
meeting possible, he would be remembered as a form of joy, for he
would seem more entirely living than all other men, a personification
or summing up of the life of all other men. He would decide on this
or that by no balance of the reason but by an infallible joy, and if
born amid a rigid mechanical order, he would make for himself a
place, as a dog will scratch a hole for itself in loose earth.

Here, as at Phase 16, the ordinary condition is sometimes reversed,
and instead of ugliness, otherwise characteristic of this as of all *primary* phases, there is beauty. The new *antithetical Tincture* (the old
primary reborn) is violent. A new birth, when the product of an
extreme contrast in the past life of the individual, is sometimes so vio-

lent that lacking foreign admixture it forestalls its ultimate physical destiny. It forces upon the *primary* and upon itself a beautiful form. It has the muscular balance and force of an animal good-humour with all appropriate comeliness as in the dancing faun.[82] If this rare accident does not occur, the body is coarse; not deformed, but coarse from lack of sensitiveness and is most fitted for rough physical labour.

Seen by those lyrical poets who draw their *Masks* from early phases, the man of Phase 2 is transfigured. Weary of an energy that defines and judges, weary of intellectual self expression, they desire some 'concealment', some transcendent intoxication. The bodily instincts, subjectively perceived, become the cup wreathed with ivy.[83] Perhaps even a *Body of Fate* from any early phase may suffice to create this *Image,* but when it affects Phase 13 and Phase 14 the *Image* will be more sensuous, more like immediate experience.

> The Kings of Inde their jewelled sceptres vail,
> And from their treasures scatter pearled hail;
> Great Brama from his mystic heaven groans
> And all his priesthood moans;
> Before young Bacchus' eye-wink turning pale.[84]

III

PHASE THREE

Will—Beginning of Ambition.
Mask (from Phase 17). *True*—Innocence. *False*—Folly.
Creative Mind (from Phase 27). *True*—Simplicity. *False*—
  Abstraction.
Body of Fate (from Phase 13)—Interest.

Out of phase and copying the opposite phase, he gives himself up to a kind of clodhopper folly, that keeps his intellect moving among conventional ideas with a sort of make-believe. Incapable of consecutive thought and of moral purpose, he lives miserably seeking to hold together some consistent plan of life, patching rags upon rags because that is expected of him, or out of egotism. If on the other hand he uses his *Body of Fate* to purify his *Creative Mind* of the

Mask, if he is content to permit his senses and his subconscious nature to dominate his intellect, he takes delight in all that passes; but because he claims nothing of his own, chooses nothing, thinks that no one thing is better than another, he will not endure a pang because all passes. Almost without intellect, it is a phase of perfect bodily sanity, for, though the body is still in close contact with supersensual rhythm, it is no longer absorbed in that rhythm; eyes and ears are open; one instinct balances another; every season brings its delight.

> He who bends to himself a joy
> Does the winged life destroy,
> But he who kisses the joy as it flies
> Lives in eternity's sunrise.[85]

Seen by lyrical poets, of whom so many have belonged to the fantastic Phase 17, the man of this phase becomes an *Image* where simplicity and intensity are united, he seems to move among yellowing corn or under overhanging grapes. He gave to Landor his shepherds and hamadryads,[86] to Morris his *Water of the Wondrous Isles,*[87] to Shelley his wandering lovers and sages,[88] and to Theocritus all his flocks and pastures;[89] and of what else did Bembo think when he cried, 'Would that I were a shepherd that I might look daily down upon Urbino.'[90] Imagined in some *antithetical* mind, seasonal change and bodily sanity seem images of lasting passion and the body's beauty.

IV

PHASE FOUR

Will—Desire for Exterior World.
Mask (from Phase 18). *True*—Passion. *False*—Will.
Creative Mind (from Phase 26). *True*—First Perception of
  Character. *False*—Mutilation.
Body of Fate (from Phase 12)—Search.

When out of phase he attempts *antithetical* wisdom (for reflection has begun), separates himself from instinct (hence 'mutilation'), and tries to enforce upon himself and others all kinds of abstract or conventional ideas which are for him, being outside his experience, mere make-believe. Lacking *antithetical* capacity, and all of *primary* that is founded upon observation, he is aimless and blundering, possesses nothing except the knowledge that there is something known to others that is not mere instinct. True to phase, his interest in everything that happens, in all that excites his instinct ('search'), is so keen that he has no desire to claim anything for his own will; nature still dominates his thought as passion; yet instinct grows reflective. He is full of practical wisdom, a wisdom of saws and proverbs,[91] or founded upon concrete examples. He can see nothing beyond sense, but sense expands and contracts to meet his needs, and the needs of those who trust him. It is as though he woke suddenly out of sleep and thereupon saw more and remembered more than others. He has 'the wisdom of instinct', a wisdom perpetually excited by all those hopes and needs which concern his well-being or that of the race (*Creative Mind* from Phase 12 and so acting from that in race which corresponds to personality when personality is unified in thought). The men of the opposite phase, or of the phases nearly opposite, worn out by a wisdom held with labour and uncertainty, see persons of this phase as images of peace. Two passages of Browning[92] come to mind:

> An old hunter, talking with gods
> Or sailing with troops of friends to Tenedos.[93]

> A King lived long ago,
> In the morning of the world,
> When Earth was nigher Heaven than now:
> And the King's locks curled,
> Disparting o'er a forehead full
> As the milk-white space betwixt horn and horn
> Of some sacrificial bull—
> Only calm as a babe new-born:
> For he was got to a sleepy mood,
> So safe from all decrepitude,
> Age with its bane, so sure gone by,

(The gods so loved him while he dreamed)
That, having lived thus long, there seemed
No need the King should ever die.[94]

V

THE OPENING OF THE TINCTURES

Since Phase 26 the *primary Tincture* has so predominated, man is so sunk in Fate, in life, that there is no reflection, no experience, because that which reflects, that which acquires experience has been drowned. Man cannot think of himself as separate from that which he sees with the bodily eye or in the mind's eye. He neither loves nor hates though he may be in hatred or in love. Birdalone in *The Water of the Wondrous Isles* (a woman of Phase 3 reflected in an *antithetical* mind) falls in love with her friend's lover and he with her. There is great sorrow but no struggle, her decision to disappear is sudden as if some power over which she has no control compelled. Has she not perhaps but decided as her unknown fathers and mothers compelled, but conformed to the lineaments of her race? Is she not a child of 'Weird',[95] are not all in these most *primary* phases children of 'Weird' exercising an unconscious discrimination towards all that before Phase 1 defines their *Fate,* and after Phase 1 their race. Every achievement of their souls, Phase 1 being passed, springs up out of the body, and their work, now it is passed, is to substitute for a life, where all is Fate frozen into rule and custom, a life where all is fused by instinct; with them to hunger, to taste, to desire, is to grow wise.

Between Phase 4 and Phase 5, the *Tinctures* separate, are said to open, and reflection begins. When closed, there is an approach to absolute surrender of the *Will,* first to God, then, as Phase 1 passes away, to Nature, and the surrender is the most complete form of the freedom of the *Body of Fate* which has been increasing since Phase 22. When Man identifies himself with his *Fate,* when he is able to say 'Thy Will is our freedom'[96] or when he is perfectly natural, that is to say perfectly a portion of his surroundings, he is free even though all his actions can be foreseen, even though every action is a logical deduction from that that went before it. He is all *Fate* but has no *Destiny.*

VI

PHASE FIVE

Will—Separation from Innocence.
Mask (from Phase 19). *True*—Excess. *False*—Limitation.
Creative Mind (from Phase 25). *True*—Social Intellect. *False*—
Limitation.
Body of Fate (from Phase 11)—Natural Law.

Out of phase, and seeking *antithetical* emotion, he is sterile, passing from one insincere attitude to another, moving through a round of moral images torn from their context and so without meaning. He is so proud of each separation from experience that he becomes a sort of angry or smiling Punch[97] with a lath between his wooden arms striking here and there. His *Body of Fate* is enforced, for he has reversed the condition of his phase and finds himself at conflict with a world which offers him nothing but temptation and affront. True to phase, he is the direct opposite of all this. Abstraction has indeed begun, but it comes to him as a portion of experience cut off from everything but itself and therefore fitted to be the object of reflection. He no longer touches, eats, drinks, thinks and feels nature, but sees it as something from which he is separating himself, something that he may dominate, though only for a moment and by some fragmentary violence of sensation or of thought. Nature is half gone but the laws of nature have appeared and he can change her rhythms and her seasons by his knowledge. He lives in the moment but with an intensity Phases 2, 3 and 4 have never known, the *Will* approaches its climax, he is no longer like a man but half-awakened. He is a corrupter, disturber, wanderer, a founder of sects and peoples, and works with extravagant energy, and his reward is but to live in its glare.

Seen by a poet of the opposite phase, by a man hiding fading emotion under broken emphasis, he is Don Juan or the Giaour.[98]

VII

PHASE SIX

Will—Artificial Individuality.

Mask (from Phase 20). *True*—Justice. *False*—Tyranny.

Creative Mind (from Phase 24). *True*—Ideality. *False*—Derision.

Body of Fate (from Phase 10)—Humanity.

Example: Walt Whitman.[99]

Had Walt Whitman lived out of phase, desire to prove that all his emotions were healthy and intelligible, to set his practical sanity above all not made in his fashion, to cry 'thirty years old and in perfect health!'[100] would have turned him into some kind of jibing demagogue; and to think of him would be to remember that Thoreau when he had picked up the jaw-bone of a pig that had not a tooth missing, recorded that there also was perfect health.[101] He would, that he might believe in himself, have compelled others to believe. But using his *Body of Fate* (his interest in crowds, in casual loves and affections, in all summary human experience) to clear intellect of *antithetical* emotion (always insincere from Phase 1 to Phase 8), and haunted and hunted by the now involuntary *Mask,* he creates an *Image* of vague, half-civilised man, while all his thought and impulse is a product of democratic bonhomie, of schools, of colleges, of public discussion. Abstraction has been born but it is the abstraction of a community, of a tradition, a synthesis starting, not as with Phases 19, 20 and 21 with logical deduction from an observed fact, but from some experience or from the whole experience of the individual or of the community: 'I have such and such a feeling. I have such and such a belief. What follows from feeling, what from belief?' While Thomas Aquinas,[102] whose historical epoch was nearly of this phase, would sum in abstract categories all possible experience, not that he may know but that he may feel, Walt Whitman makes catalogues of all that has moved him, or amused his eye, that he may grow more poetical. Experience is all absorbing, subordinating, observed fact, drowning even truth itself (where truth is conceived of as something apart from impulse and instinct and from the *Will,* where impulse or instinct begins to be all in all). In a little while, though not yet, impulse and instinct, sweeping away catalogue and category, will fill the mind with terror.

VIII

PHASE SEVEN

Will—Assertion of individuality.[103]
Mask (from Phase 21). *True*—Altruism. *False*—Efficiency.
Creative Mind (from Phase 23). *True*—Heroic sentiment.
   False—Dogmatic sentimentality.
Body of Fate (from Phase 9)—Adventure that excites the individuality.
Examples: George Borrow, Alexandre Dumas, Thomas Carlyle, James Macpherson.[104]

At Phases 2, 3 and 4 the man moved within traditional or seasonable limits, but since Phase 5 limits have grown indefinite; public codes, all that depend upon habit, are all but dissolved, even the catalogues and categories of Phase 6 are no longer sufficient. If out of phase the man desires to be the man of Phase 21; an impossible desire, for that man is all but the climax of intellectual complexity and all men, from Phase 2 to Phase 7 inclusive, are intellectually simple. His instincts are all but at their apex of complexity, and he is bewildered and must soon be helpless. The dissolving character, out of phase, desires the breaking personality, and though it cannot possess, or even conceive of personality, seeing that its thoughts and emotions are common to all, it can create a grandiloquent phantom and by deceiving others deceive itself; and presently we shall discover Phase 21, out of phase, bragging of an imaginary naiveté.

Phase 7 when true to phase surrenders to the *Body of Fate* which, being derived from the phase where personality first shows itself, is excited into forms of character so dissolved in *Will*, in instinct, that they are hardly distinguishable from personality. These forms of character, not being self-dependent like personality, are however inseparable from circumstance: a gesture, or a pose born of a situation and forgotten when the situation has passed; a last act of courage, a defiance of the dogs that must soon tear the man into pieces. Such men have a passion for history, for the scene, for the adventure. They delight in actions, which they cannot see apart from setting sun or a storm at sea or some great battle, and that are inspired by emotions that move all hearers because such that all understand.

Alexandre Dumas was the phase in its perfection, George Borrow when it halts a little, for Borrow was at moments sufficiently out of phase to know that he was naive and to brag of imaginary intellectual subjectivity, as when he paraded an unbelievable fit of the horrors, or his mastery of many tongues. Carlyle like Macpherson showed the phase at its worst. He neither could, nor should have cared for anything but the personalities of history, but he used them as so many metaphors in a vast popular rhetoric, for the expression of thoughts that seemed his own and were the work of preachers to angry ignorant congregations. So noisy, so threatening that rhetoric, so great his own energy that two generations passed before men noticed that he had written no sentence not of coarse humour that clings to the memory. Sexual impotence had doubtless weakened[105] the *Body of Fate* and so strengthened the False *Mask*, yet one doubts if any mere plaster of ant's eggs could have helped where there was so great insincerity.

IX

PHASE EIGHT

Will—War between race and individuality.
Mask (from Phase 22). *True*—Courage. *False*—Fear.
Creative Mind (from Phase 22). *True*—Versatility. *False*—
    Impotence.
Body of Fate (from Phase 8)—The beginning of strength.
Example: The Idiot of Dostoyevsky[106] perhaps.

Out of phase, a condition of terror, when true to phase, of courage unbroken through defeat.

From Phase 1 to Phase 7, there has been a gradual weakening in the character of all that is *primary.* Character has taken the disguise of individuality (the *will* analysed in relation to itself), but now, though individuality persists through another phase, personality (the *Will* analysed in relation to the *Mask*) must predominate. So long as the *primary Tincture* predominated, the *antithetical Tincture* accepted its manner of perception; and character has been enlarged by the vegetative and sensitive faculties[107] excited by the *Body of Fate,* which are the nearest a *primary* nature can come to *antithetical* emotion. But now the bottle must be burst. The struggle of idealised, or habitual theologised thought with instinct, and that between mind and body, of the waning *primary* with the growing *antithetical,* must be decided, and the vegetative and sensitive faculties must for a while take the sway. Only then can the *Will* be forced to recognise the weakness of the *Creative Mind* when unaided by the *Mask,* and so to permit the involuntary *Mask* to change into the voluntary. Every modification or codification of morality has been its attempt, acting through the *Creative Mind,* to set order upon the instinctive and vegetative faculties, and it must now feel that it can create order no longer. It is the very nature of a struggle, where the soul must lose all form received from the objectively accepted conscience of the world, that it denies us an historical example. One thinks of possible examples only to decide that Hartley Coleridge[108] is not amongst them, that the brother of the Brontës[109] may only seem to be because we know so little about him, but that Dostoyevsky's Idiot is almost certainly an example. But Dostoyevsky's Idiot was too matured a type, he had passed too many times through the twenty-eight phases to help our understanding. Here for the most part are those obscure wastrels who seem powerless to free themselves from some sensual temptation—drink, women, drugs— and who cannot in a life of continual crisis create any lasting thing. The being is often born up to four times at this one phase, it is said, before the *antithetical Tincture* attains its mastery. The being clings like a man drowning to every straw, and it is precisely this clinging, this seemingly vain reaching forth for strength, amidst the collapse of all those public thoughts and habits that are the support of *primary* man, that enables it to enter at last upon Phase 9. It has to find its strength by a transformation of that very instinct which has hitherto been its weakness and so to gather up the strewn and broken members. The union of *Creative Mind* and *Mask* in opposition to *Body of*

Fate and *Will*, intensifies this struggle by dividing the nature into halves which have no interchange of qualities. The man is inseparable from his fate, he cannot see himself apart, nor can he distinguish between emotion and intellect. He is will-less, dragged hither and thither, and his unemotionalised intellect, gathered up into the mathematical Phase 22, shows him perpetually for object of desire, an emotion that is like a mechanical energy, a thought that is like wheel and piston. He is suspended; he is without bias, and until bias comes, till he has begun groping for strength within his own being, his thought and his emotion bring him to judgment but they cannot help. As those at Phase 22 must dissolve the dramatising *Mask* in abstract mind that they may discover the concrete world, he must dissolve thought into mere impersonal instinct, into mere race that he may discover the dramatising *Mask*: he chooses himself and not his *Fate*. Courage is his True *Mask*, and diversity, that has no habitual purpose, his True *Creative Mind*, because these are all that the phase of the greatest possible weakness can take into itself from the phase of the greatest possible strength. When his fingers close upon a straw, that is courage, and his versatility is that any wave may float a straw. At Phase 7, he had tried out of ambition to change his nature, as though a man should make love who had no heart, but now shock can give him back his heart. Only a shock resulting from the greatest possible conflict can make the greatest possible change, that from *primary* to *antithetical* or from *antithetical* to *primary* again. Nor can anything intervene. He must be aware of nothing but the conflict, his despair is necessary, he is of all men the most tempted—'Eloi, Eloi, why hast thou forsaken me?'[110]

There are two human types found at each phase and called *Victim* and *Sage*,[111] the first predominantly emotional, the other predominantly intellectual. Though not necessary to a first understanding of 'The Wheel', they must be touched on when describing Phase 22 (a phase of such great importance at the present moment of history that it will be described at greater length than the other phases), and for this reason it is necessary to say that they have an interchange at Phase 8 or at Phase 22, corresponding to the interchange of the *Tinctures*. Their diagram will be given, while expounding another portion of the system.

X

PHASE NINE

Will—Belief instead of individuality.
Mask (from Phase 23). *True*—Facility. *False*—Obscurity.
Creative Mind (from Phase 21). *True*—Self-Dramatisation.
   False—Anarchy.
Body of Fate (from Phase 7)—Enforced sensuality.
Example: An unnamed artist.[112]

Out of phase, blundering and ignorant, the man becomes when in phase powerful and accomplished; all that strength as of metallic rod and wheel discovered within himself. He should seek to liberate the *Mask* by the help of the *Creative Mind* from the *Body of Fate*—that is to say, to carve out and wear the now voluntary *Mask* and so to protect and to deliver the *Image*. In so far as he does so, there is immense confidence in self-expression, a vehement self, working through mathematical calculation, a delight in straight line and right angle; but if he seek to live according to the *primary Tincture*, to use the *Body of Fate* to rid the *Creative Mind* of its *Mask*, to live with objective ambition and curiosity, all is confused, the *Will* asserts itself with a savage, terrified violence. All these phases of incipient person-ality when out of phase are brutal, but after Phase 12, when true per-sonality begins, brutality gives place to an evasive capricious coldness—'false, fleeting, perjured Clarence'[113]—a lack of good faith in their *primary* relation, often accompanied in their *antithetical* relation by the most self-torturing scruples. When an *antithetical* man is out of phase, he reproduces the *primary* condition, but with an emotional inversion, love for *Image* or *Mask* becomes dread, or after Phase 15, hatred, and the *Mask* clings to the man or pursues him in the *Image*. It may even be that he is haunted by a delusive hope, cherished in secret, or bragged of aloud, that he may inherit the *Body of Fate* and *Mask* of a phase opposed to his own. He seeks to avoid *antithetical* conflict by accepting what opposes him and his *antithetical* life is invaded. At Phase 9, the *Body of Fate* that could alone purify the mind of a Carlyle, or of a Whitman, is the enemy of a unity which it breaks with sensuality (the rising flood of instinct from Phase 7) and the man if out of phase, instead of master-ing this through his dramatisation of himself as a form of passionate self-mastery, and of seeking some like form as *Image*, grows stupid and blundering. Hence one finds at this phase, more often than at any other, men who dread, despise and persecute the women whom they love. Yet behind all that muddy, flooded, brutal self, there is per-haps a vague timid soul knowing itself caught in an antithesis, an alternation it cannot control. It is said of it, 'the soul having found its weakness at Phase 8 begins the inward discipline of the soul in the fury of Phase 9'. And again, 'Phase 9 has the most sincere belief any man has ever had in his own desire'.

There is a certain artist who said to a student of these symbols, speaking of a notable man, and his mistress and their children, 'She no longer cares for his work, no longer gives him the sympathy he needs, why does he not leave her, what does he owe to her or to her children?'[114] The student discovered this artist to be a cubist of pow-erful imagination and noticed that his head suggested a sullen obsti-nacy, but that his manner and his speech were generally sympathetic and gentle.

XI

PHASE TEN

Will—The Image Breaker.
Mask (from Phase 24). *True*—Organisation. *False*—Inertia.
Creative Mind (from Phase 20). *True*—Domination through emotional construction. *False*—Reformation.
Body of Fate (from Phase 6)—Enforced emotion.
Example: Parnell.[115]

If he live like the opposite phase, conceived as *primary* condition—the phase where ambition dies—he lacks all emotional power (False *Mask*: 'Inertia'), and gives himself up to rudderless change, reform without a vision of form. He accepts what form (*Mask* and *Image*) those about him admire and, on discovering that it is alien, casts it away with brutal violence, to choose some other form as alien. He disturbs his own life, and he disturbs all who come near him more

than does Phase 9, for Phase 9 has no interest in others except in relation to itself. If, on the other hand, he be true to phase, and use his
intellect to liberate from mere race (*Body of Fate* at Phase 6 where
race is codified), and so create some code of personal conduct, which
implies always 'divine right', he becomes proud, masterful and practical. He cannot wholly escape the influence of his *Body of Fate,* but
he will be subject to its most personal form; instead of gregarious
sympathies, to some woman's tragic love[116] almost certainly. Though
the *Body of Fate* must seek to destroy his *Mask,* it may now impose
upon him a struggle which leaves victory still possible. As *Body of
Fate* phase and *Mask* phase approach one another they share somewhat of each other's nature; the effect of mutual hate grows more diffused, less harsh and obvious. The effect of the *Body of Fate* of
Phase 10 for instance is slightly less harsh and obvious than that of
the 'enforced sensuality' of Phase 9. It is now 'enforced emotion'.
Phase 9 was without restraint, but now restraint has come and with
it pride; there is slightly less need to insist upon the brutal facts of life
that he may escape from their charm; the subjective fury is less
uncalculating, and the opposition of *Will* and *Mask* no longer produces a delight in an impersonal precision and power like that of
machinery (machinery that is emotion and thought) but rather a kind
of burning restraint, a something that suggests a savage statue to
which one offers sacrifice. This sacrifice is code, personality no
longer perceived as power only. He seeks by its help to free the creative power from mass emotion, but never wholly succeeds, and so
the life remains troubled, a conflict between pride and race, and
passes from crisis to crisis. At Phase 9 there was little sexual discrimination, and now there is emotion created by circumstance rather
than by any unique beauty of body or of character. One remembers
Faust, who will find every wench a Helen, now that he has drunk the
witches' dram, and yet loves his Gretchen with all his being.[117] Perhaps one thinks of that man who gave a lifetime of love, because a
young woman in capricious idleness had written his name with her
parasol upon the snow.[118] Here is rage, desire to escape but not
now by mere destruction of the opposing fate; for a vague abstract
sense of some world, some image, some circumstance, harmonious to
emotion, has begun, or of something harmonious to emotion that
may be set upon the empty pedestal, once visible world, image, or cir-

cumstance has been destroyed. With less desire of expression than at Phase 9, and with more desire of action and of command, the man (*Creative Mind* from Phase 20, phase of greatest dramatic power) sees all his life as a stage play where there is only one good acting part; yet no one will accuse his of being a stage player for he will wear always that stony *Mask* (Phase 24 'The end of ambition' *antithetically* perceived). He, too, if he triumph, may end ambition through the command of multitudes, for he is like that god of Norse mythology, who hung from the cliff's side for three days a sacrifice to himself.[119] Perhaps Moses when he descended the mountain-side had a like stony *Mask,* and had cut out of the one rock *Mask* and table.[120]

John Morley says of Parnell,[121] whose life proves him of the phase, that he had the least discursive mind he had ever known, and that is always characteristic of a phase where all practical curiosity has been lost wherever some personal aim is not involved, while philosophical and artistic curiosity are still undiscovered. He made upon his contemporaries an impression of impassivity, and yet after a speech that seemed brutal and callous, a follower has recorded that his hands were full of blood because he had torn them with his nails.[122] One of his followers was shocked during the impassioned discussion in Committee Room No. 15,[123] that led to his abandonment, by this most reticent man's lack of reticence in allusion to the operations of sex, an indifference as of a mathematician dealing with some arithmetical quantity, and yet Mrs Parnell tells how upon a night of storm on Brighton pier, and at the height of his power, he held her out over the waters and she lay still, stretched upon his two hands, knowing that if she moved, he would drown himself and her.[124]

XII

PHASE ELEVEN

Will—The Image Burner.

Mask (from Phase 25). *True*—Rejection. *False*—Moral Indifference.

Creative Mind (from Phase 19). *True*—Moral reformation. *False*—Self-Assertion.

Body of Fate (from Phase 5)—Enforced belief.
Examples: Spinoza, Savonarola.[125]

While Phase 9 was kept from its subjectivity by personal relations, by sensuality, by various kinds of grossness; and Phase 10 by associations of men for practical purposes, and by the emotions that arise out of such associations, or by some tragic love where there is an element of common interest; Phase 11 is impeded by the excitement of conviction, by the contagion of organised belief, or by its interest in organisation for its own sake. The man of the phase is a half solitary, one who defends a solitude he cannot or will not inhabit, his *Mask* being from a phase of abstract belief, which offers him always some bundle of mathematical formulae, or its like, opposed to his nature. It will presently be seen that the man of Phase 25, where the *Mask* is, creates his system of belief, just as Phase 24 creates his code, to exclude all that is too difficult for dolt or knave; but the man of Phase 11 systematises, runs to some frenzy of conviction, to make intellect, intellect for its own sake, possible, and perhaps, in his rage against rough-and-ready customary thought, to make all but intellect impossible. He will be the antithesis of all this, should he be conquered by his *Body of Fate* (from Phase 5, where the common instinct first unites itself to reflection) being carried off by some contagion of belief, some general interest, and compelled to substitute for intellectual rage some form of personal pride and so to become the proud prelate of tradition.

In Spinoza one finds the phase in its most pure and powerful shape. He saw the divine energy in whatever was the most individual expression of the soul, and spent his life in showing that such expression was for the world's welfare and not, as might seem, a form of anarchy. His *Mask,* under the influence of his *Body of Fate,* would have forced him to seek happiness in submission to something hard and exterior; but the *Mask,* set free by a *Creative Mind* that would destroy exterior popular sanction, makes possible for the first time the solitary conception of God. One imagines him among the theologians of his time, who sought always some formula perhaps, some sheep-dog for common minds, turning himself into pure wolf, and making for the wilderness. Certainly his pantheism, however pleasing to his own bare bench of scholars, was little likely to help the oratory of any bench of judges or of bishops. Through all his cold definitions, on whose mathematical form he prided himself, one divines some quarrel, not recorded in his biography, with the thought of his fathers and his kin, forced upon him almost to the breaking of his heart: no nature without the stroke of fate divides itself in two.

XIII

THE OPENING OF THE TINCTURE[126], ETC.

Just before the place in the Great Wheel, where the word *Heart* is written, the splitting or opening of each *Tincture* begins, and increases till Phase 15 and then decreases, until the place where *Head* is written; at which point they close once more. The *antithetical Tincture* is said to open at Phase 11, the *primary* at Phase 12. When the *Tinctures* open, that is to say when observation gives place to experience, when the being attains self knowledge or its possibility, the *Four Faculties* reflect themselves in the experience or knowledge as the *Four Qualities,* the *Will* as *instinct* (or race), the *Mask* as *emotion,* the *Creative Mind* as *reason,* the *Body of Fate* as *desire.*

Before the interchange of the *Tinctures* at Phase 15 the *antithetical* is reflected as *reason* and *desire,* the *primary* as *emotion* and *instinct,* while after Phase 15 this is reversed. *Emotion* and *instinct* when acting as one are *love, reason* and *desire hatred;*[127] and in all phases before Phase 11 and after Phase 19, except those between Phase 26 and Phase 4, and especially in those phases round Phase 8 and Phase 22 the man knows himself through acted *love* and acted *hate.* Between Phase 26 and Phase 4 *love* and *hate* should be themselves unknown being only known as one, as that which is fated.

By *love* is meant love of that particular unity towards which the nature is tending, or of those images and ideas which define it, and by *hate,* hate of all that impedes that unity. In the phases between Phase 12 and Phase 18, the unity sought is Unity of Being, which is not to be confused with the complete subjectivity of Phase 15, for it implies a harmony of *antithetical* and *primary* life, and Phase 15 has no *primary.* Between Phase 12 and Phase 18 the struggle for this unity becomes conscious and its attainment possible. All the *antithet-*

ical control over *primary* faculties increases; and the being may become almost wholly predestined, as distinguished from the *primary* phases which are fated. It struggles within itself, for it must now harmonise its *instinct* with its *emotion,* its *reason* with its *desire,* and not in relation to, or for the sake of, some particular action; but in relation to a conception of itself as Unity. With this change sexual love becomes the most important event of the life, for the opposite sex is nature chosen and fated—*Image* and *Body of Fate.*

At the approach of Unity of Being the greatest beauty of literary style becomes possible, for thought becomes sensuous and musical. All that moves us is related to our possible Unity; we lose interest in the abstract and concrete alike, only when we have said, 'My fire', and so distinguished it from 'the fire' and 'a fire', does the fire seem bright.[128] Every emotion begins to be related, as musical notes are related, to every other. It is as though we touched a musical string that set other strings into sympathetic vibration.

XIV

PHASE TWELVE

Will—The Forerunner.
Mask (from Phase 26). *True*—Self-exaggeration. *False*—Self-
   abandonment.
Creative Mind (from Phase 18). *True*—Subjective Philosophy.
   False—War between two forms of Expression.
Body of Fate (from Phase 4)—Enforced Intellectual Action.
Example: Nietzsche.[129]

The man of this phase is out of phase, is all a reaction, is driven from one self-conscious pose to another, is full of hesitation; or he is true to phase, a cup that remembers but its own fullness. His phase is called the 'Forerunner' because fragmentary and violent. The phases of action where the man mainly defines himself by his practical relations are finished, or finishing, and the phases where he defines himself mainly through an image of the mind begun or beginning; phases of hatred for some external fate are giving way to phases of self-hatred. It is a phase of immense energy because the *Four Faculties* are equidistant. The *oppositions* (*Will* and *Mask, Creative Mind* and *Body of Fate*) are balanced by the *discords* and these, being equidistant between *identity* and *opposition,* are at their utmost intensity. The nature is conscious of the most extreme degree of *deception,* and is wrought to a frenzy of desire for truth of self. If Phase 9 had the greatest possible 'belief in its own desire', there is now the greatest possible belief in all values created by personality. It is therefore before all else the phase of the hero, of the man who overcomes himself, and so no longer needs, like Phase 10, the submission of others, or like Phase 11 conviction of others to prove his victory. Solitude has been born at last, though solitude invaded, and hard to defend. Nor is there need any longer of the bare anatomy of Phase 11; every thought comes with sound and metaphor, and the sanity of the being is no longer from its relation to facts, but from its approximation to its own unity, and from this on we shall meet with men and women to whom facts are a dangerous narcotic or intoxicant. Facts are from the *Body of Fate,* and the *Body of Fate* is from the phase where instinct, before the complications of reflection, reached its most persuasive strength. The man is pursued by a series of accidents, which, unless he meet them *antithetically,* drive him into all sorts of temporary ambitions, opposed to his nature, unite him perhaps to some small protesting sect (the family or neighbourhood of Phase 4 intellectualised); and these ambitions he defends by some kind of superficial intellectual action, the pamphlet, the violent speech, the sword of the swashbuckler. He spends his life in oscillation between the violent assertion of some commonplace pose, and a dogmatism which means nothing, apart from the circumstance that created it. If, however, he meets these accidents by the awakening of his *antithetical* being there is a noble extravagance, an overflowing fountain of personal life. He turns towards the True *Mask* and having by philosophic intellect (*Creative Mind*) delivered it from all that is topical and temporary, announces a philosophy, which is the logical expression of a mind alone with the object of its desire. The True *Mask,* derived from the terrible Phase 26, called the phase of the Hunchback,[130] is the reverse of all that is emotional, being emotionally cold; not mathematical, for intellectual abstraction ceased at Phase 11, but marble pure. In the presence of the *Mask,* the *Creative Mind* has the isolation of a fountain under moonlight; yet one must always distinguish between the emotional *Will*—now approaching the greatest subtlety of sensitiveness, and more and more conscious of its frailty—and that which it would be, the lonely, imperturbable, proud *Mask,* as between the *Will* and its *discord* in the *Creative Mind* where is no shrinking from life. The man follows an *Image,* created or chosen by the *Creative Mind* from what fate offers; would persecute and dominate it; and this *Image* wavers between the concrete and sensuous *Image.* It has become personal; there is now, though not so decisively as later, but one form of chosen beauty, and the sexual *Image* is drawn as with a diamond, and tinted those pale colours sculptors sometimes put upon a statue. Like all before Phase 15 the man is overwhelmed with the thought of his own weakness and knows of no strength but that of *Image* and *Mask.*

XV

PHASE THIRTEEN

Will—Sensuous Ego.
Mask (from Phase 27). *True*—Self-expression. *False*—Self-absorption.
Creative Mind (from Phase 17). *True*—Subjective Truth. *False*—Morbidity.
Body of Fate (from Phase 3)—Enforced Love.
Examples: Baudelaire, Beardsley, Ernest Dowson.[131]

This is said to be the only phase where entire sensuality is possible, that is to say sensuality without the intermixture of any other element. There is now a possible complete intellectual unity, Unity of Being apprehended through the images of the mind; and this is opposed by the fate (Phase 3 where body becomes deliberate and whole) which offers an equal roundness and wholeness of sensation. The *Will* is now a mirror of emotional experience, or sensation, according to whether it is swayed by *Mask* or *Fate.* Though wax to every impression of emotion, or of sense, it would yet through its passion for truth (*Creative Mind*) become its opposite and receive from the *Mask* (Phase 27), which is at the phase of the Saint, a virginal purity of emotion. If it live objectively, that is to say surrender itself to sensation, it becomes morbid, it sees every sensation separate from every other under the light of its perpetual analysis (*Creative Mind* at a phase of dispersal). Phase 13 is a phase of great importance, because the most intellectually subjective phase, and because only here can be achieved in perfection that in the *antithetical* life which corresponds to sanctity in the *primary*: not self-denial but expression for expression's sake. Its influence indeed upon certain writers has caused them in their literary criticism to exalt intellectual sincerity to the place in literature, which is held by sanctity in theology. At this phase the self discovers, within itself, while struggling with the *Body of Fate,* forms of emotional morbidity, which others recognise as their own; as the saint may take upon himself the physical diseases of others. There is almost always a preoccupation with those metaphors and symbols and mythological images through which we define whatever seems most strange or most morbid. Self-hatred now reaches its height, and through this hatred comes the slow liberation of intellectual love. There are moments of triumph and moments of defeat, each in its extreme form, for the subjective intellect knows nothing of moderation. As the *primary Tincture* has weakened the sense of quantity has weakened, for the *antithetical Tincture* is preoccupied with quality.

From now, if not from Phase 12, and until Phases 17 or 18 have passed, happy love is rare for seeing that the man must find a woman whose *Mask* falls within or but just outside his *Body of Fate* and *Mask,* if he is to find strong sexual attraction, the range of choice grows smaller, and all life grows more tragic. As the woman grows harder to find, so does every beloved object. Lacking suitable objects of desire, the relation between man and *Daimon* becomes more clearly a struggle or even a relation of enmity.

XVI

PHASE FOURTEEN

Will—The Obsessed Man.
Mask (from Phase 28). *True*—Serenity. *False*—Self-distrust.

Creative Mind (from Phase 16). *True*—Emotional Will. *False*—
  Terror.
Body of Fate (from Phase 2)—Enforced Love of the World.
Examples: Keats, Giorgione, Many Beautiful Women.[132]

As we approach Phase 15 personal beauty increases and at Phase
14 and Phase 16 the greatest human beauty becomes possible. The
aim of the being should be to disengage those objects which are
images of desire from the excitement and disorder of the *Body of
Fate,* and under certain circumstances to impress upon these the
full character of the *Mask* which, being from Phase 28, is a folding
up, or fading into themselves. It is this act of the intellect, begun at
conception, which has given the body its beauty. The *Body of Fate,*
derived from the phase of the utmost possible physical energy, but of
an energy without aim, like that of a child, works against this folding up yet offers little more of objects than their excitement, their
essential honey. The images of desire, disengaged and subject to the
Mask, are separate and still (*Creative Mind* from a phase of violent
scattering). The images of Phase 13 and even of Phase 12 have in a
lesser degree this character. When we compare these images with
those of any subsequent phase, each seems studied for its own sake;
they float as in serene air, or lie hidden in some valley, and if they
move it is to music that returns always to the same note, or in a
dance that so returns into itself that they seem immortal.
  When the being is out of phase, when it is allured by *primary*
curiosity, it is aware of its *primary* feebleness and its intellect
becomes but a passion of apprehension, or a shrinking from solitude;
it may even become mad; or it may use its conscious feebleness and
its consequent terror as a magnet for the sympathy of others, as a
means of domination. At Phase 16 will be discovered a desire to
accept every possible responsibility; but now responsibility is
renounced and this renunciation becomes an instrument of power,
dropped burdens being taken up by others. Here are born those
women who are most touching in their beauty. Helen[133] was of the
phase; and she comes before the mind's eye elaborating a delicate
personal discipline, as though she would make her whole life an
image of a unified *antithetical* energy. While seeming an image of
softness, and of quiet, she draws perpetually upon glass with a dia-

mond. Yet she will not number among her sins anything that does not break that personal discipline, no matter what it may seem according to others' discipline; but if she fail in her own discipline she will not deceive herself, and for all the languor of her movements, and her indifference to the acts of others, her mind is never at peace. She will wander much alone as though she consciously meditated her masterpiece that shall be at the full moon, yet unseen by human eye, and when she returns to her house she will look upon her household with timid eyes, as though she knew that all powers of self-protection had been taken away, and that of her once violent *primary Tincture* nothing remained but a strange irresponsible innocence. Her early life has perhaps been perilous because of that nobility, that excess of *antithetical* energies, which may have so constrained the fading *primary* that, instead of its becoming the expression of those energies, it is but a vague beating of the wings, or their folding up into a melancholy stillness. The greater the peril the nearer has she approached to the final union of *primary* and *antithetical,* where she will desire nothing; and already perhaps, through weakness of desire, she understands nothing yet seems to understand everything; already serves nothing, while alone seeming of service. Is it not because she desires so little and gives so little that men will die and murder in her service? One thinks of THE ETERNAL IDOL of Rodin:[134] that kneeling man with hands clasped behind his back in humble adoration, kissing a young girl a little below the breast, while she gazes down, without comprehending, under her half-closed eyelids. Perhaps could we see her a little later, with flushed cheeks casting her money upon some gaming-table, we would wonder that action and form could so belie each other, not understanding that the Fool's *Mask* is her chosen motley, nor her terror before death and stillness. One thinks too of the women of Burne-Jones, but not of Botticelli's women, who have too much curiosity, nor Rossetti's women,[135] who have too much passion; and as we see before the mind's eye those pure faces gathered about the Sleep of Arthur, or crowded upon the Golden Stair,[136] we wonder if they too would not have filled us with surprise, or dismay, because of some craze, some passion for mere excitement, or slavery to a drug.

In the poets too, who are of the phase, one finds the impression of the *Body of Fate* as intoxication or narcotic. Wordsworth, shuddering at his solitude, has filled his art in all but a few pages with common opinion, common sentiment;[137] while in the poetry of Keats there is an exaggerated sensuousness, though little sexual passion, that compels us to remember the pepper on the tongue as though that were his symbol. Thought is disappearing in image; and in Keats, in some ways a perfect type, intellectual curiosity is at its weakest; there is scarcely an image, where his poetry is at its best, whose subjectivity has not been heightened by its use in many great poets, painters, sculptors, artificers. The being has almost reached the end of that elaboration of itself which has for its climax an absorption in time, where space can be but symbols or images in the mind. There is little observation even in detail of expression, all is reverie, while in Wordsworth the soul's deepening solitude has reduced mankind, when seen objectively, to a few slight figures outlined for a moment amid mountain and lake. The corresponding genius in painting is that of Monticelli, after 1870,[138] and perhaps that of Conder,[139] though in Conder there are elements suggesting the preceding phase.

All born at *antithetical* phases before Phase 15, are subject to violence, because of the indeterminate energy of the *Body of Fate*; this violence seems accidental, unforeseen and cruel—and here are women carried off by robbers and ravished by clowns.[140]

XVII

PHASE FIFTEEN

Will.	⎫	No description
Mask (from Phase 1).	⎬	except that this is
Creative Mind (from Phase 15).	⎬	a phase of complete
Body of Fate (from Phase 1).	⎭	beauty.[141]

Body of Fate and *Mask* are now identical; and *Will* and *Creative Mind* identical; or rather the *Creative Mind* is dissolved in the *Will* and the *Body of Fate* in the *Mask*. Thought and Will are indistinguishable, effort and attainment are indistinguishable; and this is the consummation of a slow process; nothing is apparent but dreaming *Will* and the *Image* that it dreams. Since Phase 12 all images, and cadences of the mind, have been satisfying to that mind just in so far as they have expressed this converging of will and thought, effort and attainment. The words musical, sensuous, are but descriptions of that converging process. Thought has been pursued, not as a means but as an end—the poem, the painting, the reverie has been sufficient of itself. It is not possible, however, to separate in the understanding this running into one of *Will* and *Creative Mind* from the running into one of *Mask* and *Body of Fate*. Without *Mask* and *Body of Fate* the *Will* would have nothing to desire, the *Creative Mind* nothing to apprehend. Since Phase 12 the *Creative Mind* has been so interfused by the *antithetical Tincture,* that it has more and more confined its contemplation of actual things to those that resemble images of the mind desired by the *Will.* The being has selected, moulded and remoulded, narrowed its circle of living, been more and more the artist, grown more and more 'distinguished' in all preference. Now contemplation and desire, united into one, inhabit a world where every beloved image has bodily form, and every bodily form is loved. This love knows nothing of desire, for desire implies effort, and though there is still separation from the loved object, love accepts the separation as necessary to its own existence. *Fate* is known for the boundary that gives our *Destiny* its form, and—as we can desire nothing outside that form—as an expression of our freedom. Chance and Choice have become interchangeable without losing their identity.[142] As all effort has ceased, all thought has become image, because no thought could exist if it were not carried towards its own extinction, amid fear or in contemplation; and every image is separate from every other, for if image were linked to image, the soul would awake from its immovable trance. All that the being has experienced as thought is visible to its eyes as a whole, and in this way it perceives, not as they are to others, but according to its own perception, all orders of existence. Its own body possesses the greatest possible beauty, being indeed that body which the soul will permanently inhabit, when all its phases have been repeated according to the number allotted: that which we call the clarified or *Celestial Body.* Where the being has lived out of phase, seeking to live through *antithetical* phases as though they had been *primary,* there is now terror of solitude, its forced, painful and slow acceptance and a life haunted by terrible dreams. Even for the most perfect, there is a time of pain, a passage through a vision, where evil reveals itself in its final meaning. In this passage Christ, it is said, mourned over the length of time and the unworthiness of man's lot to man, whereas his forerunner mourned and his successor will mourn over the shortness of time and the unworthiness of man to his lot; but this cannot yet be understood.[143]

XVIII

PHASE SIXTEEN

Will—The Positive Man.
Mask (from Phase 2). *True*—Illusion. *False*—Delusion.
Creative Mind (from Phase 14). *True*—Vehemence. *False*—
   Opinionated Will.
Body of Fate (from Phase 28)—Enforced Delusion.
Examples: William Blake, Rabelais, Aretino, Paracelsus, some
   beautiful women.[144]

Phase 16 is in contrast to Phase 14, in spite of their resemblance of extreme subjectivity, in that it has a *Body of Fate* from the phase of the Fool, a phase of absorption, and its *Mask* from what might have been called the phase of the Child, a phase of aimless energy, of physical life for its own sake; while Phase 14 had its *Body of Fate* from the phase of the Child and its *Mask* from that of the Fool. Fate thrusts an aimless excitement upon Phase 14, while Phase 14 finds within itself an *antithetical* dream; whereas Phase 16 has a dream thrust upon it and finds within itself an aimless excitement. This excitement, and the dream, are both illusions, so that the *Will*, which is itself a violent scattering energy, has to use its intellect (*Creative Mind*) to discriminate between illusions. They are both illusions, because, so small is the *primary* nature, sense of fact is an impossibility. If it use its intellect, which is the most narrow, the most unflinching, even the most cruel in synthesis, possible to man, to disengage the aimless child (*i.e.*, to find *Mask* and *Image* in the child's toy), it finds the soul's most radiant expression and surrounds itself with some fairyland, some mythology of wisdom or laughter; its own scattering, its mere rushing out into the disordered and unbounded, after the still trance of Phase 15, has found its antithesis, and therefore self-knowledge and self-mastery. If, however, it subordinate its intellect to the *Body of Fate* all the cruelty and narrowness of that intellect are displayed in service of preposterous purpose after purpose till there is nothing left but the fixed idea and some hysterical hatred. By these purposes, derived from a phase of absorption, the *Body of Fate* drives the *Will* back upon its subjectivity, deforming the *Mask* until the *Will* can only see the object of its desire in these purposes. It does not hate because it dreads, as do the phases of increasing *antithetical* emotion, but hates that which opposes desire. Capable of nothing but an incapable idealism (for it has no thought but in myth, or in defence of myth), it must because it sees one side is all white, see the other side all black; what but a dragon could dream of thwarting a St George.[145] In men of the phase there will commonly be both natures for to be true to phase is a ceaseless struggle. At one moment they are full of hate—Blake writes of 'Flemish and Venetian demons'[146] and of some picture of his own destroyed 'by some vile spell of Stoddart's'[147]—and their hate is always close to madness; and at the next they produce the comedy of Aretino and of Rabelais or the mythology of Blake, and discover symbolism to express the overflowing and bursting of the mind. There is always an element of frenzy, and almost always a delight in certain glowing or shining images of concentrated force; in the smith's forge; in the heart; in the human form in its most vigorous development; in the solar disc; in some symbolical representation of the sexual organs; for the being must brag of its triumph over its own incoherence.

Since Phase 8 the man has more and more judged what is right in relation to time, a right action, or a right motive, has been one that he thought possible or desirable to think or do eternally; his soul would 'come into possession of itself for ever in one single moment';[148] but now he begins once more to judge an action or motive in relation to space. A right action or motive must soon be right for any other man in similar circumstance. Hitherto an action, or motive, has been right precisely because it is exactly right for one person only though for that person always. After the change, the belief in the soul's immortality declines though the decline is slow, and it may only be recovered when Phase 1 is passed.

Among those who are of this phase may be great satirists, great caricaturists, but they pity the beautiful, for that is their *Mask,* and hate the ugly, for that is their *Body of Fate,* and so are unlike those of the *primary* phases, Rembrandt for instance, who pity the ugly, and sentimentalise the beautiful, or call it insipid, and turn away or secretly despise and hate it. Here too are beautiful women, whose bodies have taken upon themselves the image of the True *Mask,* and in these there is a radiant intensity, something of 'The Burning Babe' of the Elizabethan lyric.[149] They walk like queens, and seem to carry upon their backs a quiver of arrows, but they are gentle only to those whom they have chosen or subdued, or to the dogs that follow at their heels.[150] Boundless in generosity, and in illusion, they will give themselves to a beggar because he resembles a religious picture and be faithful all their lives, or if they take another turn and choose a dozen lovers, die convinced that none but the first or last has ever touched their lips, for they are of those whose 'virginity renews itself like the moon'.[151] Out of phase they turn termagant, if their lover take a wrong step in a quadrille where all the figures are of their own composition and changed without notice when the fancy takes them. Indeed, perhaps if the body have great perfection, there is always something imperfect in the mind, some rejection of, or inadequacy of *Mask:* Venus out of phase chose lame Vulcan.[152] Here also are several very ugly persons, their bodies torn and twisted by the violence of the new *primary,* but where the body has this ugliness great beauty of mind is possible. This is indeed the only *antithetical* phase where ugliness is possible, it being complementary to Phase 2, the only *primary* phase where beauty is possible.

From this phase on we meet with those who do violence, instead of those who suffer it; and prepare for those who love some living person, and not an image of the mind, but as yet this love is hardly more than the 'fixed idea' of faithfulness. As the new love grows the sense of beauty will fade.

XIX

PHASE SEVENTEEN

Will—The Daimonic Man.
Mask (from Phase 3). *True*—Simplification through intensity.
False—Dispersal.

Creative Mind (from Phase 13). *True*—Creative imagination
through *antithetical* emotion. *False*—Enforced self-realisation.
Body of Fate (from Phase 27)—Loss.
Examples: Dante, Shelley.[153]

He is called the *Daimonic* man because Unity of Being, and consequent expression of *Daimonic* thought, is now more easy than at
any other phase. As contrasted with Phase 13 and Phase 14, where
mental images were separated from one another that they might be
subject to knowledge, all now flow, change, flutter, cry out, or mix
into something else; but without, as at Phase 16, breaking and bruis-
ing one another, for Phase 17, the central phase of its triad, is without frenzy. The *Will* is falling asunder, but without explosion and
noise. The separated fragments seek images rather than ideas, and
these the intellect, seated in Phase 13, must synthesise in vain, drawing with its compass point a line that shall but represent the outline
of a bursting pod. The being has for its supreme aim, as it had at
Phase 16 (and as all subsequent *antithetical* phases shall have) to hide
from itself and others this separation and disorder, and it conceals
them under the emotional *Image* of Phase 3; as Phase 16 concealed
its greater violence under that of Phase 2. When true to phase the
intellect must turn all its synthetic power to this task. It finds, not the
impassioned myth that Phase 16 found, but a *Mask* of simplicity that
is also intensity. This *Mask* may represent intellectual, or sexual
passion; seem some Ahasuerus or Athanase;[154] be the gaunt Dante of
the *Divine Comedy*;[155] its corresponding *Image* may be Shelley's
Venus Urania,[156] Dante's Beatrice, or even the Great Yellow Rose of
the Paradiso.[157] The *Will*, when true to phase, assumes, in assuming
the *Mask*, an intensity, which is never dramatic but always lyrical and
personal, and this intensity, though always a deliberate assumption,
is to others but the charm of the being; and yet the *Will* is always
aware of the *Body of Fate*, which perpetually destroys this intensity,
thereby leaving the *Will* to its own 'dispersal'. At Phase 3, not as
Mask but as phase, there should be perfect physical well-being or balance, though not beauty or emotional intensity, but at Phase 27 are
those who turn away from all that Phase 3 represents and seek all
those things it is blind to. The *Body of Fate* therefore, derived from

a phase of renunciation, is 'loss', and works to make impossible 'simplification by intensity'. The being, through the intellect, selects some object of desire for a representation of the *Mask* as *Image,* some woman perhaps, and the *Body of Fate* snatches away the object. Then the intellect (*Creative Mind*), which in the most *antithetical* phases were better described as imagination, must substitute some new image of desire; and in the degree of its power and of its attainment of unity, relate that which is lost, that which has snatched it away, to the new image of desire, that which threatens the new image to the being's unity. If its unity be already past, or if unity be still to come, it may for all that be true to phase. It will then use its intellect merely to isolate *Mask* and *Image,* as chosen forms or as conceptions of the mind. If it be out of phase it will avoid the subjective conflict, acquiesce, hope that the *Body of Fate* may die away; and then the *Mask* will cling to it and the *Image* lure it. It will feel itself betrayed, and persecuted till, entangled in *primary* conflict, it rages against all that destroys *Mask* and *Image.* It will be subject to nightmare, for its *Creative Mind* (deflected from the *Image* and *Mask* to the *Body of Fate*) gives an isolated mythological or abstract form to all that excites its hatred. It may even dream of escaping from ill-luck by possessing the impersonal *Body of Fate* of its opposite phase and of exchanging passion for desk and ledger. Because of the habit of synthesis, and of the growing complexity of the energy, which gives many interests, and the still faint perception of things in their weight and mass, men of this phase are almost always partisans, propagandists and gregarious; yet because of the *Mask* of simplification, which holds up before them the solitary life of hunters and of fishers and 'the groves pale passion loves',[158] they hate parties, crowds, propaganda. Shelley out of phase writes pamphlets,[159] and dreams of converting the world, or of turning man of affairs and upsetting governments, and yet returns again and again to these two images of solitude, a young man whose hair has grown white from the burden of his thoughts,[160] an old man in some shell-strewn cave whom it is possible to call, when speaking to the sultan, 'as inaccessible as God or thou'.[161] On the other hand, how subject he is to nightmare! He sees the devil leaning against a tree, is attacked by imaginary assassins[162] and in obedience to what he considers a supernatural voice, creates *The Cenci* that he may give to Beatrice Cenci her incredible father.[163] His political enemies are monstrous, meaningless images. And unlike Byron, who is two phases later, he can never see anything that opposes him as it really is. Dante, who laments his exile as of all possible things the worst for such as he, and sighs for his lost solitude, and yet could never keep from politics, was such a partisan, says a contemporary, that if a child, or a woman, spoke against his party he would pelt this child or woman with stones.[164] Yet Dante, having attained, as poet, to Unity of Being, as poet saw all things set in order, had an intellect that served the *Mask* alone, and that compelled even those things that opposed it to serve, was content to see both good and evil. Shelley, upon the other hand, in whom even as poet unity was but in part attained, found compensation for his 'loss', for the taking away of his children, for his quarrel with his first wife, for later sexual disappointment, for his exile, for his obloquy—there were but some three or four persons, he said, who did not consider him a monster of iniquity[165]—in his hopes for the future of mankind. He lacked the Vision of Evil,[166] could not conceive of the world as a continual conflict, so, though great poet he certainly was, he was not of the greatest kind. Dante suffering injustice and the loss of Beatrice, found divine justice and the heavenly Beatrice, but the justice of Prometheus Unbound is a vague propagandist emotion and the women that await its coming are but clouds.[167] This is in part because the age in which Shelley lived was in itself so broken that true Unity of Being was almost impossible, but partly because being out of phase so far as his practical reason was concerned, he was subject to an *automatonism* which he mistook for poetical invention, especially in his longer poems. *Antithetical* men (Phase 15 once passed) use this *automatonism* to evade hatred, or rather to hide it from their own eyes; perhaps all at some time or other, in moments of fatigue, give themselves up to fantastic, constructed images, or to an almost mechanical laughter.

Landor has been examined in *Per Amica Silentia Lunæ*.[168] The most violent of men, he uses his intellect to disengage a visionary image of perfect sanity (*Mask* at Phase 3) seen always in the most serene and classic art imaginable. He had perhaps as much Unity of Being as his age permitted, and possessed, though not in any full measure, the Vision of Evil.

XX

PHASE EIGHTEEN

Will—The Emotional Man.
Mask (from Phase 4). *True*—Intensity through emotion.
  False—Curiosity.
Creative Mind (from Phase 12). *True*—Emotional Philosophy.
  False—Enforced lure.
Body of Fate (from Phase 26)—Enforced disillusionment.
Examples: Goethe, Matthew Arnold.[169]

The *antithetical Tincture* closes during this phase, the being is losing direct knowledge of its old *antithetical* life. The conflict between that portion of the life of feeling, which appertains to his unity, with that portion he has in common with others, coming to an end, has begun to destroy that knowledge. 'A Lover's Nocturne' or 'An Ode to the West Wind' are probably no more possible, certainly no more characteristic.[170] He can hardly, if action and the intellect that concerns action, are taken from him, recreate his dream life; and when he says 'who am I', he finds it difficult to examine his thoughts in relation to one another, his emotions in relation to one another, but begins to find it easy to examine them in relation to action. He can examine those actions themselves with a new clearness. Now for the first time since Phase 12, Goethe's saying is almost true: 'Man knows himself by action only, by thought never.'[171] Meanwhile the *antithetical Tincture* begins to attain, without previous struggle or self-analysis, its active form which is love—love being the union of emotion and instinct—or when out of phase, sentimentality. The *Will* seeks by some form of emotional philosophy to free a form of emotional beauty (*Mask*) from a 'disillusionment', differing from the 'delusions' of Phase 16, which are continuous, in that it permits intermittent awakening. The *Will*, with its closing *antithetical*, is turning away from the life of images to that of ideas, it is vacillating and curious, and it seeks in this *Mask* from a phase where all the functions can be perfect, what becomes, when considered *antithetically*, a wisdom of the emotions. At its next phase it will have fallen asunder; already it can only preserve its unity by a deliberate balancing of experiences (*Creative Mind* at Phase 12, *Body of Fate* at Phase 26), and so it must desire that phase (though that transformed into the emotional life), where wisdom seems a physical accident. Its object of desire is no longer a single image of passion, for it must relate all to social life; the man seeks to become not a sage, but a wise king, no longer Ahasuerus, and seeks a woman who looks the wise mother of children. Perhaps now, and for the first time, the love of a living woman ('disillusionment' once accepted), as apart from beauty or function, is an admitted aim, though not yet wholly achieved. The *Body of Fate* is from the phase where the 'wisdom of knowledge' has compelled *Mask* and *Image* to become not objects of desire but objects of knowledge. Goethe did not, as Beddoes said, marry his cook, but he certainly did not marry the woman he had desired,[172] and his grief at her death showed that, unlike Phase 16 or Phase 17, which forget their broken toys, he could love what disillusionment gave. When he seeks to live objectively, he will substitute curiosity for emotional wisdom, he will invent objects of desire artificially, he will say perhaps, though this was said by a man who was probably still later in phase, 'I was never in love with a serpent-charmer before';[173] the False *Mask* will press upon him, pursue him and, refusing conflict, he will fly from the True *Mask* at each artificial choice. The nightingale will refuse the thorn and so remain among images instead of passing to ideas.[174] He is still disillusioned but he can no longer through philosophy substitute for the desire that life has taken away love for what life has brought. The *Will* is near the place marked *Head* upon the great chart, which enables it to choose its *Mask* even when true to phase almost coldly and always deliberately, whereas the *Creative Mind* is derived from the phase which is called 'the wisdom of heart', and is therefore more impassioned and less subtle and delicate than if Phase 16 or Phase 17 were the place of the *Will*, though not yet argumentative or heated. The *Will* at *Head* uses the heart with perfect mastery and, because of the growing *primary*, begins to be aware of an audience, though as yet it will not dramatise the *Mask* deliberately for the sake of effect as will Phase 19.

XXI

PHASE NINETEEN

Will—The Assertive Man.
Mask (from Phase 5). *True*—Conviction. *False*—Domination.
Creative Mind (from Phase 11). *True*—Emotional Intellect.
  False—The Unfaithful.
Body of Fate (from Phase 25)—Enforced failure of Action.
Examples: Gabriele d'Annunzio (perhaps), Oscar Wilde,
  Byron, a certain actress.[175]

This phase is the beginning of the artificial, the abstract, the fragmentary, and the dramatic. Unity of Being is no longer possible, for
the being is compelled to live in a fragment of itself and to dramatise
that fragment. The *primary Tincture* is closing, direct knowledge of
self in relation to action is ceasing to be possible. The being only
completely knows that portion of itself which judges fact for the sake
of actions. When the man lives according to phase, he is now governed by conviction, instead of by a ruling mood, and is effective
only in so far as he can find this conviction. His aim is to use an intellect, which turns easily to declamation, emotional emphasis, so that
it saves conviction in a life where effort, just in so far as its object is
passionately desired, comes to nothing. He desires to be strong and
stable, but as Unity of Being and self-knowledge are both gone, and
it is too soon to grasp at another unity through *primary* mind, he
passes from emphasis to emphasis. The strength from conviction,
being derived from a *Mask* of the first quarter, is not founded upon
social duty, though that may seem so to others, but is temperamen-
tally formed to fit some crisis of personal life. His thought is
immensely effective and dramatic, arising always from some immediate situation, a situation found or created by himself, and may
have great permanent value as the expression of an exciting personality. This thought is always an open attack; or a sudden emphasis,
an extravagance, or an impassioned declamation of some general
idea, which is a more veiled attack. The *Creative Mind* being derived
from Phase 11, he is doomed to attempt the destruction of all that
breaks or encumbers personality, but this personality is conceived of

as a fragmentary, momentary intensity. The mastery of images, threatened or lost at Phase 18, may however be completely recovered, but there is less symbol, more fact. Vitality from dreams has died out, and a vitality from fact has begun which has for its ultimate aim the mastery of the real world. The watercourse after an abrupt fall continues upon a lower level; ice turns to water, or water to vapour: there is a new chemical phase.

When lived out of phase there is a hatred or contempt of others, and instead of seeking conviction for its own sake, the man takes up opinions that he may impose himself upon others. He is tyrannical and capricious, and his intellect is called 'The Unfaithful', because, being used for victory alone, it will change its ground in a moment and delight in some new emphasis, not caring whether old or new have consistency. The *Mask* is derived from that phase where perversity begins, where artifice begins, and has its discord from Phase 25, the last phase where the artificial is possible; the *Body of Fate* is therefore enforced failure of action, and many at this phase desire action above all things as a means of expression. Whether the man be in or out of phase, there is the desire to escape from Unity of Being or any approximation towards it, for Unity can be but a simulacrum now. And in so far as the soul keeps its memory of that potential Unity there is conscious *antithetical* weakness. He must now dramatise the *Mask* through the *Will* and dreads the *Image*, deep within, of the old *antithetical Tincture* at its strongest, and yet this *Image* may seem infinitely desirable if he could but find the desire. When so torn into two, escape when it comes may be so violent that it brings him under the False *Mask* and the False *Creative Mind*. A certain actress is typical, for she surrounds herself with drawings by Burne-Jones in his latest period,[176] and reveres them as they were holy pictures, while her manners are boisterous, dominating and egotistical. They are faces of silent women, and she is never silent for a moment; yet these faces are not, as I once thought, the True *Mask* but a part of that incoherence the True *Mask* must conceal. Were she to surrender to their influence she would become insincere in her art and exploit an emotion that is no longer hers. I find in Wilde, too, something pretty, feminine, and insincere, derived from his admiration for writers of the 17th and earlier phases, and much that is violent, arbitrary and insolent, derived from his desire to escape.

The *antithetical Mask* comes to men of Phase 17 and Phase 18 as a form of strength, and when they are tempted to dramatise it, the dramatisation is fitful, and brings no conviction of strength, for they dislike emphasis; but now the weakness of the *antithetical* has begun, for though still the stronger it cannot ignore the growing *primary*. It is no longer an absolute monarch, and it permits power to pass to statesman or demagogue whom however it will constantly change.

Here one finds men and women who love those who rob them or beat them, as though the soul were intoxicated by its discovery of human nature, or found even a secret delight in the shattering of the image of its desire. It is as though it cried, 'I would be possessed by' or 'I would possess that which is Human. What do I care if it is good or bad?' There is no 'disillusionment', for they have found that which they have sought, but that which they have sought and found is a fragment.

XXII

PHASE TWENTY

Will—The Concrete Man.
Mask (from Phase 6). *True*—Fatalism. *False*—Superstition.
Creative Mind (from Phase 10). *True*—Dramatisation of *Mask*.
   False—Self-desecration.
Body of Fate (from Phase 24)—Enforced Success of Action.
Examples: Shakespeare, Balzac, Napoleon.[177]

Like the phase before it, and those that follow it immediately, a phase of the breaking up and subdivision of the being. The energy is always seeking those facts which being separable can be seen more clearly, or expressed more clearly, but when there is truth to phase there is a similitude of the old unity, or rather a new unity, which is not a Unity of Being but a unity of the creative act. He no longer seeks to unify what is broken through conviction, by imposing those very convictions upon himself and others, but by projecting a dramatisation or many dramatisations. He can create, just in that degree in which he can see these dramatisations as separate from himself, and yet as an epitome of his whole nature. His *Mask* is derived from Phase 6, where man first becomes a generalised form, according to the *primary Tincture,* as in the poetry of Walt Whitman, but this *Mask* he must by dramatisation rescue from a *Body of Fate* derived from Phase 24, where moral domination dies out before that of the exterior world conceived as a whole. The *Body of Fate* is called 'enforced success', a success that rolls out and smooths away, that dissolves through creation, that seems to delight in all outward flowing, that drenches all with grease and oil; that turns dramatisation into desecration: 'I have made myself a motley to the view.'[178] Owing to the need of seeing the dramatic image, or images, as individuals, that is to say as set amongst concrete or fixed surroundings, he seeks some field of action, some mirror not of his own creation. Unlike Phase 19 he fails in situations wholly created by himself, or in works of art where character or story has gained nothing from history. His phase is called 'The Concrete Man', because the isolation of parts that began at Phase 19, is overcome at the second phase of the triad; subordination of parts is achieved by the discovery of concrete relations. His abstraction too, affected by these relations, may be no more than an emotional interest in such generalisations as 'God', 'man', a Napoleon may but point to the starry heavens and say that they prove the existence of God.[179] There is a delight in concrete images that, unlike the impassioned images of Phase 17 and Phase 18, or the declamatory images of Phase 19, reveal through complex suffering the general destiny of man. He must, however, to express this suffering, personify rather than characterise, create not observe that multitude, which is but his *Mask* as in a multiplying mirror, for the *primary* is not yet strong enough to substitute for the lost Unity of Being that of the external world perceived as fact. In a man of action this multiplicity gives the greatest possible richness of resource where he is not thwarted by his horoscope, great ductability, a gift for adopting any rôle that stirs imagination, a philosophy of impulse and audacity; but in the man of action a part of the nature must be crushed, one main dramatisation or group of images preferred to all others.

Napoleon sees himself as Alexander moving to the conquest of the East, *Mask* and *Image* must take an historical and not a mythological or dream form, a form found but not created; he is crowned in the dress of a Roman Emperor.[180] Shakespeare, the other supreme figure of the phase, was—if we may judge by the few biographical facts, and by such adjectives as 'sweet' and 'gentle'[181] applied to him by his contemporaries—a man whose actual personality seemed faint and passionless. Unlike Ben Jonson he fought no duels;[182] he kept out of quarrels in a quarrelsome age; not even complaining when somebody pirated his sonnets;[183] he dominated no Mermaid Tavern,[184] but—through *Mask* and *Image,* reflected in a multiplying mirror—he created the most passionate art that exists. He was the greatest of modern poets, partly because entirely true to phase, creating always from *Mask* and *Creative Mind,* never from situation alone, never from *Body of Fate* alone; and if we knew all we would find that success came to him, as to others of this phase, as something hostile and unforeseen; something that sought to impose an intuition of fate (the condition of Phase 6) as from without and therefore as a form of superstition. Both Shakespeare and Balzac used the False *Mask* imaginatively, explored it to impose the True, and what *Lake Harris, the half-charlatan American visionary, said of Shakespeare might be said of both: 'Often the hair of his head stood up and all life became the echoing chambers of the tomb.'[185]

At Phase 19 we create through the externalised *Mask* an imaginary world, in whose real existence we believe, while remaining separate from it; at Phase 20 we enter that world and become a portion of it; we study it, we amass historical evidence, and, that we may dominate it the more, drive out myth and symbol, and compel it to seem the real world where our lives are lived.

A phase of ambition; in Napoleon the dramatist's own ambition; in Shakespeare that of the persons of his art; and this ambition is not that of the solitary law-giver, that of Phase 10 (where the *Creative Mind* is placed) which rejects, resists and narrows, but a creative energy.

---

*I quote from a book circulated privately among his followers. I saw it years ago but seem to remember it, as now vague, now vulgar, and now magnificent in style.

XXIII

PHASE TWENTY-ONE

Will—The acquisitive Man.
Mask (from Phase 7). *True*—Self-analysis. *False*—Self-adaption.
Creative Mind (from Phase 9). *True*—Domination of the Intellect. *False*—Distortion.
Body of Fate (from Phase 23)—Triumph of Achievement.
Examples: Lamarck, Mr Bernard Shaw, Mr Wells, Mr George Moore.[186]

The *antithetical Tincture* has a predominance so slight that the *Creative Mind* and *Body of Fate* almost equal it in control of desire. The *Will* can scarcely conceive of a *Mask* separate from or predominant over *Creative Mind* and *Body of Fate,* yet because it can do so there is personality not character. It is better, however, to use a different word, and therefore Phases 21, 22 and 23 are described as, like the phases opposite, phases of individuality where the *Will* is studied less in relation to the *Mask* than in relation to itself. At Phase 23 the new relation to the *Mask,* as something to escape from, will have grown clear.

The *antithetical Tincture* is noble, and, judged by the standards of the *primary,* evil, whereas the *primary* is good and banal; and this phase, the last before the *antithetical* surrenders its control, would be almost wholly good did it not hate its own banality. Personality has almost the rigidity, almost the permanence of character, but it is not character, for it is still always assumed. When we contemplate Napoleon we can see ourselves, perhaps even think of ourselves as Napoleons, but a man of Phase 21 has a personality that seems a creation of his circumstance and his faults, a manner peculiar to himself and impossible to others. We say at once, 'How individual he is.' In theory whatever one has chosen must be within the choice of others, at some moment or for some purpose, but we find in practice that nobody of this phase has personal imitators, or has given his name to a form of manners. The *Will* has driven intellectual complexity into its final entanglement, an entanglement created by the continual

adaption to new circumstances of a logical sequence; and the aim of
the individual, when true to phase, is to realise, by his own complete
domination over all circumstance, a self-analysing, self-conscious
simplicity. Phase 7 shuddered at its own simplicity, whereas he must
shudder at his own complexity. Out of phase, instead of seeking this
simplicity through his own dominating constructive will, he will
parade an imaginary naiveté, even blunder in his work, encourage in
himself stupidities of spite or sentiment, or commit calculated indis-
cretions simulating impulse. He is under the False *Mask* (emotional
self-adaption) and the False *Creative Mind* (distortion: the furious
Phase 9 acted upon by 'enforced sensuality'). He sees the *antithetical*
as evil, and desires the evil, for he is subject to a sort of possession by
the devil, which is in reality but a theatrical scene. Precisely because
his adaptability can be turned in any direction, when lived according
to the *primary,* he is driven into all that is freakish or grotesque,
mind-created passions, simulated emotions; he adopts all that can
suggest the burning heart he longs for in vain; he turns braggart or
buffoon. Like somebody in Dostoyevsky's *Idiot*,[187] he will invite
others to tell their worst deeds that he may himself confess that he
stole a half-crown and left a servant-girl to bear the blame. When all
turn upon him he will be full of wonder for he knows that the con-
fession is not true, or if true that the deed itself was but a trick, or a
pose, and that all the time he is full of a goodness that fills him with
shame. Whether he live according to phase and regard life without
emotion, or live out of phase, and simulate emotion, his *Body of Fate*
drags him away from intellectual unity; but in so far as he lives out
of phase he weakens conflict, refuses to resist, floats upon the stream.
In phase he strengthens conflict to the utmost by refusing all activity
that is not *antithetical*: he becomes intellectually dominating, intellectually unique. He apprehends the simplicity of his opposite phase as
some vast systematisation, in which the will imposes itself upon the
multiplicity of living images, or events, upon all in Shakespeare, in
Napoleon even, that delighted in its independent life; for he is a
tyrant and must kill his adversary. If he is a novelist, his characters
must go his road, and not theirs, and perpetually demonstrate his
thesis; he will love construction better than the flow of life, and as a
dramatist he will create without passion, and without liking, character and situation; and yet he is a master of surprise, for one can never

be sure where even a charge of shot will fall. Style exists now but as a sign of work well done, a certain energy and precision of movement; in the artistic sense it is no longer possible, for the tension of the will is too great to allow of suggestion. Writers of the phase are great public men and they exist after death as historical monuments, for they are without meaning apart from time and circumstance.

XXIV

PHASE TWENTY-TWO

Will—Balance between Ambition and Contemplation.

Mask (from Phase 8). *True*—Self-immolation. *False*—Self-assurance.

Creative Mind (from Phase 8). *True*—Amalgamation. *False*—Despair.

Body of Fate (from Phase 22)—The Breaking of Strength.

Examples: Flaubert, Herbert Spencer, Swedenborg, Dostoieffsky.[188]

The aim of the being, until the point of balance has been reached, will be that of Phase 21 except that synthesis will be more complete, and the sense of identity between the individual and his thought, between his desire and his synthesis will be closer; but the character of the phase is precisely that here balance is reached and passed, though it is stated that the individual may have to return to this phase more than once, though not more than four times, before it is passed. Once balance has been reached, the aim must be to use the *Body of Fate* to deliver the *Creative Mind* from the *Mask*, and not to use the *Creative Mind* to deliver the *Mask* from the *Body of Fate*. The being does this by so using the intellect upon the facts of the world that the last vestige of personality disappears. The *Will*, engaged in its last struggle with external fact (*Body of Fate*), must submit, until it sees itself as inseparable from nature perceived as fact, and it must see itself as merged into that nature through the *Mask*, either as a conqueror lost in what he conquers, or dying at the moment of conquest, or as renouncing conquest, whether it come by might of logic, or might of drama, or might of hand. The *Will* since

Phase 8 has more and more seen itself as a *Mask*, as a form of personal power, but now it must see that power broken. From Phase 12 to Phase 18 it was or should have been a power wielded by the whole nature; but since Phase 19 it has been wielded by a fragment only, as something more and more professional, temperamental or technical. It has become abstract, and the more it has sought the whole of natural fact, the more abstract it has become. One thinks of some spilt liquid which grows thinner the wider it spreads till at last it is but a film. That which at Phase 21 was a longing for self-conscious simplicity, as an escape from logical complication and subdivision, is now (through the *Mask* from Phase 8) a desire for the death of the intellect. At Phase 21 it still sought to change the world, could still be a Shaw, a Wells, but now it will seek to change nothing, it needs nothing but what it may call 'reality', 'truth', 'God's Will': confused and weary, through trying to grasp too much, the hand must loosen.

Here takes place an interchange between portions of the mind which corresponds, though to represent it in the diagram of the Wheel would complicate the figure, to the interchange between the old and new *primary*, the old and new *antithetical* at Phase 1 and Phase 15. The mind that has shown a predominately emotional character, called that of the *Victim*, through the *antithetical* phases, now shows a predominately intellectual character, called that of the *Sage* (though until Phase 1 has been passed it can but use intellect when true to phase to eliminate intellect); whereas the mind that has been predominately that of the *Sage* puts on *Victimage*.*[189] An element in the nature is exhausted at the point of balance, and the opposite element controls the mind. One thinks of the gusts of sentimentality that overtake violent men, the gusts of cruelty that overtake the sentimental. At Phase 8 there is a similar interchange, but it does not display its significance at that blinded and throttled phase. A man of Phase 22 will commonly not only systematise, to the exhaustion of his will, but discover this exhaustion of will in all that he studies. If Lamarck, as is probable, was of Phase 21, Darwin[190]

---

*These terms will be explained later. They are touched on here to draw attention to a change in Swedenborg, Flaubert and Dostoieffsky at the point of balance.

was probably a man of Phase 22, for his theory of development by the survival of fortunate accidental varieties seems to express this exhaustion. The man himself is never weak, never vague or fluctuating in his thought, for if he brings all to silence, it is a silence that results from tension, and till the moment of balance, nothing interests him that is not wrought up to the greatest effort of which it is capable. Flaubert is the supreme literary genius of the phase, and his *Temptation of St Anthony* and his *Bouvard and Pécuchet* are the sacred books of the phase,[191] one describing its effect upon a mind where all is concrete and sensuous, the other upon the more logical, matter-of-fact, curious, modern mind. In both the mind exhausts all knowledge within its reach and sinks exhausted to a conscious futility. But the matter is not more of the phase than is the method. One never doubts for a moment that Flaubert was of the phase; all must be impersonal;[192] he must neither like nor dislike character or event; he is 'the mirror dawdling down a road', of Stendhal,[193] with a clear brightness that is not Stendhal's; and when we make his mind our own, we seem to have renounced our own ambition under the influence of some strange, far-reaching, impartial gaze.

We feel too that this man who systematised by but linking one emotional association to another has become strangely hard, cold and invulnerable, that this mirror is not brittle but of unbreakable steel. 'Systematised' is the only word that comes to mind, but it implies too much deliberation, for association has ranged itself by association as little bits of paper and little chips of wood cling to one another upon the water in a bowl. In Dostoyevsky the 'amalgamation' is less intellectual, less orderly, he, one feels, has reached the point of balance through life, and not through the process of his art; and his whole will, and not merely his intellectual will, has been shaken, and his characters, in whom is reflected this broken will, are aware, unlike those of *Bouvard and Pécuchet,* and those of the *Temptation* even, of some ungraspable whole to which they have given the name of God. For a moment that fragment, that relation, which is our very being, is broken; they are at Udan Adan 'wailing upon the edge of nonentity, wailing for Jerusalem, with weak voices almost inarticulate';[194] and yet full submission has not come. Swedenborg passed through his balance after fifty,[195] and a mind incredibly dry and arid, hard and tangible, like the minerals he assayed for

the Swedish government, studies a new branch of science: the economics and the natural history of Heaven, and notes that there
nothing but emotion, nothing but the ruling love exists. The desire to
dominate has so completely vanished, 'amalgamation' has pushed its
way so far into the subconscious, into that which is dark, that we call
it a vision. Had he been out of phase, had he attempted to arrange
his life according to the personal *Mask,* he would have been pedantic and arrogant, a Bouvard, or a Pécuchet, passing from absurdity to
absurdity, hopeless and insatiable. In the world of action such
absurdity may become terrible, for men will die and murder for an
abstract synthesis, and the more abstract it is the further it carries
them from compunction and compromise; and as obstacles to that
synthesis increase, the violence of their will increases. It is a phase as
tragic as its opposite, and more terrible, for the man of this phase
may, before the point of balance has been reached, become a
destroyer and persecutor, a figure of tumult and of violence; or as is
more probable—for the violence of such a man must be checked by
moments of resignation or despair, premonitions of balance—his system will become an instrument of destruction and of persecution in
the hands of others.

The seeking of Unity of Fact by a single faculty, instead of Unity
of Being by the use of all, has separated a man from his genius. This
is symbolised in the Wheel by the gradual separation (as we recede
from Phase 15) of *Will* and *Creative Mind, Mask* and *Body of Fate.*
During the supernatural incarnation of Phase 15, we were compelled to assume an absolute identity of the *Will,* or self, with its creative power, of beauty with body; but for some time self and creative
power, though separating, have been neighbours and kin. A Landor,
or a Morris,[196] however violent, however much of a child he seem, is
always a remarkable man; in Phases 19, 20 and 21 genius grows professional, something taken up when work is taken up, it begins to be
possible to record the stupidities of men of genius in a scrapbook;
Bouvard and Pécuchet have that refuge for their old age. Someone
has said that Balzac at noonday was a very ignorant man,[197] but at
midnight over a cup of coffee knew everything in the world. In the
man of action, in a Napoleon, let us say, the stupidities lie hidden, for
action is a form of abstraction that crushes everything it cannot
express. At Phase 22 stupidity is obvious, one finds it in the corre-

spondence of Karl Marx,[198] in his banal abusiveness, while to Goncourt, Flaubert, as man, seemed full of unconsidered thought.[199] Flaubert, says Anatole France, was not intelligent.[200] Dostoyevsky, to those who first acclaimed his genius, seemed when he laid down his pen an hysterical fool. One remembers Herbert Spencer dabbing the grapes upon a lodging-house carpet with an inky cork that he might tint them to his favourite colour, 'impure purple'. On the other hand, as the *Will* moves further from the *Creative Mind*, it approaches the *Body of Fate*, and with this comes an increasing delight in impersonal energy and in inanimate objects, and as the *Mask* separates from the *Body of Fate* and approaches the *Creative Mind* we delight more and more in all that is artificial, all that is deliberately invented. Symbols may become hateful to us, the ugly and the arbitrary delightful that we may the more quickly kill all memory of Unity of Being. We identify ourselves in our surroundings—in our surroundings perceived as fact—while at the same time the intellect so slips from our grasp as it were, that we contemplate its energies as something we can no longer control, and give to each of those energies an appropriate name as though it were an animate being. Now that *Will* and *Body of Fate* are one, *Creative Mind* and *Mask* one also, we are no longer four but two, and life, the balance reached, becomes an act of contemplation. There is no longer a desired object, as distinct from thought itself, no longer a *Will*, as distinct from the process of nature seen as fact; and so thought itself, seeing that it can neither begin nor end, is stationary. Intellect knows itself as its own object of desire; and the *Will* knows itself to be the world; there is neither change nor desire of change. For the moment the desire for a form[201] has ceased and an absolute realism becomes possible.

XXV

PHASE TWENTY-THREE

Will—The Receptive Man.
Mask (from Phase 9). *True*—Wisdom. *False*—Self-pity.
Creative Mind (from Phase 7). *True*—Creation through Pity.
   False—Self-driven desire.

Body of Fate (from Phase 21)—Success.
Examples: Rembrandt, Synge.[202]

When out of phase, for reasons that will appear later, he is tyrannical, gloomy and self-absorbed. In phase his energy has a character analogous to the longing of Phase 16 to escape from complete subjectivity: it escapes in a condition of explosive joy from systematisation and abstraction. The clock has run down and must be wound up again. The *primary Tincture* is now greater than the *antithetical*, and the man must free the intellect from all motives founded upon personal desire, by the help of the external world, now for the first time studied and mastered for its own sake. He must kill all thought that would systematise the world, by doing a thing, not because he wants to, or because he should, but because he can; that is to say he sees all things from the point of view of his own technique, touches and tastes and investigates technically. He is, however, because of the nature of his energy, violent, anarchic, like all who are of the first phase of a quarter. Because he is without systematisation he is without a master, and only by his technical mastery can he escape from the sense of being thwarted and opposed by other men; and his technical mastery must exist, not for its own sake, though for its own sake it has been done, but for that which it reveals, for its laying bare—to hand and eye, as distinguished from thought and emotion—general humanity. Yet this laying bare is a perpetual surprise, is an unforeseen reward of skill. And unlike *antithetical* man he must use his *Body of Fate* (now always his 'success') to liberate his intellect from personality, and only when he has done this, only when he escapes the voluntary *Mask,* does he find his true intellect, is he found by his True *Mask.* The True *Mask* is from the frenzied Phase 9 where personal life is made visible for the first time, but from that phase mastered by its *Body of Fate,* 'enforced sensuality', derived from Phase 7 where the instinctive flood is almost above the lips. It is called 'wisdom' and this wisdom (personality reflected in a *primary* mirror), is general humanity experienced as a form of involuntary emotion, and involuntary delight in the 'minute particulars' of life.[203] The man wipes his breath from the window pane, and laughs in his delight at all the varied scene. His *Creative Mind* being at Phase 7—where instinctive life, all but reaching utmost complexity, suffers an external abstract synthesis—his *Body of Fate* compelling him to intellectual life being at Phase 21; his *Will* phase that of the revolt from every intellectual summary, from all intellectual abstraction, this delight is not mere delight, he would construct a whole, but that whole must seem all event, all picture. That whole must not be instinctive, bodily, natural, however, though it may seem so, for in reality he cares only for what is human, individual and moral. To others he may seem to care for the immoral and inhuman only, for he will be hostile, or indifferent to moral as to intellectual summaries; if he is Rembrandt he discovers his Christ through anatomical curiosity, or through curiosity as to light and shade,[204] and if he is Synge he takes a malicious pleasure in the contrast between his hero, whom he discovers through his instinct for comedy, and any hero in men's minds.[205] Indeed, whether he be Synge or Rembrandt, he is ready to sacrifice every convention, perhaps all that men have agreed to reverence, for a startling theme, or a model one delights in painting; and yet all the while, because of the nature of his *Mask*, there is another summary working through bone and nerve. He is never the mere technician that he seems, though when you ask his meaning he will have nothing to say, or will say something irrelevant or childish. Artists and writers of Phase 21 and Phase 22 have eliminated all that is personal from their style, seeking cold metal and pure water, but he will delight in colour and idiosyncrasy, though these he must find rather than create. Synge must find rhythm and syntax in the Aran Islands,[206] Rembrandt delight in all accidents of the visible world; yet neither, no matter what his delight in reality, shows it without exaggeration, for both delight in all that is wilful, in all that flouts intellectual coherence, and conceive of the world as if it were an overflowing cauldron. Both will work in toil and in pain, finding what they do not seek, for, after Phase 22, desire creates no longer, will has taken its place; but that which they reveal is joyous. Whereas Shakespeare showed through a style, full of joy, a melancholy vision sought from afar; a style at play, a mind that served; Synge must fill many notebooks, clap his ear to that hole in the ceiling;[207] and what patience Rembrandt must have spent in the painting of a lace collar[208] though to find his subject he had but to open his eyes. When out of phase, when the man seeks to choose his *Mask*, the man is gloomy with the gloom of others, and tyrannical with the tyranny of others, because he cannot create. Phase 9 was dominated by desire, was described as having the greatest belief in its own desire possible to man, yet from it Phase 23 receives not desire but pity, and not belief but wisdom. Pity needs wisdom as desire needs belief, for pity is *primary*, whereas desire is *antithetical*. When pity is separated from wisdom we have the False *Mask*, a pity like that of a drunken man, self-pity, whether offered in seeming to another or only to oneself: pity corrupted by desire. Who does not feel the pity in Rembrandt, in Synge, and know that it is inseparable from wisdom. In the works of Synge there is much self-pity, ennobled to a pity for all that lived; and once an actress, playing his Deirdre, put all into a gesture. Concubar, who had murdered Deirdre's husband and her friends, was in altercation with Fergus who had demanded vengeance; 'Move a little further off,' she cried, 'with the babbling of fools'; and a moment later, moving like a somnambulist, she touched Concubar upon the arm, a gesture full of gentleness and compassion, as though she had said, 'You also live.'[209] In Synge's early unpublished work, written before he found the dialects of Aran and of Wicklow, there is brooding melancholy and morbid self-pity. He had to undergo an æsthetic transformation, analogous to religious conversion, before he became the audacious joyous ironical man we know.[210] The emotional life in so far as it was deliberate had to be transferred from Phase 9 to Phase 23, from a self-regarding melancholy condition of soul to its direct opposite. This transformation must have seemed to him a discovery of his true self, of his true moral being; whereas Shelley's came at the moment when he first created a passionate image which made him forgetful of himself. It came perhaps when he had passed from the litigious rhetoric of Queen Mab to the lonely reveries of Alastor.[211] *Primary* art values above all things sincerity to the self or *Will* but to the self active, translating and perceiving.

The quarter of intellect was a quarter of dispersal and generalisation, a play of shuttlecock with the first quarter of animal burgeoning, but the fourth quarter is a quarter of withdrawal and concentration, in which active moral man should receive into himself, and transform into *primary* sympathy the emotional self-realisation of the second quarter. If he does not so receive and transform he sinks into stupidity and stagnation, perceives nothing but his own interests, or becomes a tool in the hands of others; and at Phase 23, because there must be delight in the unforeseen, he may be brutal and outrageous. He does not, however, hate, like a man of the third quarter, being but ignorant of or indifferent to the feelings of others. Rembrandt pitied ugliness, for what we call ugliness was to him an escape from all that is summarised and known, but had he painted a beautiful face, as *antithetical* man understands beauty, it would have remained a convention, he would have seen it through a mirage of boredom.

When one compares the work of Rembrandt with that of David,[212] whose phase was Phase 21; or the work of Synge with that of Mr Wells[213]; one sees that in the one the *antithetical Tincture* is breaking up and dissolving, while in the other it is tightening as for a last resistance, concentrating, levelling, transforming, tabulating. Rembrandt and Synge but look on and clap their hands. There is indeed as much selection among the events in one case as in the other, but at Phase 23 events seem startling because they elude intellect.

All phases after Phase 15 and before Phase 22 unweave that which is woven by the equivalent phases before Phase 15 and after Phase 8. The man of Phase 23 has in the *Mask,* at Phase 9, a contrary that seems his very self until he use the discord of that contrary, his *Body of Fate* at Phase 21, to drive away the *Mask* and free the intellect and rid pity of desire and turn belief into wisdom. The *Creative Mind,* a discord to the *Will,* is from a phase of instinctive dispersal, and must turn the violent objectivity of the self or *Will* into a delight in all that breathes and moves: 'The gay fishes on the wave when the moon sucks up the dew.'[214]

XXVI

PHASE TWENTY-FOUR

Will—The End of Ambition.
Mask (from Phase 10). *True*—Self-reliance. *False*—Isolation.
Creative Mind (from Phase 6). *True*—Construction through
    humanitarianism. *False*—Authority.
Body of Fate (from Phase 20)—Objective Action.
Examples: Queen Victoria, Galsworthy, a certain friend.[215]

As the *Mask* now seems the natural self, which he must escape; the man labours to turn all within him that is from Phase 10, into some quality of Phase 24. At Phase 23, when in what seemed the natural self, the man was full of gloomy self-absorption and its appropriate abstractions, but now the abstractions are those that feed self-righteousness and scorn of others, the nearest the natural self can come to the self-expressing mastery of Phase 10. Morality, grown passive and pompous, dwindles to unmeaning forms and formulae. Under the influence of the *Body of Fate,* the unweaver and *discord* of Phase 10, the man frees the intellect from the *Mask* by unflagging impersonal activity. Instead of burning intellectual abstraction, as did Phase 23, in a technical fire, it grinds moral abstraction in a mill. This mill, created by the freed intellect, is a code of personal conduct, which being formed from social and historical tradition, remains always concrete in the mind. All is sacrificed to this code; moral strength reaches its climax; the rage of Phase 10 to destroy all that trammels the being from without is now all self-surrender. There is great humility—'she died every day she lived'[216]—and pride as great, pride in the code's acceptance, an impersonal pride, as though one were to sign 'servant of servants.' There is no philosophic capacity, no intellectual curiosity, but there is no dislike for either philosophy or science; they are a part of the world and that world is accepted. There may be great intolerance for all who break or resist the code, and great tolerance for all the evil of the world that is clearly beyond it whether above it or below. The code must rule, and because that code cannot be an intellectual choice, it is always a tradition bound up with family, or office, or trade, always a part of history. It is always seemingly fated, for its sub-conscious purpose is to compel surrender of every personal ambition; and though it is obeyed in pain—can there be mercy in a rigid code?—the man is flooded with the joy of self-surrender; and flooded with mercy—what else can there be in self-surrender?—for those over whom the code can have no rights, children and the nameless multitude. Unmerciful to those who serve and to himself, merciful in contemplating those who are served, he never wearies of forgiveness.

Men and women of the phase create an art where individuals only exist to express some historical code, or some historical tradition of action and of feeling, things written in what Raftery called the Book of the People,[217] or settled by social or official station, even as set forth in directory or peerage. The judge upon the bench is but a judge, the prisoner in the dock is but the eternal offender, whom we may study in legend or in Blue Book.[218] They despise the Bohemian[219] above all men till he turn gypsy, tinker, convict, or the like, and so find historical sanction, attain as it were to some inherited code or recognised relation to such code. They submit all their actions to the most unflinching examination, and yet are without psychology, or self-knowledge, or self-created standard of any kind, for they but ask without ceasing, 'Have I done my duty as well as so-and-so?'[220] 'Am I as unflinching as my fathers before me?' and though they can stand utterly alone, indifferent though all the world condemn, it is not that they have found themselves, but that they have been found faithful. The very Bohemians are not wholly individual men in their eyes, and but fulfil the curse, laid upon them before they were born, by God or social necessity.

Out of phase, seeking emotion instead of impersonal action, there is—desire being impossible—self-pity, and therefore discontent with people and with circumstance, and an overwhelming sense of loneliness, of being abandoned. All criticism is resented, and small personal rights and predilections, especially if supported by habit or position, are asserted with violence; there is a great indifference to others' rights and predilections; we have the bureaucrat or the ecclesiastic of satire, a tyrant who is incapable of insight or of hesitation.

Their intellect being from Phase 6, but their energy, or will, or bias, from Phase 24, they must, if in phase, see their code expressed in multiform human life, the mind of Victoria at its best, as distinguished from that of Walt Whitman. Their emotional life is a reversal of Phase 10, as what was autocratic in Victoria reversed the personal autocracy of Parnell.[221] They fly the *Mask,* that it may become, when enforced, that form of pride and of humility that holds together a professional or social order.

When out of phase they take from Phase 10 isolation, which is good for that phase but destructive to a phase that should live for others and from others; and they take from Phase 6 a bundle of race instincts, and turn them to abstract moral, or social convention, and

so contrast with Phase 6, as the mind of Victoria at its worst contrasts with that of Walt Whitman. When in phase they turn these
instincts to a concrete code, founded upon dead or living example.

That which characterises all phases of the last quarter, with an
increasing intensity, begins now to be plain: persecution of instinct—
race is transformed into a moral conception—whereas the intellectual phases, with increasing intensity as they approached Phase 22,
persecuted emotion. Morality and intellect persecute instinct and
emotion respectively, which seek their protection.

XXVII

PHASE TWENTY-FIVE

Will—The Conditional Man.
Mask (from Phase 11). *True*—Consciousness of Self. *False*—
   Self-consciousness.
Creative Mind (from Phase 5). *True*—Rhetoric. *False*—Spiri-
   tual Arrogance.
Body of Fate (from Phase 19)—Persecution.
Examples: Cardinal Newman, Luther, Calvin, George Her-
   bert, Mr George Russell (A.E.).[222]

Born as it seems to the arrogance of belief, as Phase 24 was born
to moral arrogance, the man of the phase must reverse himself,
must change from Phase 11 to Phase 25; use the *Body of Fate* to
purify the intellect from the *Mask,* till this intellect accepts some
organised belief: belief rooted in social order: the convictions of
Christendom let us say. He must eliminate all that is personal from
belief; eliminate the necessity for intellect by the contagion of some
common agreement, as did Phase 23 by its technique, Phase 24 by its
code. With a *Will* of subsidence, an intellect of loosening and separating, he must, like Phases 23 or 24, find himself in such a situation
that he is compelled to concrete synthesis (*Body of Fate* at Phase 19
the discord of Phase 11) but this situation compels the *Will*, if it pursue the False *Mask,* to the persecution of others, if found by the True
Mask, to suffer persecution. Phase 19, phase of the *Body of Fate,* is
a phase of breaking, and when the *Will* is at Phase 25 of breaking by

belief. In this it finds its inspiration and its joy. It is called the *Conditional Man*, perhaps because all the man's thought arises out of some particular condition of actual life, or is an attempt to change that condition with a moral object. He is still strong, full of initiative, full of social intellect; absorption has scarce begun; but his object is to limit and bind, to make men better, by making it impossible that they should be otherwise, to so arrange prohibitions and habits that men may be naturally good, as they are naturally black, or white, or yellow. There may be great eloquence, a mastery of all concrete imagery that is not personal expression, because though as yet there is no sinking into the world but much distinctness, clear identity, there is an overflowing social conscience. No man of any other phase can produce the same instant effect upon great crowds; for codes have passed, the universal conscience takes their place. He should not appeal to a personal interest, should make little use of argument which requires a long train of reasons, or many technical terms, for his power rests in certain simplifying convictions which have grown with his character; he needs intellect for their expression, not for proof, and taken away from these convictions is without emotion and momentum. He has but one overwhelming passion, to make all men good, and this good is something at once concrete and impersonal; and though he has hitherto given it the name of some church, or state, he is ready at any moment to give it a new name for, unlike Phase 24, he has no pride to nourish upon the past. Moved by all that is impersonal, he becomes powerful as, in a community tired of elaborate meals, that man might become powerful who had the strongest appetite for bread and water.

When out of phase he may, because Phase 11 is a phase of diffused personality and pantheistic dreaming, grow sentimental and vague, drift into some emotional abstract, his head full of images long separated from life, and ideas long separated from experience, turn tactless and tasteless, affirm his position with the greatest arrogance possible to man. Even when nearly wholly good he can scarce escape from arrogance; what old friend did Cardinal Newman cut because of some shade of theological difference?[223]

Living in the False *Creative Mind* produces, in all *primary* phases, insensitiveness, as living in the False *Mask* produces emotional conventionality and banality, because that False *Creative Mind*, having received no influence from the *Body of Fate*, no mould from individuals and interests, is as it were self-suspended. At Phase 25 this insensitiveness may be that of a judge who orders a man to the torture, that of a statesman who accepts massacre as a historical necessity. One thinks of Luther's apparent indifference to atrocities committed, now by the peasants, now against them, according to the way his incitements veered.[224]

The genius of Synge and Rembrandt has been described as typical of Phase 23. The first phase of a triad is an expression of unrelated power. They surprised the multitude, they did not seek to master it; while those chosen for examples of Phase 24 turn the multitude into a moral norm. At Phase 25 men seek to master the multitude, not through expressing it, nor through surprising it, but by imposing upon it an intellectual norm. Synge, reborn at Phase 25, might interest himself, not in the *primary* vigour and tragedy of his Aran Island countrymen but in their beliefs, and through some eccentricity (not of phase but horoscope) not in those they hold in common with fellow Catholics, as Newman would, but of those they share with Japanese peasants, or in their belief as a part of all folk belief considered as religion and philosophy. He would use this religion and philosophy to kill within himself the last trace of individual abstract speculation, yet this religion and this philosophy, as present before his mind, would be artificial and selected, though always concrete. Subsidence upon, or absorption in, the *spiritual primary* is not yet possible or even conceivable.

Poets of this phase are always stirred to an imaginative intensity by some form of propaganda. George Herbert was doubtless of this phase; and Mr George Russell (A.E.), though the signs are obscured by the influence upon his early years of poets and painters of middle *antithetical* phases. Neither Mr Russell's visionary painting, nor his visions of 'nature spirits' are, upon this supposition, true to phase. Every poem, where he is moved to write by some form of philosophical propaganda, is precise, delicate and original, while in his visionary painting one discovers the influence of other men, Gustave Moreau, for instance.[225] This painting is like many of his 'visions', an attempt to live in the *Mask*, caused by critical ideas founded upon *antithetical* art. What dialect was to Synge, his practical work as a co-operative organiser is to him, and he finds precise ideas and sincere emotion in the expression of conviction. He has learned practically, but not theoretically, that he must fly the *Mask*. His work should neither be consciously æsthetic nor consciously speculative but imitative of a central Being—the *Mask* as his pursuer—consciously apprehended as something distinct, as something never imminent though eternally united to the soul.[226]

His False *Mask* has shown him what purport to be 'nature spirits' because all phases before Phase 15 are in nature, as distinguished from God, and at Phase 11 that nature becomes intellectually conscious of its relations to all created things. When he desires the *Mask*, instead of flying that it may follow, it gives, instead of the intuition of God, a simulated intuition of nature. That simulated intuition is arrayed in ideal conventional images of sense, instead of in some form of abstract opinion, because of the character of his horoscope.[227]

XXVIII

PHASE TWENTY-SIX

Will—The Multiple Man, also called 'The Hunchback'.[228]

Mask (from Phase 12). *True*—Self-realisation. *False*—Self-abandonment.

Creative Mind (from Phase 4). *True*—Beginning of Supersensual thought. *False*—Fascination of Sin.

Body of Fate (from Phase 18)—The Hunchback is his own *Body of Fate*.

The most difficult of the phases, and the first of those phases for which one can find few or no examples from personal experience. I think that in Asia it might not be difficult to discover examples at least of Phases 26, 27 and 28, final phases of a cycle. If such embodiments occur in our present European civilisation they remain obscure, through lacking the instruments for self-expression. One must create the type from its symbols without the help of experience.

All the old abstraction, whether of morality or of belief, has now been exhausted, but in the seemingly natural man, in Phase 26 out of phase, there is an attempt to substitute a new abstraction, a simulacrum of self-expression. Desiring emotion the man becomes the most completely solitary of all possible men, for all emotional communion with his kind, that of a common study, that of an interest in work done, that of a code accepted, that of a belief shared, has passed; and without personality he is forced to create its artificial semblance. It is perhaps a slander of history that makes us see Nero so, for he lacked the physical deformity which is, we are told, first among this phase's inhibitions of personality.[229] The deformity may be of any kind, great or little, for it is but symbolised in the hump that thwarts what seems the ambition of a Cæsar or of an Achilles.[230] He commits crimes, not because he wants to, or like Phase 23 out of phase, because he can, but because he wants to feel certain that he can;[231] and he is full of malice because, finding no impulse but in his own ambition, he is made jealous by the impulse of others. He is all emphasis, and the greater that emphasis the more does he show himself incapable of emotion, the more does he display his sterility. If he live amid a theologically minded people, his greatest temptation may be to defy God, to become a Judas,[232] who betrays, not for thirty pieces of silver, but that he may call himself creator.

In examining how he becomes true to phase, one is perplexed by the obscure description of the *Body of Fate,* 'the Hunchback is his own *Body of Fate*'. This *Body of Fate* is derived from Phase 18, and (being reflected in the physical being of Phase 26), can only be such a separation of function—deformity—as breaks the self-regarding False *Mask* (Phase 18 being the breaking of Phase 12). All phases from Phase 26 to Phase 11 inclusive are gregarious; and from Phase 26 to Phase 28 there is, when the phase is truly lived, contact with supersensual life, or a sinking in of the body upon its supersensual source, or desire for that contact and sinking. At Phase 26 has come a subconscious exhaustion of the moral life, whether in belief or in conduct, and of the life of imitation, the life of judgment and approval. The *Will* must find a substitute, and as always in the first phase of a triad energy is violent and fragmentary. The moral abstract being no longer possible, the *Will* may seek this substitute through the knowledge of the lives of men and beasts, plucked up, as it were, by the roots, lacking in all mutual relations; there may be hatred of solitude, perpetual forced bonhomie; yet that which it seeks is without social morality, something radical and incredible. When Ezekiel lay upon his 'right and left side' and ate dung, to raise 'other men to a perception of the infinite',[233] he may so have sought, and so did perhaps the Indian sage or saint who coupled with the roe.[234]

If the man of this phase seeks, not life, but knowledge of each separated life in relation to supersensual unity; and above all of each separated physical life, or action,—that alone is entirely concrete— he will, because he can see lives and actions in relation to their source and not in their relations to one another, see their deformities and incapacities with extraordinary acuteness, and we shall *discover, when we come to consider the nature of *victimage*, that their images beset him in states analogous to hypnogogic vision. His own past actions also he must judge as isolated and each in relation to its source; and this source, experienced not as love but as knowledge, will be present in his mind as a terrible unflinching judgment. Hitherto he could say to *primary* man, 'Am I as good as So-and-So?'[235] and when still *antithetical* he could say, 'After all I have not failed in my good intentions taken as a whole'; he could pardon himself; but how pardon where every action is judged alone and no good action can turn judgment from the evil action by its side. He stands in the presence of a terrible blinding light, and would, were that possible, be born as worm or mole.[236]

XXIX

PHASE TWENTY-SEVEN

Will—The Saint.

Mask (from Phase 13). *True*—Renunciation. *False*—Emulation.

Creative Mind (from Phase 3). *True*—Spiritual Receptivity. *False*—Pride.

Body of Fate (from Phase 17)—None except Impersonal Action.

Examples: Socrates, Pascal.[237]

---

*This topic belongs to the psychology of the system, which I have not yet mastered. I have yet to put together and study many obscure scattered passages in the documents.—W.B.Y., July, 1925.

In his seemingly natural man, derived from *Mask*, there is an extreme desire for spiritual authority; and thought and action have for their object display of zeal or some claim of authority. Emulation is all the greater because not based on argument but on psychological or physiological difference. At Phase 27, the central phase of the soul, of a triad that is occupied with relations of the soul, the man asserts when out of phase his claim to faculty or to supersensitive privilege beyond that of other men; he has a secret that makes him better than other men.

True to phase, he substitutes for emulation an emotion of renunciation, and for the old toil of judgment and acknowledgment of sin, a beating upon his breast and an ecstatical crying out that he must do penance, that he is even the worst of men. He does not, like Phase 26, perceive separated lives and actions more clearly than the total life, for the total life has suddenly displayed its source. If he possess intellect he will use it but to serve perception and renunciation. His joy is to be nothing, to do nothing, to think nothing; but to permit the total life, expressed in its humanity, to flow in upon him and to express itself through his acts and thoughts. He is not identical with it, he is not absorbed in it, for if he were he would not know that he is nothing, that he no longer even possesses his own body, that he must renounce even his desire for his own salvation, and that this total life is in love with his nothingness.

Before the self passes from Phase 22 it is said to attain what is called the 'Emotion of Sanctity', and this emotion is described as a contact with life beyond death. It comes at the instant when synthesis is abandoned, when fate is accepted. At Phases 23, 24 and 25 we are said to use this emotion, but not to pass from Phase 25 till we have intellectually realised the nature of sanctity itself, and sanctity is described as the renunciation of personal salvation. The 'Emotion of Sanctity' is the reverse of that realisation of incipient personality at Phase 8, which the *Will* related to collective action till Phase 11 had passed. After Phase 22 the man becomes aware of something which the intellect cannot grasp and this something is a supersensual environment of the soul. At Phases 23, 24 and 25 he subdues all attempts at its intellectual comprehension, while relating it to his bodily senses and faculties, through technical achievement, through morality, through belief.[238] At Phases 26, 27 and 28 he permits those senses and those faculties to sink in upon their environment. He will, if it be possible, not even touch or taste or see: 'Man does not perceive the truth; God perceives the truth in man'.[239]

XXX

PHASE TWENTY-EIGHT

Will—The Fool.
Mask (from Phase 14). *True*—Oblivion. *False*—Malignity.
Creative Mind (from Phase 2). *True*—Physical Activity. *False*—Cunning.
Body of Fate (from Phase 16)—The Fool[240] is his own *Body of Fate.*

The natural man, the fool desiring his *Mask,* grows malignant, not as the Hunchback, who is jealous of those that can still feel, but through terror and out of jealousy of all that can act with intelligence and effect. It is his true business to become his own opposite, to pass from a semblance of Phase 14 to the reality of Phase 28, and this he does under the influence of his own mind and body—he is his own *Body of Fate*—for having no active intelligence he owns nothing of the exterior world but his mind and body. He is but a straw blown by the wind, with no mind but the wind and no act but a nameless drifting and turning, and is sometimes called 'The Child of God'.[241] At his worst his hands and feet and eyes, his will and his feelings, obey obscure subconscious fantasies, while at his best he would know all wisdom if he could know anything. The physical world suggests to his mind pictures and events that have no relation to his needs or even to his desires; his thoughts are an aimless reverie; his acts are aimless like his thoughts; and it is in this aimlessness that he finds his joy. His importance will become clear as the system elaborates itself, yet for the moment no more need be said but that one finds his many shapes on passing from the village fool to the fool of Shakespeare.

Out of the pool,
Where love the slain with love the slayer lies,
Bubbles the wan mirth of the mirthless fool.[242]

PHASE ONE

Will.
Mask (from Phase 15).
Creative Mind (from Phase 1).
Body of Fate (from Phase 15).
} No description
except complete
plasticity

This is a supernatural incarnation, like Phase 15, because there is complete objectivity, and human life cannot be completely objective. At Phase 15 mind was completely absorbed by Being, but now body is completely absorbed in its supernatural environment. The images of mind are no longer irrelevant even, for there is no longer anything to which they can be relevant, and acts can no longer be immoral or stupid for there is no one there that can be judged. Thought and inclination, fact and object of desire, are indistinguishable (Mask is submerged in Body of Fate, Will in Creative Mind), that is to say there is complete passivity, complete plasticity. Mind has become indifferent to good and evil, to truth and falsehood; body has become undifferentiated, dough-like; the more perfect be the soul, the more indifferent the mind, the more dough-like the body;[243] and mind and body take whatever shape, accept whatever image is imprinted upon them, transact whatever purpose is imposed upon them, and are indeed the instruments of supernatural manifestation, being the final link between the living and more powerful beings. There may be great joy; but it is the joy of a conscious plasticity; and it is this plasticity, this liquefaction, or pounding up, whereby all that has been knowledge becomes instinct and faculty. All plasticities do not obey all masters, and when we have considered cycle and horoscope it will be seen how those that are the instruments of subtle supernatural will differ from the instruments of cruder energy; but all, highest and lowest, are alike in being automatic.

FINISHED AT THOOR, BALLYLEE, 1922,
IN A TIME OF CIVIL WAR.[244]

BOOK II

What the Caliph Refused to Learn

1. DESERT GEOMETRY OR THE GIFT
OF HARUN AL-RASCHID[1]

Kusta ben Luka is my name, I write
To Abd Al-Rabban[2]; fellow roysterer once,
Now the good Caliph's learned Treasurer,
And for no ear but his.
                    Carry this letter
Through the great gallery of the Treasure House
Where banners of the Caliphs hang, night-coloured
But brilliant as the night's embroidery,[3]
And wait war's music; pass the little gallery;
Pass books of learning from Byzantium[4]
Written in gold upon a purple stain,
And pause at last, I was about to say,
At the great book of Sappho's[5] song; but no!
For should you leave my letter there, a boy's
Love-lorn, indifferent hands might come upon it
And let it fall unnoticed to the floor.
Pause at the Treatise of Parmenides[6]
And hide it there, for Caliphs to world's end
Must keep that perfect, as they keep her song,
So great its fame.
                    When fitting time has passed,
The parchment will disclose to some learned man
A mystery that else had found no chronicler
But the wild Bedouin[7]. Though I approve
Those wanderers that welcomed in their tents
What great Harun Al-Raschid, occupied
With Persian embassy or Grecian war,

Or those who need his bounty or his law,[8]
Must needs neglect; I cannot hide the truth
That wandering in a desert, featureless
As air under a wing, can give bird's wit.
In after time they will speak much of me
And speak but phantasy. Recall the year
When our beloved Caliph put to death
His Vizir Jaffer[9] for an unknown reason.
'If but the shirt upon my body knew it
I'd tear it off and throw it in the fire.'
That speech was all that the town knew, but he
Seemed for a while to have grown young again;
Seemed so on purpose, muttered Jaffer's friends,
That none might know that he was conscience struck—
But that's a traitor's thought. Enough for me
That in the early summer of the year
The mightiest of the princes of the world
Came to the least considered of his courtiers;
Sat down upon the fountain's marble edge,
One hand amid the goldfish in the pool:
And thereupon a colloquy took place
That I commend to all the chroniclers
To show how violent great hearts can lose
Their bitterness and find the honeycomb.

'I have brought a slender bride into the house;
You know the saying "Change the bride with Spring",
And she and I, being sunk in happiness,
Cannot endure to think you tread these paths
When evening stirs the jasmine, and yet
Are brideless.'

                    'I am falling into years.'

'But such as you and I do not seem old
Like men who live by habit. Every day
I ride with falcon to the water's edge
Or carry the ringed mail upon my back,

Or court a woman; neither enemy,
Gamebird, nor woman does the same thing twice;
And so a hunter carries in the eye
A mimicry of youth. Can poet's thought
That springs from body and in body falls
Like this pure jet, now lost amid blue sky,
Now bathing lily leaf and fishes' scale,
Be mimicry?'

          'What matter if our souls
Are nearer to the surface of the body
Than souls that start no game and turn no rhyme!
The soul's own youth and not the body's youth
Shows through our lineaments. My candle's bright;
My lantern is too loyal not to show
That it was made in your great father's reign.'

'And yet the jasmine season warms our blood.'

'Great prince, forgive the freedom of my speech;
You think that love has seasons, and you think
That if the spring bear off what the spring gave
The heart need suffer no defeat; but I
Who have accepted the Byzantine faith
That seems unnatural to Arabian minds,
Think when I choose a bride I choose for ever;
And if her eye should not grow bright for mine,
Or brighten only for some younger eye,
My heart could never turn from daily ruin
Nor find a remedy.'

          'But what if I
Have lit upon a woman who so shares
Your thirst for those old crabbed mysteries,
So strains to look beyond our life, an eye
That never knew that strain would scarce seem bright;
And yet herself can seem youth's very fountain,
Being all brimmed with life.'

'Were it but true
I would have found the best that life can give,
Companionship in those mysterious things
That make a man's soul or a woman's soul
Itself and not some other soul.'

'That love
Must needs be in this life and in what follows
Unchanging and at peace, and it is right
Every philosopher should praise that love;
But I being none can praise its opposite.
It makes my passion stronger but to think
Like passion stirs the peacock and his mate,
The wild stag and the doe; that mouth to mouth
Is a man's mockery of the changeless soul.'

And thereupon his bounty gave what now
Can shake more blossom from autumnal chill
Than all my bursting springtime knew. A girl
Perched in some window of her mother's house
Had watched my daily passage to and fro;
Had heard impossible history of my past;
Imagined some impossible history
Lived at my side; thought Time's disfiguring touch
Gave but more reason for a woman's care.
Yet was it love of me, or was it love
Of the stark mystery that has dazed my sight,
Perplexed her phantasy and planned her care?
Or did the torchlight of that mystery
Pick out my features in such light and shade
Two contemplating passions chose one theme
Through sheer bewilderment? She had not paced
The garden paths, nor counted up the rooms,
Before she had spread a book upon her knees
And asked about the pictures or the text;
And often those first days I saw her stare
On old dry writing in a learned tongue,
On old dry faggots that could never please

The extravagance of spring; or move a hand
As if that writing or the figured page
Were some dear cheek.
            Upon a moonless night
I sat where I could watch her sleeping form,
And wrote by candle-light; but her form moved,
And fearing that my light disturbed her sleep
I rose that I might screen it with a cloth.
I heard her voice 'Turn that I may expound
What's bowed your shoulder and made pale your cheek';
And saw her sitting upright on the bed;
Or was it she that spoke or some great Djinn?
I say that a Djinn spoke. A live-long hour
She seemed the learned man and I the child;
Truths without father came, truths that no book
Of all the uncounted books that I have read,
Nor thought out of her mind or mine begot,
Self-born, high-born, and solitary truths,
Those terrible implacable straight lines
Drawn through the wandering vegetative dream,
Even those truths that when my bones are dust
Must drive the Arabian host.
            The voice grew still,
And she lay down upon her bed and slept,
But woke at the first gleam of day, rose up
And swept the house and sang about her work
In childish ignorance of all that passed.
A dozen nights of natural sleep, and then
When the full moon swam to its greatest height
She rose, and with her eyes shut fast in sleep
Walked through the house. Unnoticed and unfelt
I wrapped her in a heavy hooded cloak, and she
Half running, dropped at the first ridge of the desert
And there marked out those emblems on the sand
That day by day I study and marvel at,
With her white finger. I led her home asleep
And once again she rose and swept the house
In childish ignorance of all that passed.

Even to-day, after some seven years
When maybe thrice in every moon her mouth
Has murmured wisdom of the desert Djinns,
She keeps that ignorance, nor has she now
That first unnatural interest in my books.
It seems enough that I am there; and yet,
Old fellow student, whose most patient ear
Heard all the anxiety of my passionate youth,
It seems I must buy knowledge with my peace.
What if she lose her ignorance and so
Dream that I love her only for the voice,
That every gift and every word of praise
Is but a payment for that midnight voice
That is to age what milk is to a child!
Were she to lose her love, because she had lost
Her confidence in mine, or even lose
Its first simplicity, love, voice, and all,
All my fine feathers would be plucked away
And I left shivering. The voice has drawn
A quality of wisdom from her love's
Particular quality. The signs and shapes;
All those abstractions that you fancied were
From the great Treatise of Parmenides;
All, all those gyres and cubes and midnight things[10]
Are but a new expression of her body
Drunk with the bitter-sweetness of her youth.
And now my utmost mystery is out:
A woman's beauty is a storm-tossed banner;
Under it wisdom stands, and I alone—
Of all Arabia's lovers I alone—
Nor dazzled by the embroidery, nor lost
In the confusion of its night-dark folds,
Can hear the armed man speak.

1923.

2. THE GEOMETRICAL FOUNDATION
OF THE WHEEL

I

THE GYRE

Flaubert talked much of writing a story called 'La Spirale' and died before he began it, but since his death an editor has collected the scheme from various sources. It would have concerned a man whose dreams during sleep grew in magnificence as his life became more and more unlucky. He dreamt of marriage with a princess when all went wrong with his own love adventure.[11] Swedenborg wrote occasionally of gyrations, especially in his *Spiritual Diary*, and in *The Principia*[12] where the physical universe is described as built up by the spiral movement of points, and by vortexes which were combinations of these; but very obscurely except where describing the physical universe, perhaps because he was compelled as he thought to keep silent upon all that concerned Fate. I remember that certain Irish countrymen whom I questioned some twenty years ago had seen Spirits departing from them in an ascending gyre[13]; and there is that gyring 'tangle of world lines in a fourth dimensional space'[14] of later discoverers, and of course Descartes[15] and his vortex, Boehme[16] and his gyre, and perhaps, were I learned enough to discover it, allusions in many writers back to antiquity. Arrived there I am attracted to a passage in Heraclitus[17] which I can, I think, explain more clearly than his English commentators.

II

EXPANDING AND CONTRACTING GYRES

Having the concrete mind of the poet, I am unhappy when I find myself among abstract things, and yet I need them to set my experience in order. I must speak of time and space, though as I accept the argument of Berkeley I think of them as abstract creations of the human mind, limits which it has chosen for itself.[18]

A line is the symbol of time and it expresses a movement—without extension in space—and because emotion has no extension in that space, however much connected with objects that have, a line symbolises the emotional subjective mind, the self in its simplest form. A plane cutting the line at right angles constitutes, in combination with the moving line, a space of three or more dimensions, and is the symbol of all that is objective, and so for certain purposes of nature and, because intellect is the understanding of objects in space, of intellect as opposed to emotion.[19] Line and plane are combined in a gyre, and as one tendency or the other must be always the stronger, the gyre is always expanding or contracting. For simplicity of representation the gyre is drawn as a cone. Sometimes this cone represents the individual soul, and that soul's history—these things are inseparable—sometimes general life. When general life, we give to its narrow end, to its unexpanded gyre, the name of *Anima Hominis,* and to its broad end, or its expanded gyre, *Anima Mundi*[20]; but under-

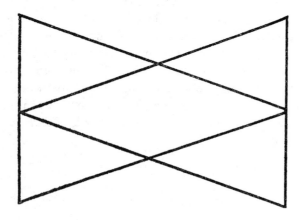

standing that neither the soul of man nor the soul of nature can be expressed without conflict or vicissitude we substitute for this cone two cones, one which is the contact of the mind with *Fate,* and the other the contact of the mind with *Destiny. Destiny* being understood to mean all external acts and forms created by the *Will* itself and out of itself, whereas *Fate* is all those acts or forms imposed upon the *Will* from without. It is as though the first act of being, after creating limit, was to divide itself into male and female, each dying the other's life living the other's death.[21]

These cones are associated with the line and the space wherein it moves respectively, as though the first gyre met with another and opposing gyre which has its greatest expansion, not in space, as we perceive it by the senses, but in a space perceived by the mind only. We can consider the cones as fixed and use disks or lines to represent the opposing gyres. It will be seen presently that these opposing gyres are also beauty and truth, value and fact, particular and universal, quality and quantity, the bundle of separated threads as distinguished from those still in the pattern, abstracted types and forms as distinguished from those that are still concrete, Man and *Daimon,* the living and the dead, and all other images of our first parents.

When the life of man is growing more predestined, there is something within the depth of his being that resists, that desires the exact contrary; and if his life is growing more fated it desires the exact contrary of that also. As these contraries become sharper in their contrast, as they pull farther apart, consciousness grows more intense,

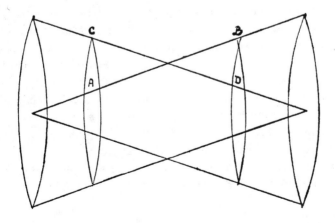

for consciousness is choice. The energy of the one tendency being in exact mathematical proportion to that of the other, the wide gyre marked B for instance in the cone of *Fate* is at exactly the same distance from its widest expanse that the gyre marked C is from its widest expansion. When each gyre has reached the widest expansion, the contradiction in the being will have reached its height. But beside these two expanding gyres there are the two narrowing gyres, marked A D in the figure. As man's intellect, say, expands, the emotional nature contracts in equal degree and vice versa; when, however, a narrowing and a widening gyre reach their limit, the one the utmost contraction the other the utmost expansion, they change places, point to circle, circle to point, for this system conceives the world as catastrophic, and continue as before, one always narrowing, one always expanding, and yet bound for ever to one another. Of this fourfold—two expanding gyres, in nature opposite to one another and two contracting gyres, opposite to one another—we consider the one we identify with the *Will* as deciding the nature of the being. If now we consider these opposing gyres or cones as expressing Man and *Daimon*—those two first portions of being that suffer vicissitude into which *Anima Hominis* and *Anima Mundi* resolve—we can explain much in Parmenides and Empedocles, but especially this in Heraclitus: 'I shall retrace my steps over the paths of song that I have travelled before, drawing from my saying a new saying. When Strife was fallen to the lowest depth of the vortex.'[22] ('Not as might be supposed,' Birkett explains, 'the centre but the extreme bound.') 'and love has reached the centre of the whirl, in it do all things come together so as to be one only; not all at once, but coming together gradually from different quarters; and as they came together Strife retired to the extreme boundary . . . but in proportion as it kept rushing out, a soft immortal stream of blameless love kept running in.'[23] So far all is plain, and it may be this very passage that suggested Flaubert's dreaming man whose life goes wrong as his dream comes right. 'For of a truth they (Love and Strife) were afore time and shall be, nor ever can (?) boundless time be emptied of the pair, and they prevail in turn as the circle comes round, and pass away before one another and increase in their appointed time.'[24]

And had we more than a few fragments of Empedocles and his

school it might not be hard to relate the four gyres of our symbol to heat and cold, light and dark, the pairs of opposites, whether in the moral or physical universe, which permeate his thought. The single cone whose extreme limits are described as *Anima Hominis, Anima Mundi,* is said in our documents to be formed by the whirling of a sphere which moves onward leaving an empty coil behind it; and the double cones by the separating of two whirling spheres that have been one, and it may be that we have here what suggested to Parmenides thoughts that seemed to forestall certain of our latest mathematical speculations. 'Where then it has its furthest boundary it is complete on every side, equally poised from the centre in every direction like the mass of a rounded sphere, for it cannot be greater or smaller in one place than another . . . and there is not, and never shall be any time, other than that which is present, since Fate has chained it so as to be whole and immoveable.'[25]

III

BLAKE'S USE OF THE GYRES[26]

Blake, in the "Mental Traveller",[27] describes a struggle, a struggle perpetually repeated between a man and a woman, and as the one ages, the other grows young. A child is given to an old woman and

> Her fingers number every nerve
> Just as a miser counts his gold;
> She lives upon his shrieks and cries
> And she grows young as he grows old.
> Till he becomes a bleeding youth
> And she becomes a virgin bright;
> Then he rends up his manacles
> And bends her down to his delight.

Then he in his turn becomes 'an aged shadow' and is driven from his door, where 'From the fire on the hearth a little female babe doth spring'. He must wander 'until he can a maiden win' and then all is repeated for

The honey of her infant lips
The bread and wine of her sweet smile
The wild game of her roving eye
Does him to infancy beguile.

  •   •   •   •   •   •   •

Till he becomes a wayward babe
And she a weeping woman old

When Edwin J. Ellis and I had finished our big book[28] on the philosophy of William Blake, I felt that we had no understanding of this poem: we had explained its details, for they occur elsewhere in his verse or his pictures, but not the poem as a whole, not the myth, the perpetual return to the same thing; not that which certainly moved Blake to write it; but when I had understood the double cones, I understood it also. The woman and the man are two competing gyres growing at one another's expense, but with Blake it is not enough to say that one is beauty and one is wisdom, for he conceives this conflict as that in all love—whether between the elements as in Parmenides[29], 'the wanton love' of Aristotle,[30] or between man and woman—which compels each to be slave and tyrant by turn. In our system also it is a cardinal principle that anything separated from its opposite—and victory is separation—'consumes itself away'. The existence of the one depends upon the existence of the other.

Blake and his wife signed, in 1789, a document approving the foundation of the Swedenborgian Church, his brother remained a Swedenborgian to the end of his life, his friend Flaxman was a Swedenborgian and a very learned man, and it is possible therefore that he found among fellow-believers a knowledge of gyres and vortexes obtained from Swedenborg himself, though at that time inaccessible in print.[31] Or, upon the other hand, those beings which gave that knowledge as it is in *The Spiritual Diary*[32] may have given it to Blake also.

IV

THE PAIRS OF OPPOSITES AND THE DANCE
OF THE FOUR ROYAL PERSONS

One must fix the character of the pairs of opposites, Blake's tyrant and slave, or, to follow Empedocles to the end, 'Fire and Water, Earth and the mighty height of Air'.[33] Our documents arrange them as in diagram.

The cone of *Fate* and *Mind* is shaded,[34] and all that is external to the *Will* is assumed to be dark, for the light that makes all things visible to the mind comes from the *Will* itself, our perception of objects,

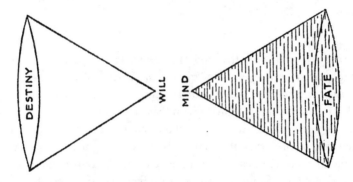

being, as Plotinus[35] insisted, not a passive reception but a state of activity. *Destiny* is here the utmost range possible to the *Will* if left in freedom, and its other name is beauty, whereas *Fate* is the utmost range of the mind when left in its freedom and its other name is truth. But we are no longer dealing with the simple elements but with mixtures, and so we impose these cones, or gyres, upon certain other cones or gyres, which remain fixed and are their containing sphere, and which for simplicity of representation we may place end to end though they are in reality one within the other,—as in the first figure in Sec. II.

By moving the two dotted cones in and out, we can express to the eye the unalterable relation between A which is the energy, and B which is its *Destiny* or beauty, and that between C, which is mind, and D which is its *Fate* or Truth. As B B approaches the wide end of the right hand cone, A approaches the narrow end of its cone, and when this movement is reversed, and B B recedes from the wide end,

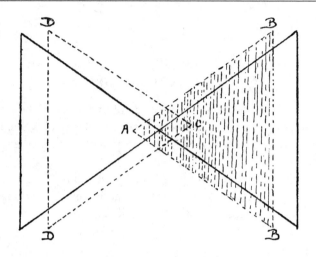

A recedes from the narrow end of its cone. That is to say when B is
three quarter *primary* and one quarter *antithetical* A is three quarter
antithetical and one quarter *primary,* and so on; and the movements
of D D and C coincide exactly with these movements. That is to say
each gyre, for the extremities of the moving cones are gyres in the
fixed cones, preserves its relation to its own opposite unbroken,
though the nature of each perpetually changes. In the documents the
fixed cones are left out and the relation between the opposites symbolised by the various relations of the approaching and separating

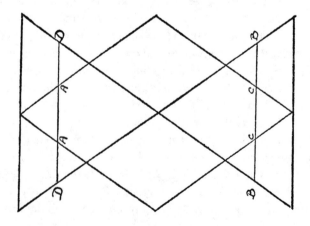

cones; or the approaching and separating cones are left out and the opposites represented by lines cutting the fixed cones.

It is, however, cumbersome to use four gyres if two will serve, as they do if we combine two sets of cones so that one line includes B B, C C, and another D D, A A, and so that the same movement causes one line to contract as the other expands.

We reach the same end if we consider both sides of the fixed cones as having different meanings, and these fixed cones as placed one within the other. We now obtain our pairs of opposites by considering the four points touched by the two gyres.

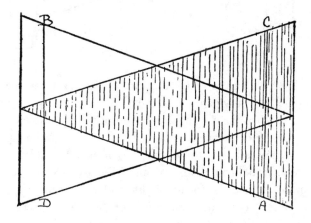

The pairs A B and C D are now so placed that opposites confront one another from opposite sides of the figure, and if we study their movements we have those of the Great Wheel or the Dance of the Four Royal Persons.

Will is *Will,* Mind is *Creative Mind, Destiny* is *Mask, Fate* is *Body of Fate.* They are the *Four Faculties,* and I must leave the definition of their function, given in the section describing the Great Wheel, to explain itself as the system grows familiar, that I may not write at too great length. The figure in the two diagrams just given is that of a person at Phase 12, and as each gyre is now considered as a whirling disc, passing through both inner and outer cones it shows the exact proportion of *antithetical* and *primary* in each of the *Four Faculties.* This proportion is represented in the Great Wheel by the size of the illuminated portion of the Lunar disc at each particular

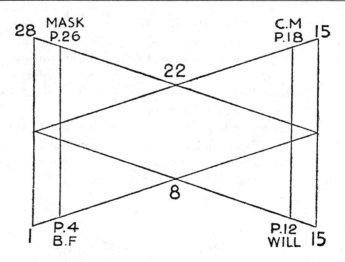

phase. At Phase 12 the Moon is approaching the full in the exact measure as that in which the gyre A C is approaching its greatest expansion. When the greatest expansion of the gyre is reached the phase is Full Moon and so on, and *Will* and *Creative Mind* pass each other at its greatest expansion exactly as in the Great Wheel. When we make a symbol combining Sun and Moon, we express the same thing more completely, for as we have already seen the *primary* may be called Solar, the *antithetical* Lunar. The converse is not always true, for the *Tinctures* belong to a man's life while in the body, and Solar and Lunar may transcend that body. The Great Wheel is not, however, an arbitrary symbol for it is a single gyre of a great cone containing, as we shall see presently, twelve cycles of embodiment. Every gyre of every cone is in the same way equal to an entire cone revolving through twenty-eight phases or their equivalent.

V

BLAKE AND THE GREAT WHEEL

We interpret the symbol differently from Blake[36] because his tyrant and slave, slave and tyrant are man and woman out of phase, and their youth occurs at Phases 8 and 22 of our symbol because there is the greatest passion, whereas their old age is at Phase 1 and Phase 15 respectively because at those phases the *primary Tincture* and the *antithetical Tincture* conquer completely and passion ceases. With us these are the moments of the greatest Beauty and Wisdom respectively because we have mainly studied men true to phase, and when man is true to phase he attains at Phase 1 and Phase 15 relation with his opposite not through conflict but, in so far as one *Faculty* or group of *Faculties* is concerned, through harmony, and is in a Sphere and not a cone. Had I studied men out of phase mainly, I would have had constantly to use Blake's interpretation, as indeed Homer did when he put into the same poem Helen and the Siege of Troy,[37] and as Avicenna did when he wrote 'All life proceeds out of corruption.'[38] As it is, the system constantly compels us to consider beauty an accompaniment of war, and wisdom of decay.

VI

THE SYMBOLISM OF THE SUN'S PRECESSION[39] AND ANNUAL MOVEMENTS[40]

Hitherto I have considered the Wheel in relation to the symbolic days of the months, but there are also the twelve symbolic months of the

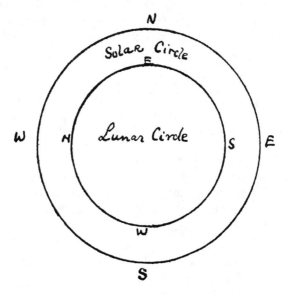

Lunar and Solar year, and the Solar day. All circles are but a single archetypal circle[41] seen according to different measures of time, and Solar East, West, the spring and autumn equinoxes, and sunrise and sunset, the critical points between the two Solar extremes, are held to fall upon Phases 15 and 1 respectively of the Lunar circle; and for simplicity we sometimes call Phase 22 Lunar East because of the Moonrise, Phase 8 Lunar West, Phase 15 Lunar South, and Phase 1 Lunar North. The fullness of *antithetical* life at Phase 15, and of *primary* life at Phase 1, fall at moments of extreme strain and shock in all that the Solar circle symbolises. We may represent the two qualities of life by two circles one within the other which move in opposite directions, the Lunar from West to East according to the Moon's zodiacal movements, the Solar from East to West according to the Sun's daily movement, or as we shall presently see, according to his precessional movement.[42]

The Solar circle represents all that comes from outside the man and is therefore the Bride, the Enemy, the Spiritual Life, the Physical World, though it is only through the *Faculties,* separated form, that he apprehends it. Because there is between the Lunar or natural world and the Solar or spiritual world conflict, the creation of philosophy 'from experience' is said 'to burn'[43] (? 'to consume itself away'[44]) whereas that from revelation gives life. For the same reason spiritual beings are said 'to deceive us if they can'.[45] The condition of truth is that neither world separate from the other and become 'abstract'.[46]

VII

THE GYRES AND LUNAR MONTHS OF THE GREAT YEAR[47]

When we come to number gyres and Lunar months in relation to the signs we consider the first gyre as coinciding with the first Lunar phase and as beginning at the centre of a zodiacal sign. We mean by the zodiacal signs not the constellations but mathematical divisions which we shall presently consider.[48]

    I. Phase One (Mid Autumn,[49] Lunar North, Cancer, Solar West, Libra).

II. Phases Two, Three and Four.
III. Phases Five, Six and Seven.
IV. Phase Eight (Mid Winter).
V. Phases Nine, Ten and Eleven.
VI. Phases Twelve, Thirteen and Fourteen.
VII. Phase Fifteen (Mid Spring, Solar East, Aries, Lunar South, Capricorn).
VIII. Phases Sixteen, Seventeen and Eighteen (First Lunar Month of Great Year).
IX. Phases Nineteen, Twenty and Twenty-one.
X. Phase Twenty-two (Mid Summer).
XI. Phases Twenty-three, Twenty-four and Twenty-five.
XII. Phases Twenty-six, Twenty-seven and Twenty-eight.

The Solar Months coincide with the signs.

Such a figure as that on page 113 is, however, without movement, for it is without error, it is but the frame, the circle which encloses all, and to show reality[50] we create another figure in the midst consisting of two more circles, the one Solar and the other Lunar, reflections as it were of the Fixed Circles. But for convenience sake I substitute cones for these two inner circles, and when the equinoctial point has just entered Aries—is at Aries 30 that is[51]—superimpose them one

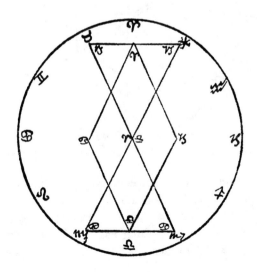

upon another and assume that the Solar or Diamond shaped cone
has a movement from East to West, and that like an Hour-Glass
from West to East.

VIII

THE CONES OF THE LUNAR AND SOLAR YEAR

I use two cones with their narrow ends meeting for *Mask* and *Will,*
which I will call the Lunar cones, and two with their broad ends
meeting for the *Creative Mind* and *Body of Fate* which I will call the
Solar cones. At the present moment as the equinox is in Pisces, the
Creative Mind, which is always identified with the East and so with
the equinoctial point, has moved from the historical starting point in
Aries 30 through somewhat more than one twelfth of the entire circle.

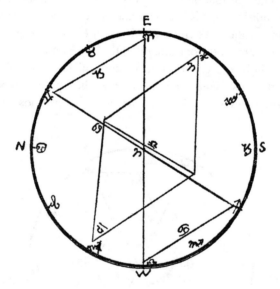

When the Sun at the vernal equinox passed from Taurus into
Aries, Eternal Man had his *Will* and *Mask* at Phase 15 and Phase 1
respectively, and so at Lunar South and North, and his *Creative
Mind* and his *Body of Fate* at Solar East and West. During the passage of *Creative Mind* through one sign, starting from solar East, the

interior gyre of these Solar and Lunar cones will have made one rotation out of the twelve that complete their circles, and in the Lunar cones that has been a passage from South to North and from North to South again.

It is necessary to notice that as Aries 30, let us say, is the extreme end or East of the Solar cone, and Capricorn 30 the extreme end of the Lunar cone, the 15th Lunar Phase does not begin at Solar East, but that its central moment corresponds to East and so to Aries 30. This means that each of the twelve Lunar divisions begins in the middle of one of the twelve Solar divisions. Starting at East and South we say that the gyre or division corresponding to Phase 15 ends and that corresponding to Phases 16, 17 and 18 begins in the middle of the Solar division that corresponds to Aries, or, if we turn it all into astronomical symbolism, that the first new Moon occurs one half of a Solar month after the Sun has entered Aries. Our figure is based on the Great Year of some twenty-six thousand years, and therefore the Sun enters Aries at the 30th degree and not at o as in the annual movement. But the new Moon is always North for it is at the beginning of the twenty-eight phases, and so we get the symbolism of the Cardinal Points once more, for each Solar division begins at East and has West for its central point. The *Will* of Eternal Man during the civilisation that climaxed in Athens and in Rome was passing through a gyre which corresponded to Phase 15 of the Lunar cone and had therefore the greatest possible artistic capacity, and at the foundation of Christianity entered upon the gyre of Phases 16, 17 and 18, while His *Creative Mind* entered upon that of Phases 14, 13 and 12; and at the foundation of the next civilisation His *Will* will have entered the gyre of Phases 19, 20 and 21, while His *Creative Mind* at the moment when the Solar equinox touches the central point of Pisces will have entered that of Phases 11, 10 and 9. As the Great Year begins at its vernal equinox—Aries 30 not Aries o—the next civilisation will correspond to its second lunar month. These revolving cones, however, as we shall see presently, belong to all periods, whether of history or of individual life, which involve the interaction of *primary* and *antithetical*.

When the Lunar and Solar cones are considered together, there are two gyres in the Lunar for *Mask* and *Will* respectively, and two in the Solar for *Creative Mind* and *Body of Fate*, and they complete their revolutions once in the course of the Great Year. The *Creative Mind* and the *Body of Fate* are only present in the Lunar cones as an outward limit or obstruction—we shall return to them presently—as they should act through *Will* and *Mask*; and the *Will* and *Mask* are present in the same way in the Solar cones as they should act through *Creative Mind* and *Body of Fate*. During the *antithetical* half of the circle, the mind of the man, as we shall see presently, is in the Lunar cones, and during the *primary* half in the Solar. When they are considered separately, each can move at its own will for it is a complete being, but we can still keep the same two cones, putting four gyres into each, and in this case the *Faculties* are not defined by the points where the gyres touch but by the gyres themselves, or we may use a double set of cones in each case with two gyres in each.

And now the essential movement is that when *Will* and *Mask* in the Hour-glass, moving from North to South respectively, reach 'the centre of the whirl' or East and West respectively, the gyres of *Creative Mind* and *Body of Fate* start from the extreme ends of the Diamond, each that is 'from the lowest depths of the vortex'.[52] Sometimes man is said to have only one gyre in the Solar cones and this is because that of the *Body of Fate* lies outside his mind, whereas both *Mask* and *Will* are within the mind of *antithetical* man. The *Body of Fate* is of course the *Creative Mind* of the *Daimon*, whereas the man's *Creative Mind* is the *Daimon's Body of Fate*, and so outside the being of the *Daimon*. When the Lunar and Solar cones are considered sep-

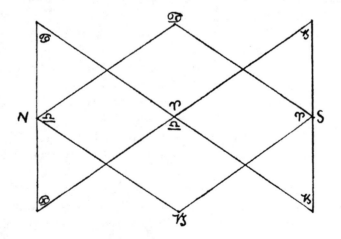

arately, we call the first the cone of the *Faculties* and the second the cone of the *Principles*; and we divide that of the *Faculties* into two cones, the one Solar and the other Lunar; and divide the cone of the *Principles* in the same way. The *Four Principles* are *Spirit, Celestial Body, Husk* and *Passionate Body*—we shall describe each presently— and they correspond to *Creative Mind, Body of Fate, Will* and *Mask* respectively. In the cone of the *Faculties* we place *Will* and *Mask* in the Lunar cone or the Hour-glass, *Creative Mind* and *Body of Fate* in the Diamond or Solar cone; and in the cone of the *Principles, Husk* and *Passionate Body* in the Hour-glass, *Spirit* and *Celestial Body* in the Diamond. In each set the revolutions of Diamond and Hour-glass round one another create the months, the Solar month being in the cone of the *Principles* which is superimposed.

Upon the diagram of the Great Wheel the words *Head, Heart, Loins* and *Fall* are written, and they correspond to *Spirit, Passionate Body, Husk* and *Celestial Body* at the opening of the next civilisation, which will be reached when the *Will* of the Great Year is between Phase 18 and Phase 19. These points have, however, no direct connection with the Great Wheel itself and imply another figure obtained by reducing two pairs of cones to one cone each and crossing them at right angles.

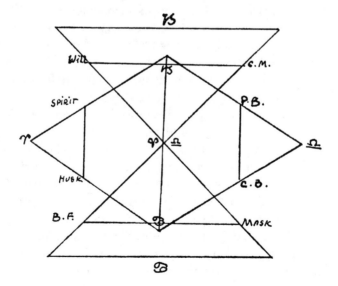

This arrangement is not used by me and is only described here because if superimposed upon the Great Wheel it explains the position upon it by *Head, Heart, Loins* and *Fall.* They are very confusing unless one remembers that they are made necessary if a single Zodiac with Cancer and Capricorn at North and South respectively is made to represent an entire Wheel.

The Diamond in this figure represents a form of existence which lasts through the entire period of twenty-six thousand years, and the Hour-glass—really Hour-glass and Diamond—the Great Wheel or period of twenty-eight embodiments, say 2200 years, a single gyre made by the whirling of the two parts of the Diamond or cone of 26,000 years. The *Faculties* and *Principles* marked upon the figure keep their position almost unchanged through the Wheel's domination.

IX

THE MONTHS ALTERNATELY PRIMARY
AND ANTITHETICAL

But each month in addition to its separate passage through the phases from 1 to 28 is part of a period of two months which is itself an entire cone or wheel, and therefore the months are alternately *antithetical* and *primary,* the lunar months corresponding to 16, 17 and 18, and so to our civilisation, being for instance *primary.* The *Principles* are properly speaking beyond the *Tinctures,* which are physical, but they have a corresponding change, and so it follows that we may say that Christ gave a *primary* revelation at the climax of an *antithetical* civilisation and will be followed by His contrary.[53] Measured by the single month, considered as the Divine influx of that month alone, He is always the Eternal Sage—Libra—but measured on the wheel or cone of the double months He is now *Victim* and now *Sage,* at East always *Victim,* the sacrificial ram, He who offers himself in sacrifice to the pitiless *antithetical* mind, for in this the life of the *Principle* resembles that of the *Faculty* and at East strength is renounced. But each quarter of the Great Year is also a cone, and so we say that the months are in sets of three; and measured by this measure He is first *Victim* and then *Sage,* and then once more *Victim,* and so we say that He is *Three Fountains*,[54] the first born of Aries and Taurus, the second of Libra and Scorpio, and the third of Aries and Taurus once more; and the greater circle is always *primary* in relation to that which turns more quickly and within.

I see the Lunar and Solar cones first, before they start their whirling movement, as two worlds lying one within another— nothing exterior, nothing interior, Sun in Moon and Moon in Sun— a single being like man and woman in Plato's Myth,[55] and then a separation and a whirling for countless ages, and I see man and woman as reflecting the greater movement, each with zodiac, precession, and separate measure of time, and all whirling perpetually. But this whirling, though it is creative, is not evil, for evil is from the disturbance of the harmony, so that those that should come in their season come all at once or straggle here and there, the gyres thrown together in confusion, and hatred takes possession of all.

X

THE GREAT YEAR IN CLASSICAL ANTIQUITY[56]

Before further explaining these cones which the reader must have found very troublesome, I would discover if Antiquity had similar measures. Remembering that elaborate geometry of the Timaeus and certain numerical calculations in the Republic of which modern scholars have seventeen incompatible explanations, we may be certain that a Platonist would have found our measures naive in their simplicity.[57]

Milton was the first English writer who made philosophical use of the obliquity of the ecliptic, but it was the Sun's annual and not his precessional movement that enabled Milton in the tenth book of *Paradise Lost* to explain the sudden ruin of the climate when Adam was driven out of Eden.[58] Yet he must have known of the precession for he had in his library the Byzantine historian Georgius Syncellus who comments upon it and upon the Great Year that it defines.[59] It is only now when we realise the antiquity of man that we can know how vast and how important was the conception of that Year.

Certain English and German scholars associate the changes of ancient mythology with the retreat of the Sun through the Zodiacal

Signs, and attribute to his passage at the Vernal Equinox through
Gemini such double Gods and Worthies as Castor and Pollux, Adam
and Eve, Cain and Abel; and all Ox-like Deities to his passage
through Taurus and so on, and discover in the Zodiac a history of
the human soul through life and death, sin and salvation,[60] and
consider that Babylonian and other Antiquity meant the Constellations when it spoke of the Book of Life, the zodiacal constituting the
text and those to North and South the commentary.[61] There are
indeed later scholars—I think of M. Cumont[62] especially—who
write about this view as if they were Protestant theologians denounc-
ing the errors of Rome, and insist that nobody knew anything about
the equinoctial precession until Hipparchus discovered it a hundred
and fifty years before Christ. Dr Alfred Jeremias and Dr Fritz Hommel, however, writing, the one upon the Babylonian Calendar, the
other upon the Babylonian Ages of the world, in *The Encyclopaedia
of Religion and Ethics,* proffer recent evidence and declare that the
older view is proved.[63] Dr Hommel fixes the date of the first Vernal
rising of the various signs as Cancer 7000 B.C., Gemini 5000 B.C.,
Taurus 3000 B.C., and Aries 1000 B.C.[64] He evidently prefers these
round numbers to the actual periods of a little under 2200 years
because we do not know precisely where the ancient mathematical
divisions of the Zodiac, if such there were, began and ended; or even
where the ancient constellations began and ended; and the symbolism expounded in this book is based upon the same dates and round
numbers. He defines a mathematical division or sign for the opening
month of the Great Year which does not correspond with any possible month of the ordinary year, for the first month of the ordinary
year, as we shall presently see, has its symbolical starting point—its
o of Aries—at his 15th or central degree, if anything so vague as his
division can have degrees.

Our authorities for the Greek and Roman use of the Great Year
which was, Dr Alfred Jeremias and Dr Fritz Hommel think, founded
like the Babylonian upon the precessional movement through the
signs, are passages in the Timaeus—39.D.ff.—in the Republic—
545.C.ff.—in Cicero's *Dream of Scipio,* and, for its relation to
another smaller cycle, in the Fourth Eclogue of Virgil,[65] and in various commentators upon them. The Babylonian Great Year began
when Aries rose at the Vernal Equinox,[66] and Syncellus says that this

was the doctrine of the 'Greeks and Egyptians . . . as stated in the Genica of Hermes, and in the Cyrannid Books',[67] but words put by Cicero into the mouth of a shade give no especial significance to any particular sign: 'By common custom men measure the year merely by the return of the Sun, or in other words by the revolutions of one star. But when the whole of the constellations shall return to the positions from which they once set forth, thus after a long interval re-making that first map of the Heavens, that may indeed be called the Great Year wherein I scarce dare say how many are the generations of men. As when in old days, at the coming of Romulus into this sacred house, the Sun seemed to fail and to be extinguished, so shall the Sun at the same time and position fail once more and the signs of the Zodiac all return to their first position and the stars be recalled, and then shall the cycle of the Great Year be full, and of that vast cycle know that not one twentieth part has passed away.'[68] Macrobius translated Cicero's Greek into Latin at the end of the fifth century[69] and said in his commentary that Cicero considered that the Great Year began with an eclipse that coincided with the death of Romulus. 'The World Year' or 'Revolution of the Universe', as he names it also, 'developed only in a profusion of centuries and the idea of it is as follows. All the luminaries and stars that seem fixed in Heaven and whose individual motion human wisdom is unable to perceive or detect are moved for all that. . . . The end of the Great Year is then when all the luminaries and other fixed stars have returned to some one definite position.' Thereupon he adds,—and Plato has the same thought which five minutes' arithmetic would have refuted—'The luminaries and the five planets must be in the same position that they were at the beginning of the world year.'[70] And this will come about, he thinks, in *fifteen thousand years. Twelve thousand, nine hundred and fifty-four, however, is the number Tacitus gives, quoting from a lost work of Cicero's,[71] but to-day we know that the true number is some twenty-six thousand years.

The Fourth Eclogue seems at first sight contradictory for it announces not that the Year has but lately begun but that it is com-

---

*The Greek or Roman Great Year if derived from Hipparchus would surely have been founded upon that 36'' which he thought the least possible annual movement.

ing to an end. 'The latest age of Cumean Song is at hand; the cycles
in their vast array begin anew; Virgin Astrea comes, the reign of Saturn comes, and from the heights of Heaven a new generation of
mankind descends . . . Apollo now is King and in your consulship, in
yours, Pollio, the age of glory shall commence and the mighty
months begin to run their course.'[72]

Virgil had in his mind not the Great Year as it seems but a period
of Ten Ages of upon an average a hundred years apiece, and if we
call them a Year, or as I prefer half a Year, it can but be because as
Macrobius says 'a month is the Moon's Year'.[73] This period which
was as Mr Kirby Flower Smith says 'divided according to the ancient
solar year'[74] probably began, when a Roman period, at the Foundation of Rome or at the death of Romulus;[75] and among the Etruscans
according to tradition at 966 B.C., the date of their coming into Italy
perhaps.[76] May I not consider it as stretching from the beginning of
the Great Year according to the dates selected for that event by
Etruscan and Roman respectively, to the moment when the equinox
reaches the centre of Hommel's Aries?[77] Macrobius may have named
fifteen thousand years for its length because the time from the Foundation of Rome to what may have seemed to him the end of the
Tenth Age—4 B.C.*—was exactly one-twentieth of the whole, that
is to say one half of a Solar month if he divided the Great Year by
ten.[78] Popular thought may have seen in the Ten Ages the life period
of the Etruscan polity alone, for it is known that the Etruscans
divided a man's life into ten ages and considered that the tenth
began with his seventieth year when, even though he lived to be
ninety, soul and body parted,[79] but I assume that in the Temples, or
among those that spoke through the Sibyl's mouth,[80] the larger
measures of time were known. One might consider that the Great
Year and the lesser period had but an accidental connection were it
not that Virgil announced for the dawn of the Tenth Age an event
too great to be expected once in a thousand years, and certainly
expected elsewhere as the supreme event of the world. Plutarch
records a trumpet shrilling from the sky to announce the Ninth

---

*Some one gave this date for close of Tenth Age, perhaps some Etruscan, but
I am correcting these pages at Thoor Ballylee and there is not a reference book in
the house.—*July* 1925.

Age, Sulla's rise, the long misery of the Roman Civil War, and Servius, a contemporary of Macrobius, quotes from the Memoirs of Augustus to prove that the Tenth or Solar Age and a comet came together in 44 B.C., a little before Virgil wrote his Eclogue; while a scholar of the third century remembers that Etruscan soothsayers foretold that the Tenth Age would bring the Etruscan State to an end.[81] That age brought to the one state death, and to the other rebirth as Empire and three hundred years of peace. So considered Virgil's prophecy ceases to be an act of individual genius and is united to something more profound and mysterious, to an apprehension of a mathematical world order. Salomon Reinach upon discovering therein thoughts from some Dionysian mystery of Magna Grecia refused to consider it a poem of compliment upon the expected birth of Cæsar,[82] but I am ready to believe that Virgil[83] to find familiar form for strange and perhaps hitherto unknown emotions summoned up in the same instant the *Spiritual* and the *Physical primary.* Upon the other hand I see no reason to explain away a prophecy which only differs from many others by its connection with an ancient sidereal faith.[84] Kepler foretold the rise of Gustavus Adolphus and even the exact year in which he would die,[85] and Savonarola the Sack of Rome and in what Pope's reign it would be,[86] and many obscure people foresee in the night's dream or the day's premonition events great or trivial.

Cicero's belief that the Sun must be eclipsed upon the same place once more, and that of Macrobius that after fifteen thousand years the planets must return to the same position,[87] and that of somebody else that a line drawn from the centre of the earth must thereon pass through them all,[88] suggests that the doctrine of the Great Year was accepted without examination because of its antiquity. Greek and Chaldean astronomers had known for centuries the periods which bring the planets back to the same point, and Macrobius enumerates them[89]—Mars returns in 'two of our years', Jupiter in twelve years, and Saturn in thirty, and so on; and that no one, not even Plato with all his mathematical calculations, calculated the periods back through the World Year implies an acceptance or half acceptance of that Year, not for its astronomical but for its moral value. Our interest in Plato's comment is precisely that he does use it as we use the lunar phases, as if it were the moving hands upon a vast clock, or a

picturesque symbolism that helped him to make more vivid, and perhaps date, developments of the human mind that can be proved
dialectically. In the *Republic* he identifies the passage of his typical
community through Timocracy, Oligarchy, Democracy, Tyranny,
and so back to Aristocracy again, as a passage through Ages of
Gold, Silver, etc., that may have seemed to the eyes of the Sibyl and
perhaps to the eyes of Virgil identical with some classification of the
Ten Ages:[90] he saw what had seemed *Fate* as *Destiny*. In another passage[91] he makes his typical community bring its different periods to
an end by carrying some character to excess, and attributes the
changes of the year to a like cause.

Machiavelli may but have spoken as Plato's disciple when he
contended that all States must decay, and that all the reformer can do
to check decay is bring them back to an earlier condition, his thought
being too summary to show him that to push the State backward
could but leave it out of phase and so in illusion.[92]

Though I have assumed that the Birth of Christ took place at the
symbolic centre of the first Solar month of the Great Year, I do not
think it likely that He was born at its exact centre. Indeed the documents from which I have worked say two or three times that the age
which preceded the Birth of Christ was longer than that which followed, but as I am unable to find an explanation of this statement—
they insist that there is a mathematical explanation—I have ignored
it.[93] We have considered that every Divine Birth occurs at a symbolical New Moon, and as that of Christ occurred at or near the middle
of the first Solar Month we may describe it as marking the First Day
of the Lunar Great Year.[94] A departure from symmetry, a separation
between the Full Moon and the first day of the Solar Month, and of
the New Moon from its Fifteenth Day, would according to our system accompany the discord of life. What we have called the First
Day of the Lunar Great Year falls at a remarkable place among the
Constellations. The Constellations being of varying lengths and
sometimes overlapping have but a vague connection either with the
Twelve Divisions of the Solar Great Year, or with the Twelve Divisions of the ordinary year, but they must have dominated the ancient
imagination much more than any abstract division of the ecliptic.
When I find the position of the vernal equinox at the birth of Christ
upon the only star map within my reach which has the ancient

mythological Zodiacal creatures—Plate 3 in E. M. Plunket's *Ancient Calendars*—it falls exactly upon the line dividing the Horn of the Ram from the Side of the Fish.[95] Probably the Zodiacal creatures were never drawn precisely alike on any two maps but the difference was not great, the stars of Ram and Fish are packed particularly close to one another, and neither Virgil nor his Sibyl, if they knew anything of the Great Year, could have failed to find the position of the precessional Sun significant. Three hundred years, two degrees of the Great Year, would but correspond to two days of the Sun's annual journey, and his transition from Pisces to Aries had for generations been associated with the ceremonial death and resurrection of Dionysus. Near that transition the women wailed him, and night showed the full moon separating from the constellation Virgo, with the star in the wheatsheaf, or in the child, for in the old maps she is represented carrying now one now the other. It may be that instead of a vague line, the Sibyl knew some star that fixed the exact moment of transition. I find but four explanations compatible with man's agency, and all four incredible, for Christ being born at or near the moment of transition: that it came of pure chance—that prophecy founded upon observation of the stars created a so general expectation that prophecy brought its own fulfilment—that there has been from time immemorial so exact and unvarying correspondence between the history of mankind and the passage of the constellations men could date at some remote millennium, perhaps when the first month was first described as the month of the Sacrifice of Righteousness, and given the sacrificial Ram as its symbol, the rise and fall of civilisations as the manager of an office can tell what his clerks will be doing after lunch by a morning consideration of the clock,—that Christianity, like the religion of Serapis at the time of Ptolemy Soter, was deliberately created by unknown men out of what they found.[96]

To show a Redeemer was expected for the middle of a period—in our system the first solar month of an Age, and I suggest in that of Rome—we have not only the Stoical argument that improvement in the arts and sciences was at the expense of the individual soul,[97] and that therefore the moment of maturity was the moment of the soul's need, but the early Christian doctrine that Christ was born in the middle of the sixth period from Adam,[98] and the Persian that Zarathustra was born in the middle of a period of six thousand years 'as the heart in the middle of the body'.[99] One remembers too, 'Times and times and half a time.'[100] The Persian and Christian doctrines were identical in essentials, for the Age is a microcosm of the whole. However I but suggest and wait judgment, being no scholar; and it may be, but seek a background for my thought,[101] a painted scene.

The alternation of *antithetical* and *primary* months is certainly Platonic, for his Golden Age men are born old and grow young, whereas in that which follows they are born young and grow old.[102] He, however, made Gold *antithetical*; upon the other hand the Babylonians had the same alternation but began we are told with Silver and the Moon.[103]

XI

THE DEAD AND THE FIXED STARS

Because the visible world is the sum of the *Bodies of Fate* of all living things, or the sum of the *Creative Minds* of all *Daimons* whether of the living or the dead, what we call *Fate* is, as much as our most voluntary acts, a part of a single logical stream; and the Fixed Stars being the least changing things are the acts of whatever in that stream changes least, and therefore of all souls that have found an almost changeless rest. Berkeley thought if his study table remained when he closed his eyes it could only be because it was the thought of a more powerful spirit which he named God,[104] but the mathematician Poincaré considers[105] time and space the work of our ancestors. With the system in my bones I must declare that those ancestors still live and that time and space would vanish if they closed their eyes.

XII

THE CONES OF INDIVIDUAL LIFE

When we consider the Lunar and Solar cones in relation to individual life, the lower half of one or other, according to whether that life be *primary* or *antithetical,* is the individual phase, and the opposite half the *Mask* or the *Body of Fate* as the case may be, and during the waking life while in the body, the man may not pass beyond the central point. The opposite state of his being, that which is the activity of his *Daimon*, meets him at the centre, and contact with it is now death and now creation. After death, or in a trance or in ordinary sleep, he enters into that state, as man is always *antithetical* in relation to his *Daimon* whatever his own phase may be, or whatever that of his *Daimon*, and to die or to sleep is to pass from the Lunar to the Solar cones.

When we translate this into the life of the *Faculties* we mean that in the cones of the *Faculties*, *Will* starting at lunar South, physical maturity, reaches lunar East (Phase 22) at death, and that then life passes into the *Creative Mind* which is in the solar cones—the Diamond—and that, instead of *Will* and *Mask* dominating the being, *Creative Mind* and *Body of Fate* are dominant until the *Will* reaches lunar West (Phase 8) at birth. If we translate it into the life of the *Principles*, which are those of spiritual life and, while Natural life continues, of subconscious life, life remains in the *Husk* until East is reached and then passes into *Spirit* which is in the Solar cones at Capricorn. Then the *Spirit* together with the *Celestial Body* which is at Cancer, dominate instead of *Passionate Body* and *Husk*, and continue to do so, moving as we have already described until the *Husk* reaches lunar *West*.

The *Principles* and the *Faculties* change quality and operation according to the side of the cone upon which they travel, for the sides of the Lunar cone where Aries is are associated with *Spirit* or *Creative Mind*, and those where Libra is with *Celestial Body* or *Body of Fate*; whereas in the Solar cones the sides where Capricorn is are associated with *Husk* or *Will*, and those where Cancer is with *Passionate Body* or *Mask*. This change of quality or operation chiefly concerns us in the part of the cones where the mind is, and, as we shall presently see, *Spirit* during all the first part of the life after death struggles to separate itself from the *Passionate Body* upon whose side of the cone it travels, whereas in the second part of that life it reunites itself with *Husk*; and during later natural life the *Mask* travels upon the side of its cone influenced by the *Celestial Body*, whereas in the earlier part upon that side influenced by the *Husk*.

It is sometimes said that there is only one gyre in the Diamond, but that means that man can know but one gyre, that of *Spirit* or of *Creative Mind* as the case may be, and sees the *Celestial Body* or

Body of Fate as beyond himself; whereas a man during natural life is in both *Will* and *Mask,* and after death—if *Husk* and *Passionate Body* be sublimated and transformed—he may enter through *Spirit* and *Celestial Body* into the nature of both, and that is why *antithetical* man after death is in good and evil, or in light and dark, whereas *primary* man is in good or evil, light or dark.[106]

XIII

THE FOUR PRINCIPLES

The *Husk* is sensuous and instinctive, almost the physical body during life, and after death its record.

The *Passionate Body* is passion, but unlike the *Mask*—which if permitted to govern the mind is isolating passion,—is without solitude.

The *Celestial Body* is the portion of Eternal Life which can be separated away.

The *Spirit* is almost abstract mind, for it has neither substance nor life unless united to the *Passionate Body* or *Celestial Body.*

Unlike the *Faculties* they do not create separated or abstracted form.

XIV

LIFE AFTER DEATH[107]

After death the consciousness or choice passes into the *Spirit* and that should turn wholly to the *Celestial Body* and submit to it; not to the *Passionate Body* which is now inseparable from the *Body of Fate* and inaugurates what is called the *Dreaming Back.* If for the sake of simplicity I count the life before death and the life after as the two halves of a single Wheel and measure it upon that, this state probably lasts till that part which corresponds to Phase 25 is over. It is succeeded by a state called the *Shiftings* which lasts until the *Spirit* escapes from the *Passionate Body,* and the *Celestial Body* from the *Husk* and they face one another in contemplation and in rest. Then comes a brief state called *Beatitude* corresponding perhaps to that moment of contemplation and to Phase 1. This is followed by the

Going Forth and the *Foreknowing* during which the *Spirit* is reunited to the *Husk*, and *Celestial Body* to *Passionate Body*—now love, not passion—and after Phase 4 the Soul is dominated by the thought of the coming life. While the Soul was passing first through the lower half and then through the upper half of the cone, the cone itself moved so that the Soul is born a phase further on than that of its previous embodiment. I have touched upon these things to set them in their place in the system and touched upon them only, for I shall describe them in detail later on.

XV

THE SUN'S ANNUAL JOURNEY AND THE CHRISTIAN YEAR

When we adopt, as in the Christian Calendar, the Sun's annual journey as the symbol, we identify the *Celestial Body* with the Sun, because it moves from Aries to Pisces and not in reverse order like the *Spirit* and the *Creative Mind*; and we attribute the Birth of Christ to the winter solstice when the *Husk* is at Phase 8, and His Conception and also His Crucifixion—He is 'slain on the stems of generations'[108]—to the moment when, at the vernal equinox, the *Husk* is at Phase 15. At least that is the way we put it in our symmetrical system, but to the early Christian the problem was more difficult, for he, or those from whom he learnt, was perplexed by the different beginning and end of the lunar and solar Years. They tried to settle the matter by a tradition that the world, and one may conclude the Sun, was created at the vernal equinox, and the Moon created at the full two days later,[109] and that as Christ's life must copy the Great Year so begun, His Crucifixion and His Conception took place two days after the vernal equinox. They did not, however, celebrate the anniversaries of these events upon a fixed date but, as if to draw attention to the annual symbolism and so to the events as always present and recurrent, they selected for their Easter Ceremonies the first full Moon after the Vernal equinox no matter what the day of the month, or the Sunday nearest to that moon.[110] One notices with surprise, however, that though the date of Conception changed from year to year the Date of Christ's Birth did not. For the first four hundred years of our era Jan-

uary the 6th was kept Holy as the day of His Birth.[111] The Christian
explanation of the date was an arbitrary and fantastic calculation, or
some childish allegory. Sometimes they calculated the age of the
world, and so Christ's relation to the Great Year, by putting together
the lives of Patriarchs,[112] and sometimes pointed out that January 6th,
being twelve days after the winter solstice, glorified the Twelve
Apostles.[113] They had plainly received the date, as I think Macrobius
and Cicero had the doctrine of the Great Year, from the learned men
of an older civilisation, from Greeks and Chaldeans perhaps, perhaps
even from those worshippers of Kore at Alexandria who upon that
day carried up from a Temple Crypt a wooden figure marked upon
head and hands and knees with a Cross and a Star, crying out 'The
Virgin has given Birth to the God.'[114] If, however, one counts nine
lunar months, allowing as the Greeks did twenty-nine and thirty days
for each alternately,[115] from the first new Moon after the Annunciation, one finds that the night of the 6th of January is the first upon
which the faint Crescent of the Tenth Moon could have shown.
The nine and a half months of gestation had passed by, and the
Divine Life had been identified with that of the Seasons.

> The White hand of Moses from the bough
> Puts forth, and Jesu from the ground suspires.[116]

The choice of the date, the hesitation which after four centuries
chose the winter solstice itself for the birth of Christ, seem much the
same choice and hesitation that we ourselves would have gone
through, if compelled to decide between Phase 8, where the need for
personality first arises, and Phase 9 where personality displays itself.
When I was a boy it was customary to consider that the association
of events in the Life of Christ with one or other of the four solstices,
was the result of competition with Pagan Festivals, but we know
now that the association came before competition and that Christianity itself is part of the Sidereal Faith.[117]

Did the great victims of Antiquity, Christ, Cæsar, Socrates[118]—
Love, Justice, Truth—die under the first full Moon after the vernal
equinox? Christ did, as the date of Easter shows; Cæsar did,—
Beware the Ides of March[119]—and the sentence upon Socrates was
pronounced when the Sacred Ship sailed for what recent research

considers a March Festival at Delos,[120] the renewal of Apollo and the Earth. Did that Festival begin at the new Moon, and the Moon show all but full on the Piræus when the Ship put in to port, and was it full when Socrates drank the Hemlock? When I write these words, and recall the place of the precessional Sun, should there not be a stirring in the roots of my hair? What did ancient Thaumaturgy guard in silence?

According to St Chrysostom, John the Baptist was conceived at the Autumnal and Christ at the Spring Equinox,[121] which makes them respectively *primary* and *antithetical* when considered in relation to one another, a mid-summer and a mid-winter child. Did Da Vinci, when he painted a St John that seemed a Dionysus, know that St John's father begot him when the grape was ripe, and that his mother bore him at the Mediterranean ripening of the corn?[122]

XVI

THE OPENING AND CLOSING OF THE TINCTURES

The closing of the *Tinctures* as described in the section about the Great Wheel is caused by the preoccupation with one another of the *Celestial Body* and the *Spirit*, of the *Creative Mind* and the *Body of Fate*, when the *Will* is between Phase 26 and Phase 4, where Unity with God is possible; whereas their opening between Phases 12 and 18 is caused by the fact that the *Faculties* can be apprehended in their separation within the united being. The fact that one *Tincture* opens or closes before the other is no doubt the effect of the gyres mounting a little higher upon one side of the cone than upon the other.

XVII

THE GYRES OF THE GREAT MYTHOLOGIES

A religion or a civilisation belongs also to the lower half of the double cone, and the religion which is the originating cause of the civilisation is begotten and dies at the centre. When the lower half of the double cone is separated off and becomes itself a double cone, what was the centre is now its North. When it reaches South of this cone,

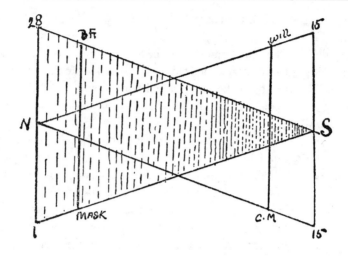

which I shall now call the History Cone, it finds its doctrinal unity and vigour, its form of Unity of Being. When later on I study this movement in detail I will divide this history cone yet once more so that there is one cone from North to South and yet another from South to North again. Whereas when I examine the life after death and compare it with this life I shall symbolise each state as one half of a double cone for I have neither the knowledge nor the talent for an analysis which would approach the *Divine Comedy* in complexity.

These are the historical cones in their simplest form, the ordinary double cone of the phases.

Will leaves North at the birth of Christ, and the *Body of Fate* leaves South, and then when *Will* reaches South and *Body of Fate* North they change sides and return: at, say 1200 A.D., they show the position in the figure. But we can also arrange them thus for the same date.[123]

Will starting at A.D. 1 travels along the lower side of the shaded cone, reaches 1000 A.D. or South and then moves upon the upper side. The *Creative Mind* starting at 1 A.D. moves along the upper side of the cone till it reaches 1000 A.D. at South and then travels down the lower side. The *Mask* and the *Body of Fate* start also from the North, but whereas the other two *Faculties* had started from the wide ends of the shaded cone, they travel from the narrow end of the unshaded cone. They also travel to South and there

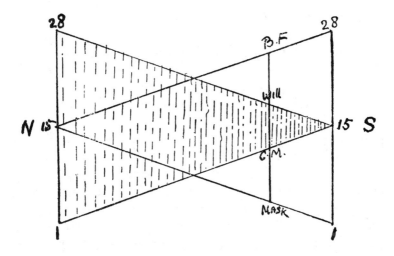

change sides and return towards the North. A single line is in this way made to show the position of all the *Four Faculties* as those *Faculties* are placed on the cone of the entire Era of two thousand years, for if this line be itself divided into 28 divisions the 15th in the centre and the 1st at the point nearest the starting point of the *Will* at A.D. 1, it will be found that the points where the sides of cones intersect will show the place of the *Four Faculties* on this greater cone. When the *Will* is so placed that any of the other *Faculties*, if placed upon the line, would lie in the future the corresponding date in a previous Millennium is taken. When the two thousand years are divided into cones of a millennium each this line has the same office as *Head, Heart, Loins* and *Fall* upon the Great Wheel, it shows the relation of the lesser to the greater division.[124]

We show the *antithetical* or *primary* nature of a *Faculty* at a particular period of time by the converging or diverging nature of the line where it is, without forgetting that each cone has its general *primary* or *antithetical* character. If we consider this figure with a similar figure, which represents the upper half of the cone, there will be two lines parallel, each marking the place of the *Four Faculties* of its half, and we shall get the third diagram in Sec. IV.

Our figure is the ground work of the historical diagram on page 147 and was probably chosen for it, because it shows at a glance what epochs are affected by what *Faculties*, and there, as it covers two thousand years and shows a movement from North to North (or if you count it upon the whole Wheel from centre to centre) it is divided into two portions of twenty-eight phases. It is upon this figure that the documents I work from place historical events with 'approximate accuracy'.[125] The movement to South of the entire era is a sinking wave of civilisation, a mounting physical or religious wave; the movement to North the converse. At South of each millennium is a period of artistic creation, that of the first millennium of mainly religious art, that of the other of mainly secular. And as North of the era is solar West, the South solar East, in the first thought is growing more Eastern, and in the second more Western. In the similar period before Christ, that of the Fifth Century B.C., thought was growing Western. Epoch, however, influences epoch as part of the cone of the entire era, by supersensual or ghostly interaction. The diagram on page 147 is drawn for our epoch and the place of *Will* is affected through its *Creative Mind* by the Age of Constantine, and when I was at Oxford a few years ago, a distinguished scholar, now dead, showed me much elaborate written evidence to prove that an apparition seen by herself and a friend in the Louvre was the Emperor Constantine.[126] This influence of age upon age is said to be through the agency of certain *[127] spirits who have come to possess what is called a simulacrum, or permanent illusionary body, created from the representation of themselves most present to the imagination of their time.

But this figure differs in form from that which preceded it and symbolised the preceding period of two thousand years, and will differ in form from any figure drawn to record the influence of a *Second Fountain*. This difference is caused by a movement analogous to the exchange of the *Tinctures* but instead of the words *primary* and *antithetical* we substitute Solar and Lunar. At each Fountain the civilisation gyres, those of *Creative Mind* and *Will* which in this connection

---

*I once heard Sir William Crookes tell how he was informed through an automatic writer that if he would make a certain incense 'The Magi would be present', and that there followed words in an unknown tongue which turned out to be ancient Persian. When read with great difficulty they proved to be a list of herbs, but no one living seemed to know to what herbs the names applied. I suspect that the link between periods arising from their place among the gyres is never broken, no matter how great the passage of time.

we call Lunar, and the gyres of *Mask* and *Body of Fate* which we call Solar, change cones. Before the birth of Christ, for instance the Lunar gyres came to the narrow end of their cone, and at His birth passed into the broad end of the other cone and so continued to converge. The Solar gyre upon the other hand passed from broad to narrow. The Solar is religious and physical and the Lunar emotional and intellectual. This means that as the civil life grew more and more *antithetical* in nature the religious grew more and more *primary* till the instant of creation was reached. At South, however, there is no interchange, but a return, a change of direction, the gyres which diverged now converge and vice versa, and this change is called *reflex* to distinguish it from that of the North which is *active*.

XVIII

THE THREE FOUNTAINS[128]
AND THE CYCLES OF EMBODIMENT

The Fountains fall into four sets of three, three in each quarter of Wheel, first of each set beginning at centre of Phases 1, 8, 15, 22 respectively, second at centre of next three, third at centre of last three phases of each quarter. They may correspond to gold, silver, copper ages adopted by the Greek poet Aratus instead of Hesiod's four.[129] But what is most clear is that they are alternately *Victim* and *Sage*, the *Victim* being called the strong soul because he attains the greatest strength and renounces it, and the *Sage* the frail soul because his strength is in that which surrounds him, in his doctrine let us say. Christ, though *Sage*—discovery of strength, the frail soul—when measured upon the Great Wheel, when placed as one of the Three Fountains of His quarter, is *Victim*, Aries, surrenders strength, and He that is to come will be the frail soul, and as Christ was the *primary* revelation to an *antithetical* age, He that is to come will be the *antithetical* revelation to a *primary* age. The cycles of human rebirth, unlike those of the Eternal Man, are measured upon the Lunar cone, and the first is at Lunar North, and these months or cycles had at first their symmetrical relation to the Solar months of the Great Year, each Lunar cycle starting in the middle of Solar, but a wheel does not cease to turn when its first revolution is over, and so it comes about at last that all the months Solar and Lunar, as it were fell together and were confused one with the other, and yet as if by a kind of crystallisation these months so arranged themselves that all the twelve Lunar months had their beginning in a certain order within each era. So we say that the first cycle sent its first soul into the world at the birth of Christ, and that the twelfth will send its last soul immediately before the birth of the New Fountain. Then there will come the first of a new series, the Thirteenth Cycle, which is a Sphere and not a cone. And yet when I say the first and last souls of a cycle, I do not mean that that cycle comes to an end for it is always beginning and always ending. When we arrange these beginnings within the two thousand years of an era we find that three cycles have their approximate beginning in each five hundred years, and so give that time their character.

There is much else that I must leave to my student, if such there be, to discover as he compares symbol with symbol. His task will be easier than mine, for I had to discover all from unconnected psychological notes and from a few inadequate diagrams. These few pages have taken me many months of exhausting labour, but never once have note and diagram failed to support each other. In judging a man one should not only know his phase but his cycle, for every cycle has a different character, but into these characters I cannot go at present, for I lack information. We retain the same sex for a cycle,[130] and then change it for another cycle, and there are said to be certain cycles between which love is more fortunate than between others, and some where physical beauty is greater and some where mental. The general law is that they follow the same development as the phases.

XIX

CONES OF NATIONS AND MOVEMENTS OF THOUGHT

We have to remember that among the solar and lunar cones that revolve in the circle of the Great Year are the cones of each separate nation and of every school of thought and action. We give to these cones the name of *Covens*.[131] The *Covens* depend exactly as individuals do upon contact for their intensity, and separated from their opposites 'Consume themselves away'. Four *Covens*, constituting four *Faculties*, may for instance move round the Wheel and pass through their phases as do individual men and women. When a movement of thought, the philosophy of religious spiritualism for instance, becomes vague and sentimental, that may be because contact through the *physical* or *spiritual primary* with some school of psychological investigation at the place, say, of the *Creative Mind* has come to an end. The *Covens* are formed by their *Daimons* out of groups of men and women who become the bodies of the *Daimons* and the *Daimon* of each *Coven* seeks to impress his will upon the three associated *Covens*. When a *Coven* has carried its creative life as far as phase and historical epoch permit, there is a re-birth, or a movement to the next phase.

I myself chose the name *Coven*, that being the name of the groups of Scotch Witches described in the witch trials, for I imagine the Nations and Philosophies as having each, as it were, a witches' cauldron of medicinal or devil's broth in the midst.[132] That which we must deduce from the doctrine is that there can be no philosophy, nation, or movement that is not a being or congeries of beings, and that which we call the proof of some philosophy is but that which enables it to be born. The world is a drama where person follows person, and though the dialogue prepares for all the entrances, that preparation is not the person's proof, nor is Polonius disproved when Hamlet seems to kill him.[133] Once the philosophy, nation or movement has clearly shown its face, we know that its chief characteristic has not arisen out of any proof, or even out of all the past, or out of the present tension of the drama, or out of any visible cause whatever, but is unique, life in itself. There can be neither cause nor effect when all things are co-eternal.

XX

THE CONES OF SEXUAL LOVE[134]

I can but touch upon the symbolism of sexual love as it needs more detailed consideration than I can give it in this book. In all pairs of lovers each is to himself or herself, *Will*, and the other *Body of Fate*. The cones of their passion are constituted, as the solar and lunar cones are, out of the first fixed circles, and its progress should mirror the cones containing the three Fountains or if we consider the matter differently and take a smaller Wheel, those from Fountain to Fountain. Love which in this way mirrors the fated and predestined, has three forms of crisis, each at the end of a constituent cone, called the first and second *Critical Moments* and the *Beatific Vision*. Such love has a relation with the dead similar to that of the Fountains and comes at each crisis under the sway of the thirteenth cone. That is to say there is harmonisation or the substitution of the sphere for the cone. The *Four Faculties* of passion, before harmonisation, are Desire, which is *Creative Mind*, Cruelty, which is *Body of Fate*, Service, which is *Will*, and Domination, which is *Mask*. After harmonisation the *Creative Mind* becomes Wisdom, *Body of Fate* Truth, *Will* Love, and *Mask* Beauty. There are also *Initiatory Moments* which create the domination of the symbol, as *Critical Moments* destroy that domination, and these fall where the gyres touch the sides of cones—North and South—and are of an indefinite number.[135] All *antithetical* life, for *primary* life has but a single movement, is seen as if it were a form of sexual life. It becomes vital through conflict and happy through harmonisation, and without either is self-consumed. Harmonisation is made possible by the recognition of fate—the Lunar cone's recognition of the Solar—but as each is Solar to the other, the destiny of the one is the fate of the other. It is the recognition by Lunar man of the Solar spiritual opposite that is called faith, and it inaugurates religious emotional and philosophical experience.

XXI

COMPLEMENTARY DREAMS[136]

I use in the section about the state of man after death the term *complementary dream*. When two people meditate upon the one theme, who have established a supersensual link, they will invariably in my experience, no matter how many miles apart, see pass before the mind's eye complementary images, images that complete one another. One for instance may see a boat upon a still sea full of tumultuous people, and the other a boat full of motionless people upon a tumultuous sea. Even when the link is momentary and superficial this takes place, and sometimes includes within its range a considerable number of people. One, for instance, will receive from a dream figure a ripe apple, another an unripe; one a lighted and one an unlighted candle, and so on.

On the same night a mother will dream that her child is dead or dying, the child that her mother is dead, while the father will wake in the night with a sudden inexplicable anxiety for some material treasure. I put an experience of the kind into the poem that begins—

> Was it the double of my dream,
> The woman that by me lay
> Dreamed, or did we halve a dream
> Under the first cold gleam of day.[137]

A whole age may be bound in a single dream, or wheel, so that its creations have all the same character though there is no visible influence.

XXII

The whole world is regarded as a single being with a relation between East and West like that between *complementary dreams,* Europe being *antithetical* and Asia *primary.* The cardinal points in the Solar and Lunar cones are not merely symbols of the Sun and Moon's path, but are held to refer to the actual geographical points. Probably those in the Solar cones refer to the movement of ideas, and their places of origin, and I shall so consider them, and those in the Lunar cones to the origin of the races themselves in so far as they keep the impression of their first surroundings.

When Joseph Strzygowski says 'the inhabitants of the South from the very beginning applied pictorial art to the representation of living creatures' he describes the *antithetical* nature of the South, and he defines the *primary* North when he attributes to it geometrical form and various 'non-representational' decorations derived from handicrafts, and he certainly describes the symbolic East when he attributes to his eastern nations conceptions that dazzle and astonish by an impression of power whether in Priest or King. Perhaps too in his description of the West as that which absorbs and uses, and is a kind of matrix, he describes our symbolic West also.[138]

XXIII

THE CONES—HIGHER DIMENSIONS

One of the notes upon which I have based this book says that all existence within a cone has a larger number of dimensions than are known to us, and another identifies *Creative Mind, Will* and *Mask* with our three dimensions, but *Body of Fate* with the unknown fourth, time externally perceived. When I saw this I tried to understand a little of modern research into this matter but found that I lacked the necessary training. I have therefore ignored it hitherto in writing this book. The difference between a higher and a lower dimension explains, however, the continual breaking up of cones and wheels into smaller cones and wheels without changing the main movement better than Swedenborg's vortex, his gyre made up of many gyres.[139] Every dimension is at right angles to all dimensions below it in the scale. If the Great Wheel, say, be a rotating plane, and the movement of any constituent cone a rotation at right angles to that plane the second movement cannot affect the first in any way. In the same way the rotation of the sphere will be a movement at right angles to a circumference which includes all movements known to us. We can only imagine a perpetual turning in and out of that sphere, hence the sentence quoted by Aherne about the great eggs which turn inside out without breaking the shell.[140]

It seems that ancient men except the Persian and the Jew who looked to an upward progression, held Nietzsche's doctrine of the eternal return,[141] but if religion and mathematics are right, and time an illusion, it makes no difference except in the moral effect.

XXIV

THE FOUR PRINCIPLES AND NEO-PLATONIC PHILOSOPHY[142]

I have not considered the ultimate origin of things, nor have my documents thrown a direct light upon it. The word *Anima Mundi* frequently occurs and is used very much as in the philosophy of Plotinus. I am inclined to discover in the *Celestial Body,* the *Spirit,* the *Passionate Body,* and the *Husk,* emanations from or reflections from his One, his Intellectual Principle, his Soul of the World, and his Nature respectively. The *Passionate Body* is described as that which links one being to another, and that which rescues the *Celestial Body* from solitude, and this is part of the office of the Soul of the World in Plotinus. As actually used in the documents *Anima Mundi* is the receptacle of emotional images when purified from whatever unites them to one man rather than to another. The 13th, 14th and 15th cycles are described as Spheres, and are certainly emanations from the Soul of the World, the Intellectual Principle and the One respectively, but there is a fundamental difference, though perhaps only of expression, between the system and that of Plotinus. In Plotinus the One is the Good, whereas in the system Good and Evil are eliminated before the Soul can be united to Reality, being that stream of phenomena that drowns us.

BOOK III

Dove or Swan [1]

THE HISTORICAL CONES.

The numbers in brackets refer to phases, and the other numbers to dates AD. The line cutting the cones a little below 250, 900, 1180 and 1927 shows four historical *Faculties* related to the present moment.

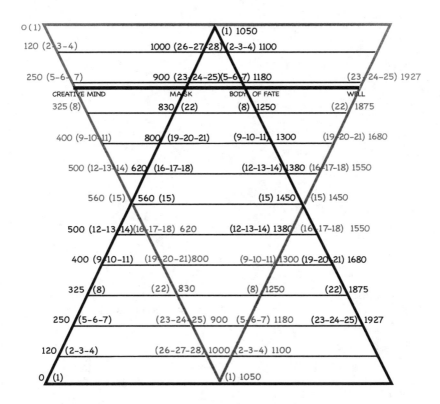

147

1. LEDA.[2]

A sudden blow: the great wings beating still
Above the staggering girl, her thighs caressed
By the dark webs, her nape caught in his bill,
He holds her helpless breast upon his breast.

How can those terrified vague fingers push
The feathered glory from her loosening thighs,
And how can body, laid in that white rush,
But feel the strange heart beating where it lies;
A shudder in the loins engenders there
The broken wall, the burning roof and tower
And Agamemnon[3] dead.
                              Being so caught up,
So mastered by the brute blood of the air,
Did she put on his knowledge with his power
Before the indifferent beak could let her drop?

2. THE GREAT WHEEL AND HISTORY.

I

STRAY THOUGHTS

One must bear in mind that the Christian Era, like the two thousand years, let us say, that went before it, is an entire wheel, and each half of it an entire wheel, that each half when it comes to its 28th Phase reaches the 15th Phase of the entire era.[4] It follows therefore that the 15th Phase of each millennium, to keep the symbolic measure of time, is Phase 8 or Phase 22 of the entire era, that Aphrodite rises from a stormy sea, that Helen could not be Helen but for beleaguered Troy.[5] The era itself is but half of a greater era and its Phase 15 comes also at a period of war or trouble. The greater number is always more *primary* than the lesser and precisely because it contains it. A millennium is the symbolic measure of a being that attains its flexible maturity and then sinks into rigid age.

A civilisation is a struggle to keep self-control, and in this it is like some great tragic person, some Niobe who must display an almost superhuman will or the cry will not touch our sympathy.[6] The loss of control over thought comes towards the end; first a sinking in upon the moral being, then the last surrender, the irrational cry, revelation—the scream of Juno's peacock.[7]

II

2000 B.C. TO 1 A.D.[8]

I imagine the annunciation that founded Greece as made to Leda, remembering that they showed in a Spartan Temple, strung up to the roof as a holy relic, an unhatched egg of hers; and that from one of her eggs came Love and from the other War.[9] But all things are from antithesis, and when in my ignorance I try to imagine what older civilisation she refuted I can but see bird and woman blotting out some corner of the Babylonian mathematical starlight.[10]

Did the older civilisation like the Jewish think a long life a proof of Heavenly favour that the Greek races should affirm so clearly that those whom the Gods love die young, hurling upon some age of crowded comedy their tragic sense?[11] Certainly their tribes, after a first multitudinous revelation—dominated each by its *Daimon* and oracle-driven—broke up a great Empire and established in its stead an intellectual anarchy.[12] At some 1000 years before Christ I imagine their religious system complete and they themselves grown barbaric and Asiatic. Then came Homer,[13] civil life, a desire for civil order dependent doubtless on some oracle, and then (Phase 10 of second Greek millennium) for independent civil life and thought. At, let me say, the sixth century B.C. (Phase 12) personality begins, but there is as yet no intellectual solitude. A man may rule his tribe or town but he cannot separate himself from the general mass. With the first discovery of solitude (Phases 13 and 14) comes, as I think, the visible art that interests us most to-day, for Phidian art, like the art of Raphael, has for the moment exhausted our attention.[14] I recall a Nike at the Ashmolean Museum with a natural unsystematised beauty like that before Raphael, and above all certain pots with strange half supernatural horses dark on a light ground.[15] Self-realisation attained will bring desire of power—systematisation for its instrument—but as yet clarity, meaning, elegance, all things separated from one another in luminous space, seem to exceed all other virtues. One compares this art with the thought of Greek Philosophers before Anaxagoras, where one discovers the same phases, always more concerned with the truth than with its moral or political effects. One longs for the lost dramatists, the plays that were enacted before Aeschylus and Sophocles arose, both Phidian men.[16]

But one must consider not the movement only from the beginning to the end of the historical cone, but the gyres that touch its sides, the horizontal movement. There is that continual oscillation which I have symbolised elsewhere as a King and Queen, who are Sun and Moon also, and whirl round and round as they mount up through a Round Tower.[17]

Side by side with Ionic elegance there comes after the Persian wars a Doric vigour, and the light-limbed dandy of the potters, the Parisian-looking young woman of the sculptors, her hair elaborately curled, give place to the athlete.[18] One suspects a deliberate turning away from all that is Eastern, or a moral propaganda like that which turned the poets out of Plato's Republic,[19] and yet it may be that the preparation for the final systematisation had for its apparent cause the destruction, let us say, of Ionic studios by the Persian invaders,[20] and that all came from the resistance of the *Body of Fate* to the growing solitude of the soul. Then in Phidias Ionic and Doric influence unite—one remembers Titian[21]—and all is transformed by the full moon, and all abounds and flows.[22] With Callimachus pure Ionic revives again, as Furtwängler has proved, and upon the only example of his work known to us, a marble chair, a Persian is represented, and may one not discover a Persian symbol in that bronze lamp, shaped like a palm, known to us by a description in Pausanias?[23] but he was an archaistic workman, and those who set him to work brought back public life to an older form.[24] One may see in masters and man a momentary dip into ebbing Asia.

Each age unwinds the thread another age had wound, and it amuses one to remember that before Phidias, and his westward moving art, Persia fell, and that when full moon came round again, amid eastward moving thought, and brought Byzantine glory, Rome fell; and that at the outset of our westward moving Renaissance Byzantium fell; all things dying each other's life, living each other's death.

After Phidias the life of Greece, which being *antithetical* had moved slowly and richly through the *antithetical* phases, comes rapidly to an end. Some Greek or Roman writer whose name I forget will soon speak of the declining comeliness of the people,[25] and in the arts all is systematised more and more, and the antagonist recedes.

Aristophanes' passion-clouded eye falls before what one must believe, from Roman stage copies, an idler glance. (Phases 19, 20, 21).[26] Aristotle and Plato end creative system—to die into the truth is still to die—and formula begins.[27] Yet even the truth into which Plato dies is a form of death, for when he separates the Eternal Ideas from Nature and shows them self-sustained he prepares the Christian desert and the Stoic suicide.[28]

I identify the conquest of Alexander and the break-up of his kingdom, when Greek civilisation, formalised and codified, loses itself in Asia, with the beginning and end of the 22nd Phase, and his intention recorded by some historian to turn his arms westward shows that he is but a part of the impulse that creates Hellenised Rome and Asia.[29] There are everywhere statues where every muscle has been measured, every position debated, and these statues represent man with nothing more to achieve, physical man finished and complacent, the women slightly tinted, but the men, it may be, who exercise naked in the open air, the colour of mahogany. Every discovery after the epoch of victory and defeat (Phase 22) which substitutes mechanics for power, is an elimination of intellect by delight in technical skill (Phase 23), by a sense of the past (Phase 24) by some dominant belief (Phase 25). After Plato and Aristotle, the mind is as exhausted as were the armies of Alexander at his death, but the Stoics can discover morals and turn philosophy into a rule of life. Among them doubtless—the first beneficiaries of Plato's hatred of imitation—we may discover the first benefactors of our modern individuality, sincerity of the trivial face, the mask torn away. Then in the last three phases of the wheel, a Greece that Rome has conquered, and a Rome conquered by Greece, must adore, desire being dead, physical or spiritual force.[30] This adoration which begins in the second century before Christ creates a world-wide religious movement as the world was then known, which, being swallowed up in what came after, has left no adequate record. One knows not into how great extravagance Asia, accustomed to abase itself, may have carried what soon sent Greeks and Romans to stand naked in a Mithraic pit, moving their bodies as under a shower-bath that those bodies might receive the blood of the bull even to the last drop.[31] The adored image took everywhere the only form possible as the *antithetical* age died into its last violence—a human or animal form. Even before Plato that collective image of man dear to Stoic and Epicurean alike, the moral double of bronze or marble athlete, had been invoked by Anaxagoras when he declared that thought and not the warring opposites created the world.[32] At that sentence the heroic life, passionate fragmentary man, all that had been imagined by great poets and sculptors began to pass away, and instead of seeking noble antagonists, imagination moved towards divine man and the ridiculous devil. And now sages lure men away from the arms of women because in those arms man becomes a fragment; and all is ready for revelation. When revelation comes athlete and sage are merged; the earliest sculptured image of Christ is copied from that of the Apotheosis of Alexander the Great;[33] the tradition is founded which declares even to our own day that Christ alone is exactly six feet high,[34] perfect physical man. Yet as perfect physical man He must die, for only so can *primary* power reach *antithetical* mankind shut within the circle of its senses, touching outward things alone in that which seems most personal and physical. When I think of the moment before revelation I think of Salome—she too, delicately tinted or maybe mahogany dark—dancing before Herod and receiving the Prophet's head in her indifferent hands,[35] and wonder if what seems to us decadence was not in reality the exultation of the muscular flesh and of civilisation perfectly achieved. Seeking images, I see her anoint her bare limbs according to a medical prescription of that time, with lion's fat, for lack of the sun's ray, that she may gain the favour of a king, and remember that the same impulse will create the Galilean revelation and deify Roman Emperors whose sculptured heads will be surrounded by the solar disk.[36] Upon the throne and upon the cross alike the myth becomes a biography.[37]

III

A.D. 1 TO A.D. 1050[38]

God is now conceived of as something outside man and man's handiwork, and it follows that it must be idolatry to worship that which Phidias and Scopas made, and seeing that He is a Father in Heaven that Heaven will be found presently in the Thebaid,[39] where the world is changed into featureless clay and can be run through the fingers; and these things are testified to from books that are outside human genius, being miraculous, and by a miraculous church, and this church, as the gyre sweeps wider, will make man also featureless as clay or sand. Night will fall upon man's wisdom now that man has been taught that he is nothing.[40] He had discovered, or half-discovered, that the world is round and one of many like it,[41] but now he must believe that the sky is but a tent spread above a level floor, and—that he may be stirred into a frenzy of anxiety and so to moral transformation—blot out the knowledge or half-knowledge that he has lived many times, and think that all eternity depends upon a moment's decision, and Heaven itself—transformation finished—must appear so vague and motionless that it seems but a concession to human weakness.[42] It is even essential to this faith to declare that God's messengers, those beings who show His will in dreams or announce it in visionary speech were never men. The Greeks thought them often great men of the past but now that concession to mankind is forbidden.[43] All must be narrowed into the sun's image cast out of a burning-glass and man be ignorant of all but the image.

The mind that brought the change, if considered as man only, is a climax of whatever Greek and Roman thought was most a contradiction to its age; but considered as more than man He controlled what Neo-Pythagorean and Stoic could not—irrational force. He could announce the new age, all that had not been thought of or touched or seen, because He could substitute for reason, miracle.

The sacrifice of the 22nd Phase is voluntary and so we say of Him that He was love itself, and yet that part of Him which made Christendom was not love but pity, and not pity for intellectual despair, though the man in Him, being *antithetical* like His age, knew it in the Garden, but *primary* pity, that for the common lot, man's death seeing that He raised Lazarus, sickness seeing that He healed many, sin seeing that He died.[44]

Love is created and preserved by intellectual analysis, for we love only that which is unique, and it belongs to contemplation not to action, for we would not change that which we love. A lover will admit a greater beauty than that of his mistress but not its like, and surrenders his days to a delighted laborious study of all her ways and looks, and he pities only if something threatens that which has never been before and can never be again. Fragment delights in fragment and seeks possession, not service; whereas the Good Samaritan[45] discovers himself in the likeness of another, covered with sores and abandoned by thieves upon the roadside, and in that other serves himself. The opposites are gone; he does not need his Lazarus; they do not each die the other's life, live the other's death.

It is of course impossible to do more than select a more or less arbitrary general date for the beginning of Roman decay (Phases 2 to 7, A.D. 1 to A.D. 250).[46] Roman sculpture—sculpture made under Roman influence whatever the sculptor's blood—did not for instance reach its full vigour, if we consider what it had of Roman as distinct from Greek, until the Christian Era.[47] It even made a discovery which affected all sculpture to come. The Greeks painted the eyes of marble statues and made out of enamel or glass or precious stones those of their bronze statues, but the Roman was the first to drill a round hole to represent the pupil, and because, as I think, of a preoccupation with the glance characteristic of a civilisation in its final phase.[48] The colours must have already faded from the marbles of the great period, and a shadow and a spot of light, especially where there is much sunlight, are more vivid than paint, enamel, coloured glass or precious stone. They could now express in stone a perfect composure, the administrative mind, alert attention where all had been rhythm, an exaltation of the body, uncommitted energy. May it not have been precisely a talent for this alert attention that had enabled Rome and not Greece to express those final *primary* phases? One sees on the pediments troops of marble Senators, officials serene and watchful as befits men who know that all the power of the world moves before their eyes, and needs, that it may not dash itself to pieces, their unhurried unanxious never-ceasing care. Those riders upon the Parthenon[49] had all the world's power in their moving bodies, and in a movement that seemed, so were the hearts of man and beast set upon it, that of a dance; but presently all would change and measurement succeed to pleasure, the dancing-master outlive the dance. What need had those young lads for careful eyes? But in Rome of the first and second centuries where the dancing-master himself has died, the delineation of character as shown in face and head, as with us of recent years, is all in all, and sculptors seeking the custom of occupied officials stock in their workshops toga'd marble bodies upon which can be screwed with the least possible delay heads modelled from the sitters with the most scrupulous realism.[50] When I think of Rome I see always those heads with their world-considering eyes, and those bodies as conventional as the metaphors in a leading article, and compare in my imagination vague Grecian eyes gazing at nothing, Byzantine eyes of drilled ivory staring upon a vision, and those eyelids of China and of India, those veiled or half-veiled eyes weary of world and vision alike.[51]

Meanwhile the irrational force[52] that would create confusion and uproar as with the cry 'The Babe, the Babe, is born'[53]—the women speaking unknown tongues, the barbers and weavers expounding Divine revelation with all the vulgarity of their servitude, the tables that move or resound with raps[54]—still but creates a negligible sect.

All about it is an *antithetical* aristocratic civilisation in its completed form, every detail of life hierarchical, every great man's door crowded at dawn by petitioners, great wealth everywhere in few men's hands, all dependent upon a few, up to the Emperor himself who is a God dependent upon a greater God, and everywhere in court, in the family, an inequality made law, and floating over all the Romanised Gods of Greece in their physical superiority.[55] All is rigid and stationary, men fight for centuries with the same sword and spear, and though in naval warfare there is some change of tactics to avoid those single combats of ship with ship that needed the seamanship of a more skilful age, the speed of a sailing ship remains unchanged from the time of Pericles to that of Constantine.[56] Though sculpture grows more and more realistic and so renews its vigour, this realism is without curiosity. The athlete becomes the boxer that he may show lips and nose beaten out of shape, the individual hairs show at the navel of the bronze centaur, but the theme has not changed.[57] Philosophy alone, where in contact with irrational force—holding to Egyptian thaumaturgy and the Judean miracle but at arms length—can startle and create. Yet Plotinus is as *primary*, as much a contradiction of all that created Roman civilisation as St Peter, and his thought has its roots almost as deep among the *primary* masses. The founder of his school was Ammonius Saccas, an Alexandrine porter.[58] His thought and that of Origen,[59] which I skimmed in my youth, seem to me to express the abstract synthesis of a quality like that of race, and so to display a character which must always precede Phase 8. Origen, because the Judean miracle has a stronger hold upon the masses than Alexandrian thaumaturgy, triumphs when Constantine (Phase 8) puts the Cross upon the shields of his soldiers and makes the bit of his war-horse from a nail of the True Cross,[60] an act equivalent to man's cry for strength amid the animal chaos at the close of the first lunar quarter. Seeing that Constantine was not converted till upon his deathbed I see him as half statesman, half thaumaturgist, accepting in blind obedience to a dream the new fashionable talisman, two sticks nailed together.[61] The Christians were but six millions of the sixty or seventy of the Roman Empire but, spending nothing upon pleasure, exceedingly rich like some Nonconformist sect of the eighteenth century; and the world became Christian and 'that fabulous formless darkness'[62] as it seemed to a philosopher of the fourth century, blotted out 'every beautiful thing', not through the conversion of crowds or general change of opinion, or through any pressure from below, for civilisation was *antithetical* still, but by an act of power.

I have not the knowledge (it may be that no man has the knowledge) to trace the rise of the Byzantine state through Phases 9, 10 and 11.[63] My diagram tells me that a hundred and sixty years brought that state to its 15th Phase, but I that know nothing but the arts and of these little, cannot revise the series of dates 'approximately correct' but given it may be for suggestion only.[64] With a desire for simplicity of statement I would have preferred to find in the middle, not at the end, of the fifth century Phase 12, for that was, so far as the known evidence carries us, the moment when Byzantium became Byzantine and substituted for formal Roman magnificence, with its glorification of physical power, an architecture that suggests the Sacred City in the Apocalypse of St John.[65] I think if I could be given a month of Antiquity and leave to spend it where I chose, I would spend it in Byzantium a little before Justinian opened St Sophia and closed the Academy of Plato.[66] I think I could find in some little wine shop some philosophical worker in mosaic who could answer all my questions, the supernatural descending nearer to him than to Plotinus even, for the pride of his delicate skill would make what was an instrument of power to Princes and Clerics and a murderous madness in the mob, show as a lovely flexible presence like that of a perfect human body.

I think that in early Byzantium, and maybe never before or since in recorded history, religious, aesthetic and practical life were one, and that architect and artificers—though not, it may be, poets, for language had been the instrument of controversy and must have grown abstract—spoke to the multitude and the few alike.[67] The painter and the mosaic worker, the worker in gold and silver, the illuminator of Sacred Books were almost impersonal, almost perhaps without the consciousness of individual design, absorbed in their subject matter and that the vision of a whole people. They could copy out of old Gospel books those pictures that seemed as sacred as the text, and yet weave all into a vast design, the work of many that seemed the work of one, that made building, picture, pattern, metal work of rail and lamp, seem but a single image; and this vision, this proclamation of their invisible master had the Greek nobility, Satan always the still half divine Serpent, never the horned scarecrow of the didactic Middle Ages.

The ascetic, called in Alexandria 'God's Athlete', has taken the place of those Greek athletes whose statues have been melted or broken up or stand deserted in the midst of cornfields,[68] but all about him is an incredible splendour like that which we see pass under our closed eyelids as we lie between sleep and waking, no representation of a living world but the dream of a somnambulist. Even the drilled pupil of the eye, when the drill is in the hand of some Byzantine worker in ivory, undergoes a somnambulistic change for its deep shadow among the faint lines of the tablet, its mechanical circle, where all else is rhythmical and flowing, give to Saint or Angel a look of some great bird staring at miracle.[69] Could any visionary of those days, passing through the Church named with so un-theological a grace 'The Holy Wisdom',[70] can even a visionary of to-day wandering among the mosaics of Rome and Sicily,[71] fail to recognise some one image seen under his closed eyelids? To me it seems that He, who among the first Christian communities was little but a ghostly exorcist, had in His assent to a full Divinity made possible this sinking in upon a supernatural splendour, these walls with their little glimmering cubes of blue and green and gold.

I think that I might discover an oscillation, a revolution of the horizontal gyre like that between Doric and Ionic art, between the two principal characters of Byzantine art. Recent criticism distinguishes between the figures which come from Greece and Rome,

their stern faces suggesting Greek wall-painting at Palmyra, Greco-
Egyptian painting upon the cases of mummies, where characteristic
lines are exaggerated as in much work of our time, and that decoration which seems to undermine our self-control, and is it seems of
Persian origin, and has for its appropriate symbol a vine whose ten-
drils climb everywhere and display among their leaves all those
strange images of bird and beast, those forms that represent no
creature eye has ever seen, yet are begotten one upon the other as if
they were themselves living creatures.[72] May I consider the domination of the first late *antithetical* and that of the second *primary*, and
see in their alternation the work of the horizontal gyre? Strzygowski
thinks that the church decorations where there are visible representations of holy persons were especially dear to those who believed in
Christ's double nature and that wherever Christ is represented by a
bare Cross and all the rest is bird and beast and tree, we may discover an Asiatic art dear to those who thought Christ contained
nothing human.[73]

If I were left to myself I would make Phase 15 coincide with Justinian's reign, that great age of building in which one may conclude
Byzantine art was perfected; but the meaning of the diagram may be
that a building like St Sophia where all, to judge by the contemporary description, pictured ecstasy, must unlike the declamatory St
Peter's precede the moment of climax.[74] Of the moment of climax
itself I can say nothing and of what followed from Phase 17 to
Phase 21 almost nothing, for I have no knowledge of the time; and
no analogy from the age after Phidias, or after our own Renaissance
can help.[75] We and the Greeks moved towards intellect but Byzantium and the western Europe of that day moved from it. If Strzygowski is right we may see in the destruction of images but a
destruction of what was Greek in decoration accompanied perhaps
by a renewed splendour in all that came down from the ancient Persian Paradise, an episode in some attempt to make theology more
ascetic, spiritual and abstract.[76] Destruction was apparently suggested to the first iconoclastic Emperor by followers of a Monophysite Bishop, Xenaias, who had his See in that part of the Empire
where Persian influence had been strongest.[77] The return of the
images must, as I see things, have been the failure of synthesis (Phase
22) and the first sinking in and dying down of Christendom into the

heterogeneous loam. Europe grew animal and literal; the strength of the victorious party came from zealots who were as ready as their opponents to destroy an image if permitted to grind it into powder, mix it with some liquid and swallow it as a medicine. Mankind for a season would do, not what it would, or should, but what it could, and accept the past and the current belief because they prevented thought. In western Europe I think I may see in Johannes Scotus Erigena the last intellectual synthesis before the death of philosophy, but I know little of him except that he is founded upon a Greek book of the sixth century, put into circulation by a last iconoclastic Emperor, though its Angelic Orders might have given, and perhaps did give a theme to the image makers.[78] I notice too that my diagram makes Phase 22 coincide with the break up of Charlemagne's Empire and so clearly likens him to Alexander, but I do not want to concern myself, except where I must, with political events.[79]

Then follows, as always must in the last quarter,[80] heterogeneous art; hesitation amid architectural forms, some book tells me; an interest in Greek and Roman literature; much copying out and gathering together; yet outside a few courts and monasteries I seem to discover an Asiatic and anarchic Europe. The intellectual cone has so narrowed that secular intellect has gone, and the strong man rules with the aid of local custom that needs none, and everywhere the supernatural is sudden, violent, and as dark to the intellect as a stroke or St Vitus' dance.[81] Men under the Cæsars, my documents tell me, were physically one but intellectually many, but that is now reversed, for there is one common thought or doctrine and town is shut off from town, village from village, clan from clan. The spiritual life is alone overflowing, its cone expanded, and yet this life—secular intellect extinguished—has little effect upon men's conduct, is perhaps a dream which passes beyond the reach of conscious mind but for some rare miracle or vision. I think of it as like that profound reverie of the somnambulist which may be accompanied by a sensuous dream—a romanesque stream perhaps of bird and beast images[82]—and yet neither affect the dream nor be affected by it. It is indeed precisely because this double mind is created at the South that the *antithetical* phases are but, at the best, phases of a momentary illumination like that of a lightning flash.[83] But the South that now concerns us, is not only Phase 15 of its greater era, but the final

phase, Phase 28, of its millennium and, in its physical form, human
life grown once more automatic. I knew a man once who, seeking
for an image of the absolute, saw one persistent image, a slug, as
though it were suggested to him that Being which is beyond human
comprehension is mirrored in the least organised forms of life. Intellectual creation has ceased but men have come to terms with the
supernatural and are agreed that, if you make the usual offerings, it
will remember to live and let live; even Saint or Angel does not
seem very different from themselves, a man thinks his guardian
Angel jealous of his mistress; a King, dragging some Saint's body to
a new Church, meets some difficulty upon the road, assumes a miracle, and denounces the Saint as a churl. Three Roman Courtesans
who have one after another got their favourite lovers chosen Pope
have, it pleases one's mockery to think, confessed their sins, with full
belief in the supernatural efficacy of the act, to ears that have heard
their cries of love, or received the Body of God from hands that have
played with their own bodies.[84] Interest has narrowed to what is near
and personal and, seeing that all abstract secular thought has faded,
those interests have taken the most physical forms. In monasteries
and in hermit cells men freed from the intellect at last can seek their
God upon all fours like beasts or children. Ecclesiastical Law, in so
far as that law is concerned not with government, Church or State,
but with the individual soul, is complete; all that is necessary to salvation is known, but as I conceive the age there is much apathy. Man
awaits death and judgment with nothing to occupy the worldly faculties and is helpless before the world's disorder, and this may have
dragged up out of the subconscious the conviction that the world
was about to end. Hidden, except at rare moments of excitement or
revelation, and even then shown but in symbol, the stream of *recurrence*,*[85] set in motion by the Galilean Symbol, has filled its basin,
and seems motionless for an instant before it falls over the rim, and

---

*The documents distinguish between *recurrence* which is an impulse that
begins strongly and dies out by degrees, and *sequence* where every part of the
impulse is related to every other. Every phase is a *recurrence*, and *sequence* is
related to Unity of Being. If I understand rightly Plato's perfect and imperfect
numbers they have much the same meaning. The documents distinguish both
recurrence and *sequence* from an *allusion*, or unrelated fact. A spirit at Phase 1
sees *allusion* only.

in the midst of the basin I imagine in motionless contemplation, blood that is not His blood upon His Hands and Feet, One that feels but for the common lot, and mourns over the length of years and the inadequacy of man's fate to man. Two thousand years before, His predecessor, careful of heroic men alone, had so stood and mourned over the shortness of time, and man's inadequacy to his fate.[86]

Full moon over, that last Embodiment shall grow more like ourselves, putting off that stern majesty, borrowed it may be from the Phidean Zeus—if we can trust Cefalù and Monreale—and His Mother—putting off her harsh Byzantine image—stand at His side.[87]

IV

A.D. 1050 to the Present Day[88]

When the tide changed and God no longer sufficed, something must have happened in the courts and castles of which history has perhaps no record, for with the first vague dawn of the ultimate *antithetical* revelation man, under the eyes of the Virgin, or upon the breast of his mistress, became but a fragment. Instead of that old alternation, brute or ascetic, came something obscure or uncertain that could not find its full explanation for a thousand years. A certain Byzantine Bishop had said upon seeing a singer of Antioch, 'I looked long upon her beauty, knowing that I would behold it upon the day of judgment, and I wept to remember that I had taken less care of my soul than she of her body',[89] but when in the *Arabian Nights* Harun Al-Raschid looked at the singer Heart's Miracle, and on the instant loved her, he covered her head with a little silk veil to show that her beauty 'had already retreated into the mystery of our faith'.[90] The Bishop saw a beauty that would be sanctified but the Caliph that which was its own sanctity, and it was this latter sanctity, come back from the first Crusade or up from Arabian Spain or half Asiatic Provence and Sicily, that created romance. What forgotten reverie, what initiation it may be, separated wisdom from the monastery and, creating Merlin, joined it to passion. When Merlin in Chrétien de Troyes loved Ninian he showed her a cavern adorned with gold mosaics and made by a prince for his beloved, and told her that those lovers died upon the same day and were laid 'in the chamber where they found delight'. He thereupon lifted a slab of red marble that his art alone could lift and showed them wrapped in winding sheets of white samite. The tomb remained open, for Ninian asked that she and Merlin might return to the cavern and spend their night near those dead lovers, but before night came Merlin grew sad and fell asleep, and she and her attendants took him 'by head and foot' and laid him 'in the tomb and replaced the stone', for Merlin had taught her the magic words, and 'from that hour none beheld Merlin dead or alive'.[91] Throughout the German *Parzival* there is no ceremony of the Church, neither Marriage nor Mass nor Baptism, but instead we discover that strangest creation of romance or of life, 'the love trance'. Parzival in such a trance, seeing nothing before his eyes but the image of his absent love, overcame knight after knight, and awakening at last looked amazed upon his dinted sword and shield;[92] and it is to his lady and not to God or the Virgin that Parzival prayed upon the day of battle, and it was his lady's soul, separated from her entranced or sleeping body, that went beside him and gave him victory.

The period from 1005 to 1180 is attributed in the diagram to the first two gyres of our millennium, and what interests me in this period, which corresponds to the Homeric period some two thousand years before, is the creation of the Arthurian Tales and Romanesque architecture. I see in Romanesque the first movement to a secular Europe, but a movement so instinctive that as yet there is no antagonism to the old condition. Every architect, every man who lifts a chisel, may be a cleric of some kind, yet in the overflowing ornament where the human form has all but disappeared and where no bird or beast is copied from nature, where all is more Asiatic than Byzantium itself, one discovers the same impulse that created Merlin and his jugglery. I do not see in Gothic architecture, which is a character of the next gyre, that of Phases 5, 6 and 7, as did the nineteenth century historians ever looking for the image of their own age, the creation of a new communal freedom but a creation of authority, a suppression of that freedom though with its consent, and certainly St Bernard when he denounced the extravagance of Romanesque saw it in that light.[93] I think of that curious sketchbook of Villard de Honnecourt with its insistence upon mathematical form, and I see that form in Mont St Michel—Church, Abbey, Fort and town, all that dark geometry that makes Byzantium seem a sunlit cloud—and it seems to me that the Church grows secular that it may fight a new-born secular world.[94] Its avowed appeal is to religion alone: nobles and great ladies join the crowds that drag the Cathedral stones, not out of love for beauty but because the stones as they are trundled down the road cure the halt and the blind; yet the stones once set up traffic with the enemy. The mosaic pictures grown transparent fill the windows, and draw all eyes and quarrel one with the other as if they were pretty women, and upon the faces of the statues flits once more the smile that disappeared with archaic Greece. That smile is physical, *primary* joy, the escape from supernatural terror, a moment of irresponsible common life before *antithetical* sadness begins. It is as though the pretty worshippers, while the Dominican[95] was preaching with a new and perhaps incredible sternness, let their imaginations stray and the observant sculptor, or worker in ivory, in modelling his Holy Women has remembered their smiling lips.

Are not the Cathedrals and the Philosophy of St Thomas[96] the product of the abstraction that comes a little before the Phases 8 and 22, and of the moral synthesis that at the end of the first quarter seeks to control the general anarchy? That anarchy must have been exceedingly great, or man must have found a hitherto unknown sensitiveness, for it was the shock that created modern civilisation. The diagram makes the period from 1250 to 1300 correspond to Phase 8, certainly because in or near that period, chivalry and Christendom having proved insufficient, the King mastered the one, the Church the other, reversing the achievement of Constantine, for it was now the mitre and the crown that protected the Cross.[97] I prefer, however, to find my example of the first victory of personality where I have more knowledge. Dante in the *Convito* mourns for solitude,[98] lost through poverty, and writes the first sentence of modern autobiography, and in the *Divine Comedy* imposes his own personality upon a system and a phantasmagoria hitherto impersonal; the King everywhere has found his kingdom.

The period from 1300 to 1380[99] is attributed to the fourth gyre, that of Phases 9, 10 and 11, which finds its character in painting from Giotto to Fra Angelico, in the chronicles of Froissart and in the elaborate canopy upon the stained glass of the windows.[100] Every old tale is alive, Christendom still unbroken; painter and poet alike find new ornament for the tale, they feel the charm of everything but the more poignantly because that charm is archaistic; they smell a pot of dried roses. The practical men, face to face with rebellion and heresy, are violent as they have not been for generations, but the artists separated from life by the tradition of Byzantium can even exaggerate their gentleness, and gentleness and violence alike express the gyre's hesitation. The public certainty that sufficed for Dante and St Thomas has disappeared, and there is yet no private certainty. Is it that the human mind now longs for solitude, for escape from all that hereditary splendour, and does not know what ails it; or is it that the *Image* itself encouraged by the new technical method, the flexible brushstroke instead of the unchanging cube of glass, and wearied of its part in a crowded ghostly dance longs for a solitary human body? That body comes in the period from 1380 to 1450 and is discovered by Masaccio, and by Chaucer who is partly of the old gyre, and by Villon who is wholly of the new.[101] Masaccio, a precocious and abundant man, dying like Aubrey Beardsley[102] in his six-and-twentieth year, cannot move us, as he did his immediate successors, for he discovered a naturalism that begins to weary us a little, making the naked young man awaiting baptism shiver with the cold, and St Peter grow red with exertion as he drags the money out of the miraculous fish's mouth, and Adam and Eve, flying before the sword of the Angel, show faces disfigured by their suffering.[103] It is very likely because I am a poet and not a painter that I feel so much more keenly that suffering of Villon—of the 13th Phase as man, and of it or near it in epoch—in whom the human soul for the first time stands alone before a death ever present to imagination, without help from a Church that is fading away, or is it that I remember Aubrey Beardsley, a man of like phase though so different epoch, and so read into Villon's suffering our modern conscience which gathers intensity as we approach the close of an era?[104] Intensity that has seemed to me pitiless self-judgment may have been but heroic gaiety. With the approach of solitude bringing with it an ever increasing struggle with that which opposes solitude—sensuality, greed, ambition, physical curiosity in all its species—philosophy has returned driving dogma out. Even amongst the most pious the worshipper is preoccupied with himself, and when I look for the drilled eyeball, which reveals so much, I notice that its edge is no longer so mechanically perfect, nor, if I can judge by casts at the Victoria and Albert Museum,[105] is the hollow so deep. Angel and Florentine noble must look upward with an eye that seems dim and abashed as though to recognise duties to Heaven, an example to be set before men, and finding both difficult seem a little giddy. There are no miracles to stare at, for man descends the hill he once climbed with so great toil, and all grows but natural again.[106]

As we approach the 15th Phase, as the general movement grows more and more westward in character, we notice the oscillation of the horizontal gyres, as though what no unity of being, yet possible, can completely fuse displays itself in triumph.

Donatello, as later Michelangelo, reflects the hardness and astringency of Myron, and foretells what must follow the Renaissance; while Jacopo della Quercia, and most of the painters seem by contrast, as Raphael later on, Ionic and Asiatic.[107] The period from 1450 to 1550 is allotted to the gyre of Phase 15, and these dates are no doubt intended to mark somewhat vaguely a period that begins in one country earlier and in another later. I do not myself find it possible to make more than the first half coincide with the central moment, Phase 15 of the Italian Renaissance—Phase 22 of the cone of the entire era—the breaking of the Christian synthesis as the corresponding period before Christ, the age of Phidias, was the breaking of great traditional faith. The first half covers the principal activity of the Academy of Florence which formulated the reconciliation of Paganism and Christianity.[108] This reconciliation which to Pope Julius meant that Greek and Roman Antiquity were as sacred as that of Judea, and like it 'a vestibule of Christianity', became in the theoretic exploration of Dürer who had visited Venice within the movement of the gyre, that the human norm, discovered from the measurement of ancient statues, was God's first handiwork, that 'perfectly proportioned human body' which had seemed to Dante unity of being symbolised.[109] The ascetic, who had a thousand years before attained his transfiguration upon the golden ground of Byzantine mosaic, had not turned athlete but into that unlabouring form the athlete dreamed of: the second Adam had become the first.[110] Because the 15th Phase can never find direct human expression, being a supernatural incarnation, it impressed upon work and thought an element of strain and artifice, a desire to combine elements which may be incompatible, or which suggest by their combination something supernatural. Had some Florentine Platonist read to Botticelli Porphyry upon the Cave of the Nymphs?[111] for I seem to recognise it in that curious cave, with a thatched roof over the nearer entrance to make it resemble the conventional manger, in his *Nativity* in the National Gallery.[112] Certainly the glimpse of forest trees, dim in the evening light, through the far entrance, and the deliberate strangeness everywhere, gives one an emotion of mystery which is new to painting.

Botticelli, Crivelli, Mantegna, Da Vinci,[113] who fall within the period, make Masaccio and his school seem heavy and common by something we may call intellectual beauty or compare perhaps to that kind of bodily beauty which Castiglione called 'the spoil or monument of the victory of the soul'.[114] Intellect and emotion, *primary* curiosity and the *antithetical* dream, are for the moment one. Since the rebirth of the secular intellect in the eleventh century, faculty has been separating from faculty, poetry from music, the worshipper from the worshipped, but all have remained within a common fading circle—Christendom—and so within the human soul image has been separated from image but always as an exploration of the soul itself; forms have been displayed in an always clear light, have been perfected by separation from one another till their link with one another and with common associations has been broken; but, Phase 15 past, these forms begin to jostle and fall into confusion, there is as it were a sudden rush and storm.[115] In the mind of the artist a desire for power succeeds to that for knowledge, and this desire is communicated to the forms and to the onlooker. The eighth

---

*There is a Greek inscription at the top of the picture which says that Botticelli's world is in the 'second woe' of the Apocalypse, and that after certain other Apocalyptic events the Christ of the picture will appear. He had probably found in some utterance of Savonarola's promise of an ultimate Marriage of Heaven and Earth, sacred and profane, and pictures it by the Angels and shepherds embracing, and as I suggest by Cave and Manger. When I saw the Cave of Mithra at Capri I wondered if that were Porphyry's Cave. The two entrances are there, one reached by a stair of a hundred feet or so from the sea and once trodden by devout sailors, and one reached from above by some hundred and fifty steps and used, my guide-book tells me, by Priests. If he knew that cave, which may have had its recognised symbolism, he would have been the more ready to discover symbols in the cave where Odysseus landed in Ithaca.

gyre, which corresponds to Phases 16, 17 and 18 and completes itself say between 1550 and 1650, begins with Raphael, Michelangelo and Titian, and the forms, as in Titian, awaken sexual desire[116]—we had not desired to touch the forms of Botticelli or even of Da Vinci— or they threaten us like those of Michelangelo, and the painter himself handles his brush with a conscious facility or exultation. The subject matter may arise out of some propaganda as when Raphael in the Stanza della Segnatura, and Michelangelo in the Sistine Chapel put, by direction of the Pope, Greek Sages and Doctors of the Church, Roman Sibyls and Hebrew Prophets, opposite one another in apparent equality.[117] From this on, all is changed and where the Mother of God sat enthroned, now that the Soul's unity has been found and lost, Nature seats herself, and the painter can paint what he desires in the flesh alone, and soon, asking less and less for himself, will make it a matter of pride to paint what he does not at all desire. I think Raphael almost of the earlier gyre—perhaps a transitional figure—but Michelangelo, Rabelais, Aretino, Shakespeare, Titian—Titian is so markedly of the 14th Phase as a man that he seems less characteristic—I associate with the mythopæic and ungovernable beginning of the eighth gyre. I see in Shakespeare a man in whom human personality, hitherto restrained by its dependence upon Christendom or by its own need for self-control, burst like a shell. Perhaps secular intellect, setting itself free after five hundred years of struggle has made him the greatest of dramatists, and yet because an *antithetical* art could create a hundred plays which preserved—whether made by a hundred hands or by one—the unity of a painting or of a Temple pediment, we might, had the total works of Sophocles survived—they too born of a like struggle though with a different enemy—not think him greatest. Do we not feel an unrest like that of travel itself when we watch those personages, who are so much more living than ourselves, amidst so much that is irrelevant and heterogeneous, amid so much *primary* curiosity, are carried from Rome to Venice, from Egypt to Saxon England, or in the one play from Roman to Christian mythology.

Were he not himself of a later phase, were he of the 16th Phase like his age and so drunk with his own wine he had not written plays at all, but as it is he finds his opportunity among a crowd of men and women who are still shaken by thought that passes from man to man in psychological contagion. I see in Milton who is characteristic of the moment when the first violence of the gyre has begun to sink, an attempted return to the synthesis of the Stanza della Segnatura and the Sistine Chapel. It is this attempt made too late that, amid all the music and magnificence of the still violent gyre, gives him his unreality and his cold rhetoric. The two elements have fallen apart in the hymn 'On the Morning of Christ's Nativity', the one is called sacred, the other profane, and his classical mythology has become an artificial ornament,[118] whereas no great Italian artist from 1450 to the sack of Rome saw any difference between them, and when difference came, as it did with Titian, it was God and the Angels that seemed artificial.

The gyre ebbs out in order and reason, the Jacobean poets succeed the Elizabethan, Cowley and Dryden the Jacobean as belief dies out.[119] Elsewhere Christendom keeps a kind of spectral unity for a while, now with one, now with the other element of synthesis dominant; declamatory statues deface old Churches, innumerable Tritons and Neptunes pour water from their mouths. What had been a beauty like the burning sun fades out in van Dyck's noble ineffectual faces,[120] and the Low Countries, which have reached the new gyre long before the rest of Europe, convert the world to a still limited curiosity, to certain recognised forms of the picturesque constantly repeated, chance travellers at an inn door, men about a fire, men skating, the same pose or grouping, where the subject is different, passing from picture to picture. The world begins to long for the arbitrary and accidental, for the grotesque, the repulsive and the terrible, that it may be cured of desire, and the moment has come for the ninth gyre, Phases 19, 20 and 21, and for the period that begins for the greater part of Europe with 1650 and lasts it may be to 1875.

The beginning of the gyre[121] like that of its forerunner is violent, a breaking of the soul and world into fragments, and has for a chief character the materialistic movement at the end of the seventeenth century, all that comes out of Bacon perhaps, the foundation of our modern inductive reasoning, the declamatory religious sects and controversies that first in England and then in France destroy the sense of form, all that has its very image and idol in Bernini's big Altar in St Peter's with its figures contorted and convulsed by religion as though by the devil. Men change rapidly from deduction to deduction, opinion to opinion, have but one impression at a time and utter it always, no matter how often they change, with the same emphasis.[122] Then the gyre develops a new coherence in the external scene; and violent men, each master of some generalisation, arise one after another: Napoleon, a man of the 20th Phase in the historical 21st—personality in its hard final generalisation—typical of all. The artistic life, where most characteristic of the general movement, shows the effect of the closing of the *Tinctures*. It is external, sentimental and logical,—the poetry of Pope and Gray, the philosophy of Johnson and of Rousseau—equally simple in emotion or in thought, the old oscillation in a new form.[123] Personality is everywhere spreading out its fingers in vain, or grasping with an always more convulsive grasp a world where the predominance of physical science, of finance and economics in all their forms, of democratic politics, of vast populations, of architecture where styles jostle one another, of newspapers where all is heterogeneous, show that mechanical force will in a moment become supreme.

That art discovered by Dante of marshalling into a vast *antithetical* structure *antithetical* material became through Milton Latinised and artificial—the Shades, as Sir Thomas Browne said, 'steal or contrive a body'—and now it changes that it may marshal into a still *antithetical* structure *primary* material, and the modern novel is created, but even before the gyre is drawn to its end, the happy ending, the admired hero, the preoccupation with desirable things, all that is undisguisedly *antithetical* disappears.[124]

All the art of the gyre that is not derived from the external scene, is a Renaissance echo growing always more conventional or more shadowy, but since the Renaissance—Phase 22 of the cone of the era—the 'Emotion of Sanctity',[125] that first relation to the *Spiritual primary* has been possible in those things that are most intimate and personal, but not until Phase 22 of the millennium cone will general thought be ready for its expression. A mysterious contact is perceptible first in painting and then in poetry and last in prose. In painting it comes where the influence of the Low Countries and that of Italy mingle, but always rarely and faintly. I do not find it in Watteau but there is a preparation for it, a sense of exhaustion of old interests— 'they do not believe even in their own happiness,' Verlaine said—and then suddenly it is present in the faces of Gainsborough's women as it has been in no face since the Egyptian sculptor buried in a tomb that image of a princess carved in wood.[126] Reynolds had nothing of it, an ostentatious fashionable man fresh from Rome, he stayed content with fading Renaissance emotion and modern curiosity.[127] In frail women's faces—Lady Bessborough's rises before me[128]—the soul awakes—all its prepossession, the accumulated learning of centuries swept away—and looks out upon us wise and foolish like the dawn. Then it is everywhere, it finds the village providence of the eighteenth century and turns him into Goethe, who for all that comes to no conclusion, his Faust after his hundred years but reclaiming land like some Sir Charles Grandison or Voltaire in his old age.[129] It makes the heroines of Jane Austen seek, not as their grandfathers and grandmothers would have done, theological or political truth, but simply good breeding, as though to increase it were more than any practical accomplishment.[130] In poetry alone it finds its full expression for it is a quality of the emotional nature (*Celestial Body* acting through *Mask*); and creates all that is most beautiful in modern English poetry from Blake to Arnold, all that is not a fading echo, and one discovers it in those symbolist writers like Verhaeren who substitute an entirely personal wisdom for the physical beauty or passionate emotion of the fifteenth and sixteenth centuries.[131] In painting it shows most often where the aim has been archaistic, as though it were an accompaniment of what the popular writers call decadence, as though old emotions had first to be exhausted. I think of the French portrait painter Ricard[132] to whom it was more a vision of the mind than a research, for he would say to his sitter 'you are so fortunate as to resemble your picture', and of Mr Charles Ricketts, my education in so many things. How often his imagination moves stiffly as though in fancy dress, and then there is something,—Sphinx, Danaides—that makes me remember Callimachus' return to Ionic elaboration and shudder as though I stared into an abyss full of eagles.[133] Everywhere this vision or rather this contact is faint or intermittent and it is always fragile; Dickens was able with a single book, *Pickwick*, to substitute for Jane Austen's privileged and perilous research the camaraderie of the inn parlour, qualities that every man might hope to possess, and it did not return till Henry James began to write.[134]

Certain men have sought to express the new emotion through the *Creative Mind*, though fit instruments of expression do not yet exist, and so to establish, in the midst of our ever more abundant *primary* information, *antithetical* wisdom; but such men, Blake, Coventry Patmore at moments, Nietzsche, unlike those who, from Richardson to Tolstoy, from Hobbes to Mill and Spencer, have grown in number and serenity, are full of morbid excitement and few in number.[135] They were begotten in the Sistine Chapel[136] and still dream that all can be transformed if they be but emphatic; yet Nietzsche, when the doctrine of the Eternal Recurrence drifts before his eyes, knows for an instant that nothing can be and is almost of the next gyre.[137]

The period from 1875 to 1927[138] (Phase 22)—in some countries and in some forms of thought it is from 1815 to 1927—is like that from 1250 to 1300 (Phase 8) a period of abstraction, and like it also in that it is preceded and followed by abstraction. Phase 8 was preceded by the Schoolmen and followed by legalists and inquisitors and Phase 22 was preceded by the great popularisers of physical science and economic science, and will be followed by social movements and applied science. Abstraction which began at Phase 19 will end at Phase 25 for these movements and this science will have for their object or result the elimination of intellect. Our generation has stood at the climax, at what I call in 'The Trembling of the Veil' *Hodos Chameliontos*,[139] or has witnessed a first weariness, and when the climax passes will recognise that there common secular thought began to break and disperse. Tolstoy in *War and Peace* had still preference, could argue about this thing or that other, had a belief in Providence and a disbelief in Napoleon, but Flaubert in his St Anthony[140] had neither belief, nor preference, and so it is that, even before the general surrender of the will, there came synthesis for its own sake, organisation where there is no masterful director, books where the author has disappeared, painting where some accomplished brush paints with an equal pleasure, or with a bored impartiality, the human form or an old bottle, dirty weather and clean sunshine. I too think of famous works where synthesis has been carried to the utmost limit possible, where there are elements of inconsequence or discovery of hitherto ignored ugliness, and I notice that when the limit is approached or past, when the moment of surrender is reached, when the new gyre begins to stir, I am filled with excitement. I think of recent mathematical research, and even my ignorance can compare it with that of Newton—so plainly of the 19th Phase—with its objective world intelligible to intellect; and I recognise that the limit itself has become a new dimension, and that this ever hidden thing which makes us fold our hands has begun to press down upon multitudes.[141] Having bruised their hands upon that limit men, for the first time since the seventeenth century, see the world as an object of contemplation, not as something to be remade, and some few, meeting the limit in their special study, even doubt if there is any common experience, that is to say doubt the possibility of science.[142]

It is said that at Phase 8 there is always civil war, and at Phase 22 always war, and as this war is always a defeat for those who have conquered, we have repeated the wars of Alexander.[143]

I discover already the first phase[144]—Phase 23—of the last quarter in certain friends of mine, and in writers, poets and sculptors admired by these friends, who have a form of strong love and hate hitherto unknown in the arts. It is with them a matter of conscience to live in their own exact instant of time, and they defend their conscience like theologians. They are all absorbed in some technical research to the entire exclusion of the personal dream. It is as though the forms in the stone or in their reverie began to move with an energy which is not that of the human mind. Very often these forms are mechanical, are as it were the mathematical forms that sustain the *physical primary*—I think of the work of Mr Wyndham Lewis, his powerful 'cacophony of sardine tins', and of those marble eggs, or objects of burnished steel too drawn up or tapered out to be called eggs, of M. Brancusi, who has gone further than Mr Wyndham Lewis from recognisable subject matter and so from personality; of sculptors who would certainly be rejected as impure by a true sectary of this moment, the Scandinavian Milles, Meštrović perhaps, masters of a geometrical pattern or rhythm which seems to impose itself wholly from beyond the mind, the artist 'standing outside himself'.[145] I compare them to sculpture or painting where now the artist now the model imposes his personality. I think especially of the art of the 21st Phase which was at times so anarchic, Rodin creating his powerful art out of the fragments of those Gates of Hell that he had found himself unable to hold together—images out of a personal dream, 'the hell of Baudelaire not of Dante', he had said to Symons.[146] I find at this 23rd Phase which is it is said the first where there is hatred of the abstract, where the intellect turns upon itself, Mr Ezra

Pound, Mr Eliot, Mr Joyce, Signor Pirandello, who either eliminate from metaphor the poet's phantasy and substitute a strangeness discovered by historical or contemporary research or who break up the logical processes of thought by flooding them with associated ideas or words that seem to drift into the mind by chance; or who set side by side as in *Henry IV, The Waste Land, Ulysses,* the *physical primary*—a lunatic among his keepers, a man fishing behind a gas works, the vulgarity of a single Dublin day prolonged through 700 pages—and the *spiritual primary* delirium, the Fisher King, Ulysses' wandering.[147] It is as though myth and fact, united until the exhaustion of the Renaissance, have now fallen so far apart that man understands for the first time the rigidity of fact, and calls up, by that very recognition, myth—the *Mask*—which now but gropes its way out of the mind's dark but will shortly pursue and terrify. In practical life one expects the same technical inspiration, the doing of this or that not because one would, or should, but because one can, consequent licence, and with those 'out of phase' anarchic violence with no sanction in general principles. If there is violent revolution, and it is the last phase where political revolution is possible, the dish will be made from what is found in the pantry and the cook will not open her book. There may be greater ability than hitherto for men will be set free from old restraints, but the old intellectual hierarchy gone they will thwart and jostle one another. One tries to discover the nature of the 24th Phase which will offer peace—perhaps by some generally accepted political or religious action, perhaps by some more profound generalisation—calling up before the mind those who speak its thoughts in the language of our earlier time. Péguy in his Joan of Arc trilogy displays the national and religious tradition of the French poor, as he, a man perhaps of the 24th Phase, would have it, and Claudel in his *L'Otage* the religious and secular hierarchies perceived as history.[148] I foresee a time when the majority of men will so accept an historical tradition that they will quarrel, not as to who can impose his personality upon others but as to who can best embody the common aim, when all personality will seem an impurity—'sentimentality', 'sullenness', 'egotism'—something that revolts not morals alone but good taste. There will be no longer great intellect for a ceaseless activity will be required of all; and where rights are swallowed up in duties, and solitude is difficult, creation except among avowedly archaistic and unpopular groups will grow impossible. Phase 25 may arise, as the code wears out from repetition, to give new motives for obedience, or out of some scientific discovery which seems to contrast, a merely historical acquiescence, with an enthusiastic acceptance of the general will conceived of as a present energy—'Sibyl what would you?' 'I would die.'[149] Then with the last gyre must come a desire to be ruled or rather, seeing that desire is all but dead, an adoration of force spiritual or physical, and society as mechanical force be complete at last.

> Constrained, arraigned, baffled, bent and unbent
> By those wire-jointed jaws and limbs of wood
> Themselves obedient,
> Knowing not evil or good.[150]

A decadence will descend, by perpetual moral improvement, upon a community which may seem like some woman of New York or Paris who has renounced her rouge pot to lose her figure and grow coarse of skin and dull of brain, feeding her calves and babies somewhere upon the edge of the wilderness. The decadence of the Greco-Roman world with its violent soldiers and its mahogany dark young athletes was as great, but that suggested the bubbles of life turned into marbles, whereas what awaits us, being democratic and *primary,* may suggest bubbles in a frozen pond—mathematical Babylonian starlight.[151]

When the new era comes bringing its stream of irrational force it will, as did Christianity, find its philosophy already impressed upon the minority who have, true to phase, turned away at the last gyre from the *Physical primary.* And it must awake into life, not Dürer's, nor Blake's, nor Milton's human form divine—nor yet Nietzsche's superman, nor Patmore's catholic, boasting 'a tongue that's dead'— the brood of the Sistine Chapel—but organic groups, *covens* of physical or intellectual kin melted out of the frozen mass.[152] I imagine new races, as it were, seeking domination, a world resembling but for its immensity that of the Greek tribes—each with its own *Daimon* or ancestral hero—the brood of Leda, War and Love; history grown symbolic, the biography changed into a myth.[153] Above all I imagine everywhere the opposites, no mere alternation between nothing and something like the Christian brute and ascetic, but true opposites, each living the other's death, dying the other's life.[154] It is said that the *primary* impulse 'creates the event' but that the *antithetical* 'follows it' and by this I understand that the Second Fountain will arise after a long preparation and as it were out of the very heart of human knowledge, and seem when it comes no interruption but a climax. It is possible that the ever increasing separation from the community as a whole of the cultivated classes, their increasing certainty, and that falling in two of the human mind which I have seen in certain works of art is preparation. During the period said to commence in 1927, with the 11th gyre, must arise a form of philosophy, which will become religious and ethical in the 12th gyre and be in all things opposite of that vast plaster Herculean image, final *primary* thought. It will be concrete in expression, establish itself by immediate experience, seek no general agreement, make little of God or any exterior unity, and it will call that good which a man can contemplate himself as doing always and no other doing at all. It will make a cardinal truth of man's immortality that its virtue may not lack sanction, and of the soul's re-embodiment that it may restore to virtue that long preparation none can give and hold death an interruption. The supreme experience, Plotinus' ecstasy,[155] ecstasy of the Saint, will recede, for men—finding it difficult—substituted dogma and idol, abstractions of all sorts, things beyond experience; and men may be long content with those more trivial supernatural benedictions as when Athena took Achilles by his yellow hair.[156] Men will no longer separate the idea of God from that of human genius, human productivity in all its forms.[157]

Unlike Christianity which had for its first Roman teachers cobblers and weavers, this thought must find expression among those that are most subtle, most rich in memory; that Gainsborough face floats up;[158] among the learned—every sort of learning—among the rich—every sort of riches—among men of rank—every sort of rank—and the best of those that express it will be given power, less because of that they promise than of that they seem and are. This much can be thought because it is the reversal of what we know, but those kindreds once formed must obey irrational force and so create hitherto unknown experience, or that which is incredible.

Though it cannot interrupt the intellectual stream—being born from it and moving within it—it may grow a fanaticism and a terror, and at its first outsetting oppress the ignorant—even the innocent— as Christianity oppressed the wise, seeing that the day is far off when the two halves of man can define each its own unity in the other as in a mirror, Sun in Moon, Moon in Sun, and so escape out of the Wheel.

FINISHED AT CAPRI, FEBRUARY, 1925.[159]

BOOK IV

The Gates of Pluto [1]

1. THE FOOL BY THE ROADSIDE[2]

When my days that have[3]
From cradle run to grave
From grave to cradle run instead;[4]
When thoughts that a fool
Has wound upon a spool
Are but loose thread, are but loose thread;

When cradle and spool are past
And I mere shade at last
Coagulate of stuff
Transparent like the wind,
I think that I may find
A faithful love, a faithful love.

2. THE GREAT WHEEL
AND FROM DEATH TO BIRTH⁵

I

STRAY THOUGHTS

Cornelius Agrippa in *De Occulta Philosophia* quotes from 'Orpheus'—'The Gates of Pluto cannot be unlocked, within is a people of dreams,'⁶ and from that sentence I take the name of this fourth book, in which I must consider the condition from death to birth.

I must speak much of the *Daimon*, and yet we can know nothing of the *Daimon* except by the *Complementary Dream*.⁷ She is not phasal and yet we must speak as if she were because she affects human life, now through one *Faculty* and now through another, and if we are to strengthen her influence or to moderate it we must know what these *Faculties* are. She is that being united to man which knows neither good nor evil, and shapes the body in the womb, and impresses upon the mind its form. She is revealed to man in moments of prevision and illumination and in much that we call good and evil fortune, and yet, seeing that she remains always in the Thirteenth Cycle, cannot accompany man in his wanderings, nor can her tutelage of man be eternal, seeing that after many cycles man also inhabits the Thirteenth Cycle and has in a certain way a greater power than hers.⁸ When both are as it were side by side in the same cycle, she like a spirit of the 15th Phase, can communicate with one living man,⁹ chosen still doubtless from a cycle beneath her own, whereas the man can communicate with an indefinite number of other men. We can but fall back on image and say that they are united for twelve cycles, and are then set free from one another, she being Full Moon and he Full Sun; though when we consider all with the eyes of living man he is Moon and she the Sun.[10]

Presently I must speak of the *Ghostly Self*[11] by which the creators of this system mean the permanent self, that which in the individual may correspond to the fixed circle of the figure, neither Man nor *Daimon*, before the whirling of the Solar and Lunar cones. It is the source of that which is unique in every man, understanding by unique that which is one and so cannot be analysed into anything else.

I do not think of death as separation from body but from the exclusive association with one body for in no experience possible to the human spirit, as it is known to me, does the human spirit cease to use directly or through the *Record* the senses of living men. Upon the other hand, eye and ear and touch have not always the same range for the living and the dead, nor has the brain of the living, when the dead and the living use it, the same capacity, for the dead are the wisdom of the living. Seeing that the body is a portion of the *Daimon's Body of Fate* it may be said that the *Daimon,* and therefore all associated *Daimons* or Spirits, are nearer to the body than to the intellect. Nor must the dead be thought of as living an abstract life for it is the living who create abstraction which 'consumes itself away'.[12]

II

THE VISION OF THE BLOOD KINDRED[13]

At death the man passes into what seems to him afterwards a state of darkness and sleep; there is a sinking in upon fate analogous to that of the individual cones at Phase 22. During the darkness he is surrounded by his kindred, present in their simulacrae, or in their Spirits when they are between lives, the more recent dead the more visible. Because of their presence it is called the *Vision of the Blood Kindred.*

III

THE SEPARATION OF THE FOUR PRINCIPLES[14]

The *Spirit* first floats horizontally within the man's dead body, but then rises until it stands at his head. The *Celestial Body* is also hor-

izontal at first but lies in the opposite position, its feet where the
Spirit's head is, and then rising, as does the *Spirit,* stands up at last at
the feet of the man's body. The *Passionate Body* rises straight up
from the genitals and stands in the centre. The *Husk* remains in the
body until the time for it to be separated and lost in *Anima Mundi.*
The separation of the *Principles* from the body is caused by the
Daimon's gathering into the *Passionate Body* memory of the past
life—perhaps but a single image or thought—which is always taken
from the unconscious memories of the living, from the *Record*[15] of
all those things which have been seen but have not been noticed or
accepted by the intellect, and the *Record* is always truthful.

IV

THE AWAKENING OF THE SPIRITS

The *Spirit* meanwhile has passed from the *Vision of the Blood Kindred* into meditation, but of this meditation we are told little except
that it is upon the coming 'dissolution of the *Passionate Body*'[16]
and that, though in certain cycles it may be prolonged for a very
great period, with us it ends with burial. The *Spirit* may appear to
the living during this meditation, but if it does so it will show in the
likeness of the body as that body was shortly before death. The meditation may be moved and shaped by the Burial Ritual, for the body
has become a symbol, and as the *Spirit* has entered upon a condition
that is a dream, thoughts inspired among the living by that Ritual
can influence its life. Now in its turn the *Spirit* gradually awakens,
and it is said that the awaking may begin with the sight of a flower
upon the grave where it appears shining amidst the general darkness.
In the world where it is now the human soul is seen to give forth
light which is transmitted to objects and the thought of some
mourner will illuminate the flower.[17] The *Spirit* is somewhere said to
appear as a colourless outline until at this awakening it gradually
takes upon itself something of the hues of the living man. Its coming
to self-knowledge may be long and painful. If death has been violent
or tragic, *Spirit* and *Passionate Body* may dream that death again
and again with intervals of awakening, and in some few cases so
dream for a century or more. A gambler killed in a gambling brawl

will demand his money, and a man, who has believed that nothing will remain but the decaying body may haunt the house where he has lived as an odour of decay; nor is there any reason why a man may not see reflected in a mirror some beloved ghost who, thinking herself unobserved, will powder her face as in Mr Davies' verse.

> The first night she was in her grave,
> As I looked in the glass
> I saw her sit upright in bed;
> Without a sound it was;
> I saw her hand feel in the cloth
> To fetch a box of powder forth.
>
> She sat and watched me all the while
> For fear I looked her way,
> I saw her powder cheek and chin
> Her fast corrupting clay.
> Then down my lady lay and smiled,
> She thought her beauty saved, poor child.[18]

V

THE RETURN[19]

The *Spirit* should separate itself from all such dreams of the *Passionate Body* and seek the *Celestial Body,* and only when so separate does it cease to dream and know that it is dead. There are therefore, in what is known as the *Return,* a *[20] *Waking State* and a *Sleeping State* which alternate, and these states resemble each other in that in both are sensible images or some impression of sense, but differ in that during the *Waking State* these images and impressions of sense are imposed by other beings, who are bound to the dead man by the events of some past life, and in that during the *Sleeping State* they are recovered from the *Record,* by the man's *Spirit* or *Passionate Body,*

---

*These states seem analogous to *Sage* (or teacher) and *Victim* respectively. During the *Waking State* the gyre moves but during the *Sleeping State* it is stationary.—*Sept.* 28.

and in that during the *Waking State* alone does he know that he is no longer living. During this state which is commonly called the *Teaching* he is brought into the presence, as far as possible, of all sources of the action he must presently, till he has explored every consequence, dream through. This passion for the source is brought to him from his own *Celestial Body* which perpetually, being of the nature of *Fate,* dreams the events of his life backward through time. If the thought of the past life permit, he will now perceive all those persons as they now live or as they have lived, who have influenced him, or whom he has influenced, and so caused the action, but if he has belonged to some faith that has not known rebirth he may explore sources that require symbolical expression.

As he cannot escape the symbols of his life, whatever his belief, he may now see himself surrounded by flames and persecuted by devils. One remembers the girl in the Japanese play whose Ghost tells a Priest of a slight sin which seems a great sin because of its unforeseen and unforeseeable consequences, and that she is persecuted by flames. If she but touch a pillar, she says, it bursts into flames, and the Priest who knows that these flames are but her own conscience made visible, tells her that if she cease to believe in them they must cease to exist. She thanks him, but the flames return, for she cannot cease to believe, and the play ends with a dance which is the expression of her agony.[21]

The *Teaching Spirits,* as the *Waking State* returns and the first passion declines, may offer him a guidance which seems like that of some familiar institution, hospital, or school, for they are still the human mind and keep old habits of thought, but it differs from that of an institution because these spirits have been a part of his life for perhaps many centuries. The object of the *Return* is to exhaust pleasure and pain by the display of all the good and evil of his past life, but it is always the old, never new pleasure or pain. He may sometimes visit the living, suggest thoughts or emotions that may amend the consequence of his acts, but cannot, unless through the eyes and ears of some spirit from a later condition, see any that were not a part of his own life. When in the *Meditation* he could but appear to the living in the form he last wore alive, but now he may be seen as of that age at which the event he is about to dream occurred. Most of the spirits at séances are said to belong to this condition.

When the *Spirit* has been for the moment exhausted by the phantasmagoria[22] as it is sometimes called, the *Passionate Body* attracts it to itself, and the *Sleeping State* begins. The *Passionate Body* like the *Celestial Body* never ceases to dream, moving through events, however, not in the order of their occurrence but in that of their intensity, and when the *Spirit* returns to it the *Spirit* is compelled to imitate this dream, having no life except from one or other of the bodies. The man is now in what is called the *Dreaming Back*,[23] and it is now that, according to ancient and modern tradition, the murderer may be seen committing his murder night after night,[24] or perhaps upon the anniversary of its first committal; or it may be that the dream is happy and that the seer but meets the old huntsman hunting once more amid a multitude of his friends and all his hounds, or half tragic and half happy as when the mother, as the folklore of all nations and spiritualistic annals recall, comes to her orphan children.[25] 'The Divine returns to the Divinity' through the *Celestial Body*, and to invert *Plotinus* 'the Lonely returns to the Lonely'[26] in the dream of the *Passionate Body*, for mother, murderer and huntsman are alone. If the dreamed event was once shared by many, now dead, those many may indeed be present, and yet as each but dreams again without change what happened when they were alive, each dreamer is alone. Should they exchange the thought of the moment, one with another, there would be contrast, conflict, and therefore creation, and the dream would not fade. The dream may be dreamed through by the *Spirit* once, or many times with short or long periods of awakening, but the man must dream the event to its consequence as far as his intensity permit; not that consequence only which occurred while he lived, and was known to him, but those that were unknown, or have occurred after his death. The more complete the exploration, the more fortunate will be his future life, but he is concerned with events only, and with the emotions that accompanied events. Every event so dreamed is the expression of some knot,[27] some concentration of feeling separating off a period of time, or portion of the being, from the being as a whole and the life as a whole, and the dream is as it were a smoothing out or an unwinding. Yet it is said that if his nature had great intensity, and the consequences of the event affected multitudes, he may dream with slowly lessening pain and joy for centuries.

As all the consequences of the event are discovered from the

Record made by the living—the *Spirit* finding there names, dates, and language to complete the drama, and the *Passionate Body* finding the concrete events—we may say that the dead remain a portion of the living. It is indeed said that where murderer and victim die unknown, and the crime remains unknown, the *Spirit* can find certain facts in its own *Passionate Body,* or from the *Passionate Body* of its victim, but with difficulty, and such a *Dreaming Back* is imperfect. A *Dreaming Back* may be so imperfect or so prolonged that it obsesses the next life and causes rebirth into almost the same circumstances as those already lived through, and generally into the same family. *Teaching Spirits* may assist the dreamer, and many hauntings, many inexplicable sights and sounds, are to cause, among the living, inquiries that passing into the unconscious mind of the enquirer enable the *Passionate Body* or *Spirit* of the dreamer to perfect its knowledge.

The *Spirit* can even consult books, records, of all kinds, once they be brought before the eyes or even perhaps to the attention of the living, but it can see nothing there that does not concern the dream.[28] The *Spirit* so dreaming, if it see the living thinks they are a portion of its dream, and is without reflection or the knowledge that it is dead. When the dream ends the *Spirit* withdraws from the *Passionate Body* which continues its purely animal dream. There is, however, the rare event, which may affect either the *Dreaming Back* or the *Waking State,* of renewed contact of *Spirit* and *Passionate Body* with the *Husk.* This constitutes the true ghost as distinguished from the dream of the *Spirit* and *Passionate Body.* In this state a spirit may experience for a moment once more pleasure and pain[29] that are not a fading memory. It is said to be dangerous to the living and a hindrance to the dead, and to include incubi and succubi, and perhaps most of those beings the Cambridge Platonist described, when he called the Devil 'A Body Politick',[30] and with whom witches made compacts to keep them, by a periodical offering of their blood, from fading out. Seeing that there is no punishment but the prolongation of the *Dreaming Back,* and the consequent exclusion of other states, it is among *Spirits* so united to their *Husk* that we discover tempting or evil spirits.

VI

THE RETURN IN RELATION TO THE COVENS

There are beings which have personality, though their bodies consist of a number of minds held together by a stream of thought[31] or an event, and these beings, called *Covens*, have their own *Dreaming Back*, *Record Teachings*, and so on, and hold those, who constitute their bodies, even after death and perhaps for many lives. During his individual *Teaching* or *Dreaming Back*, an individual man is among the forms of his *Coven*, the Heaven and Hell of Christianity, the Spheres of Spiritualism,[32] the Faery Hostings of Irish folk-lore,[33] and where there is little change in civilisation and belief these forms may persist for centuries, and it is through these forms that the beings of the 13th Cycle unite the individual destiny to that of a race, or a religion, and make the individual knot coincide with that of the nation and make the untying of one the untying of both.

VII

THE SHIFTINGS[34]

At the end of the *Return* which corresponds upon the diagram to the gyre associated with Phases 23, 24 and 25, the *Spirit* is freed from pleasure and pain and is ready to enter the *Shiftings* where it is freed from Good and Evil, and in this state which is a state of intellect, it lives through a life which is said to be in all things opposite to that lived through in the world, and dreamed through in the *Return*. As the documents are here more than usually obscure and strange and as I am afraid of unconsciously perverting their meaning, I will quote certain passages.[35] If the surroundings of a past life were 'good' they are now 'evil' and where 'evil' 'good', and if a man has had good motives 'they are now evil, and if evil good . . . because it is not virtue to be good knowing no evil, nor is it sin to be evil knowing no good . . . Good is not good if it is not a conquest of evil, and evil is not evil unless a conquest of good.' And this is amplified later on with the statement that if one has been in any matter good, knowing evil, or evil, knowing good, one suffers in that matter no transformation. Yet seeing that one is generally good or evil in ignorance, the state is for most men 'the best possible life in the worst possible surroundings' or the direct contrary, and this is brought about by no external law but by a craving in the *Principles* to know what life has hidden, that the *Daimon* who knows intellect but not good and evil, may be satisfied. Yet there is no suffering 'for in a state of equilibrium there is neither emotion nor sensation'; and seeing that for all, 'in the limits of the good and evil of the previous life, . . . the soul is brought to a comprehension of good and evil, neither the utmost evil nor the utmost good can force sensation or emotion.'[36] Evil is that which opposes Unity of Being[37] and seeing that man seeks his *primary* in woman, and woman her *antithetical* in man, a relationship of sex displays good and evil in their most subtle and overpowering form. Therefore it is said that in the *Shiftings* men and women relive their loves, and not as in the *Dreaming Back* to exhaust pleasure and pain, but that they may separate that which belongs to their true *primary* or true *antithetical* from that which seems to, and therefore exhaust good and evil themselves. The man would know the woman utterly and so he must relive his love in all things whereof he was ignorant, turning good fortune into complete tragedy, or tragedy into good fortune, that he may test his love in every fire; and if the woman be dead and in like condition she will be present in reality, but if not, in similitude alone. Yet whether she be there or not there, the dream will be but the same, for he can see nothing but his dream. Light loves, loves without mutual recognition, may not long delay him, for their circumstance and consequence have been exhausted in the *Dreaming Back,* and their effect upon himself has been but little, but strong love given in ignorance may be relived again and again, though not with suffering, for all now is intellect and he is all *Daimon,* and tragic and happy circumstance alike offer an intellectual ecstasy at the revelation of truth, and the most horrible tragedy in the end can but seem a figure in a dance. Yet his dream, like that of the *Dreaming Back,* is not like dreams in sleep, for though it seems to him reality, he sees beside it the love that he actually did live, a reality that seems a dream, for without that he could not bring his soul to quiescence.

In the *Waking State* of the *Shiftings* there is no reliving of the past, and though the soul is taught, there is no teaching, and there is no

Teacher but the *Celestial Body*,[38] for it is a form of life; the soul is as it were folding up into itself. We can say of it that it is no longer in space, but, in the measure of its truth to phase, in time alone, past and present being within equal reach—for so it is the documents put it—and yet it is more intelligible to say that it has now received from the *Celestial Body* the *Record* of its past existence. It has no memory of its own, apart from this *Record*, having no acquired faculties, and thinks not as man thinks but as *Daimon* thinks. Abstraction has gone, no thread of the cloth can be separated from any other thread, and the whole cloth is unwound. It is now, as the *Shiftings* close, brought by the *Celestial Body* into the presence, not of the source of its good and evil, for it must transcend good and evil, but into that of all typical qualities of its being, and all the associates of its past lives in the order of their phase that it may see their loves and its own as one single wheel; and where the *Celestial Body* is in contact with the beings of the Thirteenth Cycle it may carry to the living messages concerned with purposes that transcend individual life, or upon the other hand it may carry from its own *Celestial Body* messages that concern individual life alone. But when it goes upon these messages—remembering that it can hear but cannot see, being in time only—it must act through the intermediary of those in the *Waking State* of the *Return*, and of Spirits at Phase 1; and should it desire to appear it must by such intermediary mould into a living image the most vivid memory of itself found in the unconscious minds of the living, and this image is always that most generally known, for it is still 'suggestible'. Sometimes these messengers make their presence known by some scent or sound or sight[39] associated with them, and it is through this scent or sound or sight that they draw upon the physical vitality of a man, or upon the knowledge of the *Daimon* of this man to whom they are sent, or of that other who may help the delivery of the message. When through intermediaries they make use of our eyes, they can unlike those in the *Return* understand records which have no relation to their own past. They are most commonly sent to those with whom they have lived in some near or distant past, and they always 'take upon themselves the exact mental condition of the person they communicate with; if with some person they have injured, they take on the sense of that injury . . . sorrow, suspicion, self-doubt'.[40]

VIII

EXPIATION FOR THOSE IN THE SHIFTINGS
AND IN THE RETURN

Seeing that persons are born again and again in association, mother
and son at first it may be, then wife and husband, brother and sister,
and that our loves and friendships are many, each person is a part of
a community of spirits and our re-embodiments are governed and
caused by passions that we must exhaust in all their forms. As all
strong passions are said[41] to contain 'cruelty and deceit' and so to
require expiation, one deceived as to motive cannot pass out of the
Shiftings if unable to complete the transposition of life and surroundings, and some other who has sinned in act may be compelled
to relive his phase again and again till he has completed the expiation
which frees both souls. 'An Act' or motive that created action is 'expiated in physical life' but an intellectual defect in 'spiritual life'.[42] So
that a man who has been deceived but has not retaliated expiates in
the *Shiftings* what, must have found, had he retaliated, an expiation
during physical life. Expiation during physical life is caused by the
craving to experience that which we have done to another, to reverse
in action what the disembodied soul reverses in thought, and we owe
it not to that other but to our own *Daimon* which, but for 'cruelty or
deceit', had found the *Daimon* of that other. The expiation is followed by a prolonged or short mingling of the *Daimons*.[43] Expiation
is a harmonisation of being, and we seek out the image, reflected in
some living man or woman, of that other being, that we may achieve
it in action. It affects that other who must achieve it in thought by
Complementary Dream for the expiations are simultaneous.

Until an act has been expiated the same circumstance occurs
again and again, as though the *Dreaming Back* flowed over into the
life that followed. One woman has endured[44] a drunken husband
because of a wrong done to a husband in another life, while another
expiates, by a life of devotion to an un-loved man, a suicide whereby
under some misunderstanding she had deserted a man she loved.
During these acts of expiation the life may be embittered 'by an inhibition of the active qualities' and a suffering which is a 'physical
emotional and spiritual, and not moral purgation'.[45] And there is

always a sense of being fated. This inhibition, this sense of being fated is not always an unhappiness. A life of voluntary surrender to another may create an unconscious craving for its opposite, and this craving may produce a prosperous self-appeasing life which is fated and so expiatory. A Knot is first in the being, and is called a *Knot of Destiny,* but in the life that follows, may be in the events themselves, and uncontrollable by the being, and is then a *Knot of Fate*.[46] That the expiatory suffering, or pleasure, may affect a particular disembodied soul, the *Celestial Body* of that soul is through its *Spirit* imposed, while in the *Waking State* of the *Shiftings,* as an image upon some living man or woman, and that man or woman is then loved, not for his or her own sake but for that of the dead. Yet this image, not being imposed upon the desires but upon the unconscious mind, does not create new deception and expiation. There is indeed a condition of the soul when an image, unexhausted in the *Dreaming Back,* does impose a physical image upon the desire of the living, but this is not expiation though it may—if the same person be dominated by both images—be as it were mixed into expiation. A purgation completed brings good fortune and happiness, a consciousness of luck.[47]

A race may at times become dominated like an individual by a subconscious desire for suffering or for ease, as an expiation for acts done centuries before to some race whose *Coven* has passed into *Daimonic* life.

There are other forms of expiation with which I shall not concern myself in this book, but there is one on which I must touch later, for it is that whereby supernatural forms of the more powerful kind are created.

IX

BEATITUDE[48]

After the *Shiftings* the *Spirit* is for a short time 'out of space and time',[49] and every other abstraction, and is said not to move in a gyre but in a sphere, being as it were present everywhere at once. *Beatitude* is the result of the expiations of living man and disembodied soul, and the final harmony so established, and it is said that while still living we receive joy from those we have served—choosing tragedy they abandon to us this cast-off joy?—whereas we receive from those we have wronged, ecstasy, described as the only perfected love and as emotion born when we love that which we hate knowing that it is fated.

In life, seeing that the *Four Faculties* and the *Husk* and *Passionate Body* constrain all, we are in accident and passion; but now *Spirit* and *Celestial Body* constrain all, the one calling up all concrete universal quality and idea, and the other closing it in the unique image. Nor can I consider the *Beatitude* as any state beyond man's comprehension, but as the presence before the soul in some settled order, which has arisen out of the soul's past, of all those events or works of men which have expressed some quality of wisdom or of beauty or of power within the compass of that soul, and as more completely human and actual than any life lived in a particular body. It is the momentary union of the *Spirit* and the *Celestial Body* with the *Ghostly Self* and fades into or is preceded by what is called the *Vision of the Clarified Body*, which is indeed a Vision of our own *Celestial Body* as that body will be when all cycles end.[50]

(Mr Yeats, indulgent to Christian or *primary* prejudice, permits me to say that in the Robartes Papers I find this passage—'The *Celestial Body* is the Divine Cloak lent to all; at the Consummation the Cloak falls for the Christ is revealed.'[51] A passage that reminds me of Bardesan's 'Hymn of the Soul'[52] where a king's son asleep in Egypt is sent a cloak which is also an image of the body of him to whom it is sent—the *Celestial Body* acting through the *Mask*—and the king's son sets out to his father's kingdom clad in the cloak. I find also that the *Ghostly Self* is so named, not as it might seem because it is shadowy but because the *Beatitude* and the two states that follow correspond to the 13th, 14th and 15th Cycles which correspond in their turn to Holy Ghost, Son and Father.—Owen Aherne.)[53]

X

*54THE STATES BEFORE BIRTH, CALLED THE GOING FORTH AND THE FOREKNOWING

Were the *Spirit* strong enough, or were its human cycles finished, it would remain, as in the *Beatitude,* permanently united to its *Ghostly Self,* or would, after two more states, be reborn into a spiritual cycle where the movement of the gyre is opposite to that in our cycles, and incomprehensible to us, but it will almost certainly pass to human rebirth because of its terror of what seems to be the loss of its own being. Whether it pass to a spiritual or to a human rebirth it must receive in the *Beatitude*—in Cancer—the Cup of Lethe.55 There all thoughts or images drawn from the *Faculties* during the *Shiftings* or the *Dreaming Back,* or that have remained in the *Faculties,* must be passed into the *Ghostly Self* and so be forgotten by the *Spirit.* It has now no fixed form, or rather one should say, cannot impose a fixed form upon its intermediaries, or be represented by a fixed correspondence, for it is not in space, nor is it 'suggestible' like an inhabitant of the *Shiftings* though like this inhabitant it lives in what is to us darkness. It has, through its intermediaries and our senses and its own darkness, an almost limitless vision of concrete reality, and is in the presence of all those activities whose *Complementary Dream* is in our art, or music or literature, and of those men and women who have finished all their cycles and are called 'Those who wait'.56 We may even while we live hear their voices when in a state of trance, but speaking detached and broken sentences, and that which they say is always the greatest wisdom attainable by our soul. It is now, however, that there comes, seeing that it must recover or find its new *Husk,* a craving for deception, for pleasure and for pain, and it passes into the state called the *Foreknowing* and into space among abstracted types and forms; and there, in a reversal of the *Dreaming Back,* it sees events and people that shall influence its

---

*The Documents where they describe existence between the *Beatitude* and birth are exceedingly confused and what I have written on the subject is less founded upon what they say than upon my knowledge of the system as a whole.—*Sept.* 26.

coming life upon earth, and as it can see that influence, as can no living man, it is possessed with violent love and hate, a wilful passion
comparable to the fated passion of the *Dreaming Back*. Such souls if
drunk with prevision may become what are called *Frustrators* and
through their power over human emotion, or if helped by more
powerful beings over the *Body of Fate* of some living man, prevent,
or try to prevent, the beginnings of those things that they fear.[57]

(Robartes told me that while in Arabia his work was constantly
interfered with by illness, his own or somebody else's, and that he
came to know the presence of *Frustrators* by animal odours like that
of the excrement of some beast, or by the smell of a guttering candle.
He said that these odours were objective, for anybody who came
into the tent smelt them. He blamed the *Frustrators* for the inadequacy and confusion of all his own notes which deal with the life
between death and birth, and insisted that the original revelation to
Kusta Ben Luka had been, so far as this subject is concerned, left
unfinished for the same reason. A curious point of his was that
souls immediately before birth frequently thought of themselves as
becoming small, and that this called up an imagination of small
beasts, birds and flies. He had known, he said, two Arab women
who found, one a mouse in her shoe, the other in her bed, the night
before their first children were born.[58] He thought that mice, constrained by the imagination of the unborn, were perhaps really
there.—Owen Aherne.)[59]

In certain cycles the soul is able within limits to choose into what
body it shall be born, but in most it must accept the choice of others.
Then comes the sleep in the womb and it must be in this sleep I think
that there comes what is called the *Vision of the Friends* to distinguish it from that of the *Blood Kindred*.[60]

In the *Beatitude* and in the states that immediately follow, the
man is subject to his *Daimon* only, and there is no alternation of
sleep and waking. In the *Beatitude* communication with the living is
through that state of soul, where an extreme activity is indistinguishable from an equal passivity.

> "Mind moved but seemed to stop
> As 'twere a spinning top,"[61]

and in the *Going Forth* through those actions and emotions, which are at once conscious and automatic like sudden rage and bodily desire, and nobler emotions cut from the same piece. And yet, through intermediaries, souls in the *Going Forth* can use all forms of communication not peculiar to the *Beatitude*. The *Going Forth* lasts longer than any state except the *Return*, which may last for generations.[62]

XI

FUNERAL IMAGES, WORKS OF ART, AND THE DEAD[63]

In the other life, as we have described it, there is no creation of separated form, that being the work of the living, and until the *Beatitude* there is no deliberate selection of form. All antiquity seems to have thought the newly dead 'suggestible', compelled even to go where living men commanded. I have a story of a Sligo stable boy[64] who was dismissed by his employer because he had sent her late husband's ghost to haunt a weather-beaten lighthouse, far out in the bay. A dying Mahomedan is sometimes guarded by relatives that he may look upon no ugly woman and so compel the ghostly women he will shortly meet to take her form. A Brahmin once told Florence Farr that he disliked acting because if a man died playing Hamlet he would be Hamlet in the life to come.[65] A Galway woman told a friend of mine she had met this friend's dead husband in an old torn coat, but that if my friend gave a new coat, made to his measure, to some poor man, he would have the use of it.[66] I heard a like story in Munster but there the ghost returned to thank the giver dressed in the new clothes. A king in Herodotus burned the best clothes of the ladies in his neighbourhood that his dead wife might make her choice.[67] A man once told in my hearing[68] a long story of a ghost who appeared at his bedside in a suit of clothes that had, as he proved, by some argument I forget, been copied from a portrait. One thinks of the burial customs of antiquity, all that they hid away in tombs—boats, chairs, oars, and weapons, the realistic statue of the dead man, or the golden mask upon his face—and one may well conclude that all were there to help the *Dreaming Back* of the *Spirit* or its *Waking State* in the *Return.* At some moment of the past it was discovered by some living man, or more likely taught by some dead man, that all being but 'suggestion' the clay or wooden image would serve as well as the real boat or the real slave, or even that a painting upon the wall sufficed, for that which made the image serviceable was not its magnitude or its reality but the fervour and precision of the ceremony of dedication, that is to say the might of the 'suggestion'. The first portraits were statues buried in tombs and buried there, as we believe, to assist the *Spirit* in its *Dreaming Back,* and Strzygowski thinks that the first landscape—a landscape painted or worked in mosaic within the dome of some Mazdian Temple[69]—was 'connected with the cult of the dead, the might and majesty of departed spirits'.[70] The Christmas before last the spiritualistic paper 'Light' described how some woman had been directed by spirits to make a Christmas tree for the pleasure of spirit children.[71] After the toys had served that turn they were to be given to some children's hospital. She and a medium sat beside the tree on Christmas night and she heard the spirit children asking for this or that toy, and older spirits—*Teaching Spirits* doubtless—answering. They seemed to unloose the toy which remained, however, in its place upon the bough.* One recognises in those 'synthetic cigars' in *Raymond,* a venerable tradition;[72] but may be permitted to consider the scientific language and explanation as borrowed from the subconsciousness of the questioner, or from that of some associated person.

XII

[†73]THE SPIRITS AT FIFTEEN AND AT ONE

It is said of the Spirits at Phases 15 and 1 that the first need help and the second give it. The second give it because they are the instrument

---

*The ceremony was repeated last Christmas, and this time the name of the child for whom each toy was intended was by direction of the Spirits written near it. This made the dedication precise with the precision of antiquity.—W.B.Y.

†Much in this chapter belongs to a part of the system that requires a more detailed study than I can at present give. I may be mistaken and only include it because the Documents insist upon the importance of the form of expiation described. It is connected with those *critical* and *initiatory moments* touched on in Book II Sec. XX.

of communication between men and all orders of Spirits, where the communication shows an automatic element, and they are also said to give the 'Kiss of Life' while the first give what is called the 'Kiss of Death'.[74] The Spirits at 15 need help that, before entering upon their embodied state, they may rid themselves of all traces of the *primary Tincture,* and this they gain by imposing upon a man or woman's mind an *antithetical* image which requires *primary* expression. It is this expression, which may be an action or a work of art, which sets them free, and the image imposed is an ideal form, an image of themselves, a type of emotion which expresses them, and this they can do but upon one man or woman's mind; their coming life depending upon their choice of that mind. They suffer from the terror of solitude, and can only free themselves from terror by becoming entirely *antithetical* and so self-sufficing, and till that moment comes each must, if a woman, give some one man her love, and though he cannot, unless out of phase and obsessed to the creation of a succuba know that his muse exists, he returns this love through the intermediary of an idol. This idol he creates out of an image imposed upon his imagination by the Spirit. This Spirit is said to give the 'Kiss of Death' because though she that gives it may persecute other idols, being jealous, the idol has not come out of the man's desire. Its expression is a harmonisation which frees the Spirit from terror and the man from desire, and that which is born from the man, and from an all but completed solitude, is called an *antithetical Arcon.*[75] Such *Arcons* deal with form not wisdom. It is of that Kiss I thought when I made Emer say:

> They find our men asleep, weary with war,
> Or weary with the chase, and kiss their lips
> And drop their hair upon them; from that hour
> Our men, who yet know nothing of it all,
> Are lonely, and when at fall of night we press
> Their hearts upon our hearts, their hearts are cold.[76]

If the Spirit at 15 be a man he must give the 'Kiss of Death' to some woman.

There is yet another expiation that follows denial of experience, the wilful refusal of expression. Because of this denial the *Ghostly*

Self is famished and so in the succeeding life there comes upon the man a craving to inflict upon himself that which he has inflicted, to make what is called the expiation for the *Ghostly Self*. He will offer his love to some woman who will refuse it, or to some cause that cannot prosper, or he will seek money and find but penury, or knowledge and find but ignorance, he is full of an insatiable desire and yet that desire is unsatisfied because of the curse that is upon him and his secret craving. The *Ghostly Self* is as it were shut up in its own marmorean time-less infinity.[77] That this penury and this fullness[78] may meet in *Complementary Dream* as in marriage, other spiritual beings must intervene, using as their instruments still other spirits, evil perhaps, instruments of the *Ghostly Self*; the man must receive a violent shock from some crisis created by supernatural dramatisation. Did Dante acquire in the Thebaid[79] the frenzy that he offered to Beatrice? In *antithetical* man this form of Victimage is superimposed upon Victimage for the Dead that the harmony of human emotions that creates may be followed or accompanied by acceptance of a supernatural aim. A man feels suddenly for a woman, or a woman for a man, or—if there has been in both expiation for the dead and for the *Ghostly Self*,—each feels for the other an emotion which has become a supernatural contemplation. I so picture my own Deirdre and Naisi when at the spectacle of triumphant evil and the approach of death they sit and play at chess, and I wrote my *Hour-Glass*[80] to describe such contemplation, but there the man being *primary* makes no expiation for the dead. In the one case natural love is brought to the greatest height, and in the other intellectual search, and both reduced to nothing that the soul may love what it hates, accepting at the same moment what must happen and its own being, for the *Ghostly Self* is that which is unique in man and in his fate. This is the moment of the greatest genius possible to that man or woman, and in it a *primary* or *antithetical Arcon* of wisdom is begotten by the *Ghostly Self* upon the soul. The beings who at the bidding of the *Ghostly Self* produce these dramatisations of evil are the corrective Spirits of Strindberg's Swedenborgian play, called in its English translation *There are crimes and crimes*.[81] These beings are themselves *Arcons* born through previous dramatisations. The *Ghostly Self* comes to the man by symbol and as when that symbol or vesture is not a spirit at 15 it is a spirit from Phase 1, we may speak of the *primary Arcon* as born from and receiving its body from a spirit at Phase 1. Its soul may be that of any selected spirit. Once born it creates a stream of impersonal expression or search. In every supernatural communication or influence which has a public object there is such an *Arcon* that its supernatural body may give stability and continuity. These beings begotten in tragedy may be brought forth in joy; and all works which are new creation, and so not from desire which can but repeat that which is already known, are brought forth under their influence or under that of beings, born from men and from the spirits at Phase 15. Was it at the Crucifixion or in the Agony in the Garden that the being was begotten whose history imaged itself in that of Christendom?[82]

There are also *Arcons* born from the marriage of a spirit at Phase 1 and a spirit at Phase 15, but these *Arcons* have for their body neither expression nor search but the work of art, the philosophy, or action itself. They are the organic unity of thought.

XIII

COMMUNICATIONS WITH SPIRITS
AND THE NATURE OF SLEEP

No concrete image that comes before the mind in sleep is ever from the memory; for in sleep we enter upon the same life as that we enter between death and birth. Hence we may dream all night of a sweetheart or a friend or a father or a mother and speak to them, and be aware of affection or enmity, and yet if we examine our dream immediately upon waking and before our waking thought has had time to alter the dream, we find that another image has been *substituted, perhaps very like but more probably quite unlike, perhaps even a table or a chair, and we may discover the nature of our emotion if we study the substitution which is itself a language. The concrete images that have come before us are from one or other of the states before our birth, changed by the mind's automatic phantasy, or

---

*I cannot account for the fact that these substituted images often seem not only familiar but that their very form seems to recall the person for whom they are substituted.

from those images of *Anima Mundi* which have some personal link with ourselves, or images from our present life that have evaded the memory and entered the *Record* alone. All these concrete images are associated with the *Passionate Body*; but the abstract intellectual memory of the *Spirit*, that for names and qualities, continues to serve in our sleep, though we cannot connect its contents with recognisable facts. *Spirit* and *Passionate Body* are separating, for it was the waking mind that held them together; and when coherence is attained, as it is at rare moments, it is in some philosophical or symbolical dream where a new centre of coherence is discovered in the *Celestial Body*.[83]

(Robartes told me that at Baghdad he came across an old Judwali doctor who had taken a medical degree in France, and made under his direction certain experiments upon an Arab boy. This boy was a patient of the doctor's for some physical ailment which had no connection with the fact that he talked in his sleep and would answer questions. Sometimes Robartes carried on conversations upon the most profound problems of the soul with an automatic personality which seemed sometimes the boy's own spirit and sometimes an extraneous being. He discovered that the boy's *Passionate Body* continued to dream during these conversations, but he only became aware of this dream when some physical action arising out of it interfered with articulation. Once the sleeper lapped like a cat under the influence of some chance word spoken in his hearing before he fell asleep; upon another occasion he dreamt that his mouth was full of feathers; and so on. If afterwards Robartes asked the boy what he had dreamt it was the dream of the *Passionate Body* and that alone he remembered. Upon one occasion when the boy was lapping Robartes imitated the barking of a dog as he might for a child. The boy's terror was great, the beating of his heart violent and yet Robartes had scarcely made any attempt at mimicry. Some part of the boy's mind must have accepted the suggestion deliberately; the dream must have been a self-created terror. Robartes told me that the dream of the *Passionate Body* after death was so created and that the *Spirit* while it shared the dream could be sufficiently apart from it to see men, scenes, other spirits, though it could not act or speak outside the dream.—O. Aherne.)[84]

In our dreams we communicate with the dead in their *Waking*

State, and these dreams never come to an end though they are only known to us while we sleep. They are part of the *Automatic Faculty,* which with that plastic substance sometimes visible at séances is an element of personality which corresponds to, without being identical with, the Spirits at Phase 1. This *Automatic Faculty* prolongs, when we walk or breathe, an act which was in the first instance voluntary, and it may create, under an impulse from a spirit an automatic personality which resembles that spirit, more or less accurately, according to the intensity of the impulse and the freedom of the *Automatic Faculty* from contrary impressions.[85]

(During the sleep of the boy I described in a previous note, Robartes once arranged a code with the automatic personality. When the boy, who knew nothing of all this was wide awake, perhaps eating or at some work, the dream created being would comment upon Robartes' conversation or action by tapping with the boy's foot or with his fork or in some similar way. Sometimes he would speak through the boy's lips and at such moments the boy heard nothing, though the voice was loud and clear, and though he heard everything that Robartes said and every sound in the room and everything that he himself said except those words. Gradually as the automatic personality increased in power it made visible or other signs outside the body of the boy, a sudden light, a sudden heat or cold or some strong fragrance, that of a flower frequently, and this fragrance was generally perceptible to anybody who came into the room. Once Robartes listened to the sleeping boy talking to a number of spirits, and pausing for their answers. The boy spoke to them as though he knew who they were, their capacities, and when they lived. There was something they wanted to tell him that he might know what to do in a certain difficult matter, and that they might be able to impress it on his mind they were evidently insisting that he should go away by himself at a certain hour the next day. He reluctantly consented, being a very sociable person. Next morning he knew nothing of his dream, but when the hour came round he said he wanted to be alone and strayed away into the fields. On his return, he said that he had made up his mind what to do in that difficult matter. Robartes' comment was that he had obeyed an order received in sleep without knowing that he did so and received a thought without knowing that it was not his own, and that this

showed how strong is the control of the *Daimons* over human life.—
Owen Aherne.)[86]

The automatic personality is never perhaps a puppet in the hand
of the spirit that created it, but has always not only its own automatic life but that reflected from the man himself. When, however,
the creator's control is continuous, the thought and its expression
may reveal a mind with powers of co-ordination greater and swifter
than those of the embodied mind. One can most easily study these
powers in their physical expression, and it has long been known that
the hand of the medium can under such influences trace perfect circles or make patterns of sweeping lines with a rapidity and precision
no voluntary movement can achieve.[87] A poltergeist has been known
to hurl small flat stones through narrow slits in a shutter from a considerable distance, though no living man could have done it from but
a few feet off. One notices there and elsewhere that mathematical
clarity one would expect from *Daimonic* domination. It is possible
even that the first jugglers did not so much imitate the effect of
magic as display a sleight of hand, the result of their obsession by an
automatic personality.

Primary man in certain periods of thought, Shelley's Ahasuerus,
let us say, is able 'By dreadful abstinence and conquering penance of
the mutinous flesh'[88] to keep his *Automatic Faculty* from desire and
fear—hence the symbolic value given to chastity by *primary* philosophers—and so be both vehicle and questioner. His mind has but a
single direct movement which may be wholly dominated, whereas an
antithetical inspiration may demand a separation of vehicle and
questioner, a relation like that between Priest and Sybil, Socrates and
Diotime, wandering magician and his scryer.[89] This relation, in its
highest form, implies a constant interchange of office and such relations may so cross and re-cross that a community may grow clair-
voyant. Lover and beloved, friend and friend, son and daughter, or
an entire family and *coven,* are brought by the dramatisation of the
Arcons into such a crisis that the *primary* oppositions and harmonies of the world are exposed in their minds and fates. There must
arise in the mind of one, where the bond is between two, a need for
some form of truth so intense that the *Automatic Faculty* of the other
grows as it were hollow to receive that truth. Should the desire but
be to impose a particular form of belief upon others or upon himself

the automatic personalities may exercise their control of thought or of mechanical movement for deception; but if the man desires truth itself that which comes will be the most profound truth possible to his fate. I have, however, but spoken of the communication of truth by intelligible word and there is a continual influence of *Waking Spirits* upon man's destiny by their control of his automatic movements during ordinary life. William Morris sometimes attributes to his heroes lucky eyes and foretells of one that all that he does unwitting shall be well done.[90]

There is, however, communication of waking man and *Sleeping Spirit*, the communication during expiation and during the creation of a work of art, let us say. Self-exhaustion of a man's creative power can make his *Automatic Faculty* plastic to the *Waking* Spirits but it can only be roused into that extremity of creation and so of exhaustion, by conflict. Exhaustion and creation should follow one another like day and night, his creation bringing contact with one form of the *spiritual primary*, his exhaustion with another, and this can only come from a choice forced by conflict with the *physical primary*. When the conflict is sexual and the man and woman each *Victim* for the Dead and for the *Ghostly Self*—each miracle working idol and an object of desire, they give one another a treble love, that for the dead, that for the living, that for the never living. And if those two for whom the victimage had been undertaken be born of the man and of the woman then there is created, both before and after the birth, the position known as that of the *Four Daimons*,[91] and each of the four has been set free from fate.

XIV

THE RECORD AND THE MEMORY[92]

I find[93] a statement that for the supreme magical work no word or symbol can be used that is still a part of living tradition, whether that tradition is known to the questioner or to the vehicle or not. Certainly when sleep is interrupted by vision the seer goes back to remote times, and the seer amidst brilliant light discovers myths and symbols that can only be verified by prolonged research. He has escaped from the individual *Record* to that of the race. In even a comparatively superficial communication, in so far as the actual mind of the spirit is present, words and symbols are from the individual *Record* and not from the individual memory. Those things which have no intellectual element, sound of wind and sea for instance, as distinguished, let us say, from speech—constantly pass into the *Record* without passing through the memory, and therefore come most easily to the communicators, hence frequent symbolism even where direct statement is possible. However all images, languages, forms of every kind used in communications from spirits, have passed through living minds whether in the past or in the present.[94] All forms are from the *Record,* and almost always from that made by those who are still living, rarely from that made by the spirit itself while living. Sometimes, however, a spirit may come into contact with his own *Husk,* and through that with his own personal *Record,* or with the *Husk* of another if that other has completely separated himself from it. It may mistake that *Husk* for its own for it finds it difficult to distinguish between *Husk* and *Husk.* The recovery, let us say, of a language from such a *Husk* except in the form of whole sentences imprinted upon the *Record* with their associated meaning is difficult, and a spirit with knowledge so acquired may write or speak accurately sentences in Greek or Latin because the *Husk* when living read or wrote or spoke such sentences, but will seldom be able to form the simplest Greek or Latin sentence for itself.[95] It is easier to recover the concrete image than an abstraction.

XV

THE HERRING FISHERS

Much of this book is abstract, because it has not yet been lived, for no man can dip into life more than a moiety of any system. When a child, I went out with herring fishers one dark night, and the dropping of their nets into the luminous sea and the drawing of them up has remained with me as a dominant image. Have I found a good net for a herring fisher?[96]

XVI

MYTHOLOGY[97]

A book of modern philosophy may prove to our logical capacity that there is a transcendental portion of our being that is timeless and spaceless, and therefore immortal, and yet our imagination remain subjected to nature as before. The great books—Berkeley's *Principles of Human Knowledge* let us say—beget new books, whole generations of books, but life goes on unchanged. It was not so with ancient philosophy because the ancient philosopher had something to reinforce his thought,—the Gods, the Sacred Dead, Egyptian Theurgy, the Priestess Diotime.[98] He could assume, perhaps even prove, that every condition of mind discovered by analysis, even that which is timeless, spaceless, is present vivid experience to some being, and that we could in some degree communicate with this being while still alive, and after our death share in the experience. We can believe that every school child possesses in some degree all natural faculty displayed by even the greatest man, for every such child can, if it will, understand some few lines of Milton or Shakespeare. That we may believe that all men possess the supernatural faculties I would restore to the philosopher his mythology.

FINISHED AT SYRACUSE, JANUARY, 1925.[99]

3. ALL SOULS' NIGHT[100]

Midnight has come and the great Christ Church[101] bell,
And many a lesser bell, sound through the room;
And it is All Souls' Night
And two long glasses brimmed with muscatel
Bubble upon the table. A ghost may come;
For it is a ghost's right,
His element is so fine
Being sharpened by his death,
To drink from the wine-breath
While our gross palates drink from the whole wine.

I need some mind that, if the cannon sound
From every quarter of the world, can stay
Wound in mind's pondering,
As mummies in the mummy-cloth are wound;
Because I have a marvellous thing to say,
A certain marvellous thing
None but the living mock;
Though not for sober ear;
It may be all that hear
Should laugh and weep an hour upon the clock.

X——'s the first I call. He loved strange thought
And knew that sweet extremity of pride
That's called platonic love,
And that to such a pitch of passion wrought
Nothing could bring him, when his lady[102] died,
Anodyne for his love.

Words were but wasted breath;
One dear hope had he:
The inclemency
Of that or the next winter would be death.

Two thoughts were so mixed up I could not tell
Whether of her or God he thought the most,
But think that his mind's eye,
When upward turned, on one sole image fell;
And that a slight companionable ghost
Wild with divinity,
Had so lit up the whole
Immense miraculous house,
The Bible promised us,
It seemed a gold-fish swimming in a bowl.

On Florence Emery[103] I call the next,
Who finding the first wrinkles on a face
Admired and beautiful,
And knowing that the future would be vexed
With 'minished beauty, multiplied commonplace,
Preferred to teach a school
Away from neighbour or friend
Among dark skins, and there
Permit foul years to wear,
Hidden from eyesight, to the unnoticed end.[104]

Before that end much had she ravelled out
From a discourse in figurative speech
By some learned Indian
On the soul's journey.[105] How it is whirled about
Wherever the orbit of the moon can reach,
Until it plunge into the sun,
And there—free and yet fast,
Being both Chance and Choice—
Forget its broken toys
And sink into its own delight at last.

And I call up MacGregor[106] from the grave,
For in my first hard spring-time we were friends,
Although of late estranged.
I thought him half a lunatic, half knave,
And told him so; but friendship never ends,
And what if mind seem changed,
And it seemed changed with the mind,
When thoughts rise up unbid
On generous things that he did
And I grow half contented to be blind.

He had much industry at setting out,
Much boisterous courage, before loneliness
Had driven him crazed;
For meditations upon unknown thought
Make human intercourse grow less and less;
They are neither paid nor praised.
But he'd object to the host,
The glass because my glass;
A ghost-lover he was
And may have grown more arrogant being a ghost.

But names are nothing. What matter who it be,
So that his elements have grown so fine
The fume of muscatel
Can give his sharpened palate ecstasy
No living man can drink from the whole wine.
I have mummy truths to tell
Whereat the living mock;
Though not for sober ear
For maybe all that hear
Should weep and laugh an hour upon the clock.

Such thought—such thought have I that hold it tight
Till meditation master all its parts,
Nothing can stay my glance
Until that glance run in the world's despite
To where the damned have howled away their hearts,

And where the blessed dance;
Such thought, that in it bound
I need no other thing,
Wound in mind's wandering,
As mummies in the mummy-cloth are wound.

OXFORD, *AUTUMN, 1920.*[107]

NOTES

Editors' Introduction

1. The date of publication as printed in the text is 1925, and the book is often identified by this date rather than the year of its actual appearance. Henceforth, W. B. Yeats is abbreviated WBY; George Yeats (née Hyde Lees) is abbreviated GY.

2. Letter from WBY to T. Werner Laurie, 27 July [1924], Special Collections, Miller Library, Colby College, Waterville, Maine.

3. Letter from WBY to T. Werner Laurie, 13 March 1923, Special Collections and Archives, Robert W. Woodruff Library, Emory University, Atlanta, Georgia.

4. Prospectus for *A Vision,* Laurie's Privately Printed Library, Special Collections and Archives, Robert W. Woodruff Library, Emory University, Atlanta, Georgia. The sum was well over £100 in today's currency.

5. The materials now reside in the National Library of Ireland; the catalogue may be accessed through http://www.nli.ie. When George Mills Harper and Walter Kelly Hood prepared their edition (*CVA*), the materials had not yet been catalogued; the notes to this edition give the new NLI numbers if possible. The AS, many notebooks, and the card file, as well as early drafts of the book, have been edited in *YVP*.

6. Letter from WBY to T. Werner Laurie, ? August [1925], Special Collections and Archives, Robert W. Woodruff Library, Emory University, Atlanta, Georgia.

7. Letter from WBY to T. Werner Laurie, 16 January [1926], Special Collections and Archives, Robert W. Woodruff Library, Emory University, Atlanta, Georgia.

8. Several of these dialogues have been edited as part of volume 4 of *YVP*.

9. *YVP* 1:252. See also this "Definition" as copied by GY into a notebook: "A *philosophy* created from experience, burns & destroys; one which is created from search, leads" (3:174). See also page 114 and Book II, n. 43.

10. Elsewhere in *AVA,* the title of the fictitious book (the spelling of which WBY corrected eventually to *Hominum*) is spelled "Hominorum" (see page lxi). See also the note to the frontispiece (Dedication and Introduction, n. 1).

11. Richard Ellmann, "*A Vision* before Revision," *Books and Bookmen* 24, no. 7 (April 1979): 52.

12. Ann Saddlemyer, *Becoming George: The Life of Mrs W. B. Yeats* (Oxford: Oxford University Press, 2002). Herein abbreviated Saddlemyer.

13. Foreword by Gerald Yorke to Ellic Howe, *The Magicians of the Golden Dawn: A Documentary History of a Magical Order 1887–1923* (London: Routledge & Kegan Paul, 1972), ix.

14. The best introduction to Yeats and this tradition is Kathleen Raine, *Yeats the Initiate* (Mountrath, Ireland: Dolmen Press; London: George Allen & Unwin, 1986).

15. The Yeatses owned a typescript of over two hundred pages of Moses's automatic script (NLI, 36,261/2/1–3).

16. "Preliminary Examination of the Script of E[lizabeth] R[adcliffe]," edited by George Mills Harper and John Kelly (*YO*, 130–71).

17. "The Manuscript of 'Leo Africanus,' " ed. Steve L. Adams and George Mills Harper (*YA* 1 [1982]: 3–47); " 'The Poet and the Actress': An Unpublished Dialogue by W. B. Yeats," ed. David R. Clark (*YA* 8 [1991]: 123–43).

18. In this series, *Per Amica* appears in *LE*, 1–33.

19. See *YVP* 3:399–400 and George Mills Harper, *W. B. Yeats and W. T. Horton: The Record of an Occult Friendship* (London: Macmillan, 1980), 59–63.

20. *L*, 644. "Ross" is Sir Edward Denison Ross, director of the School of Oriental Studies in London University. Yeats probably consulted him when he and GY returned to London after their honeymoon, possibly on 8 December 1917, in part to check on the success of the part-time job Yeats had arranged for Iseult Gonne at the school. Some manuscripts, possibly the earliest, contain blanks for title and author of the mythical book, which were filled in after Ross had given Yeats the Latin and Arabic he needed.

21. For two other accounts, see the introductions to *CVA* and *YVP* 4.

22. Edited by Walter Kelly Hood, this text appears in *YO*, 210–15.

23. Much of this material comprises *YVP* 4.

24. *Michael Robartes and the Dancer* (Dundrum, Ireland: Cuala Press, 1920), 30.

25. WBY reworked VersB extensively to arrive at Book A; see *CVA*, xxxvii–xxxviii for a detailed summary of the revisions, expansions, and reorganizations.

26. The corrected typescript is reproduced in Hobby, 165–69; see 26 July 1923 below.

27. Letter of 13 March 1923, Special Collections and Archives, Robert W. Woodruff Library, Emory University, Atlanta, Georgia.

28. Unpublished letter, Special Collections and Archives, Robert W. Woodruff Library, Emory University, Atlanta, Georgia.

29. John Kelly, *A W. B. Yeats Chronology* (Basingstoke, UK: Palgrave Macmillan, 2003), 230.

30. Unpublished letter, Special Collections and Archives, Robert W. Woodruff Library, Emory University, Atlanta, Georgia.
31. Ibid.
32. Margherita G. Sarfatti, *The Life of Benito Mussolini*, trans. Frederic Whyte (New York: Frederick A. Stokes, 1925).
33. Donald H. Reiman, *Romantic Texts and Contexts* (Columbia: University of Missouri Press, 1987), 169, 170, quoted in George Bornstein, "Introduction: Why Editing Matters," *Representing Modernist Texts: Editing as Interpretation*, ed. George Bornstein (Ann Arbor: University of Michigan Press, 1991), 6–7.
34. Bornstein, "Introduction: Why Editing Matters," 7.
35. Richard J. Finneran, "On Editing Yeats: The Text of *A Vision* (1937)," *Texas Studies in Literature and Language* 19 (1977): 121–22.
36. For a more detailed treatment of the corrections made in proofs, see Connie Kelly Hood, "A Search for Authority: Prolegomena to a Definitive Critical Edition of W. B. Yeats's *A Vision* (1937)," Ph.D. diss., University of Tennessee, 1983, pp. 108–11.

Dedication and Introduction

1. (fig. 1) Edmund Dulac made the portrait of Giraldus and the designs of the Great Wheel (fig. 4) and the unicorn (fig. 5), printed on brown paper in the original book. The Yeatses decided very early to ascribe the "solar" or Western exposition of the system to this fictional figure. An AS on 12 January answers the question "Two Cycles" with the information "Gyraldus primary / Arab Anti" (*YVP* 1:250). The "Arab" is probably Kusta ben Luka; see Dedication and Introduction n. 52 below. Giraldus has several possible historical antecedents, including Giraldus Cambrensis (Gerald de Barry), a twelfth-century Cambro-Norman historian who wrote about Ireland; Gerard of Cremona (1114–87), a translator from Arabic into Latin and a scholar of Arabic science; and Lilio Gregorio Giraldi of Ferrara (1479–1552), a Latin poet, philosopher, and scholar, who was a friend of Pico della Mirandola and other prominent humanists (see Kathleen Raine, *Yeats the Initiate* [Mountrath, Ireland: Dolmen Press; London: George Allen & Unwin, 1986], 408–30).

   Soon after the script began (see introduction), WBY also asked Dulac to produce a portrait of the semifictitious author and a diagram for the cover of the dialogues. WBY admired Dulac's illustrations for *Sinbad the Sailor and Other Stories from the Arabian Nights* (ed. Laurence Houseman [London: Hodder and Stoughton, 1907]); their Oriental exoticism may have contributed to WBY's sense that Dulac would be the best designer for a portrait of someone mysteriously connected with Eastern wisdom (Hobby, 77, 80). In a letter dated 15 February 1918, Dulac sent WBY a sketch of Giraldus, asking if Giraldus Cambrensis were the model (*LWBY*, 344). WBY replied in the

negative. WBY received a sketch of Giraldus that he thought "a masterpiece" in February 1918 (Hobby, 109) and asked Dulac to produce the
"planisphere" (the Great Wheel) in March 1921 (Hobby, 153). Dulac
did not complete the work immediately, but on 24 July 1923 he wrote
saying that he had "done a sketch in pencil of the portrait of Gyraldus
by an unknown artist of the early sixteenth century" (*LWBY,* 439).
WBY wrote Dulac on 26 July without specific information about a historical placement for Giraldus: "The date is nothing, if you want early
sixteenth century let it be 1524 or any date you please. I have not
thought of any particular divine. He would certainly be an astrologer
and a mathematician and that is about all I know" (Hobby, 157).
Dulac sent a sketch of the Giraldus portrait on 30 September 1923,
saying, "Here is the best I can do with Gyraldus. It is a little 'early' in
style, but I think it better suited to a book of that kind than the 'Durer'
manner. One can argue that Mr Gyraldus did not go to a first class
artist as otherwise the book would be known" (*LWBY,* 439).

In correspondence, Frank Pearce Sturm pointed out to WBY that
the proper grammatical form for this caption should have read "Speculum Angelorum et Hominum." WBY wondered if he could get away
with the erroneous form as "dog Latin," but Sturm said no: "you
can't pretend Giraldus wrote dog Latin, for he was the most learned of
the 12th century translators from the Arabic." He did suggest that
WBY could change the erroneous *homenorum* to *homunculorum* or
homullorum, thereby suggesting a "manikin," "the artificial men that
the alchemists of [Giraldus's] day were forever trying to concoct in their
stew-pans. Of course the proper title: *Speculum Angelorum et
Hominum* is the more dignified" (3? February 1926, *FPS,* 94). Note
that in Owen Aherne's introduction, the title is given as "Speculum
Angelorum et Hominorum" (see p. lxi).

2. (fig. 2) In galley proofs (NLI, 36,271), the title read: ". . . Giraldus and
also Certain Doctrines . . ." This subtitle, together with Owen Aherne's
introduction and the Dulac woodcuts, promoted the deception that this
book was based on the sixteenth-century book found by Michael
Robartes (see Dedication and Introduction, n. 31 below).

Thomas Werner Laurie (1864–1944), whose independent publishing house was founded in 1904, published an eclectic list of literary,
spiritualist and psychic, travel, antiquarian, erotic, and general trade
books, including works by George Moore, Upton Sinclair, and Edgar
Lee Masters, as well as Robert Sherard's biography of Oscar Wilde and
the memoirs of the medium Hester Travers Smith. Laurie published
WBY's *The Trembling of the Veil* in 1922 as well as *A Vision* in 1926.
At his death, the firm was bought by Clarence Hatry; in 1957, it was
sold to Max Reinhardt, who, with the merchant banking firm Ans-
bacher & Co., had also successfully purchased the Bodley Head, the
press of Elkin Mathews and John Lane which published the Rhymers

Club volumes as well as James Joyce's *Ulysses* and Gertrude Stein's *The Autobiography of Alice B. Toklas*. Laurie's daughter Joan Werner Laurie (1920–64), a book and magazine editor, was also the life partner of journalist, author, and radio and television personality Nancy Brooker Spain (1917–64).

3. (fig. 3) "The Phases of the Moon" was first published in *The Wild Swans at Coole* (1919), and then in *Later Poems* (Macmillan, 1922).

4. The dedication refers to Mina (later Moina) Bergson Mathers (1865–1928), sister of Henri Bergson and widow of Samuel Liddell (MacGregor) Mathers, founding Chief of the Golden Dawn (see Book IV, n. 106). She was known as Vestigia or Vesty, for *Vestigia Nulla Retrorsum*, "No traces behind," her motto in the Golden Dawn. For a biographical sketch, see Mary K. Greer, *Women of the Golden Dawn: Rebels and Priestesses* (Rochester, VT: Park Street Press, 1995). Note parallels to "All Souls' Night" (intended as the epilogue). WBY also kept a rejected prose version of an epilogue addressed "To Vestigia."

5. These are approximate numbers. Although we do not know the precise date of the dedication's first draft, thirty years had not elapsed since he had last seen Moina in Paris. (He stayed with the Matherses in April 1898.) A letter from her dated 5 January 1924 suggests that he had talked with her since her return to London (see *LWBY*, 446–48).

6. S. L. MacGregor Mathers explains "The Schemahamphorasch or Divided Name," basic study material in the Golden Dawn, in *The Kabbalah Unveiled* ([London: George Redway, 1887], 170–71; O'Shea 1292, 1293), a book that both WBY and GY knew well. Each verse of Exodus 14:19–21 has seventy-two Hebrew characters. Placing the three verses one above another in Hebrew and reading downward produces seventy-two columns of three letters, each expounding the powers of the name Jehovah (the common European rendering of the "sacred tetragrammaton"). This is also related to the seventy-two rungs in Jacob's ladder. One of the three preserved manuscript copies of "The Schemahamphorasch" was copied by GY (NLI, 36,281/3).

7. Florence Farr Emery (1860–1917), known in the Golden Dawn as *Sapientia Sapienti Dono Data*, "Wisdom is given as a gift to the wise," was an English actress and served in the Golden Dawn for a time as Mathers's "Representative in the Second Order in London" (*YGD*, 21). She performed Aleel in the first production of *The Countess Cathleen* (1892) and was involved in WBY's musical experiments with the psaltery in 1902. In 1912 Emery left England to teach in India; in a letter of July 1917, WBY noted her death (*L*, 628).

8. Analytical chemist and student of theosophy Allan Bennett (1872–1923, *Iehi Aour*, "Let there be light") was a member of the Golden Dawn until he moved to Burma (see *L*, 499 and *YGD*, 197), where he became a *bhikku* or Theravaedin monk. He was good friends with the notorious Aleister Crowley.

9. WBY corresponded sporadically from 1896 to 1919 with William Thomas Horton (1864–1919; *Spes Mea Christus*, "Christ is my hope"), a member of the Golden Dawn. Horton's mystical drawings were influenced by William Blake and Aubrey Beardsley. WBY wrote the introduction for Horton's *A Book of Images* (London: The Unicorn Press, 1898; O'Shea 918; Wade, 255) and drew on many of Horton's works.

10. For what few details are known of Amy Audrey Locke (1881–1916), see *L*, 260–63 and *YO*, 190–203.

11. In a very late letter, WBY wrote that "Man can embody the truth but he cannot find it" (Saddlemyer, 559; the word "find" is misquoted as "know" in *L*, 922). The research for *AVA* demonstrates that the Yeatses hoped to find, in the words GY wrote from the control Thomas of Dorlowicz on 14 January 1918, "a philosophy . . . which leads . . . a light which you follow not one which will burn you," since "a philosophy created from experience burns—one which is created from search leads" (*YVP* 1:252).

12. George Mills Harper suggests that this may be West Yorkshire watchmaker and clockmaker Thomas Henry Pattinson, a member of the Theosophical Society, the Golden Dawn (his motto was *Vota Vita Mea*, or "My life is devoted"), and the Societas Rosicruciana in Anglia (*YGD*, 197n80).

13. The Latin term literally means "the highest good." Spiritual alchemists sought "the Stone of the Wise," and the Adepti of the Golden Dawn focused on their quest for the *Summum Bonum* (see *YGD*, 161). In the AS (11 October 1918), WBY asked "What is the sumum bonum?" to which the control Thomas replied, "Subjectifying of personal & spiritual objective or oneness with God" (*YVP* 2:74). WBY then asked what "the personal objective" is, and GY wrote Thomas's answer: "All desire all impulse all individual."

14. WBY wrote that the communicators' change from automatic writing to automatic speaking came on a train in Southern California (*AVB*, 9). One notebook of sleeps suggests that it may actually have occurred "on way to San Francisco" from Portland, Oregon, on 24 March 1920.

15. WBY added this sentence in the galley proofs. *Hodos Chamelionis* is the title by which the Introducing Adept in the Adeptus Minor (5 = 6) Ritual of the Golden Dawn is known, and also the name given to the newly installed Aspirant to the rank. At the climax of the ceremony, the Chief greets the new Adeptus Minor with the words, "And therefore do I greet thee with the Mystic Title of 'Hodos Chamelionis,' the Path of the Chamelion, the Path of Mixed Colours . . ." (Israel Regardie, *The Golden Dawn. A Complete Course in Practical Ceremonial Magic. Four Volumes in One. The Original Account of the Teachings, Rites and Ceremonies of the Hermetic Order of the Golden Dawn [Stella Matutina]*, 6th ed. [Saint Paul, MN: Llewellyn Publications, 1992], 225, 242). WBY uses the phrase as the title of a section of *The Trem-*

bling of the Veil, written as the Yeatses worked on the system: he describes being "lost" in the confused path of the chameleon, "that region a cabbalistic manuscript, shown to me by MacGregor Mathers, had warned me of" (*Au,* 215). The spelling is not standard; family friend and Trinity College don Louis C. Purser informed WBY that "the genitive is chameleontos" if used as a Greek word (*LWBY,* 436), and WBY changed the spelling. Concerning the use of the manual in the Golden Dawn, see *YGD,* 177.

16. See chap. 12, "Qualities and Defects of Dante," in Boccaccio's *Life of Dante,* in Philip Henry Wicksteed, trans., *The Early Lives of Dante* (London: Chatto and Windus, 1907; O'Shea 232). This biography by Giovanni Boccaccio (1313–75), the scholar, poet, and author of *The Decameron,* which presented Florentine poet and writer Dante Alighieri (1265–1321) as a poet of the people rather than a man of classical learning, experienced a surge of popularity in English-speaking countries around the turn of the century, thanks to no less than four new translations which appeared between 1898 and 1904. See also a reference in *Per Amica Silentia Lunae* (*LE,* 7).

17. A purposefully vague reference suggests the AS, generated from over 450 sittings during which the Yeatses, with GY acting as medium or "interpreter," received from spirit communicators some 3,600 pages of script, as well as messages received in trance or "sleep" and recorded in notebooks (see introduction). WBY was informed on more than one occasion to keep the proceedings secret; for example, on 26 August 1918, he was informed that the book he was writing "must be written on another understanding than that under which you have so far spoken"; that is, "that you must acknowledge without indicating the means the supernormal origin of the system" (*YVP* 2:25).

18. References are to Swedish philosopher and mystic Emanuel Swedenborg (1688–1772) and English Romantic poet and visionary painter William Blake (1757–1827). Cf. WBY's note (written in 1924) to "The Friends of the People of Faery": "A countryman near Coole told me of a spirit so ascending. Swedenborg, in his *Spiritual Diary,* speaks of gyres and spirits, and Blake painted Jacob's Ladder as an ascending gyre" (*Myth1,* 123; *Myth2,* 81). Here, as elsewhere, "gyres" are used to mark the rise, development, and fall of civilizations.

19. This poem, which appears as an epilogue to *A Vision,* was first printed in *The New Republic* (9 March 1921) and *The London Mercury* (March 1921) and later as the closing poem of *The Tower* (1928). WBY notes that he composed this poem in autumn 1920, while at Oxford, and during the period in which he and GY were transitioning from automatic writing sessions to other methods such as "sleeps" and discussions (see Dedication and Introduction, nn. 14 and 17 above). On the spirit revelations disclosed during the Yeatses' time at Oxford, see Foster 2:157–62.

20. See *AVB*, 12–20. WBY frequently regretted his lack of a formal education, but his instructors warned him not to read philosophy during the AS and sleeps. See, for example, the injunction, "dont deliberately read—bad—bad," given on 12 January 1918 (*YVP* 1:250).

21. In a letter of 1931 to Olivia Shakespear, WBY similarly commented

> I write very much for young men between twenty and thirty, as at that age, and younger, I wanted to feel that any poet I cared for—Shelley let us say—saw more than he told of, had in some sense seen into the mystery. I read more into certain poems than they contained, to satisfy my interest. The young men I write for may not read my *Vision*—they may care too much for poetry—but they will be pleased that it exists. Even my simplest poems will be the better for it. . . . Apart from these young men—who will only glance at *A Vision*—I shall have a few very devoted readers. . . . (*L*, 781)

22. Later, in the description of Phase 18, a similar remark is attributed to Goethe: 'Man knows himself by action only, by thought never' (p. 66).

23. Indeed, revisions to *A Vision* would continue for a dozen years after this book's publication, and WBY pondered the system in thought and practice for the rest of his life.

24. Barbara J. Frieling has noted that the "Beatific Vision" is one of four "Moments of Crisis" that appear in the AS of 20 March–5 April 1919 and after (" 'Moments of Crisis' in the *Vision* Papers," *YAACTS* 10 (1992): 281–95). See *YVP* 2:200–235, 518–19; 3:1–142, 272–76; *MYV* 2:228–46. The Moments are part of the "personal" aspects of the system, which George Mills Harper estimates comprise about seventy-five percent of the script. They are "often intimate, and could not be used in the book" (*MYV* 1:x).

    WBY intended a more extended treatment of the Beatific Vision, which together with Initiatory Moments, Critical Moments, and undefined "OMs" represent sudden flashes of defining intensity within each human life. One card in the CF explains: "Solar Vision followed by Lunar V. brings B.V. Solar—15, lunar—one, B.V. apex (center)" (*YVP* 3:245; see also *YVP* 3:246). The Solar represents understanding of the Head; the Lunar, of the Heart; the Beatific, the Soul. See the brief mention on p. 140 and the discussion of the Beatitude on pp. 193–94.

25. About "The Phases of the Moon" and two other poems, WBY wrote in 1922: "To some extent I wrote these poems as a text for exposition" (*Poems*, 604).

26. WBY said of *The Player Queen* (1922): "I wasted the best working months of several years in an attempt to write a poetical play where

every character became an example of the finding or not finding of what I have called the Antithetical Self" (Plays, 698).

27. For WBY's reading of this edition, see S. B. Bushrui, "Yeats's Arabic Interests," in A. Norman Jeffares and K. G. W. Cross, eds., In Excited Reverie: A Centenary Tribute to William Butler Yeats (London: Macmillan, 1965), 291–92. As with several other foreign-language books, WBY evidently found the language of this particular edition exciting. See also Book III, n. 90.

28. Both Augustus and Tiberius built villas—the Villa Augustus and the Villa Jovis, respectively—on the Italian island of Capri, remains of which are still extant. The Yeatses went to Capri in January–February 1925 while traveling in Italy with Ezra and Dorothy Pound (Foster 2:279).

29. The quotation, if not the idea, seems to be WBY's own. See a passage from the VersB manuscript in explication of phase 25: "I gave up my desire to understand suppersentual reality, now I must give up my desire to possess it. I must be nothing—an insect in the roots of the grass" (YVP 4:233). The phrase also occurs in ms. in a first draft of what later became the two poems "At Algeciras—a Meditation upon Death" and "Mohini Chatterjee" (Poems, 250, 251–52); see David R. Clark, ed., Words for Music Perhaps and Other Poems: Manuscript Materials (Ithaca and London: Cornell University Press, 1999), 215, lines 18–19. It appears again in the introduction to the Vision-related play The Resurrection: "Perhaps we shall learn to accept even innumerable lives with happy humility—'I have been always an insect in the roots of the grass'—and putting aside calculating scruples be ever ready to wager all upon the dice" (Plays, 725). David S. Thatcher (Nietzsche in England, 1890–1914: The Growth of a Reputation [Toronto: University of Toronto Press, 1970], 172) suggests that these remarks evoke the eternal return in Also sprach Zarathustra (see also p. 142).

30. WBY wrote or reworked many sections of A Vision during his 1925 trip to Italy with the Pounds. The Yeatses spent time in southern Italy in January and February 1925, visiting Sicily with Ezra and Dorothy Pound, continuing on to Naples, Capri, and Rome. For details of their itinerary, see Russell Elliott Murphy, " 'Old Rocky Face, look forth': W. B. Yeats, the Christ Pantokrator, and the Soul's History (The Photographic Record)," YAACTS 14 (1996): 69–117.

31. WBY invented the characters of Owen Aherne (sometimes called John Ahern, who was also, variably, Owen's brother) and Michael Robartes for the stories "Rosa Alchemica" (1896), "The Tables of the Law" (1896), and "The Adoration of the Magi" (1897); Robartes, a Rosicrucian magician, was used also at one point as a named speaker for three poems in The Wind among the Reeds (1899), although in the notes to the volume, WBY identified the speakers "more as principles of mind than as actual personages. It is probable that only students of the magical tradition will understand me when I say that 'Michael

Robartes' is fire reflected in water . . . [or] the pride of the imagination brooding upon the greatness of its possessions, or the adoration of the Magi" (*VP*, 803). The characters were resurrected for several poems in the volume *The Wild Swans at Coole* (1919) and poems and notes to the volume *Michael Robartes and the Dancer* (1921).

In part at least, Aherne was modeled on Lionel Johnson (1867–1902). Sources for Michael Robartes include MacGregor Mathers (see the sketch of him in *Au*, 159–63), possibly George Russell (or Æ 1865–1935), and perhaps also Captain Roberts, a Dublin black magician. For discussion of the characters Robartes and Aherne, see Michael J. Sidnell, "Mr Yeats, Michael Robartes and Their Circle" (*YO*, 225–54); concerning other possible sources for Aherne, see Warwick Gould, " 'Lionel Johnson Comes the First to Mind': Sources for Owen Aherne" (*YO*, 255–84), and *Myth2*, 399–400n1. For background on Robartes, see also *Myth2*, 367–68n1.

On 26 July 1923, WBY sent Dulac "my preface, in the rough, or rather Owen Aherne's. It will give you all the facts as I see them" (Hobby, 157).

32. London's National Gallery, on Trafalgar Square, was established in 1824 and houses the British national collection of Western painting. From the beginning, access to the gallery was free of charge, and the site was chosen to provide easy access to poor East Enders on foot and to more affluent West Londoners by carriage.

33. See Dedication and Introduction, n. 31 above.

34. The Pre-Raphaelite Brotherhood was founded in 1848 by the painters William Holman Hunt, Sir John Everett Millais, and Dante Gabriel Rossetti. They rejected academicism, which they perceived to have descended from the Bolognese followers of Raphael, and returned to nature for their inspiration, also using the Bible, Shakespeare, and Keats for their sources. Such artists as William Morris, Arthur Hughes, and Sir Edward Burne-Jones were later associated with the movement. WBY was much influenced by the Pre-Raphaelites (see Elizabeth Bergmann Loizeaux, *Yeats and the Visual Arts* [New Brunswick and London: Rutgers University Press, 1986], 5–33).

35. This three-painting series, painted from about 1490–1500 by the Master of the Story of Griselda, narrates the final story of Boccaccio's *Decameron,* in which a marquis marries a peasant woman (Griselda), torments her, and, finding she endures it all with patience, loves her all the more. The story also appears in "The Clerk's Tale" in Chaucer's *Canterbury Tales.* The painting was acquired by the National Gallery in 1874.

36. Robartes and Aherne appear as prominent characters in three early stories—"Rosa Alchemica" (1896), "The Tables of the Law" (1896), and "The Adoration of the Magi" (1897). Here WBY refers only to the first story, which appeared in *The Savoy* in April 1896 and then in *The*

Secret Rose (1897) (Wade, 21). See *Myth*2, 367, and *The Secret Rose, Stories by W. B. Yeats: A Variorum Edition*, edited by Warwick Gould, Phillip L. Marcus, and Michael J. Sidnell, 2nd ed. (London: Macmillan, 1992), xv–xix, 126–50.

37. (fig. 4) Like the portrait of Giraldus and the image of the unicorn, this illustration was made by Edmund Dulac. On 5 May 1925, WBY wrote to Dulac, "The designs are exactly right. 'The Wheel' would take in the whole British Museum" (Hobby, 174). In the original publication, it is printed on brown paper and page-sized, positioned opposite the opening of the Introduction.

38. John M. Watkins (1862–1947) edited *Book-notes* (March 1893–February 1897), published the writings of the Theosophical Society, and was a seller of new and used occult books. He moved his bookselling business from Charing Cross to the shop at No. 21 Cecil Court in 1901. His son Geoffrey N. Watkins notes that his store was a center for "tea, talk, and theosophy" ("Yeats and Mr Watkins' Bookshop," *YO*, 307–10).

39. "Rosa Alchemica" ends with an explanation of the "tragic end" of Michael Robartes. The narrator, an urban aesthete, has been taken to a magical initiation by Robartes. He wakes after a night of transformative ecstasy in the Temple of the Alchemical Rose, an ancient-seeming house on a pier somewhere in the rural west of Ireland. He is unable to wake Robartes from a deep sleep or trance before he must flee from an angry mob of local fishermen and women who have gathered to expel the heretical sect of outsiders from their village. Robartes is left to the violent crowd. In notes to the poems "The Phases of the Moon," "The Double Vision of Michael Robartes," and "Michael Robartes and the Dancer," WBY explains the fiction beyond a fiction he develops for *A Vision*, derived from his choice to revive the characters of Robartes and Aherne from the story "Rosa Alchemica":

> Years ago I wrote three stories in which occur the names of Michael Robartes and Owen Aherne. I now consider that I used the actual names of two friends, and that one of these friends, Michael Robartes, has but lately returned from Mesopotamia, where he has partly found and partly thought out much philosophy. I consider that Aherne and Robartes, men to whose namesakes I had attributed a turbulent life or death, have quarrelled with me. They take their place in a phantasmagoria in which I endeavour to explain my philosophy of life and death. (*Poems*, 604)

40. The Golden Dawn studied works of these alchemists and spiritualists, who made trips to Poland in 1583–85. WBY seems to have known English alchemist and geographer Dr. John Dee's (1527–1608) published diary (see *FPS*, 98). Edward Kelly (or Kelley), assistant to Dee, claimed

to speak to angels using Dee's scrying stone. Alchemy was an early pro-toscientific practice combining metallurgy, chemistry, mysticism, art, symbology, physics, and medicine in an attempt to learn how to turn any metal into gold, find a panacea to cure all diseases and grant immortality, and create human life. Scrying is clairvoyance using a reflec-tive medium, such as water, a crystal ball, a mirror, or polished stones.

41. The story of the discovery of this book is part of the deception that the material presented in *A Vision* derives from these old sources.

42. This imaginary volume's title may be translated as "Mirror of Angels and Men." Grammatically, *hominorum* should be *hominum,* as F. P. Sturm pointed out to WBY (*FPS,* 93–94); see Dedication and Introduc-tion, n. 1 above. In the earliest versions, WBY used *hominis.* As the title is noted under the frontispiece (see p. l), it is written "Speculum Angelorum et Homenorum."

43. See Dedication and Introduction, n. 1 above.

44. Cracow was a center of printing in the early sixteenth century rather than the seventeenth. Concerning the date, see Dedication and Intro-duction, n. 1 above. WBY wrote to Dulac on 14 October, "your Kra-cow artist would not have drawn them very carefully. I can give the *speculum* what date you please" (*L,* 700). The irrelevance of the date signifies; Cracow may have been chosen because Dee and Kelly (see Dedication and Introduction, n. 40 above) had traveled there in 1584 and again in 1585, because it was the city where Hannibal Rosselius's six-volume commentary on the *Divinus Pymander Hermetis Mercurii Trismegisti* was published (1585–90), or because of the connection that the alchemist Michael Sendivogius (1566–1636) had with the city.

45. The CF contains a list of "Symbols of Phases" for all twenty-eight phases except 12 and 25. Several suggest the three "curious allegorical pictures": "(3) Eagle over sea with one foot caught in back of sea lion one foot caught by Dolphin. Eagle drags both"; "(9) leopard. Eagle on head plucking out eyes"; "(15) man with arrow & stone one in each hand"; "(26) Hunch back fighting his shadow on ground which bleeds" (*YVP* 3:400–401). In the DMR-TS, Robartes notes that the *Speculum* "was indeed full of curious allegorical woodcuts, astronom-ical diagrams, where drawings of Noah's Ark and the Tables of the Law were mixed up with Zodiacal signs and phases of the moon and geometrical diagrams where cones containing gyres sprang out of each other like strange vegetables" (*YVP* 4:16). The unicorn was one of the most important symbols used in the Golden Dawn. Upon passing the examination, the Aspirant took the symbolic title of *Monoceros de Astris,* translated by Father John as "the unicorn from the stars" in WBY's play by that title (*Plays,* 208). WBY told his sister Lolly in 1920 that "it is a private symbol belonging to my mystical order. . . . It is the soul" (*L,* 662). In the AS (31 May 1919), the control Thomas (recently renamed Eurectha because of a "new state") revealed that the unicorn

was also the daimon. When WBY asked if he could "apply symbol of Unicorn to New Avatar," the control said "*NO*" (*YVP* 2:294–95). This reference to the New Avatar suggests the use of the symbol in connection with the New Adam in *The Player Queen*. The play was begun in 1910 but dropped; WBY worked on it again beginning in 1915 and continued while the script arrived. The play was staged in 1919 and published, after more revision, in 1922. The unicorn is a prominent symbol in the play, signifying, as the character Septimus announces, "the end of the Christian Era, the coming of a New Dispensation, that of the New Adam, that of the Unicorn" (*Plays*, 358). In the autumn of 1920, the unicorn was discussed in sleeps on the topic of groups; GY wrote, "asked leave to alter terminology. 'COVEN' for group 'UNICORN' for group mind" (*YVP* 3:57), but the next day, WBY wrote that the term "Dragon" would be used for group mind, and "Unicorn to be kept for Daimon" (*YVP* 3:58). See also Book II, nn. 131, 132; Book IV, n. 31. For the woman with stone and arrow, see *Au*, 486.

46. WBY describes the woodcut of the Great Wheel as containing "an apple, an acorn, a cup, and what looked like a sceptre or wand" (*AVB*, 38). These four symbols correspond generally to the tarot suits of cups, wands, swords, and pentacles. The woodcut actually includes only three of these symbolic objects, at points on the wheel corresponding to Pulchritudo (beauty), Sapientia (wisdom), Temptatio (temptation), and Violentia (violence), substituting a flower (perhaps a rose) for the apple or the acorn (the image is ambiguous). In the AS (24 September 1918), three visions of the coming avatar are "The arrow / The flower / The cup" (*YVP* 2:70).

47. The plot may follow Joseph Glanvill's story from *The Vanity of Dogmatizing* (1661) of the wandering gypsy, made famous by Matthew Arnold's poem "The Scholar-Gypsy." WBY quotes Glanvill's account in his essay "Magic" (*EE*, 32).

48. The Church of the Holy Sepulchre, within the old walled city of Jerusalem, is built on ground venerated by Christians as Golgotha, the hill of Calvary, where Jesus is said to have been crucified. It is also said to contain the place where Jesus was buried. Damascus, capital of Syria, is the oldest continuously inhabited city in the world. Mecca, site of the Ka'bah (believed by Muslims to have been built by Abraham and Isaac) and birthplace of the Prophet Muhammad, is considered the holiest city in Islam.

49. Called Bacleones in an early manuscript (*YVP* 4:122), this fictitious group may get its name (which, WBY explains, means "makers of measures, or as we would say, of diagrams" [*VP*, 825]) from Sir Edward Denison Ross (1871–1940), a great Orientalist. Ross may have invented the slightly incorrect Arabic term when WBY approached him for help with the "fable"; see Bushrui in *In Excited Reverie*, 295–99.

50. WBY wrote to Lady Gregory (2 June 1900) that George Russell "and

I are the opposite of one another. I think I understand people easily and easily sympathize with all kinds of characters and easily forgive all kinds of defects and vices. I have the defect of this quality. Apart from opinions, which I judge too sternly, I scarcely judge people at all and am altogether too lax in my attitude towards conduct" (*L, 345*). See also *Au, 320.*

51. This fictitious title derives from two books given to WBY by friends: W. T. Horton's *The Way of the Soul, a Legend in Line and Verse* (London: William Rider, [1910]; O'Shea 920) and Cecil French's *Between Sun and Moon: Poems and Wood-Cuts* (London: The Favil Press, 1922; O'Shea 712), dedicated to WBY (see *LWBY*, 424). WBY probably also knew that Tennyson sometimes called *In Memoriam* "The Way of the Soul." Robartes notes that he "went to Damascus to speak with a student of 'The Way of the Soul.' " This title was changed in the DMR-TS to "The way of souls between the moons and the suns," following a blank where WBY wanted to insert an Arabic translation (*YVP* 4:17), apparently supplied by Sir Edward Denison Ross, director of the School of Oriental Languages at the University of London: "I have got the title in Arabic," WBY noted, "but cannot find it for the moment" (*MYV* 2:82). As the DMR-MS (*YVP* 4:70) and VersB (*YVP* 4:143) are presented in *YVP*, the Arabic text (probably طريقة النُفوس بينَ القَمَر والشُموس) has been transliterated TARĪQAT UN-NUFŪS BAYN AL-QUMÚR WA'L SHUMUS, a closer translation of which would be "the way of souls between the moon and the suns."

52. Under the reign of the Abbasid caliph Harūn al-Rashid (هارون الرّشيد , ca. 763–809 CE), the fifth and most famous Abbasid caliph, Baghdad became the world's preeminent center of trade, learning, and culture. WBY might have discovered Harūn in *The Arabian Nights* (see page lvi), where his reign and fabulous court are immortalized, and in Gibbon. WBY owned two separate editions of the *Arabian Nights* (O'Shea 251 and 676). Kusta ben Luka (قُسطا إبن لوقا , Qusṭā ibn Luqā, 820–912 CE) was a doctor and translator of Greek and Syrian texts into Arabic; WBY may have encountered him in Robert Burton's *Anatomy of Melancholy.*

   Although he did not note that it would have been chronologically impossible for these men even to meet, Frank Pearce Sturm did point out to WBY, in a letter of 11 October 1924, the difficulty of these characters' dates:

> Fifty seven years after the death of Harun-al-Rashid the *Mechanica* of Hero of Alexandria was translated into Arabic by Costa ibn Luca, whom you call Kusta ben Luka. He therefore could not have been an old man when the Caliph made him a present of the sleep-walking girl, unless he lived to a very great age indeed. I know you hate pedantry, & so do I, but if 'A Vision' is

to be founded on supposedly existing *MS*, the dates will have to be right. The Caliph died in 809. Kusta was still hard at work with his pen in 866. (*FPS*, 83)

53. In pre-Islamic Arabian mythology, djinn (or jin, جن) a race of spirits of vanished ancient peoples who acted during the night and disappeared with the first light of dawn; they could make themselves invisible or change shape into animals at will. In sorcery books, djinn are classified into four races after the classical elements, Earth, Air, Fire, and Water. Bushrui (in *In Excited Reverie*, 305–6) relates the djinns to WBY's daimons, much discussed in the AS.

54. WBY kept a residence at No. 18 Woburn Buildings, London, from March 1896 until December 1917.

55. In the DMR-TS, Robartes and Aherne decided not to come in because of the probable presence of American poet Ezra Pound (1885–1972), "a very violent talker" who had been rude to Aherne (*YVP* 4:17).

56. "The Tables of the Law" was first published in *The Savoy* 7 (November 1896), [79]–87, and then in *The Tables of the Law. The Adoration of the Magi* (London: private printing, 1897; Wade, 24). It was republished many times with significant revisions; the full publication history is traced in *Myth2*, 399. Owen Aherne's dwelling on Dominick Street, near Four Courts, is described in *Myth1*, 304f., *Myth2*, 198f.; see also *Myth2*, 402n9.

57. WBY bought this Norman tower near Gort in 1916. The Yeatses lived from May to September 1918 in Ballinamantane, a cottage on Lady Gregory's Coole Park estate, during the restoration of Ballylee, where they lived for less than a week in September, returning June to September 1919, and then not again until April 1922. "Thoor" (*túr*), which WBY liked to include in the designation, is the Irish word for tower.

58. "The Phases of the Moon" (1918; see pp. 3–9), was written at Ballinamantane in the early summer of 1918; WBY wrote to Pound on 6 June about two "philosophical poems" he had finished ("The Phases of the Moon" and "The Double Vision of Michael Robartes"); see Foster 2:126. There is imagery resonant with that of the poem in an AS of 25 November 1917 (*YVP* 1:120). See also *MYV* 2:19, 420n11, 421n19.

59. There is no orthodox support for the remarks about either Clement of Alexandria (not actually a saint) or Archbishop Passavalli; WBY may have relied on a biased occultist article. Clement of Alexandria (Titus Flavius Clemens, b. mid-second century, d. 211–16), was one of the most distinguished teachers of the Church of Alexandria. He is well known for his trilogy of writings, the *Protrepticus* (Exhortation), the *Paedagogus* (Instructor), and the *Stromata* (Miscellanies). Long venerated as a saint, he was struck from the calendar by Pope Clement VIII in the sixteenth century. In identifying Clement of Alexandria as a saint, WBY may have confused him with Saint Clement I of Rome, either the

third or fourth pope, considered one of the Apostolic Fathers. The Italian Capuchin Luigi Puecher Passavalli gave the opening sermon for the Vatican Council of 1869. A mitre is a traditional ceremonial headdress of bishops in the Roman Catholic Church, and the right to wear the mitre is, by the canon law of the Roman Catholic Church, confined to the pope, cardinals, and bishops—though by papal privilege it may be worn by others such as abbots. In the DMR-TS, Aherne notes that a church council found metempsychosis heretical; "however," he adds, "Leo XII gave me exemption from the Index and I make a distinction between what I investigate as philosopher and what I believe as Christian" (*YVP* 4:20). WBY confused his popes: Leo XII was pope from 1823 to 1829 and Leo XIII, from 1878 to 1903.

60. Both terms refer to possible destinations for souls after death. In Roman Catholic theology, limbo describes the temporary status of the souls of good persons who died before the resurrection of Jesus, and the permanent status of the unbaptised who die in infancy (without having committed any personal sins, but without having been freed from original sin). As a hypothesis, limbo waned in popularity during the latter half of the twentieth century, and in 2005 an international theological commission recommended to Pope Benedict XVI that the concept be set aside. Purgatory is a process of purification after judgment and before entry into paradise, an intermediate step for those who have died after repenting of their sins but not expiating them.

61. These words are central to *AVA*, suggesting the feeling appropriate for a new influx. The AS of 2 August 1919 has several questions concerned with terror, glossed as "the other serenity of isolation" and related to the masculine form of phase 15. Asked "What causes the terror," the control Ameritus responds, "Isolation before serenity is achieved." At the end of the session, WBY notes "I find it hard to distinguish between terror & terror caused by terror" (*YVP* 2:353–54). On 26 April 1919, when WBY asked the control Thomas why the AS had to be "joyous"—i.e., "an affirmation of life"—Thomas replied, "because this script has its origin in human life—all religious systems have their origin in God & descend to man—this ascends" (*YVP* 2:269). See also *LE*, 231, about the use of "terror" in *A Vision*; WBY's comment to Edith Shackleton Heald in 1937 that poet Charles Williams was the first reviewer of *A Vision* to see "the greatness and terror of the diagram" (*L*, 901); WBY's treatment of the terror in Edith Sitwell's poetry in "Modern Poetry: A Broadcast" (*LE*, 96); and cf. the "terrible beauty" of "Easter, 1916" (*Poems*, 182–84).

62. Originally a Greek name adapted from Old Persian and meaning "the land between the two rivers," this region of Southwest Asia is, strictly speaking, the alluvial plain between the Tigris and Euphrates rivers, in modern Iraq and Syria. More commonly, the term includes these river plains as well as the surrounding lowland territories. Mesopotamia was

settled by, and conquered by, numerous ancient civilizations. Cultures in this region were among the first to engage in agriculture, and the earliest written works in the world originate here, giving it its reputation as the "cradle of civilization."

63. On 11 November 1918, Germany formally capitulated to the Allied forces, ending World War I. In several of the drafted Robartes-Aherne dialogues, Robartes is presented as caring little about the war: he comments that "It is a mistake to attribute a high degree of reality to the great War. . . . I am here because many brave Turks and Englishmen disturbed the desert by letting off their cannon, but I do not think that I have thereby been disturbed by serious life. The world is at present yawning and stretching itself, its mouth is very wide open and it [is] making a very boorish sound" (*YVP* 4:18).

64. WBY probably intended this passage to contain mystification appropriate to Aherne, but see Sections VII ("The Gyres and Lunar Months of the Great Year") and VIII ('The Cones of the Lunar and Solar Year") of "The Geometrical Foundation of the Wheel" (pp. 114–20).

65. On the symbol of the egg, see Giorgio Melchiori, *The Whole Mystery of Art: Pattern into Poetry in the Work of W. B. Yeats* (London: Routledge and Kegan Paul, 1960), 164–99; on the symbol in WBY and Blake, see Raine, *Yeats the Initiate*, 111–48. See also Section XXIII ("The Cones— Higher Dimensions") of "The Geometrical Foundation of the Wheel": "We can only imagine a perpetual turning in and out of that sphere, hence the sentence quoted by Aherne about the great eggs which turn inside out without breaking the shell" (p. 142). In "Discoveries" (1906), WBY wrote: "We must find some place upon the Tree of Life for the Phœnix nest, for the passion that is exaltation and the negation of the will, for the wings that are always upon fire, set high that the forked branches may keep it safe, yet low enough to be out of the little wind-tossed boughs, the quivering of the twigs" (*EE*, 199). Derived from Egyptian mythology, the phoenix is a traditional Christian and Romantic symbol of rebirth, as in Carlyle's *Sartor Resartus,* bk. 3, chap. 5.

66. Although the introduction was written much earlier than this date, the book itself was finished in early 1925 and sent to Laurie at the end of April. A letter from GY to Laurie dated 14 April 1925 informs him that " 'A Vision' is finished but there is a week's work to be done on the typescript" and that she hopes "to be able to send it to you, through Mr Watt, in ten days time" (Special Collections and Archives, Robert W. Woodruff Library, Emory University, Atlanta, Georgia). See also Foster 2:293.

Book I: What the Caliph Partly Learned

1. Elsewhere called "The Phases of the Moon," this poem was first printed in *The Wild Swans at Coole* (1919). About the relationship

between the writing of this poem and the AS, see *MYV* 2:19, 2:420n11, 2:421n19. See also Owen Aherne's reference to it on p. lxii of his introduction. In the summer of 1918, WBY sent this poem and "The Double Vision of Michael Robartes" to Ezra Pound for publication in *The Little Review*; Ann Saddlemyer notes that Pound wrote to John Quinn of these poems that WBY had gone "queer in his head about 'moon' " (Saddlemyer, 178). In *Later Poems* (1922), and then in *The Collected Poems* (1933), WBY attached a note about this poem and two others from *A Vision*: see Dedication and Introduction, n. 39.

2. Connemara is a region in the west of Ireland (County Galway), known for its rugged yet beautiful landscape of mountains, rivers, and bogs. Historically, it was a very poor part of Ireland and many of its inhabitants suffered terribly during the famine. Until today, it has remained a rural area and contains the largest of the Gaeltacht (or Irish-speaking) regions.

3. The setting of the poem is Ballylee.

4. "Milton's platonist" refers to the title character of John Milton's *Il Penseroso* (1632). This passage refers to lines 85–92:

> Or let my Lamp at midnight hour,
> Be seen in some high lonely T'wer,
> Where I may oft outwatch the *Bear*,
> With thrice great *Hermes*, or unsphere
> The spirit of *Plato* to unfold
> What Worlds, or what vast Regions hold
> The immortal mind that hath forsook
> Her mansion in this fleshly nook. . . . (Milton, 74)

5. The "visionary prince" is the title character of Percy Bysshe Shelley's "Prince Athanase" (1817). In lines 187–90 of that poem, Shelley echoes the lines from Milton above:

> The Balearic fisher, driven from shore,
> Hanging upon the peaked wave afar
> Then saw their lamp from Laian's turret gleam,
> Piercing the stormy darkness, like a star. . . . (Shelley, 163)

6. English printmaker and landscape painter Samuel Palmer (1805–81) was known especially for works produced in Kent and inspired by the style of Blake. WBY refers here to the engraving entitled *The Lonely Tower* illustrating *Il Penseroso* in *The Shorter Poems of John Milton* (London: Seeley, 1889).

7. English essayist and critic Walter Pater (1839–94) was known for the richness and depth of his language, and for such works as *The Renaissance* (1873), a collection of essays about Renaissance humanists and

artists. His *Marius the Epicurean* (1885) displays Pater's ideal of the aesthetic life, his cult of beauty as opposed to bare asceticism, and his theory of the pursuit of beauty as an ideal of its own. WBY owned a copy as printed in two volumes (London: Macmillan, 1902); O'Shea 1537.

8. Robartes's death is alluded to in "The Adoration of the Magi" (*Myth1*, 308–15; *Myth2*, 201–5).

9. This phrase, which is slightly misquoted, is from the second edition of John Milton's *The Doctrine and Discipline of Divorce* (London, 1644; see Milton, 696–715). WBY also used it in his essay "J. M. Synge and the Ireland of his Time," published in *The Cutting of an Agate* (1912; *EE*, 226–47). Wayne Chapman notes that "mine author" is Plato ("The Miltonic Crux of 'The Phases of the Moon,'" *YA* 8 [1991]: 65–66).

10. The phrase is enumerated in the chapter entitled "The Twenty-Eight Embodiments" (pp. 34–94). "The full" refers to phase 15; "the moon's dark" is phase 1; "all the crescents" include phases 2–8, 8–14, 16–22, and 22–27; "but six-and-twenty" indicates that phase 1 and phase 15 are not phases of human life; "the first crescent to the half" embraces phases 2–8; "the moon is rounding" refers to phases 9–14.

11. In *Iliad* 1.197, Athena grabs Achilles by the hair and then urges him to curb his passion rather than battle Agamemnon.

12. After Hector kills Achilles' friend Patroclus, Achilles, overly enraged, kills Hector and desecrates his body, dragging it before the walls of Troy and refusing it funeral rites. See *Iliad* 22.330–405.

13. German philosopher Friedrich Nietzsche (1844–1900) is listed as an example for phase 12 (see p. 52), perhaps because of Nietzsche's idea of the *Übermensch*, which establishes a natural hierarchy of the strong over the weak, or because of his concept of "will to power," a process of expansion and venting of creative energy that he believed was the basic driving force of nature. See Book I, n. 129 below.

14. According to Exodus 19:1–25, Sinai is the mountain where God gave the Ten Commandments to Moses. Whether this place is the same as the modern Jabal Musa on the Sinai Peninsula, is a matter of contention. See also Exodus 34 and 35.

15. Compare DMR-TS: Robartes says that in *Per Amica Silentia Lunae*, WBY "contends that a man of genius works at whatever task—among those not impossible—is hardest to him, for in that way he finds his direct opposite, that which most stirs his desire, and so the greater the opposition the greater the genius." "Yes," says Aherne, "I remember thinking that the one original thing in the book" (*YVP* 4:14). See also *LE*, 8–9.

16. Hugh Kenner has suggested ("A Possible Source in Coleridge for 'The Phases of the Moon,'" *YAACTS* 3 [1985]: 173–74) that WBY may here be remembering a passage in the *Biographia Literaria* (James Engell and Walter Jackson Bate, eds., *The Collected Works of Samuel Taylor Coleridge* 7 [London: Routledge and Kegan Paul; Princeton: Princeton

University Press, 1973], pt. 1, p. 231) where Coleridge translates a passage from Herder's *Briefe, das Studium der Theologie betreffend* (1790):

> With the greatest possible solicitude avoid authorship. Too early or immoderately employed, it makes the head *waste* and the heart empty; even were there no other worse consequences. A person, who reads only to print, in all probability reads amiss; and he, who sends away through the pen and press every thought, the moment it occurs to him, will in a short time have sent all away, and will be a mere journeyman of the printing-office, a *compositor.*

WBY owned a copy of the *Biographia Literaria* (London: George Bell, 1876; O'Shea 401).

17. The reference is to phases 26–28; see pp. 89–93.
18. (fig. 5) Like the portrait of Giraldus and the image of the Great Wheel, this woodcut was made by Edmund Dulac and was printed on brown paper in the original book. Its placement, pasted into the book at this point, remedied a small confusion. As Dulac explained to WBY in a letter of 30 April 1925 accompanying his finished diagram of the Great Wheel,

> When it [the diagram] was done I remembered that in your description of it you mention that the square in the center is occupied by a design of a unicorn. Thence the accompanying design of the Animal in question. If it is not absolutely necessary that the Diagram should incorporate it leave it as it is, but if its presence in the Diagram is of vital importance, the engraver can make the two blocks and fit that of the Unicorn in its proper place for purposes of printing. Otherwise it may be used as a tail piece somewhere else in the book. (*LWBY,* 462)

This same illustration appears on the title page of *Stories of Michael Robartes and his Friends: An Extract from a Record Made by his Pupils: And a Play in Prose* by W. B. Yeats (Dublin: Cuala, 1931).

19. Called in an early typescript "Arabian Account of the Origin of the Great Wheel, or as They Have Named it of the Dance of the Four Royal Persons" (NLI, 36,265/7). Melchiori notes that occult literature often uses the phrase "Royal Persons" in reference to alchemical symbols (*The Whole Mystery of Art* 4). The four quarters of the Great Wheel are reminiscent of other Yeatsian quaternaries (pp. 27–33). The caliph's name was El Mukledir in an early version. WBY seems to have identified his own family with "the King, the Queen, the Prince and the Princess of the Country of Wisdom." In a record of a sleep for 24 March 1920, GY is called the Queen of Cups, WBY the King of

Wands (*YVP* 2:536). Numerous sessions of the AS suggest that the Yeatses will have two children, a daughter and a son, who are connected with the third and fourth daimons. VersB shows a connection with "the four suits of the Tarot" (*YVP* 4:153).

20. See fig. 4.

21. Caliph is the title for the Islamic leader of the *ummah*, or community of Islam. It is an Anglicized/Latinized version of the Arabic word خَلِيفة (khalifa), meaning "successor"—that is, successor to the Prophet Muhammad. In an early version, the caliph is called El Mukledir; perhaps WBY intended him to be Al-Muqtadir, (المُقتَدِر, d. 932), who was Abbasid caliph in Baghdad from 908 to 932. For Harun Al-Raschid, see Dedication and Introduction, n. 52.

22. A vizir (وَزير, sometimes spelled *vizier* or *wazir*) is a Persian term for a high-ranking religious and political adviser, often to a king or sultan. The name literally means "one who bears burdens."

23. This passage is reminiscent of one in *SB* (2:75–76). From an entry dated 4 June 1909 in the Maud Gonne Notebook, it is clear that WBY connected the symbolic dance and the teachings and rituals of the Golden Dawn:

> Felkin told me that he had seen a Dervish dance a horoscope. He went round & round on the sand bar & then circled to center. He whirled round at the planets making round holes in the sand by doing so. He then danced the connecting lines between planets & fell into a trance. This is what I saw in a dream or vision years ago.

Dr. Robert Felkin was Chief of the Stella Matutina, a branch of the Golden Dawn succeeding the unitary Order and founded after the disintegration of the Golden Dawn in the crisis years of 1900 to 1903. For further treatment of the dance, see *YGD*, 118, and also Frank Kermode, *Romantic Image* (London: Routledge and Kegan Paul, 1957), 49–91.

24. This line almost matches line 824 of WBY's play *The King's Threshold* (*Plays*, 148). At one point, WBY added the following note, signed by Owen Aherne, to a rejected version of "The Dance": "According to the Robartes MSS the Dance of the Four Royal Persons is one of the names for the first figure drawn by the Judwaylis elders for the instruction of youth. It is, it seems, identical with 'The Great Wheel' of Gyraldus" (fig. 4).

25. Mentioned on pp. 202–4; see Book IV, n. 84.

26. This poem (written 1923, published January 1924) appears at the beginning of Book II (pp. 97–102) and offers a thinly disguised biographical parallel to WBY's own marriage to GY: Harun Al-Raschid gives Kusta ben Luka a bride who unexpectedly speaks and writes words of otherworldly wisdom while asleep, shortly after their wedding.

27. It seems that the grammarian is of WBY's own invention, intended to characterize the pedantic and literal Aherne.

28. This date may not point to a date of composition, but it does further the fiction that Aherne wrote the essay after WBY's book manuscript was finished, so that Aherne can make reference to and pass judgment upon it.

29. The Yeatses preserved a copy of a sheet in GY's hand of lines 1117–125 and 1129–134 of Chaucer's "The Franklin's Tale," as presented in the edition of W. W. Skeat (*The Canterbury Tales* [Oxford: Clarendon Press, 1894], 4.493–94). She drew double vertical lines beside the second passage, about the workings of the twenty-eight mansions of the moon. Beneath the excerpt, she wrote, "Note by Skeat on this passage" and copied his note for line 1130 (5.392) with some changes. Skeat's note quotes from his own preface to Chaucer's *Astrolabe* and reads:

> The twenty-eight 'moon-stations' of the Arabs are given in Ideler's Untersuchungen über die Bedeutung der Sternnamen, p. 287. He gives the Arabic names, the stars that help to fix their positions, &c. See also Mr Brae's edition of the Astrolabe, p. 89. For the influence of the moon in these mansions, we must look elsewhere, viz. in lib. i. cap. 11, and lib. iv. cap. 18 of the Epitome Astrologiae of Johannes Hispalensis. Suffice it to say that there are 12 temperate mansions, 6 dry ones, and 10 moist ones. The number 28 corresponds with the number of days in a lunation.

Beside the lines citing Hispalensis's *Epitome Totius Astrologiae*, she again drew double vertical lines. Jeffares notes that GY typed out these passages from Chaucer, "whom [WBY] had read carefully in 1910" (*A Commentary on the Collected Poems of W. B. Yeats* [London: Macmillan, 1968], 195). WBY had studied lunar-solar symbolism in the Theosophical Society, the Golden Dawn, and many books, such as John Rhys's *Lectures on the Origin and Growth of Religion* (1886).

On other sources for the Yeatses' knowledge of the mansions of the moon, and particularly concerning GY's exploration of the encyclopedic writings of seventeenth-century Jesuit scholar Athanasius Kircher, see Neil Mann, "George Yeats and Athanasius Kircher," *YA* 16 (2005): 163–93.

30. The unification of these traditional solar and lunar symbols represents perfection, the aim of the alchemist.

31. This name for the OED refers to its first editor (from 1879), Scottish lexicographer Sir James Augustus Henry Murray (1837–1915).

32. This passage seems only to address the bound dictionary volumes, because the fascicle covering the alphabetic span *Su-subterraneous* was issued in December 1914.

33. The OED gives this term's alchemical meaning as "a supposed spiritual principle or immaterial substance whose character or quality may be infused into material things, which are then said to be tinctured; the quintessence, spirit or soul of a thing." Although the concept of *primary* and *antithetical* Tinctures was there from the first week of AS, the term itself is used for the first time on 8 October 1918 (*YVP* 2:71).

34. (fig. 6) Responding to Frank Pearce Sturm's assertion that he could not make sense of *A Vision* because of its numerous errors, WBY wrote to him on 20 January 1926, "If you master the diagram on Page 13 & the movements of the Four Faculties therein you will understand most of the book" (*FPS*, 90).

35. In addition to its more general meanings, "strife" here has a Heraclitean sense (see p. 106), implying an irreconcilable battle of opposites that is the basis of human life.

36. This four-part division of the personality is central to the conception of the self in the system: it is also crucial to Blake's prophetic books and serves as the basis of Golden Dawn rituals and occult doctrines. *Will*, the final term for a concept sometimes called "ego" or "self" in the AS and other early documents, is the essential definition of personality; it is pure choice and defines the self. *Mask* is what *Will* chooses as an ideal personality. *Creative Mind*, sometimes called "creative genius," "genius," or "intellect," is the ability to make conceptual sense of the world. That world, perceived as external to the self but in fact part of it, is the *Body of Fate*, also called "personality," "persona," or "vehicle of fate" in the genetic materials. There are also "Four Principles," or transcendent aspects of human personality. See Book I, n. 70 below.

37. As WBY's confusing note reveals, WBY reckoned with a genuine conflict between the material from the AS and what he might have written on his own. While for WBY Creative Mind is largely a rational faculty, the roughly equivalent Latin *genius* and the Greek *daimon* connote a total self. On 15 January 1918, WBY asked the control Thomas for the "equivalent in our system to spiritistic guide & Greek daimon" but received an ambiguous answer (*YVP* 1:258). Blake's terms "self" and "selfhood" carry with them implications of selfishness, egotism, or egoism: happening in heaven, the sin of selfhood precipitated the Fall.

38. Apparently the Mask is more freely chosen than the image, which is offered by an external fate (see p. 54). As used in the AS, the term "image" is usually related to symbolic artistic creation.

39. This passage refers less to seventeenth-century epistemology than to a conception of the intellect as something that shapes, formulates, constitutes, and is equivalent to the imagination (rather than the fancy) of Coleridge's *Biographia Literaria* (James Engell and Walter Jackson Bate, eds., *The Collected Works of Samuel Taylor Coleridge* 7 [London: Routledge and Kegan Paul; Princeton: Princeton University Press, 1973], pt. 1, p. 304); cf. O'Shea 401.

40. This opposition between fate and destiny recurs in this text; while fate is determined by forces outside the self, destiny expresses a choice of the self (see p. 39). This distinction is also emphasized frequently in the AS.

41. The Yeatses explored these distinctions twice in the AS. Using the term "allusion" to denote concrete images, GY wrote that "the fire" = abstract, "a fire" = concrete, and "my fire" = sensuous (14 October 1919, *YVP* 2:447). WBY posed a rhetorical question two nights later that makes an epistemological progression not communicated in *AVA*: "When *the* Fire becomes *a* fire & afterwards *my* fire you mean I conclude *my* fire in this life—that it is to say present sensuous memory on which is in some way impressed the shape as it were of something in a past life" (*YVP* 2:449).

42. This is fig. 6.

43. "Fate" instead of "Fall" is used in earlier drafts. Despite the term's lack of anatomical parallelism, WBY had used the term "Fall" (as in, from grace) as early as 1893, in *WWB*, edited by Edwin John Ellis and himself (1:262–64; see also 1:347). In the AS for 22 November 1917, GY drew a diagram (not reproduced in *YVP*) with Head, Heart, Fall, and Loins at four quarters and correlated them to Mars, Saturn, Venus, and the Moon, respectively. WBY asked the control Thomas if he was familiar with Blake's terms "Head, Heart Loins," and Thomas later said, "no but if I can get it from yourselves I may be able to." WBY responded, "What do you mean by fall," to which Thomas replied, "The beginning of anger and the departure from wisdom," adding later, "Head and Heart = anti–loins and fall = prim[ary]" (*YVP* 1:103–4). See also WBY's later development in "The Four Ages of Man" and also his letter to Olivia Shakespear of 24 July 1934 (*L*, 823–25).

44. See p. 119, where WBY connects these points to the transcendental Principles.

45. Italian commedia dell'arte is a form of improvisational theater still performed today, but popular from the sixteenth through eighteenth centuries. Performances include juggling, acrobatics, and humorous plays based on a repertoire of established characters. In the AS for 17 January 1918, in response to the statement of the control Thomas (assisted by Fish), "The Ego in his part chooses the part he plays & writes the words," WBY said, "You have described Commedia Dell Arte." Thomas replied, "That is like the Noh partially a dramatisation of the soul—it is all great art" (*YVP* 1:270).

46. This is one of WBY's most frequent allusions (see also p. 165). Dante Alighieri's *Il Convito* (1304–7), also known as the *Convivio* (or *The Banquet*), is one of two prose works written immediately following his exile from Florence. The work is a synthesis of philosophical readings presented as a series of commentaries on previously composed canzoni.

Although WBY's exact reference to Dante has not been identified, there are two illuminating passages (trans. Philip H. Wicksteed [London: J. M. Dent, 1903]):

(1) Amongst the effects of divine wisdom man is the most marvellous, seeing how the divine power has united three natures in one form, and how subtly harmonized his body must be harmonized for such a form, having organs for almost all its powers. Wherefore, because of the complex harmony amongst so many organs which is required to make them perfectly answer to each other, few of all the great number of men are perfect. (3.8, p. 178)

(2) And when it [the body] is well ordained and disposed, then it is beauteous as a whole and in its parts; for the due order of our members conveys the pleasure of a certain wondrous harmony. . . . And so, to say that the noble nature beautifies its body, and makes it comely and alert, is to say not less than that it adjusts it to the perfection of order. (4.25, p. 358)

GY owned a copy of this translation in the widely read Temple Classics edition of Dante and was very familiar with it. Unlike WBY's copies of Dante's works, whose pages are for the most part unmarked and some of which are even uncut, hers, including the *Convito,* contain much marginalia, including corrections of the translation (O'Shea 466–77). On 13 October 1919, the control Ameritus informed WBY and GY, "I want you both to read the whole of Dante's Convito—only a little every day—she can read it to you" (*YVP* 2:445). That they took Ameritus's advice immediately is evident here and on p. 234, as well as the essay "A People's Theatre," which appeared the following month (*IDM,* 128). The AS contains numerous discussions of Unity of Being. It "is a harmony," GY wrote in a SDNB on 30 June 1920: "All the being vibrates to the note, it is like striking a chord. It is like sounding on the piano certain harmonic notes which are responded to by others in their sequence" (*YVP* 3:27). Later, she recorded that it is "a co-equality of Primary & Antithetical" (SDNB8, 7 October 1921, *YVP* 3:99). The most important definition was given on 3 September 1918, well before the injunction to read (or reread) *Il Convito*: WBY asked, "What is unity of being?" to which the control Thomas replied, "Complete harmony between physical body intellect & spiritual desire—*all may be imperfect* but if harmony is perfect it is unity" (*YVP* 2:41). This concept, given through GY's hand and out of her knowledge, was crucial to WBY's philosophy of art and life from this point forward. See also *Au,* 164, 200, and 227; *Plays,* 714; *LE,* 162 and 179. See also pp. 26, 167.

47. Thomas à Kempis (1380–1471), a German monk, is widely accepted to be the author of *The Imitation of Christ* (ca. 1418). He was a follower

of Geert Groote and Florentius Radewijns, founders of the Brethren of the Common Life.

48. The opposition between *character* and *personality* recurs in the system and its various expositions, as well as elsewhere in WBY's corpus; for example, the preface to *Plays for an Irish Theatre* (1911) connects character, comedy, and individuality, in contradistinction to personality, tragedy, and universality (*VPl*, 1296–99). The twenty-eight phases are much concerned with personality, which waxes and wanes with the lunar progression in the form of the Mask. In the AS for 17 October 1918, WBY asked, "May I define Mask as personality," and received a positive reply (*YVP* 2:82). In the course of many discussions, personality was further defined (see, for example, *YVP* 3:69). Similar to the Faculty that uses the term to describe the chosen drama of a human life, Personality of Fate, personality is always assumed and performed, even in late phases when it may have "almost the rigidity, & seems at times to have the permanence & of character, but it is not character for it is always assumed" (*YVP* 4:207). In VersB, the quality of choice is the determining factor between the unenforced and the enforced Mask, alternative terms for *personality* and *character* (*YVP* 4:159).

49. Walter Savage Landor (1775–1864), poet, prose writer, and intellectual, is the author of *Imaginary Conversations of Literary Men and Statesmen* (1824–46). See p. 65.

50. Maximilien François Marie Isidore de Robespierre (1758–94) was one of the best-known leaders of the French Revolution, an influential member of the Committee of Public Safety during the period known as the Reign of Terror.

51. See *YVP* 1:94, 332.

52. The terms "Good and Bad Masks" are used in VNB2, and then changed to "Good and Evil Masks," before the present terms were adopted (*YVP* 3:193–200).

53. WBY misquotes slightly from Blake's "Auguries of Innocence," lines 1–2 (Erdman, 490; *WWB* 3:76).

54. This term replaces the earlier "Creative and Evil Genius" (see VNB2, *YVP* 3:193–200).

55. Water is related to Heart, air to Head, fire to Loins, and earth to Fall in VNB2 (*YVP* 3:202).

56. In William Shakespeare's *Julius Caesar*, and speaking of the prospect of dishonor, Brutus says, "I had rather be a dog and bay the moon / Than such a Roman" (4.3.27–28).

57. A. Norman Jeffares (*A Commentary on the Collected Poems of W. B. Yeats*, 109–10) has noted a similar image in "Upon a House Shaken by the Land Agitation," which includes passages from several of Blake's poems. The contrast between these two images is expanded in WBY's note to *Calvary*: "Certain birds, . . . such lonely birds as the heron, hawk, eagle, and swan, are the natural symbols of subjectivity, espe-

cially when floating upon the wind alone or alighting upon some pool or river, while the beasts that run upon the ground, especially those that run in packs, are the natural symbols of objective man" (*Plays*, 696).

58. Windmills were usually built with four sails.

59. See especially "The Cones of Sexual Love," Part XX of "The Geometrical Foundation of the Wheel" (pp. 139–40).

60. This section, one of the most focused on questions of gender, is eliminated from *AVB* (see Janis Tedesco Haswell, "The Sexual Dynamic of W. B. Yeats's *Vision*," YAACTS 12 [1994]: 102–18, esp. pp. 112–14).

61. This note, added at the galley proof stage, may draw on H. P. Blavatsky's *The Secret Doctrine* (2 vols [1888; rpt., Pasadena: Theosophical University Press, 1963], vol. 1, chap. 9).

62. *Daimon* is one of the more confusing Yeatsian terms, whose meaning changed over time. Before *Per Amica Silentia Lunae* (1918), WBY tended to use the etymologically identical term "demon" in the common sense of a malevolent spirit (see *Myth1*, 284–86; *Myth2*, 187). By the time he came to write *Per Amica Silentia Lunae*, having had the experience of writing the "Leo Africanus" letters, the daimon had developed into a term with distinctive meaning as an anti-self connected with the mask and the *Anima Mundi*, the two main topics of that monograph. It developed still further in the AS as GY's philosophical knowledge was added to WBY's own. The daimon of *AVA* has source material in a plethora of classical and occult texts and traditions. These include Plato, who discusses daimons as wise spirits in *Cratylus* (397e), in terms of the soul in *Phaedo*, and with reference to inspiration for art in *Ion* (cf. *UP1*:399). Other influential Platonic ideas include spirit intermediaries in *Symposium*, a third term of divinity within humanity in *Timaeus*, and the myth of souls and their chosen genii in *Republic* 10. Two other classical sources are critical: Plotinus, who discusses tutelary spirits in the fourth tractate of the third *Ennead*, and Plutarch (see Saddlemyer, 45 and 284). Plutarch's essay "On the Genius of Socrates" is a named source for WBY's 1914 essay "Swedenborg, Mediums, and the Desolate Places" in Lady Gregory's *Visions and Beliefs in the West of Ireland*, and the notes that were also included in that volume (*LE*, 65–66, 269; O'Shea 1598). Also relevant are Heraclitus's fragment 121, Empedocles' *Purifications*, v. 369ff. (*LE*, 11–12, 28–29; see also Burnet, *Early Greek Philosophy*, 141, 233–34, 270), and the work of various Neoplatonists in addition to Plotinus (see *LE*, 67–68), as well as later figures such as Cornelius Agrippa (*LE*, 24), Blake (Erdman, 1), Henry More (*LE*, 22), and Golden Dawn teachings (see Book I, n. 64 below).

See also Virginia Moore, *The Unicorn: William Butler Yeats' Search for Reality* (New York: Macmillan, 1954), 287–88, 368; F. A. C. Wilson, *W. B. Yeats and Tradition* (New York: Macmillan, 1958), 244–45; Janis Tedesco Haswell, *Pressed Against Divinity: W. B. Yeats's Feminine

Masks, chaps. 1 and 2; and Margaret Mills Harper, *Wisdom of Two: The Spiritual and Literary Collaboration of George and W. B. Yeats* (Oxford: Oxford University Press, 2006), 299–315.

63. According to Eusebius, Saint Peter was crucified upside down. Blake writes, "The Modern Church Crucifies Christ with the Head Downwards" (Erdman, 564; *WWB* 2:401). Concerning this matter, see "William Blake and His Illustrations to *The Divine Comedy*" (*EE,* 102). In the tarot deck, the Hanged Man (no. 12) is also crucified upside down.

64. This Latin phrase was WBY's motto in the Golden Dawn. It may be translated as "A demon is the inverse of God," though the word "demon" may mean daimon or personal deity as readily as demon or devil. WBY may have found it in H. P. Blavatsky's *Isis Unveiled* or *The Secret Doctrine,* where the motto heads a chapter concerning solar and lunar deities. Madame Blavatsky writes that ancient philosophers "defined evil as the lining of God or Good: *Demon est Deus inversus,* being a very old adage. Indeed, evil is but an antagonizing blind force in nature; it is *reaction, opposition,* and *contrast,*—evil for some, good for others. There is no *malum in se*: only the shadow of light, without which light could have no existence, even in our perceptions. . . . This is the 'Astral Light', of DEMON EST DEUS INVERSUS" (1:413, 424). WBY's motto demonstrates his supposedly Heraclitean belief that man and god live each other's death, die each other's life, that a man and his guardian angel can easily envy one another, and that seasons are antithetical in the fairyland and this world.

65. "Love thou the Gods—and withstand them, lest thy fame should fail in the end" is how William Morris translates Brynhild's instructions to Sigurd in *The Story of Sigurd the Volsung and the Fall of the Niblungs,* in *The Collected Works of William Morris: With Introductions by His Daughter May Morris* (London: Longmans Green and Co., 1911), 12:127. The Yeatses bought twenty-four volumes of this collection as a Christmas gift to each other in 1919 (O'Shea 1389).

66. In the *Convito,* Dante complains that exile diminishes solitude and therefore damages fame. Wicksteed's translation reads: "And this is why every prophet is less honoured in his own country; this is why a man of excellence should grant his presence to few and his intimacy to fewer, that his name may have acceptance and not be despised" (1.4, p. 20). The idea of "that passage of the convito in which he laments his lack of solitude" (*YVP* 3:27) recurs, even as late as February 1937, when WBY wrote to Ethel Mannin: "When the rivers are poisoned, take to the mountain well; or go with Dante into exile" (*L,* 882). See Book I, n. 46 above.

67. Beatrice Portinari (1266–90), with whom Dante says he fell in love at first sight at age nine, was the basis for his *Vita nuova* and the ultimate spiritual guide and symbol of salvation in the *Commedia.*

68. GY knew well the work of Guido Cavalcanti (ca. 1255–1300), the Florentine poet and contemporary of Dante, who was also active in politics and exiled briefly in 1300. She may have been introduced to Cavalcanti by Ezra Pound, who gave her a presentation copy of his translation of *Sonnets and Ballate of Guido Cavalcanti* (London: Stephen Swift, 1912; O'Shea 356a); she also bought a copy of Cavalcanti's *Rime* (Lanciano: R. Carabba, 1910; O'Shea 355) when she was in Rome in 1913 and compared her own translation with that of her friend (Saddlemyer, 39). Many years later, Pound gave her another edition of *Rime* (Genova: Edizione Marsano S. A., 1931). WBY's knowledge of Cavalcanti came by way of GY and Pound (see, for instance, Saddlemyer, 394).

69. WBY is compared to Dante: both belonged to phase 17, a phase where Unity of Being is possible, had loved hopelessly, had been exiled, and hated abstraction, "that quality in every phase which impedes unity of being" (AS, 30 January 1919, *YVP* 2:195). Both were also favorites of GY: her well-used copies of the Temple Classic editions of Dante's *Comedy, Vita nuova,* and Latin works date from 1910–12 and contain her own translations as well as marginalia in French, Italian, German, and English (O'Shea 470–72, 477, 475). See also Book I, n. 46 above.

70. In the AS from 24 November 1917, WBY asked, "What are the 28 stages," receiving the response, "I will give their meanings later." The session later that evening included a diagram of a circle of numbers from 1 to 28, followed by the direction, "No—draw a circle for me into 28." Then follows a list with descriptions for the Will for each of the phases of the moon. This list, with few changes, moved into the table here. The AS in following months included a diagram of the four cardinal directions with diagonal lines indicating Head, Heart, Loins, and Fall; lists of Good and Bad Masks (changed to True and False Masks); Evil and Creative Geniuses (later called True and False Creative Mind); and Personas of Fate (*YVP* 1:115–16, 192, 203, and 2:466, 522). See also Margaret Mills Harper, "The Medium as Creator: George Yeats's Role in the Automatic Script," *YAACTS* 6 (1988): 49–71.

   WBY worked extensively on this table's contents and arrangement. In an entry in VNB2 (the notebook itself is dated 9 July 1923 on its first page), he set up the first eight phases in five columns with the rest in six. The headings were very different from those printed in the published book: Ego, Good Mask, Evil Mask, Evil Genius, Creative Genius, and Passionate Fate (*YVP* 3:197–200). Ego changed to Will, Good and Evil Masks were combined, Passionate Fate was changed to Body of Fate. That notebook is primarily devoted to the Four Faculties and various other quaternaries, such as Four Automatisms, Four Types of Wisdom, Four Conditions of the Mask, Four Elements, and so forth.

71. "Law" should be "lure," as given in the AS of 3 January 1918 (*YVP* 1:192); the error is corrected in *AVB*, 97.

72. These are not the only quaternaries that were considered for inclusion in
    A Vision. VNB2 contains WBY's notes about Four Memories, probably
    intended for Section XIII (Mask = Conditional, Ego = Personal, Creative
    Genius = Spiritual, Passionate Fate = Emotional) (*YVP* 3:201). He also
    contemplated adding the four daimons (Self = Love, Creative Genius =
    Wisdom, Mask = Beauty, Passionate Fate = Truth) (*YVP* 3:195). See also
    CF (phase 8), which links the Four Memories to the Four Faculties in life
    and death, as well as in time and space (*YVP* 3:351).

73. See *YVP* 1:183, 2:98, 3:207, for AS and notebook entries about the
    four types of wisdom.

74. In an earlier version, this heading was "Genius of the devisions of
    phases in wheel & cone" (VNB2; *YVP* 3:207). See also *YVP* 2:97 for
    the arrival of the information in the AS. WBY refers in his note to "the
    old tenfold year," the Roman ten-month calendar. Because the system
    has an essentially four-part vision of the cosmos, it was troublesome
    that these two tables were "divided into ten divisions" instead of
    twelve. A list of "Automatism of 12 Cycles at phases" was rejected
    (VNB2; *YVP* 3:208).

75. For consistency with the rest of the table, the last numerals in this series
    should read 5, 4, 3, but this order is retained in *AVB*, 101.

76. See *YVP* 2:101–2 for the first appearance of this information; see also
    YVP 3:201 for its "codification" in VNB2. Note that "Breathing" is
    "Aspiration" in the original forms.

77. Two septenary tables were originally planned, to appear probably
    after Section XV: (1) Planes (Physical, Passionate, Spirits of Dead,
    Celestial Body, Guides, etc., Angels, Invisible); (2) Colours (Prayer =
    Amber, Truth = Blue, Peace = Gray, Heir = Purple, Position = Green,
    Negation = Red, Space = Yellow) (VNB2; *YVP* 3:209).

78. The phasal essays that comprise this section were some of the earliest
    parts of *A Vision* to be composed, after WBY had abandoned the dia-
    logue form of the earliest drafts. The essays were for a time intended to
    be the majority of the book and remain rhetorically central. They also
    remained more textually stable than many other sections after 1926 as
    WBY revised *A Vision* for its second edition. For an early version, see
    VersB, *YVP* 4:139–237.

79. This is line 8 of WBY's "The Magi"; in the poem's text, "upon" is
    replaced by "on" (*Poems*, 125).

80. This passage is taken from Blake's "The Mental Traveller," lines 93–96
    (Erdman, 486; *WWB* 2:33). See also p. 157, where this line is quoted
    slightly differently.

81. This passage is taken from Genesis 1:2, in reference to the formless
    darkness that preceded God's creation of light.

82. This is the old name for the *Drunken Faun* of Rome's Capitoline
    Museums. The sculpture is made of *rosso antico* marble, the faun
    accompanied by a goat and smiling, holding up in his right hand a

bunch of grapes and in his left a cane and more fruit. It has been displayed in the eponymous Hall of the Faun of the Capitoline Museums' Palazzo Nuovo since 1817. The piece has long aroused admiration of travelers and cataloguers alike: it appears in chapter 2 of Nathaniel Hawthorne's *The Marble Faun* (1859, 1860) and in Blake's *A Descriptive Catalogue of Pictures, Poetical and Historical Inventions* (Erdman, 544; *WWB* 2:375). (It should not be confused with the Capitoline's also much admired *Resting Satyr*, a copy of a sculpture by Praxiteles.) In Roman mythology, fauns were place-spirits (*genii*) of untamed woodland; like the the Greek satyrs, they were wild and orgiastic drunken followers of Dionysus/Bacchus, with the result that they have come to represent physical strength and beauty unguided by intelligence.

83. This image of the cup of Bacchus also appears in Matthew Arnold's "Strayed Reveller" (lines 84–85). Note that the passage from John Keats's *Endymion* from which WBY quotes below also mentions Dionysus's ivy.

84. These lines are from John Keats's *Endymion* 4.263–37.

85. These lines are very similar to those in Blake's "Eternity" (lines 1–4) and his "Several Questions Answered" (lines 1–4), although in both places the first line of the passage reads "He who binds to himself a joy" (Erdman, 470, 474).

86. "The Hamadryad" (meaning "tree nymph") is one of the best-known poems of Walter Savage Landor's *Hellenics* (1847). WBY admired Landor, in particular his *Imaginary Conversations*, and Landor's name appears many times in the AS. See also Book I, n. 49 above.

87. WBY knew William Morris and admired such medieval romances as *The Water of the Wondrous Isles* (1897). For WBY's view of Morris's work, see "The Happiest of the Poets" (*EE*, 42–50). See also Book I, n. 65 above, and Dedication and Introduction, n. 34.

88. The allusion may be to various characters from poems by Shelley, including the poet of *Alastor; or the Spirit of Solitude* (1816) and Ahasuerus, the Wandering Jew of *Hellas* (1821). In an earlier version of the dedication, WBY quotes two lines (155–56) about Ahasuerus from *Hellas* (NLI, 36,264/3), and Alastor is the name of one of the controls in the sleeps of 1920, arriving on 6 October (*YVP* 3:50).

89. The reference is to Theocritus's idylls about rustic life in his native Sicily, the widely imitated first examples of pastoral poetry in Greek.

90. Pietro Bembo (1470–1547) was a native of Venice but a proponent of the Florentine language as a literary norm. His great facility in Latin, Greek, and Tuscan made him successful as a literary pundit, poet, and courtier. The city-state of Urbino, in the Marche region of Italy, was a cultural center during the fifteenth and sixteenth centuries, although it endured a volatile political history during this time. Both Bembo and Urbino figure symbolically in WBY's work, as Urbino stood as an example of a well-run cultural center; for example, see "To

a Wealthy Man who promised a second Subscription to the Dublin Municipal Gallery if it were proved the People wanted Pictures" (*Poems*, 106–7). WBY knew of both Bembo and Urbino from L. E. Opdycke's translation of Baldassare Castiglione's *The Book of the Courtier* (written 1508–18; published 1528; translated by Opdycke 1902). Castiglione's book presents a series of conversations among courtiers, including Bembo, who were guests at the palace of Urbino in March 1507. WBY repeated this untraced exclamation in "The Bounty of Sweden" (*Au*, 400).

91. In his famous "All the world's a stage" speech from Shakespeare's *As You Like It* (2.7.139–66), Jaques describes the seven ages of man, including the fifth, imagined as a justice, "In fair round belly with good capon lined, / With eyes severe and beard of formal cut, / Full of wise saws and modern instances" (153–56). In this usage, "saws" means "sayings."

92. The poet Robert Browning (1812–1889) is known for his dramatic monologues, his long blank-verse *Sordello*, and such plays as *Pippa Passes*. On 22 August 1923, WBY wrote that GY was guided by a spirit voice to pull Browning from the shelf and turn to a particular line in volume 1, page 45 (in *The Poetical Works of Robert Browning*, ed. by Augustine Birrell and Sir Frederic G. Kenyon, 2 vols. [London: John Murray, 1919]). WBY then corrected: GY was directed, "line 13 (line corrected as my edition is wrong) is the 2 vol (1919) & the quotation is [of] great significance" (VNB2; *YVP* 3:185). On page 45 of volume 1, lines 10 to 14 in the first column contain a passage from *Paracelsus* that was apparently what the voice had in mind. Festus speaks to Paracelsus: "They praise you here as one whose lore, already / Divulged, eclipses all the past can show, / But whose achievements, marvellous as they be / Are faint anticipations of a glory / About to be revealed." (The first volume is the correct reference: page 45 in the second volume contains part of book 3 of *The Ring and the Book*, "The Other Half-Rome," but WBY continues that "George had never read Paracelsus from which the quotation came & I not that part since boyhood & never in this edition"). WBY owned this book (see O'Shea 298); he also had in his library volume 3 of an 1865 edition that belonged to his father, in which *Paracelsus* is much annotated (O'Shea 297).

93. This passage is slightly misquoted from Robert Browning's "Pauline" (lines 323–25); WBY uses this same passage in "Bishop Berkeley" (*LE*, 111) and *P&I*, 127.

94. This passage reproduces a song from Robert Browning's *Pippa Passes* (3.164–77).

95. "Weird" here means fate (which concept in Old English was spelled *wyrd*). In William Morris's medieval romance *The Water of the Wondrous Isles* (1897), Birdalone falls in love with the Black Squire Sir Arthur, also her friend Atra's lover. Deciding to leave the situation

rather than wreck it, Birdalone says, "Now hast thou [Atra] forgiven me that Weird dragged me in betwixt thy love and thy goodhap; and I have forgiven thee that I am led away by Weird into the waste and wilderness of love. Farewell" (Morris, *Collected Works*, 20:256). Other references to "Weird" in that work appear on pp. 203, 211, 313, 314.

96. This line adapts Dante's *"E'n la sua volontade è nostra pace"* (*Paradiso* 3.85), which WBY quotes in "Edmund Spenser" (*EE*, 266) and "Prometheus Unbound" (*LE*, 120). He significantly substitutes "freedom" for "peace."

97. The Punch-and-Judy show was a popular British glove puppet show originating in the seventeenth century, featuring stock characters and a storyline derived from Italian commedia dell'arte. Punch wears a jester's motley, is hunchbacked, and his hooked nose almost meets his curved, jutting chin. He carries a stick as large as himself, which he freely uses upon all the other characters in the show.

98. In *AVB*, 113, WBY inserts "Byron's" before the titles of these two poems. The figures are the title characters of *Don Juan* (1821) by George Gordon, Lord Byron, about the legendary libertine, and of *The Giaour* (1813), an Orientalizing romance. *Giaour* is the Turkish word for infidel or nonbeliever and is similar to the Arabic word *kāfir* (كافر).

99. American Romantic poet Walt Whitman (1819–92) wrote *Leaves of Grass* and "Song of Myself." The simplicity of the phase accords with WBY's description of Whitman and Emerson in "Ireland after Parnell" as "writers who have begun to seem superficial precisely because they lack the Vision of Evil" (*Au*, 200). It should be noted that although it is possible to locate the phase of the moon under which a person is born, the examples in *A Vision* are symbolic and do not correspond to any actual lunar phases. It is also noteworthy that human examples begin with this phase; in a sleep of 6 July 1920, recorded by GY, the Yeatses were informed that "Till five, or was it till after 5? no eminent famous personality is possible" (*YVP* 3:29).

100. This line is slightly misquoted from line 8 of Whitman's "Song of Myself," where the speaker notes his age as thirty-seven.

101. See paragraph 11 of "Higher Laws" in Henry David Thoreau's *Walden* (1854), which was an influence for "The Lake Isle of Innisfree" (*Au*, 139). WBY owned a copy (O'Shea 2133).

102. Saint Thomas Aquinas (1225–74) was an Italian philosopher and theologian in the Scholastic tradition, and the originator of the Thomistic school of philosophy, long the primary philosophical approach of the Roman Catholic Church. In some drafts, Aquinas is suggested for the list of examples for phase 6. Frank Pearce Sturm suggested to WBY in a letter of 19 January 1926 that "St Thomas Aquinas was very interested in gyres, and his opinions would make a very apposite footnote when *A Vision* is reprinted in your collected works." WBY wrote back, "I am most grateful to you for that quotation from St Thomas. It

is the exact thought of my work for at harmonization the soul is in a sphere not in a gyre. The sphere is his circle. I believe that I have been given a simplification of ancient thought" (*FPS*, 87).

103. In VersB, the description for Self (not yet changed to be called Will) makes clear why human examples begin to multiply beginning with phase 7: here occurs the "First realization of Self (?Premonition of personality)" (*YVP* 3:177).

104. George Borrow (1803–81) primarily wrote novels and travelogues about his journeys around Europe. In the DMR-TS, WBY noted Borrow's "insistence in Lavengro upon his recurring attack of the horrors . . ." (*YVP* 4:30), referring to chapter 84 of Borrow's largely autobiographical novel. It may be that WBY was reading or rereading *Lavengro* around this time, as he refers to it in a letter to Olivia Shakespear dated 28 June 1923, calling some of the novel's events "a little heightened" (*L*, 699).

The reference seems to be to French novelist Alexandre Dumas (1802–70), who wrote such tales of high adventure as *The Three Musketeers* (1844) and *The Count of Monte Cristo* (1845–46), among many others, rather than to Dumas' son of the same name (1824–95), who penned a number of commercially successful novels, including *The Lady of the Camellias* (1848), which served as the basis of *La Traviata*.

Thomas Carlyle (1795–1881) was an influential Scottish essayist and historian, best known as the author of *Sartor Resartus* (1831).

The Scottish poet James Macpherson (1736–96) is best known as the "translator" of Ossianic poems about Finn mac Cumhail, including *Fingal, an Ancient Epic Poem in Six Books, together with Several Other Poems composed by Ossian, the Son of Fingal, translated from the Gaelic Language* (1761), *Temora* (1763), and a collected edition, *The Works of Ossian* (1765). The authenticity of the translated documents was challenged by Samuel Johnson, and although Macpherson insisted on their genuineness, he never published his originals.

105. This assertion might be rooted in J. A. Froude's posthumous *My Relations with Carlyle* (1903) or Frank Harris's "Talks with Carlyle" (*English Review*, 1911; reproduced in *Contemporary Portraits*, 1915). WBY's assessment of Carlyle's work as abstraction and empty rhetoric occurs also in a letter of 14 March 1916, which also presents a comparison with Macpherson's *Ossian* (*L*, 608).

106. Prince Lyov Nikolaievich Myshkin, the main character of Fyodor Dostoyevsky's *The Idiot* (1869), is a character whose mental condition is unclear: when younger he had blackouts and learning difficulties, but what his society views as idiocy may simply be honesty and trustfulness. WBY seems to have read *The Possessed* and *The Idiot* by 1922 (*Au*, 176, 199), but Gabriel Fallon recalls Lady Gregory responding to WBY's mention of Dostoyevsky by saying, "You know, Willie, you never read a novel by Dostoievsky" and promising to send him a copy

of *The Idiot* (*Sean O'Casey: The Man I Knew* [London: Routledge, 1965], 21–22). See also Book I, n. 187 below.

107. In the early modern way of understanding humanity's relationship to nature and God, a human being was a microcosm of all creation, in possession of three souls: with plants and animals were shared the vegetative and sensitive souls, but the possession of a rational soul made a human godlike, distinguished from the lower orders of creation.

108. The eldest son of Samuel Taylor Coleridge, Hartley Coleridge (1796–1849), wrote poetry, biographies, and literary criticism, as well as the unfinished lyric drama *Prometheus*. He is less known for his slight literary reputation than for his intemperate life and early death.

109. Patrick Branwell Brontë (1817–48), the only brother of the famous writers Charlotte, Emily, and Anne, was an artist but also an alcoholic and perhaps a drug addict, and his early death is blamed on these addictions.

110. These are the final words of the crucified Christ, combining the original Aramaic and an English translation. See Mark 15:34, "And at the ninth hour Jesus cried with a loud voice, 'Eloi, Eloi, la ma sabachthani?' which means, 'My God, my God, why hast thou forsaken me?'" A similar passage occurs in Matthew 27:46. Psalm 22:1, a prayer for deliverance from a mortal illness, begins, "My God, my God, why hast thou forsaken me? / Why art thou so far from helping me, and from the words of my groaning?" See also *Per Amica Silentia Lunae* (*LE,* 13). In the AS, Judas appears at phase 8 and Christ at phase 22, in phasal opposition (see *YVP* 1:291, 3:161, and Janis Haswell, "Resurrecting *Calvary:* A Reconstructive Interpretation of W. B. Yeats's Play and Its Making," *YA* 15 [2002]: 162–75).

111. In the AS, the Yeatses focused extensive attention on distinguishing the viewpoints of the sage or teacher, who is primary, and the victim, who is antithetical. GY's hand first made the distinction on 21 February 1918, noting that artists are teachers, in that they reveal "unanalysed emotion in the sinner or sinned against"; a teacher "creates a vehicle for the victim but is not a victim himself" (*YVP* 1:359). Other significant discussions were held in the early months of 1919, in the course of discussions of *Calvary,* Critical Moments (the patterning of life-altering occasions in individual lives, an important concept in the AS that does not remain in *A Vision*), and daimons. On 28 March 1919, the Yeatses learned that "the victim is the intellectual subjective nature—the teacher the emotional & objective" (*YVP* 2:219); on 6 April, it was affirmed that the teacher is "a higher order of daimon" (*YVP* 2:236). The concepts are summarized in the card file (*YVP* 3:412, 421–24). Cf. p. 185, WBY's note. WBY's below-mentioned "diagram" does not exist.

112. An early draft had no example; the "unnamed artist" is likely Wyndham Lewis. See Book I, n. 114 below.

113. In William Shakespeare's *Richard III*, George, Duke of Clarence, tells of a dream in which he visits the underworld, encountering, among others, the shade of Prince Edward, son of Henry VI. As Clarence describes the dream to the Keeper in the Tower, "Then came wand'ring by / A shadow like an angel, with bright hair / Dabbled in blood, and he shriek'd out aloud, / 'Clarence is come—false, fleeting, perjur'd Clarence, / That stabb'd me in the field by Tewksbury: / Seize on him, Furies, take him unto torment!' " (1.4.52–57).

114. The "certain artist" is the British painter and writer Wyndham Lewis (1882–1957) and the "notable man" Welsh painter Augustus John (1878–1961). In the DMR-TS, Robartes says, "I wonder too if I should not place at ten or eleven the genius of Augustus John the images of whose art unlike those of Rembrandt or Velazquez, men of late phases whose intellectual egos have separated themselves from the images of their art, seem accidental and instinctive as though their creator saw from within the race, his soul unfixed and floating" (*YVP* 4:31). In the discussion of phase 9 in VersB, WBY writes, "Last night after I wrote these words I was sitting in the Cafe Royal when I got into conversation with a bullet headed young man, who had that short neck which I associate with passion." Lewis spoke to WBY (not to a "student of these symbols") of "a certain notable man" and his mistress. WBY noted that this young man was "a cubist artist of powerful imagination," adding, "There I thought is my example" for phase 9 (*YVP* 4:183). Robartes says that "in Gyraldus' allegorical woodcut that phase is symbolised by an eagle tearing out a man's eyes" (DMR-TS, *YVP* 4:30).

115. Charles Stewart Parnell (1846–91) was an Irish nationalist leader whose Irish Parliamentary Party fought in the 1880s for Home Rule for Ireland and Irish land reform in the British House of Commons. He was mythologized by many as a national hero, but his career was ruined by a combination of forces, the most dramatic of which was the revelation of his longstanding affair with Katharine O'Shea. By the time that WBY and GY were generating the system, Parnell's reputation had been largely resurrected, a process that began with his death and intensified especially after the Irish party reunited in 1900 under John Redmond.

116. The reference is to Mrs. Katharine O'Shea, Parnell's mistress and later wife, whose shocking divorce trial was the catalyst for Parnell's downfall. She gives her account in *Charles Stewart Parnell: His Love Story and Political Life* (2 vols. [London: Cassell, 1914]).

117. Gretchen appears in Goethe's *Faust*, not in Marlowe's. In his reference to Helen of Troy, WBY draws on lines 2603–4 of Goethe's work, where Mephistopheles says that after drinking a diabolical drink, Faust will see Helen in every woman.

118. In Victor Hugo's *The Toilers of the Sea* (1866), Déruchette writes Gilliatt's name in the snow, albeit with her finger rather than a parasol

(bk. 1, chap. 1). This incident serves as an example in Walter Pater's essay "Romanticism" (in *Appreciations*). WBY wrote that he "read all Victor Hugo's romances" in his youth (*Au,* 95).

119. Odin, according to the *Hamaval* in the *Elder Edda*, committed a self-sacrifice by wounding himself and then hanging himself from the branches of the ash tree Yggdrasil, the world tree. After nine days and nights, Odin saw some runes below him, and in lifting them was set free by their magical power, soon discovering himself filled with new youth and vigor. WBY refers to this same incident in *Mem,* 146; *Plays,* 704, and *EE,* 233 ("the sacrifice of a man to himself"). WBY may have encountered the story in various contexts: by 1917, GY had read the *Eddas* (*L,* 635), and Powys Mathers mentioned the passage in the Golden Dawn Flying Roll No. X (in Francis King [ed.], *Astral Projection: Ritual Magic and Alchemy by S. L. MacGregor Mathers and Others, Being Hitherto Unpublished Golden Dawn Material* [New York: Samuel Weiser, 1971], 121): "Recall to your mind that passage in one of the Eddas 'I hung on the Tree three days and three nights, wounded with a spear, myself a sacrifice offered to (highest) Self,— Odin unto Odin.' " The passage also appears in Sir James George Frazer's *The Golden Bough* (12 vols., 3rd ed. [1907–15; rpt., New York: Macmillan, 1951], 5:290; O'Shea 700). Frazer's source seems less immediate, because unlike the Golden Dawn source, it retains the original nine days and nights, but the Yeatses discussed *The Golden Bough* in the automatic experiments on several occasions.

120. Moses brings down the Ten Commandments from Mount Sinai in Exodus 34:29.

121. Viscount John Morley writes of Parnell in *Recollections* (2 vols. [New York: Macmillan, 1917]) that "In ordinary conversation he was pleasant, without much play of mind; temperament made him the least discursive of the human race" (1:238).

122. See Katharine O'Shea, *Charles Stewart Parnell,* 1:176–77, and *Poems,* 674–75.

123. In the months following Parnell's trial for adultery, his rejection by William Gladstone's Liberal Party, and his loss of popular Catholic Irish support, Parnell fought to retain his hold on parliamentary power. From 1 to 6 December 1890, the Irish party famously met in Committee Room 15 of the House of Commons to consider whether to retain him as leader. After several days of angry discussion, during which Parnell used his position as chair to prevent the issue from coming to a vote, a majority of members left the room and declared his deposition. A minority remained in the room with Parnell, splitting the party and ensuring Parnell's political downfall.

124. This description follows Katharine O'Shea's account, as given in *Charles Stewart Parnell,* 2:153.

125. Although WBY thought of the pantheistic philosopher Baruch de Spi-

noza (1632–77) as a mystic, he was less fond of his rationalism (*L,* 650). An early manuscript seems to describe Spinoza as one who embraces "some abstract system of belief, some bundle of almost mathematical principles and convictions." Robartes is more precise in the DMR-TS: "at eleven one discovers now a Pantheistic image of man little more precise than my own legs when I study them through the water where I am bathing and now the reason[ed] conviction of Spinoza" (*YVP* 4:31).

The Dominican friar Girolamo Savonarola (1452–98) rose to power in Florence after the exile of Piero de' Medici in 1494, becoming a spokesman for a moral crusade damning the ruling families for such vices and frivolity as theater and the fine arts. For WBY's sense of him, see *EE,* 167. In an AS from 3 January 1918, Savonarola appears in phase 11 (*YVP* 1:193). An important list of people who are examples of each phase, with astrological associations and identification of the cycle associated with them, was compiled by GY and filed with the AS for 2 June 1918. On this list, Schopenhauer appears in phase 11 (*YVP* 1:549).

126. The VersB manuscript titles this section "The meaning of the word 'heart' on the diagram," and then retitles it "The splitting of Antithetical & Primary" (*YVP* 4:187).

127. See *YVP* 2:99 and 3:209 for these concepts.

128. See Book I, n. 41 above, concerning this epistemological distinction.

129. WBY was particularly concerned with this phase "because the hero's crescent is the twelfth" (see p. 5). Over time, different names appeared as this phase's examples. The AS of 3 January 1918 leaves this phase blank (*YVP* 1:191–95), and the sheet in GY's hand filed with the AS for 2 June 1918 lists Nietzsche, Pound, Virgil, Keats, and Tennyson, the latter two later crossed out, and Robespierre added later still (*YVP* 1:549). The DMR-TS includes an important passage about Pound that WBY cut, although he kept Pound as an example until the galleys. In that TS, Robartes says, "His enemy is that which opposes isolation some form of collective thought & many among whom I would be sorry to include your enemy Ezra Pound, by the frenzy of their attack increase more & more the power of the vehicle, & so bring the creative power to its death & remain themselves not transfigured but transfixed" (*YVP* 4:31–32; see also the references to Pound in the DMR-MS, *YVP* 4:86–88). WBY asked on 23 May 1918, "Ezra of violence, Nietzsche violence?" although the control Thomas did not respond (*YVP* 1:454). In a letter to Ethel Mannin, WBY illuminates somewhat the intellectual hatred in Pound that fascinated WBY: "I am a forerunner of that horde that will some day come down the mountains" (*L,* 873), a comment in which, Davis S. Thatcher has observed, WBY was echoing language from *The Will to Power* by German philosopher Friedrich Nietzsche (1844–1900) (*Nietzsche in England,* 157).

130. The description of this phase and of the Hunchback appears on pp. 89–91.

131. The examples listed are French poet Charles Baudelaire (1821–67), English illustrator and poet Aubrey Beardsley (1872–98), and English poet and member of the Rhymers Club Ernest Dowson (1867–1900). Baudelaire and Verlaine were the two examples given in the sheet in GY's hand filed with the AS for 2 June 1918 (*YVP* 1:549) and the DMR-TS (*YVP* 4:32). In this list, Beardsley accompanied Blake and others at phase 16 (*YVP* 1:549, 4:35). Dowson was added later.

132. The role of English Romantic poet John Keats (1795–1821) in WBY's thinking was well established prior to the AS, and he is discussed in many automatic sessions. See his appearances in "Ego Dominus Tuus" (1915) (*Poems*, 161) and *Per Amica Silentia Lunae* (*LE*, 7). In 1918, WBY set up a contrast between Romantic poets Keats (see Book III, n. 134) and Shelley (see Book I, n. 153 below) that is borne out in their placement on the wheel (see p. 63): "If you accept metempsychosis, Keats was moving to greater subjectivity of being, and to unity of that being, and Shelley to greater objectivity and to consequent break-up of unity of being" (*L*, 653). In the AS of 6 and 21 December 1917, Keats appears in phase 12 (*YVP* 1:146, 169), although on 2 June 1918 he is first in phase 12 then moved to phase 14 with Wordsworth, Iseult Gonne, and Tennyson because they all loved the world, or nature (*YVP* 1:549). WBY frequently cites "Ode to a Nightingale" as an example of the daimonic influence on an artwork already in the *Anima Mundi*. "Thoughts & images received by Keats . . . still remain & can be transfered [*sic*] to us" (CF, *YVP* 3:413). Venetian painter Giorgione (Giorgio Barbarelli da Castelfranco, ca. 1477–1510) was one of the most important figures of the High Renaissance. The "Many Beautiful Women" include Iseult Gonne and Helen of Troy.

133. In Greek myth, Helen was daughter of Leda and Zeus, wife of Menelaus, and reputed to be the most beautiful woman in the world. Her abduction by Paris brought about the Trojan War. In the DMR-TS, Robartes notes "that Helen would never have set Troy afire if she were not of this phase" (*YVP* 4:34).

134. This statue by French sculptor Auguste Rodin (1840–1917) resides in the Musée Rodin in Paris. For a reproduction, see *YVP* 4:93.

135. The references are to portraits of women painted by English Pre-Raphaelite painter Sir Edward Burne-Jones (1833–98), Florentine painter Sandro Botticelli (Alessandro Filipepi [di Mariano di Vanni], ca. 1445–1510), and English painter and poet Dante Gabriel (Gabriel Charles Dante) Rossetti (1828–82). In the sheet in GY's hand filed with the AS of 2 June 1918, Rossetti appears first in phase 14 and then is moved to phase 17 (*YVP* 1:549).

136. Sir Edward Burne-Jones painted *The Golden Stair* (in the Tate Britain) and the late work *The Sleep of King Arthur in Avalon* (begun 1881; in

the Museo de Arte de Ponce, Puerto Rico). The DMR-TS mentions *Briar Rose* (1870–90; exhibited 1890), Burne-Jones's popular series of four large paintings, instead of *The Golden Stair* (*YVP* 4:35).

137. The description of the "soul's deepening solitude" in Wordsworth comes almost exactly from the DMR-TS, in which Wordsworth was still placed in phase 14 (*YVP* 4:35). In January 1915, WBY and Pound proposed "to read through the whole seven vols of Wordsworth in Dowden's edition" (*L,* 590). In February 1917, in "Anima Hominis," WBY depicted "Wordsworth withering into eighty years, honoured and empty-witted . . ." (*LE,* 16).

138. Adolphe Joseph Thomas Monticelli (1824–86), French painter of the Barbizon school, returned to his native Marseilles after the outbreak of the Franco-Prussian War (1870) and there developed his mature style, often painting with Paul Cézanne.

139. English painter Charles Conder (1868–1909) was an acquaintance of WBY and a member of the Decadent movement (see *L,* 508–9, and *Au,* 250, 266).

140. This paragraph was added to a late typescript (NLI, 36,265/10; 36,268/1).

141. Phase 15 is that of complete beauty, so it can contain no human life. The phase description stresses the connection between physical and spiritual beauty. In the DMR-TS, Robartes emphasizes that "all beauty has been, would be or will be physical and that is why those creatures at the Fifteenth phase—though invisible to our eyes—are ponderable and plant their feet upon this earth and why, no longer limited by thought their eyes have such an eagle gaze." A bit later WBY inserted a note by John Aherne: "It is one of the doctrines of Kusta ben Luka that the retina of the eye has an incalculable range and that it is limited by our expectations alone. He explained many miraculous phenomena in this way." Touch and hearing have "a like range" (*YVP* 4:37–38).

142. A recurring set of polarities; see, for example, "Solomon and the Witch" (*Poems,* 179–80).

143. A primary man and Teacher, Christ desired the other world, while his "forerunner" (identified as Buddha in a late typescript), an antithetical man and Victim, connected the physical beauty of this world with the spiritual. Another avatar, of which there can be only one "to each cycle," is Krishna, according to the AS of 2 June 1918 (*YVP* 1:468, summarized on *YVP* 3:339). "This cannot yet be understood" until the "successor" (also called "New Messiah," "Initiate," or "Avatar" in the AS) appears at the end of the present cycle of two thousand years. This concept was often discussed in the AS, beginning as early as 21 November 1917 (*YVP* 1:94–95); see, for example, the AS for 26 May 1918 (*YVP* 1:458–62). See Book IV, n. 82.

144. The examples are English Romantic poet and visionary painter William Blake (1757–1827); French author of *Gargantua and Pantagruel*

François Rabelais (ca. 1493–1553); Italian author, poet, playwright, and satirist Pietro Aretino (1492–1556); and the alchemist, physician, astrologer, and general occultist Paracelsus (1493–1541; born Theophrastus Bombastus von Hohenheim). The names on this list varied at different stages: the sheet accompanying the AS of 2 June 1918 names Blake, Beardsley, Stephens, Madame Gonne, Cervantes (*YVP* 1:549), while the DMR-TS includes "Blake and Beardsley and perhaps Boehme" (*YVP* 4:35), and VersB gives only Blake and Rabelais (*YVP* 4:193). The relationships among these examples may be explained by WBY's belief that the list should contain (1) satirists who hate the ugly and pity the beautiful (Blake and Rabelais), (2) "certain rare sages" (Paracelsus or the rejected Boehme and Cervantes), and (3) beautiful women (Maud Gonne). In the DMR-TS, Robartes says, "if a man has not loved a woman of the fourteenth or of the Sixteenth phase he has not known the greatest earthly beauty" (*YVP* 4:37).

145. The story of Saint George (ca. 275–303) slaying a dragon in order to end its demands for regular human sacrifice (and, in the process, converting a city to Christianity) is often read as an allegory about the victory of Christianity over Satan.

146. Blake so speaks of schools of art in *A Descriptive Catalogue*, Number IX: "These Pictures . . . were the result of temptations and perturbations, labouring to destroy Imaginative power, by means of that infernal machine, called Chiaro Oscuro, in the hands of Venetian and Flemish Demons . . ." (Erdman, 547; *WWB* 2:377).

147. For a narration of this incident, see Alexander Gilchrist, *Life of William Blake,* ed. Ruthven Todd (London: J. M. Dent, 1942), 241; and G. E. Bentley, *Blake Records* (Oxford: Clarendon, 1969), 180–81.

148. In "Swedenborg, Mediums, and the Desolate Places," WBY quotes Villiers de l'Isle-Adam quoting Thomas Aquinas as saying, "Eternity is the possession of one's self, as in a single moment" (*LE,* 52); see also *Per Amica Silentia Lunae* (*LE,* 19, 26) and "On the Boiler" (*LE,* 247). The passage in the first English translation of *Axël* (1890), published in 1925 with WBY's preface, reads, "For eternity, as Saint Thomas well remarks, is merely the full and entire possession of oneself in one and the same instant" (trans. H. P. R. Finberg [London: Jarrolds, 1925], 60; O'Shea 2201). In the *Summa theologica,* Aquinas tests the Boethian position that eternity is "interminabilis vitae tota simul et perfecta possessio" (part 1, *quaestio* 10, referring to *De consolatione philosophiae* 5:6).

149. "The Burning Babe" is a poem by the Elizabethan Jesuit martyr and poet Robert Southwell (1561–95).

150. See the DMR-TS:

> One marble shape rises before me a French Diana of the 16th Century her exquisite head alert she lies half sitting amid the

wild deer that in a moment she will destroy, dogs and deer alike gathered about her in fascinated affection: A king's mistress, a quiver of arrows to symbolise that bitter wit that kept ministers in dread, whom the artist solitary it may be as herself saw transfigured as the goddess lingering amid her woodland court after all Olympus elfs had vanished, Was she in truth Diana of Poitiers, was a King of France great enough to love such a beauty and did he turn away at last from that never empty quiver? (*YVP* 4:36–37)

This sculpture of Diana, known as *The Fountain of Diana* and *Diana of Anet* (mid-sixteenth century), is in the Louvre. It was long incorrectly attributed to Jean Goujon, but because it was heavily restored in the eighteenth century its original artist is unknown. It is often seen as praising Diane de Poitiers, mistress of Henry II of France. It appeared reproduced in plate 2 between pages 496 and 497 of the *Encyclopaedia Britannica*, 11th ed., a copy of which WBY owned (O'Shea 629–30). For a reproduction, see *YVP* 4:36, where it is attributed perhaps to Ponce Jacquiot. WBY almost certainly intended Maud Gonne to be the archetypal queen, since she is the only woman named in phase 16 in the AS and in early versions of *AVA*.

151. This unidentified quotation appears twice in *AVB*, on pp. 24, 140.

152. Hephaestus, the Greek analogue of the Roman god of the fire and volcanoes, is often depicted as lame from birth, ill-made in both legs, with twisted feet and stumbling gait. The early Roman god Vulcan later took on qualities from the Greek god, including his marriage to Venus/Aphrodite.

153. While this printed list includes Dante (see Dedication and Introduction, n. 16) and the Romantic poet Percy Bysshe Shelley (1792–1822), the earliest list of examples (AS, 2 June 1918) names WBY, Shelley, Landor, Dante, Homer, Botticelli, Burne-Jones, Rossetti (*YVP* 1:549). Elsewhere in the AS and CF, WBY appears here. A sleep dated 6 July 1920 notes "M[aud]G[onne], 16, my self 17" (*YVP* 3:128), and a detailed diagram in the CF notes, "individual horoscope 'WBY' being placed to show ascendant at 17" (*YVP* 3:296). He does not use his own name in the description of phase 17 in the DMR-TS or other early drafts, although numerous passages show him thinking of himself. As Landor's name appears under phase 17 in *AVB*, 141, his omission here appears to be accidental.

154. These are both characters from Shelley's work. Ahasuerus appears in *Hellas* and *Queen Mab; A Philosophical Poem* (1813) and Athanase in "Prince Athanase: A Fragment."

155. If Dante's Mask is "gaunt," then his Will is the opposite, as WBY had suggested in the poem "Ego Dominus Tuus," written in December 1915 and published in the Cuala edition of *The Wild Swans at Coole*

and also *Per Amica Silentia Lunae.* The primary voice in the dialogue
of the poem, "Hic," notes that Dante's *Commedia* has made "that hollow face of his / More plain to the mind's eye than any face / But that
of Christ"; but the antithetical voice "Ille" counters, "is that spectral
image / The man that Lapo and that Guido knew?" "Ille" continues,

> Being mocked by Guido for his lecherous life,
> Derided and deriding, driven out
> To climb that stair and eat that bitter bread,
> He found the unpersuadable justice, he found
> The most exalted lady loved by a man. (*Poems*, 162)

The AS contains further discussion of the idea that Dante created an
opposite for the self-named subject of his work; see, for example, a passage in SDNB6. "We took Dante as an example" of the movement of
the soul through the Faculties, GY wrote, thus discovering that a True
Mask "accepts its doom, is 'Doom-eager' Dante sees himself in his exile
as the tragic Dante of the Poems. He sees him self as he is fated &
desires that self" (*YVP* 3:27).

156. Mary Shelley's note to Percy Bysshe Shelley's "Prince Athanase" suggests that the poem traces a development from material to transcendent
love, and the distinction between earthly (Aphrodite Pandemos) and
heavenly love (Aphrodite Urania) comes from Plato's *Symposium,*
(Shelley, 158–59n1). See *EE,* 67, and George Bornstein, *Yeats and
Shelley* (Chicago: University of Chicago Press, 1970), 72–73.

157. About Beatrice, see Book I, n. 67 above. The Great Yellow Rose
appears in canto 30 of *Paradiso* (line 113) and served as standard
Rosicrucian background in such works as A. E. Waite's *The Brotherhood of the Rosy Cross* (London: W. Rider, 1924), 94.

158. WBY used the phrase "pale passion loves" several times (see *EE,* 171,
271). The line "Fountaine heads, and pathlesse Groves, / Places which
pale passion loves" is from the song "Hence all you vaine Delights,"
praising "sweetest melancholy," from the play *The Nice Valour* by
John Fletcher and possibly Thomas Middleton, 3.3.46–47 (*The Dramatic Works in the Beaumont and Fletcher Canon,* Fredson Bowers,
gen. ed. [Cambridge: Cambridge University Press, 1966–96], 7:468).

159. The reference might be to Shelley's "Address to the Irish People"
(1812), "Declaration of Rights" (1812), "Letter to Lord Ellenbor-
ough" (1812), and "Vindication of Natural Diet" (1813).

160. See Shelley's *Alastor,* lines 248–50, 413, 471, 534–35 (Shelley, 20, 24,
25, 26).

161. See Shelley's *Hellas,* lines 164–65: "less accessible / Than thou or
God!" (Shelley, 456). This section of *Hellas* is also quoted at length in
Au, 152–53.

162. See Edward Dowden's *The Life of Percy Bysshe Shelley* (1886; rpt.,

New York: Barnes and Noble, 1966; see *Au,* 95). Although some did not believe him, Shelley in 1813 claimed to have been attacked, and in a letter he used the word "assassination" (Dowden, 184). The wife of one witness said that Shelley, who thought he had been fired upon through a window, "bounced out on the grass, and there he saw leaning against a tree the ghost, or, as he said, the devil . . ." (Dowden, 188).

163. *The Cenci* (1819), Shelley's verse drama about incest and revenge, relates the tale of Beatrice Cenci (1577–99), killed with the rest of her family for murdering her abusive and violent father, the Roman patriarch Francesco Cenci.

164. The contemporary here is Boccaccio; see Wicksteed, *The Early Lives of Dante,* 80 and cf. x.

165. Shelley wrote to Thomas Love Peacock in a letter dated 6 April 1819, "I am regarded by all who know or hear of me, except, I think, on the whole five individuals as a rare prodigy of crime & pollution whose look even might infect" (*Letters of Percy Bysshe Shelley,* ed. Frederick L. Jones [Oxford: Clarendon, 1964], 2:94).

166. Emerson and Whitman are similarly described in *Au,* 200. Based on cabalistic learning, WBY saw evil as an imbalance of opposing forces (see pp. 121 and 143; *LE,* 25). The AS of 10 June 1918 lays out the necessity of oppositions and the nature of evil: "In so far as knowledge of evil is attained," the control Thomas said, "one becomes good but in as far as one is good the visible world becomes evil because it is no virtue to be good knowing no evil—& it is no sin to be evil knowing no good" (*YVP* 1:492). See also Book IV, n. 35.

167. Shelley's play *Prometheus Unbound* (1820) was inspired by *Prometheus Bound,* traditionally attributed to Aeschylus.

168. Walter Savage Landor appears twice in this 1916 monograph (*LE,* 6, 15).

169. The examples are German novelist, dramatist, philosopher, and humanist Johann Wolfgang von Goethe (1749–1832) and Victorian poet and cultural critic Matthew Arnold (1822–88). The list of examples for this phase on the sheet filed with the AS of 2 June 1918 was longer: Zarathustra, GY, Goethe, Dulac, George Frederic Watts, Villon, Plutarch, Montaigne, Dürer, Titian, and two indecipherable names (*YVP* 1:549). As with WBY himself and phase 17, numerous aspects of the following essay suggest that WBY had GY, the philosophically minded receiver, interpreter, and organizer of the material and its uses, in mind as he wrote.

170. WBY slightly misquotes the titles of Rossetti's "Love's Nocturne" (see *EE,* 213, and *Au,* 234) and Shelley's "Ode to the West Wind."

171. Paraphrased from Goethe's *Wilhelm Meisters Wanderjahre:* "Wie kann man sich selbst kennen lernen? Durch Betrachten niemals, wohl aber durch Handeln" (*Goethes Werke,* ed. Erich Trunz et al. [Hamburg: Christian Wegner Verlag, 1964–67], 8:283).

172. Thomas Lovell Beddoes notes, "Goethe married his maid servant &

drinks brandy" (*Works of Thomas Lovell Beddoes*, ed. H. W. Donner [London: Oxford, 1935], 626), but it is unclear how WBY knew this passage before 1925, since the letter in Edmund Gosse's edition of *The Letters of Thomas Lovell Beddoes* (1894; rpt., New York: Benjamin Blom, 1971, 119–25) does not include this passage. Goethe loved Charlotte von Stein, but she was married to the Duke of Saxe-Weimar's Master of the Horse.

173. These words were spoken by Arthur Symons (*Au*, 257, and *Mem*, 97; and see *L*, 298). In VersB, WBY wrote that "The one man of this phase I have known intimately, the serpent charming lover, was a connosseur [*sic*] in several arts, a man of great tecnical [*sic*] mastery who saw art, life, literature as tecnical [*sic*] problems, & his life had lacked all momentum but for his bodily lusts" (*YVP* 4:200).

174. This passage may refer to the proverb "To sit (or sing) like a nightingale with a thorn against one's breast," or to that proverb's appearance in *The Spanish Tragedy* by Thomas Kyd, *The Rape of Lucrece* by William Shakespeare, and elsewhere.

175. Italian poet, novelist, and nationalist politician Gabriele d'Annunzio (1863–1938) led a seizure of the city of Fiume (Rijeka in Croatia) in 1919, maintaining control of the "independent state" until December 1920; his approach foreshadowed many aspects of Italian fascism. The Anglo-Irish playwright, critic, and novelist Oscar Wilde (1854–1900) was one of the most successful writers of his day, but he was also famous for his involvement in the Queensberry scandal and his trial in 1895 for "committing acts of gross indecency with other male persons." For WBY's assessment of Wilde, see *Au*, 124–30.

The examples also include English Romantic poet George Gordon, Lord Byron (1788–1824), of whose life WBY knew partly from Ralph Milbank, Earl of Lovelace's *Astarte: A Fragment of Truth Concerning George Gordon Byron, Sixth Lord Byron* (London: Chiswick Press, 1905), which WBY read in 1906 (*L*, 468), and he may have been aware of the second edition in 1921. WBY was aware of Byron's sexual relationship with his half sister, Augusta Leigh.

"A certain actress" refers to Mrs. Patrick Campbell, whom WBY saw in Maeterlinck's *Bluebird* (*L*, 544) and who performed the part of Mélisande in *Pelléas and Mélisande* (in 1898 and July 1904). In the AS of 21 November 1917, the control Thomas calls her one in whom the antithetical is "losing" to the primary. WBY asked: "Am I right in supposing that Mrs C violent egotism is aroused by the intensity of her consciousness of Materlinck emotion," to which Thomas responded, "The egotism in its endeavour to anihilate the meterlinc emotion becomes more violent until it has achieved its purpose when it becomes more normal" (*YVP* 1:93; see also *YVP* 2:17). This information is transferred to "Tinctures" in the CF (*YVP* 3:419), and a rejected section of VersB addresses George Bernard Shaw and Mrs. Campbell

(*YVP* 4:200–202). In *Per Amica Silentia Lunae*, WBY enforced the distinction between Mrs. Campbell's selfless presence as a Maeterlinck queen and her personal egotism (*LE*, 5). The list for this phase in the AS of 2 June 1918 differed significantly, naming Browning, Velázquez, Cromwell (*YVP* 1:549).

176. Mrs. Campbell's collection of Burne-Jones engravings drew attention from many. See *LE*, 217 (quoting from "Yeux Glauques" from Ezra Pound's *Hugh Selwyn Mauberley*), and Penelope Fitzgerald, *Edward Burne-Jones: A Biography* (London: Michael Joseph, 1975), 244.

177. This list contains English playwright and poet William Shakespeare (1564–1616), French novelist Honoré de Balzac (1799–1850), and French general and emperor Napoleon Bonaparte (1769–1821). The list on the sheet filed with the AS of 2 June 1918 names Dickens, Shakespeare, Chaucer, Plato, Fielding, Meredith, Anatole France (*YVP* 1:549). WBY struck through Fielding in VersB, replacing him with "Balzac. Perhaps Ben Johnson" (*YVP* 4:203).

178. See Shakespeare, Sonnet 110.

179. This episode derives from the *Mémoires* of Napoleon's secretary Bourrienne, but WBY may have encountered it in the sixth lecture of Carlyle's *On Heroes, Hero-Worship, and the Heroic in History*; see also Emil Ludwig, *Napoleon*, trans. Eden and Cedar Paul (Garden City, NJ: Garden City Publishing Company, 1926), 120. In the DMR-TS, Robartes comments on the changing unity of phase 19, saying "Balzac said of Napoleon that he was always the second lieutenant meaning that he was coarse and crude whom he admired extravagantly" (*YVP* 4:39).

180. Napoleon often looked to the trappings of the Roman Empire to dress up his regime. WBY wrote in "Four Years" (1921):

> Napoleon was never of his own time, as the naturalistic writers and painters bid all men be, but had some Roman emperor's image in his head and some condottiere's blood in his heart; and when he crowned that head at Rome with his own hands he had covered, as may be seen from David's painting, his hesitation with that emperor's old suit. (*Au*, 139)

181. Both words appear in Ben Jonson's eulogy attached to the First Folio.

182. Jonson killed an actor of Philip Henslowe's theatrical company in a duel and was for a short time imprisoned as a result.

183. The 1609 quarto text of Shakespeare's sonnets, widely accepted as the standard text, is generally understood to have been pirated.

184. Shakespeare, Jonson, and others gathered at this tavern.

185. Thomas Lake Harris, slightly misquoted, thus writes in *The Wisdom of the Adepts: Esoteric Science in Human History* (privately printed, Fountain Grove, 1882), 442. WBY repeats this quotation in *Au*, 217

(see also *Au,* 193–94; *LE,* 49, 70, 111). W. T. Horton introduced WBY to Harris's religious writing, much of which was automatic, including epic poems. After a brief time with the Golden Dawn, Horton joined an occult religious order called the Brotherhood of the New Life, founded by Harris. In 1896, Horton tried to convince WBY to follow suit and loaned him books by Harris, of which two titles can be identified from correspondence: *God's Breath in Man and in Humane Society* and *The Arcana of Christianity.*

186. The figures associated with phase 21 are the French naturalist Jean-Baptiste Lamarck (1744–1829); Irish playwright George Bernard Shaw (1856–1950); British novelist and science fiction writer Herbert George Wells (1866–1946); and the Irish novelist, poet, and critic George A. Moore (1852–1933). For the connection between "distortion" and "the mischievous malicious pranks of George Moore," see the sleep of 10 September 1920 (*YVP* 3:43). The list on the sheet filed with the AS for 2 June 1918 reads: Milton, Horace, Dr. Johnson, Flaubert, Napoleon, Richelieu. Dickens is marked through (*YVP* 1:549). Writing in 1934, WBY called Shaw, Wilde, and Moore "the most complete individualists in the history of literature, abstract, isolated minds, without a memory or a landscape" (*Poems,* 673).

187. WBY also refers to this passage, which mentions the character Ferdyshchenko and an incident occurring in part 1, chapters 13 and 14, of Dostoyevsky's *The Idiot,* in *Au,* 320–21, and echoes it in an oddly similar personal passage (*Mem,* 227), which may have been written before he had read the novel (see Book I, n. 106 above).

188. The figures listed are French novelist Gustave Flaubert (1821–80), English classical liberal philosopher Herbert Spencer (1820–1903), Swedish philosopher and mystic Emanuel Swedenborg (1688–1772), and Russian novelist Fyodor Dostoyevsky (1821–81). In the DMR-TS, Robartes mentions Flaubert's belonging "to the terrible Twenty-second phase" (*YVP* 4:43). The list filed with the AS of 2 June 1918 included Swedenborg, Dostoyevsky, and F. [W. H.] Myers, mentioned elsewhere in the AS and in other contexts during the time of the Yeatses' spiritualistic experiments. A founder and early president of the Society for Psychical Research, and an authority on automatic writing, Myers was the author of *Human Personality and Its Survival of Bodily Death* (1903), a book WBY knew well.

189. These terms are sketched on p. 45; see also p. 185 and Book I, n. 111 above.

190. The British naturalist Charles Darwin (1809–82), famous for his theories of evolution and natural selection, acknowledged Lamarck as an early proponent of ideas about evolution.

191. Two novels by Gustave Flaubert: *La tentation de Saint Antoine* (1874), written in the form of a play script, focuses on one night in which Saint Anthony the Great (ca. 251–356/7), the Egyptian founder of Christian

monasticism, is faced with great temptations; *Bouvard et Pécuchet* (published posthumously 1881), although incomplete, follows two narrow-minded Parisian copy clerks in their search for a suitable intellectual pursuit, parodying their findings along the way. The Yeatses owned copies of both these works (O'Shea 679, 682).

192. In *Art and Life* (London: Methuen, 1910; O'Shea 1361), T. Sturge Moore writes about Flaubert and "Impersonal Art," beginning the essay with an epistolary quotation from Flaubert: "I believe that great art is scientific and impersonal" (79).

193. The phrase is from the epigraph of part 1, chapter 13, of *Le Rouge et le Noir* by Stendhal (see also part 2, chapter 14). John Butler Yeats brought this passage to WBY's attention (see *Passages from the Letters of John Butler Yeats,* ed. Ezra Pound [Dublin: Cuala Press, 1917], 46), and WBY repeated it several times (*Au,* 270; *LE,* 194; *Ex,* 333; and *Plays,* 703). VersB has "sauntering" instead of "dawdling" (*YVP* 4:213).

194. The first part of this inexact quotation is in Blake's *Visions of the Daughters of Albion,* plate 7, line 15 (Erdman, 50; the plate is reproduced in facsimile in volume 3 of *WWB*). The Lake of Udan-Adan is featured in Blake's *Jerusalem.*

195. WBY refers to Swedenborg's entry into a new phase of his spiritual life. See *LE,* 49.

196. For Landor, see Book I, nn. 49, 86, 153, 168 above. The writer, designer, and socialist William Morris (1834–96) was one of the principal founders of the British Arts and Crafts movement; he and his work were among the most significant early as well as lasting influences upon WBY (see Book I, nn. 65, 87, 95 above).

197. Balzac usually worked at night, sleeping during the day. He wrote about his use of specially prepared coffee in "Traité des excitants modernes," or "Treatise on Modern Stimulants" (1838; *Études analytiques* [Paris: Les Bibliophiles de l'Originale, 1968]), 260–65. See also *LE,* 40.

198. German economist and philosopher Karl Marx (1818–83).

199. WBY may be drawing on T. Sturge Moore's *Art and Life,* where remarks by Edmond and Jules Goncourt are quoted on pp. 133 and 280 (see Book I, n. 192 above). He may have been confusing the brothers with Rémy de Gourmont, from whose *Problem of Style* Moore also quotes: "Far from its being his [Flaubert's] work which is impersonal, the roles are here reversed: it is the man who is vague and a tissue of incoherences; it is the work which lives, breathes, suffers, and smiles nobly . . ." (301).

200. In *Art and Life,* Moore writes: "Artists cannot be rigidly intellectual, since logic to become practical must yield something to the sensuous illusion in which life is immersed. Anatole France was perhaps feeling after this fact when he made the clumsy assertion that Flaubert was unintelligent" (134–35).

201. The words "a form" are an error: see VersB, where the phrase reads "The desire of reform has ceased" (*YVP* 4:216).

202. Dutch painter Rembrandt van Rijn (1606–69) joins Irish playwright and poet John Millington Synge (1871–1909). In "The Bounty of Sweden" (1923–24), WBY wrote: "Synge has described, through an exaggerated symbolism, a reality which he loved precisely because he loved all reality" (*Au*, 417). The sheet accompanying the AS of 2 June 1918 also lists as examples Michelangelo, Balzac (marked through), and Daniel O'Connell (*YVP* 1:549).

203. WBY frequently quoted or paraphrased this line from Blake's *Jerusalem*: "You shall want all the Minute Particulars of Life" (plate 88, line 43; Erdman, 247; the plate is reproduced in facsimile in volume 3 of *WWB*). In addition to the appearance here and in the manuscript draft, he rephrased the image in line 42 of "The Double Vision of Michael Robartes" to read, "the minute particulars of mankind" (*Poems*, 173). That poem originated in the AS of 7 January 1919 (*YVP* 2:162–64).

204. This passage might refer to the anatomically represented image of Christ in Rembrandt's *Descent from the Cross* (there is one in Munich and one in St. Petersburg) or of the more literal representation of anatomical discovery in *The Anatomy Lesson of Dr. Nicholaes Tulp*. Rembrandt's dramatic use of light and shade, or chiaroscuro, is rightly famous.

205. Synge's play *The Playboy of the Western World* contrasts its hero Christy Mahon with a traditional hero.

206. WBY was proud to have urged Synge, in late 1896, to "Go to the Aran Islands. Live there as if you were one of the people themselves; express a life that has never found expression" (see Synge 3:63; see also *Au*, 262). Beginning in 1898, Synge spent six summers in the Aran Islands collecting stories and folklore and perfecting his Irish.

207. Synge writes in the preface to *The Playboy of the Western World*, "I got more aid than any learning could have given me, from a chink in the floor of the old Wicklow house where I was staying, that let me hear what was being said by the servant girls in the kitchen" (Synge 4:53).

208. Many of Rembrandt's portraits show minute details of bourgeois clothing.

209. These characters are in Synge's play *Deirdre of the Sorrows* (1910); WBY slightly misquotes the line, "Draw a little back with the squabbling of fools when I am broken up with misery" (Synge 4:267). The actress may be Maire O'Neill, who was successful with Dublin audiences, if not with WBY (see *Au*, 386–87).

210. In the VersB treatment of phase 23, this observation is longer and more personal: "When I went through Synges work I marked many dialogues & paragraphs & one whole play as not to be published, or used except by the critic or historian. They were Synge before he found his genius, through Arran & dialect" (*YVP* 4:220).

211. *Queen Mab* was Shelley's earliest long poetic work, laying out his theory of revolution. *Alastor,* on the other hand, is an early expression of Shelley's doctrine of love, expressing a conflict between a desire for an ideal vision of love and an actual human (and imperfect) lover.

212. Jacques-Louis David (1748–1825) was a French Neoclassical painter.

213. Herbert George Wells is best known for novels like *The Time Machine* (1895) and *The War of the Worlds* (1898); see also Book I, n. 186 above.

214. This slightly misquoted line from Blake's *Europe* (plate 14, line 3; Erdman, 65; the plate is reproduced in facsimile in volume 3 of *WWB*) did not appear in the drafted essay in VersB but was also quoted in *Myth*1, 282, *Myth*2, 185.

215. Victoria (1819–1901), queen of Great Britain and Ireland from 1837 until her death, joins English novelist and playwright John Galsworthy (1867–1933). "A certain friend" is Lady Gregory, and she is named in *AVB,* 169. The AS (2 June 1918) lists Mazarin and Lady Gregory, dubbed "Placens uxor" (or "pleasing wife") (*YVP* 1:549). In the AS on 2 January 1918, WBY asked, without naming, "Where does Placens uxor come" and received the answer "24" (*YVP* 1:190). The Latin comes from Horace's *Odes* (book 2, no. 14, ll. 20–21), about death's inevitability. VersB lists Queen Victoria and "a certain personal friend," "personal" later crossed out (*YVP* 4:223). This phase was extensively revised, but its original opening seems to be an indirect tribute to Lady Gregory: "The most obviously impressive of all the phases when true to phase" (*YVP* 4:223).

216. WBY used this line from *Macbeth* (4.3.111) to describe Lady Gregory in *Mem,* 162, and *Au,* 336 (see also *Myth*1, 116; *Myth*2, 77). The manuscript draft reads: "There is great pride, but an impersonal pride, that of the code it self, & as great humility, a perpetual murmer 'in servant of servants'. Of such Shakespear wrote she died every day she lived" (*YVP* 4:223).

217. This passage describes Anthony Raftery (Antoine Ó Raifteiri, ca. 1748–1835), a blind Gaelic poet, in *Myth*1, 22–30; *Myth*2, 14–19. Lady Gregory, in her essay "Raftery," writes of "The truths of God that he strove in his last years . . . 'to have written in the book of the people' " (*Poets and Dreamers: Studies and Translations from the Irish* [Dublin: Hodges, Figgis, 1903], 21–22; O'Shea 807). WBY also uses the phrase in *IDM,* 103, and line 44 of "Coole and Ballylee, 1931" (*Poems,* 249).

218. Named for the color of its covers, a blue book is an official report of Parliament or the Privy Council.

219. According to the OED, this term, which originally referred specifically to a native of Bohemia, and later became a synonym for Gypsy, came to be used in the mid-nineteenth century for a person (especially an artist, writer, or actor) who leads a free or irregular life, without being particular as to the society he or she frequents.

220. WBY uses similar phrasing in *Au*, 201, and in his characterization of Mary Bell in *AVB*, 46.

221. Katharine O'Shea wrote that Parnell's "will was autocratic, and once he had made up his mind to any course he would brook no interference, nor suffer anything to stand in the way" (*Charles Stewart Parnell*, 2:243).

222. The figures listed are Anglican priest and later convert to Catholicism John Henry Cardinal Newman (1801–90); German theologian and ecclesiastical reformer Martin Luther (1483–1546); Christian theologian John Calvin (Jean Chauvin, 1509–64); English metaphysical poet George Herbert (1593–1633); and Irish nationalist, critic, poet, and mystical writer George William Russell (Æ, 1867–1935), described as "my friend AE" in VersB (*YVP* 4:232). The sheet accompanying the AS of 2 June 1918 lists as examples "Luther. Calvin. Ignatius Loyola. George Herbert. G. Russell" (*YVP* 1:549), although VersB includes only Newman and Luther (*YVP* 4:229). The list suggests that Herbert, Æ, and the others named are religious reformers. All are Teachers and Sages, not Victims, and primary instead of antithetical. There are many references to Æ in the AS (see, for example, *YVP* 2:17–18 and a discussion of Russell's "Irish avatar," *YVP* 2:67–68). On 6 February 1896, Æ had written to WBY that "the gods have returned to Erin and have centred themselves in the sacred mountains. . . . I believe profoundly that a new Avatar is about to appear . . ." (George Russell, *Letters from AE*, ed. Alan Denson [London: Abelard-Schuman, 1961], 17).

223. Possibilities for this reference include Newman's *A Letter Addressed to the Rev. E. B. Pusey, D. D., on Occasion of His Eirenicon of 1864* (1866). Prior to Newman's conversion, Pusey was one of Newman's fellows in the Oxford Movement, which sought a renewal of Roman Catholic practice in the Church of England. Pusey was trying to bring the two churches closer together, but Newman resented Pusey's representation of the Catholic doctrine of the Blessed Virgin. WBY got some of his knowledge of Newman from Lionel Johnson, but WBY later discovered that Johnson had imagined some of the meetings he described (*Au*, 236–37).

224. In the Peasants' War of 1524–26, the lower classes in Germany revolted against repressive measures against them. Although many viewed Luther as a revolutionary, he opposed the peasants. WBY revised this passage in VersB. He wrote "One thinks of Luthers rage," then "One thinks of Luthers incitment by, & later represssion of the peasantry & of accusations that followed Newman all his life" (*YVP* 4:230).

225. See similar ideas and wording in *Au*, 197–98. Æ was a talented amateur painter, and his paintings reflect a sense of the insubstantiality of the visible world. Gustave Moreau (1826–98) was a French Symbolist painter.

226. VersB adds a final sentence to the paragraph at this point: "He is a moralist" (*YVP* 4:232).

227. See a section on "the emotion of sanctity" beginning at this point in VersB (*YVP* 4:233).

228. In the AS (3 January 1918), WBY asked, "Can there [be] nobody of note at 26 & 28," but no answer was recorded (*YVP* 1:194). The Yeatses concluded, as WBY states in VersB, that "I must create from imagination, with some help from legend & from literature" (*YVP* 4:234). His source for the hunchback is not entirely clear. Melchiori (*The Whole Mystery of Art*, 277–79) believes WBY drew from Byron's play *The Deformed Transformed*. Other sources might be Shakespeare's *Richard III*, Victor Hugo's Quasimodo (see *Au*, 95), and "an old hunchback" painted by WBY's father, John B. Yeats (*Au*, 91).

229. Nero Claudius Caesar Augustus Germanicus (reigned 54–68 CE), the fifth Roman emperor; Nero, whose original name was Lucius Domitius Ahenobarbus, replaced his stepfather Claudius in 54 CE at the latter's murder, probably by Claudius's wife and Nero's mother, Agrippina Minor. Nero became infamous for widely believed stories of his debauched life, his persecution of Christians, and his burning of Rome.

230. As examples of ambitious men, the text offers Roman military and political leader Gaius Julius Caesar (ca. 100–44 BCE), who was instrumental in transforming the Roman republic into an empire, and Achilles, the legendary Greek hero of the Trojan War.

231. WBY wrote of Florence Farr Emery:

> I formed with her an enduring friendship that was an enduring exasperation—'Why do you play the part with a bent back and a squeak in the voice? How can you be a character actor, you who hate all our life, you who belong to a life that is a vision?' But argument was no use, and some Nurse in Euripides must be played with all an old woman's infirmities and not as I would have it, with all a Sibyl's majesty, because 'it is no use doing what nobody wants', or because she would show that she 'could do what the others did'. (*Au*, 119)

232. Judas appears regularly in the AS. The control Thomas observed on 26 January 1918 that "Judas is Creative Genius," placing him in phase 8, the phasal opposite of Christ at phase 22. WBY asked how he could be "amalgamation or pity," to which Thomas replied: "because he synthesises this pity into a single action a *choice*." WBY clarified: "You mean he would force C[hrist] to act" (*YVP* 1:291; see also 3:161). On the next evening, Thomas cautioned, "Dont make your Judas the conventional bad man—make him the weak man who achieves a supreme good through his temptation" (*YVP* 1:294). The role of Judas in *Calvary* (1920) seems to grow out of this AS, devoted mostly to the rela-

tionship of Christ and Judas. On the relationship between the AS and the play, and on the phasal relationship between Christ and Judas, see Haswell, "Resurrecting *Calvary*," 162–75; and Margaret Mills Harper, *Wisdom of Two*, 204–8.

233. More than to the biblical allusion to Ezekiel 4:4–6 and 13:1–23, this passage refers to Blake's *The Marriage of Heaven and Hell* (plates 12–14; Erdman, 39; the plate is reproduced in facsimile in volume 3 of *WWB*); see *LNI*, 102.

234. In the great Sanskrit epic the *Mahabharata*, the Pandava princes (Yudhishtira, Bhima, Arjuna, Nakula, and Sahadeva), the five acknowledged sons of the king Pandu (by his two wives Kunti and Madri), are not his biological offspring but the sons of various gods. One day, while on a hunt, Pandu saw a deer coupling with its mate. He killed it and then discovered that the buck was in fact a *rishi* (a sage) in the form of a deer. The deer, changing its form, delivered a curse: that the king too would die in the act of lovemaking. The king then refrained from intercourse with his wives, but the gods granted them the boon of having sons through other means. The ancient practice of *niyoga*, or the begetting of children by proxy when a husband is unable to father them, derived from the story of this family.

235. See p. 85.

236. At this point in *AVB*, a paragraph is added and the footnote omitted.

237. The examples are Greek philosopher Socrates (ca. 470–399 BCE), a prominent figure in Plato's dialogues, and the French mathematician and physicist Blaise Pascal (1623–62). In the AS (3 January 1918), both Socrates and Pascal appeared in phase 27 (*YVP* 1:193–94). In page proofs (NLI, 36,271), WBY struck through the name of Tagore as his third example. WBY found several occasions to use the word "saint" in his introduction (1912) to Tagore's *Gitanjali* (*LE*, 165–70; O'Shea 2084). He may have determined it bad taste to canonize the living.

238. In VersB, this long passage (with some changes) appears at the end of the explanation of phase 25. WBY notes that the soul "cannot pass 25, it must reincarnate at 25 till it has turned this emotion—which is a subconscious thought—into 'sanctity' it self. That is to say it must give up the endevour to rela[te] that supersentual environment to itself" (*YVP* 4:233). This discussion ends with a poetic passage, later revised and used at the end of the dedication (see Dedication and Introduction, n. 29).

239. Arthur Symons writes in "Maeterlinck as a Mystic": "Jacob Boehme has said, very subtly, 'that man does not perceive the truth but God perceives the truth in man'; that is, that whatever we perceive or do is not perceived or done consciously by us, but unconsciously through us" (*The Symbolist Movement in Literature*, rev. ed. [New York: E. P. Dutton, 1919], 90; London: William Heinemann, 1899; O'Shea 2068).

240. The source for this figure may include the *Amadán-na-Breena*, "a fool of the forth" (see *Myth1*, 112; *Myth2*, 75; see also *Myth2*, 460, and

Lady Gregory, *Visions and Beliefs in the West of Ireland* [1920; Gerrards Cross: Colin Smythe, 1970], 250–54), in Irish *amadán na briona,* "the fool who loves fighting"; the tarot Fool known to WBY from the Golden Dawn and works by S. L. MacGregor Mathers; the fool of the East (*Au,* 196); or "the pure fool of European tradition," as exemplified in Shakespeare's *King Lear* (see *LE,* 150).

241. Unidentified; fools are widely connected with innocence and goodness. In the New Testament, followers of Christ are sometimes referred to as "children of God," and the Gospel is often referred to as seeming folly; see, for example, 1 Corinthians 1:20: "Hath not God made foolish the wisdom of this world?"

242. Misquoted from Sir William Watson's epigram on "The Play of *King Lear*" from *Wordsworth's Grave and Other Poems* (London: T. Fisher Unwin, 1890), 72, which is quoted correctly by WBY in *LNI,* 105.

243. See p. 7.

244. WBY probably finished a draft of Book I between October and December 1922, having left Ballylee for Dublin with his family in September. The Irish Civil War, which began in June 1922, was a conflict between two republican factions over whether to accept the Anglo-Irish Treaty of 1921. The anti-treaty forces, including a large section of Sinn Féin and the majority of the Irish Republican Army (IRA), called the Irregulars, fought the pro-treaty forces of the Provisional Government of the Free State under Michael Collins. The pro-treaty side eventually prevailed and hostilities had ceased by the spring of 1923, but there was no negotiated peace and consequently no official end to the war.

Book II: What the Caliph Refused to Learn

1. This poem does not appear in an early typescript of Book III, consisting of material that eventually became Books II–IV in the published book (NLI, 36,263/24/1–2). Instead, there is a section called "Where Kusta-ben-Luka got his philosophy," a prose account containing the narrative details of the poem and signed "Owen Ahearne." This account was published, with some changes and additions, as a note to "The Gift of Harun-al-Rashid" in *The Cat and the Moon and Certain Poems* (1924), where WBY described it as a "letter of Owen Ahern's, which I am publishing in 'A Vision' " (*Poems,* 700). The prose narrative is more clearly autobiographical than the poem. For instance, it notes that the "young bride" had "fallen in love with the elderly philosopher . . . to the surprise of her friends and relations." "They were married but a few days," according to the typescript, "when she began to talk in her sleep, and her wisdom was so great that he saw at once that the Caliph had acted under divine guidance, and that she had been brought to him that he who had sought wisdom in libraries might learn all the secrets from an ignorant mouth. . . . She taught him for a num-

ber of years, often walking to the border of the desert in her sleep, and there marking upon the sand innumerable intricate symbols" (cf. *Poems*, 700–701). The fiction extends even further in Book IV of the typescript, "Death, the Soul, and the Life after Death," which starts with the story "Michael Robartes and the Judwali Doctor," a shorter version of which appears in the published book (see pp. 202 and 203–4). Unlike Kusta's wife, however, GY was no "ignorant mouth."

This poem does not appear in *AVB*, where WBY noted that "as my wife was unwilling that her share should be known, and I to seem sole author, I had invented an unnatural story of an Arabian traveler which I must amend and find a place for some day because I was fool enough to write half a dozen poems that are unintelligible without it" (*AVB*, 19). The poem was first published in *English Life and The Illustrated Review* (January 1924) and in *The Dial* (June 1924) and was later included in *The Tower* (1928).

2. This character, called "Faristah" in the poem's first printing, remains untraced. The name was probably invented for the purpose of the poem.

3. Writing in 1924, WBY remarked that "The banners of the Abbasid Caliphs were black as an act of mourning for those who had fallen in battle at the establishment of the Dynasty" (*VP*, 461, 829).

4. The eastern section of the Roman Empire had its capital in Constantinople from 330 to 1453, until the city was besieged by the Ottoman Turks, becoming Istanbul. The full flowering of Byzantine culture and apex of its power, according to the system, is located in the historical cones precisely halfway between the primary and the antithetical poles, at the midpoint of the two-thousand-year cycle. See pp. 158–60 and *AVB*, 279–81.

5. Sappho (b. 630–612 BCE) was an ancient Greek lyric poet from the city of Eressos on the island of Lesbos, a cultural center in the seventh century BCE. Her poetry survives only in fragments, although WBY said in a note of 1924 that "Gibbon says the poems of Sappho were extant in the twelfth century" (*VP*, 829).

6. Parmenides of Elea (fifth century BCE) was a Greek philosopher reported to have been a student of Xenophanes. He is one of the most significant of the pre-Socratic philosophers, arguing that the everyday perception of reality of the physical world (the Way of Seeming) is mistaken and that the reality of the world is "One Being" (the Way of Truth): an unchanging, ungenerated, indestructible whole. As with Sappho, his writings survive only in fragments, although WBY commented in his note of 1924 that "it does not seem impossible that a great philosophical work, of which we possess only fragments, may have found its way into an Arab library of the eighth century" (*VP*, 829).

Plato's dialogue *Parmenides* concerns Socrates' theory of forms and claims to be an account of a meeting between Parmenides and Zeno of

Elea (two great philosophers of the Eleatic school) and a very young Socrates. WBY may have read *Parmenides* in the translation of Thomas Taylor, who noted that Plato intended "to conceal divine mysteries under the veil of symbols and figures" (*Works of Plato* [London, 1794], 3:3). WBY may be referring to other books he was reading at this time (see Book II, n. 25 below; also *VP*, 829).

7. *Bedouin*, meaning "desert dweller," is a term generally applied to Arab nomadic groups living throughout most of the desert belt extending from the Atlantic coast of the Sahara, via the Western Desert, Sinai, and Negev, to the eastern coast of the Arabian desert.

8. This line is omitted from the poem as printed in *VP*, 462, and *Poems*, 451.

9. Vizier Jaffer governed under the caliph Harun al-Rashid from 786–803 CE, and was then imprisoned and executed for unknown reasons.

10. In 1924, WBY wrote that " 'All those gyres and cubes and midnight things' refers to the geometrical forms which Robartes describes the Judwali Arabs as making upon the sand for the instruction of their young people, & which, according to tradition, were drawn or described in sleep by the wife of Kusta-ben-Luka" (*VP*, 830).

11. Summarizing Daphne Fullwood, Jeffares (*The Circus Animals: Essays on W. B. Yeats* [London: Macmillan, 1970], 103–14) suggests that WBY only knew of the Flaubert project through Moore's *Art and Life* (see Book I, n. 200). This section was much revised in typescript.

12. WBY knew Swedenborg well (see *LE*, 47–73); he owned copies of five of Swedenborg's works, some of which are heavily marked. His copies of *The Spiritual Diary* and *The Principia* feature fairly extensive marginalia, although he did not read all of either of these copies: only the first volumes of either book have had all the pages cut (O'Shea 2039, 2039A, 2040, 2040A, 2040B, 2040C, 2040D).

13. See *Myth1*, 123; *Myth2*, 81.

14. WBY wrote in an early version headed "The Gyres and Higher Dimensions," "I find among my documents the statement that a gyre represents a life lived in a higher dimension . . . , and we may consider the full gyre itself half a rotating four dimensional sphere" (NLI, 36,263/24/1–2). WBY borrowed this concept from Lyndon Bolton's *An Introduction to the Theory of Relativity* ([London: Methuen, 1921], 160; O'Shea 240), which he misquoted slightly in the same rejected typescript: "The whole of the physical nature is a mathematical diagram, is a mass of these world-lines, existing in a fourth dimensional continuum, like strings in a piece of jelly, and sometimes intersecting one another."

15. Concerning the vortices of French philosopher René Descartes (1596–1650), WBY may have borrowed from J. P. Mahaffy's *Descartes* (see Jeffares, *The Circus Animals*, 106), but Bolton had written that "The immediate predecessor of Newton's theory was the Cartesian the-

ory of Vortices. According to this theory, space is filled with a subtle medium or aether which is in a continual state of whirl, producing vortices which entangle bodies such as the planets and thus cause them to revolve" (*An Introduction to the Theory of Relativity,* 168).

16. WBY read the works of Christian mystic Jakob Boehme (1575–1624) in William Law's famous edition (1764–81), of which he owned a secondhand copy (O'Shea 239), one of six books by Boehme that he owned. See also *AVB,* 23–24. Blake used the same edition and wrote in *The Marriage of Heaven and Hell* that "any man of mechanical talents may from the writings of Paracelsus or Jacob Behmen, produce ten thousand volumes of equal value with Swedenborg's" (Erdman, 43; the plate [no. 22] is reproduced in facsimile in volume 3 of *WWB*).

17. The idea of the gyre was probably justified after the fact by the passages cited; on WBY's sources, see Melchiori, *The Whole Mystery of Art,* 261–70. The vortices of the system probably drew from Blake, theosophy, and especially Rosicrucianism (see, for example, Israel Regardie, *The Golden Dawn. A Complete Course in Practical Ceremonial Magic. Four Volumes in One. The Original Account of the Teachings, Rites and Ceremonies of the Hermetic Order of the Golden Dawn [Stella Matutina],* 6th ed. [Saint Paul, MN: Llewellyn Publications, 1992], 614–61). On Heraclitus, see also pp. 105, 106.

18. As Matthew Gibson has noted, this sentence incorrectly attributes to the Irish philosopher George, or Bishop, Berkeley (1685–1753) ideas about temporal and spatial forms in the mind that belonged to Immanuel Kant (1724–1804) ("Yeats, Kant, and Giovanni Gentile: The Single Gyre of Time and Space," *YA* 15 (2002): 315.

   In the section of the typescript indebted to Bolton (see Book II, n. 14 above), WBY wrote: "If I did not wish to avoid all argument wherein my concrete mind would do badly what others do well, it would amuse me to follow these arguments of Ouspensky, that birth and death, spring and summer, and all waxing and waning, are but the appearance that immoveable solids take, as we encircle them . . ."

19. This passage, perhaps borrowing from Bolton and others, appeared in a section entitled "Symbols of Time and Space" in the rejected typescript (see Book II, n. 14 above). WBY also found parallels in other sources; see *Au,* 282, as well as Regardie, who notes:

> In this diagram [of the Maltese Cross] are represented the Circle, the Point, the Line, the Cross, the Square and the Cube. For the Circle is the Abyss, the Nothingness, the AIN. The Point is Kether. Now, the Point has no dimension, but in moving, it traces the Line. This gives the first number—Unity—yet therein, lies duality unmanifest, for two Points mark its ends. The movement of the line maketh the Plane or Square thus. . . . The motion of the Point at angles to its first direction and intersecting

it maketh the Cross. So therefore, are the Square and the Cross but one Symbol, deriving from the Circle and the Point. (*The Golden Dawn,* 204–5).

20. Meaning "soul of man" and "soul of the world," these two phrases are the titles of the two main sections of *Per Amica Silentia Lunae.* WBY wrote in that text:

> If all our mental images no less than apparitions (and I see no reason to distinguish) are forms existing in the general vehicle of *Anima Mundi,* and mirrored in our particular vehicle, many crooked things are made straight. I am persuaded that a logical process, or a series of related images, has body and period, and I think of *Anima Mundi* as a great pool or garden where it moves through its allotted growth like a great water plant or fragrantly branches in the air. (*LE,* 22–23)

See also F. A. C. Wilson, *Yeats's Iconography* (London: Gollancz; New York: Macmillan, 1960), 97–98. Although the first recorded question of the AS concerns the *Anima Mundi,* and although it remains a significant term in the system, it was de-emphasized in the *Vision* documents as time went on, and there is a sense that WBY was likelier to use it than GY. On 9 January 1918, the control Thomas informed the couple, "I hate that term" (*YVP* 1:234).

21. It seems that WBY first noted this quotation from Heraclitus in his journal in 1909 (*Mem,* 216). He may have found it in Thomas Taylor, who quotes it several times, but Taylor's translation ("we live their death, and we die their life") differs from WBY's (*Thomas Taylor the Platonist: Selected Writings,* ed. Kathleen Raine and George Mills Harper [Princeton: Princeton University Press, 1969], 303). John Burnet's *Early Greek Philosophy,* which WBY owned and used as reference (O'Shea 308), is a more likely source: "Mortals are immortals and immortals are mortals, the one living the other's death and dying the other's life" (Burnet, 138). Burnet is an even more obvious source for another citation from Heraclitus (*Mem,* 216): "War is the father of all and the king of all; and some he has made gods and some men, some bound and some free" (Burnet, 136). See also *AVB,* 67 and 82. WBY apparently relied on the first edition of Burnet, rather than editions of 1908 or 1920, for other borrowings from the pre-Socratic philosophers.

22. Here begins a series of quotations from Burnet, not "Birkett." WBY had read F. C. Burkitt's *Early Eastern Christianity* (London: John Murray, 1904; see *LE,* 207; *Au,* 284–85); the error is corrected in the copy of *AVA* in which the Yeatses recorded errors in order to correct the future second edition (O'Shea 2433c; see table 3, p. 348). Similarly, although WBY mistakenly attributes the quotation to Heraclitus

(ca. 535–475 BCE), it is from Empedocles (ca. 490–430 BCE), fragments 35–36: "But now I shall retrace my steps over the paths of song that I have travelled before, drawing from my saying a new saying. When Strife was fallen to the lowest depth of the vortex, and Love had reached to the centre of the whirl, in it do all things come together so as to be one only; not all at once, but coming together gradually each from different quarters; and, as they came together, Strife retired to the extreme boundary" (Burnet, 211–12). Burnet included a note in the 1892 edition that he withdrew from all subsequent editions: "The 'lowest depth' is not, as might be supposed, the centre; but it is the same thing as the 'extreme boundary.' " WBY corrected *Heraclitus* to *Empedocles* in *AVB*, 67.

23. Empedocles, fragments 35–36 (Burnet, 211–12).

24. Burnet's translation of Empedocles reads: "For, of a truth, they [i.e., Love and Strife] were aforetime and shall be: nor ever, methinks, will boundless time be emptied of that pair. And they prevail in turn as the circle comes round, and pass away before one another, and increase in their appointed turn" (223).

25. See Parmenides in Burnet: "Where, then, it has its farthest boundary, it is complete on every side, equally poised from the centre in every direction, like the mass of a rounded sphere; for it cannot be greater or smaller in one place than in another. [Here, WBY goes back to the preceding paragraph in Burnet.] And there is not, and never shall be, any time other than that which is present, since fate has chained it so as to be whole and immovable" (187). A passage in the rejected typescript (see Book II, n. 14 above) refers to these lines:

> A book of mathematics tells me that I am to understand an obscure passage in Parmenides as the description of a higher dimensional solid under the symbol of a stick thrust into running water. The stick thrust into the surface of the water creates a series of whorls and eddies very comparable to our gyres, whereas in the mathematics of today 'The physical history of every object is its worldline'.

See Bolton, *An Introduction to the Theory of Relativity*, 160.

26. In a fairly late typescript (NLI, 36,266/6), Sections III and IV (pp. 107–112), both without headings, were interchanged.

27. For the quotations from "The Mental Traveller," see Erdman, 484–85; *WWB* 2:31–33. The poem is most important to the understanding of *A Vision*. Much of the AS of 9 April 1919 draws a parallel between Blake's poem and the system (*YVP* 2:239–41). The relationship of the poem to the cyclical theories of the system is also suggested in the record of a "meditation" of 3 October 1920: "But she [GY] had got the words continually repeated 'He grows old as she grows young'

from Blake's Mental Traveller. . . . He [the control Dionertes] said that the C[elestial]. B[ody]. grew young reaching its climax of youth at the Man's death while the P[assionate]. B[ody]. grew old, reaching its greatest age at Death. After death the PB. grew young & the CB old; until birth came round again birth being the CB's time of greatest age, while in it (birth) the youth of PB. climaxed" (*YVP* 3:50–51).

28. The reference is to *WWB*. Commentary on "The Mental Traveller" appears in 2:34–36.

29. WBY seems again to confuse pre-Socratic philosophers; Parmenides says little about love, whereas Empedocles says a great deal (see p. 106, and Burnet, 245–71).

30. Allusion untraced. In Plato's dialogue *Symposium,* the doctor Eryxi-machus famously distinguishes between the polarities of heavenly and earthly or wanton love (187c–188b).

31. G. E. Bentley's *Blake Records* illuminate these references: on the doc-ument, see p. 35; on Blake's brother, James Blake, see p. 2; on Blake's friend Flaxman, see pp. 440–41n6.

32. WBY's copy of Swedenborg's *The Spiritual Diary* (O'Shea 2040) con-tains numerous marginal comments that demonstrate WBY's connect-ing its ideas to those of Blake as well as the Yeatses' system. In *The Spiritual Diary,* Swedenborg describes a hell in which man is sur-rounded by "an encircling form, which existed from the influx of heaven; and, from this, there was an operation into the spirits and genii around man. That form was active, like a vortex, as if it revolved" (Emanuel Swedenborg, *The Spiritual Diary,* trans. George Bush and Rev. John H. Smithson [London: James Speirs, 1883–1902], 4:159–60).

33. See Burnet, "Fire and Water and Earth and the mighty height of Air," 222.

34. In a letter of 19 January 1926, Frank Pearce Sturm wrote to WBY: "On page 135 you say *the cone of fate & mind is shaded,* & you shade it to distinguish it, and on the very next page you leave it plain & shade the opposite cone[.] Until some dull dog with an eye for detail & accuracy goes over book II, it will remain incomprehensible simply because of inaccuracies in the text. I have given my life to these studies, but until Book II is rewritten I must be like the Caliph & refuse to learn. The text simply does not explain the figures." WBY responded on 21 January, "You are write [*sic*] about page 135—the cone of *fate* is the one that should be shaded throughout. This is an old error of mine—it was a mis-understanding that I corrected after recurring confusion—on the second of these pages I slipped back into it. I have made a mark in the margin that I may remember to put it right later on" (*FPS,* 87–89). The copy of *AVA* that the Yeatses used to record corrections (O'Shea 2433c) does indeed have marginal corrections on pp. 135–36. WBY changed A to C, B to D, C to A, and D to B in the sentence that begins "By moving the two dotted cones in and out"; noted by the second diagram in this sec-

tion that "cones are transposed shadow cone is that of Mind etc."; and transposed the terms *antithetical* and *primary* in the sentence that begins "That is to say when B is three quarter *primary* . . ." (table 3, p. 348).

35. See Plotinus, *Enneads* 4.6.1–2. GY studied seriously the work of Plotinus (ca. 205–70 CE) from 1913; she owned several copies of selections, and the complete set of Stephen MacKenna's important translation in the Yeatses' library has her bookplate in the first volume (O'Shea 1589–95a). She claimed to have introduced the translations of Thomas Taylor to WBY (see Saddlemyer, 45), although WBY had known MacKenna and Plotinian thought for many years before they met. WBY sometimes disapproved of Plotinus's abstract thought (see "The Tower," line 146 and note; *Poems*, 198, 598).

36. Blake writes often about wheels, which for him are almost inevitably negative symbols, connected with the evils of industrialism or deistic philosophy, with its concept of a mechanistic universe.

37. In other words, in *The Iliad* and *The Odyssey*, the supreme beauty of Helen and the horrors of the war that the Greek forces waged on Troy (which are *antithetical* and *primary*, respectively) are opposites whose relation to each other is conflictual rather than harmonic.

38. Avicenna is the common English name for the Persian philosopher and physician Abu 'Ali al-Husayn ibn 'Abd Allah ibn Sina, or Ebn e-Sina (980–1037), who was influenced by Aristotle and the Neoplatonists. Although, according to A. E. Waite's *Lives of Alchemystical Philosophers* (O'Shea 2210), he was known to be a "philosopher devoid of wisdom, and a physician without health" ([London: George Redway, (1888)], 52), this maxim is, in the words of Warwick Gould and Deirdre Toomey, "an alchemical commonplace which [WBY] had found in a number of contexts" (*Myth2*, 383n35). See also Flaubert's *The Temptation of St. Anthony* (trans. D. F. Hannigan [London: H. S. Nichols, 1895]; O'Shea 682): "existence proceeds from corruption" (162). See also *Myth1*, 276; *Myth2*, 182.

39. The "Precession of the Equinoxes" or "Precession of the Zodiac" is the term for the phenomenon that explains why the astrological signs of the zodiac do not now correspond with the actual sidereal constellations. The unequal gravitational pulls of the moon and the sun create a kind of "wobble" in the earth's rotation like a gyroscope, so that as the earth rotates once each day around its axis, the axis itself rotates in the opposite direction in a motion shaped like a cone. This motion—the precession—is very slow, so that it takes 2,160 years for the axis to rotate thirty degrees around a circle. In Western Tropical Astrology (so called because it is based on the *tropos,* or turning of the four seasons, rather than the passage of planets through the celestial constellations), the system that the Yeatses and most Western astrologers use, this 2,160 years is called an *Age.* Twelve Ages, or about twenty-five thousand years, comprise one Great Year.

40. In one typescript, this section is headed "The Equinoctial Points" (NLI, 36,269/13).

41. The AS for 22 January 1918 includes attempts to incorporate the twenty-eight phases with other divisions of a single circle: "12 = Mind / 10 = Soul / 22 = ascent." These numbers may signify the ten limbs on the Tree of Life and ten degrees in the Golden Dawn, the twelve signs of the zodiac, and the twenty-two petals in the Rosicrucian rose. On the recto of the pages recording the session from 18 January, a diagram presents five concentric circles and cardinal directions. The circles are labeled "Horoscope," "phases," "days," and "Equinoxes" (NLI, 36,253/12; see *YVP* 1:275, 531nn214, 215.

42. On 19 January 1926, Sturm wrote to WBY concerning this sentence:

> In order that I may write about your book with some appearance of intelligence it will be necessary to explain what you mean here, if you will help me. The Moon doesn't move from West to East; she is never retrograde; but moves along the Zodiac in the same direction as the Sun, not in the opposite direction. You base so much on the opposite movements of the Lunar & Solar circles, when no opposite movement exists, that some kind of explanation is needed to smooth out the wrinkles here.

WBY responded on 20 January that "You will get all mixed up if you think of my symbolism as astrological or even astronomical in any literal way." He added,

> You should think of the moons movement through the 28 phases & the suns movement through the zodiac as two ways of symbolizing—a mere language. . . . The symbolism is consistent with itself—if it is not at any point that is my fault not the fault of its makers—but it is not a natural symbolism.

He noted in a postscript,

> I notice that on P 141 I spoke of the zodiacal movement. I was thinking of the moons passage through the signs, as compared to the [sun symbol] diurnal journey, but it would have been less confusing if I had stuck to my symbolism & said 'phasal movement'—I was thinking of the picture to the eye. If you master the diagram on Page 13 & the movements of the Four Faculties therein you will understand most of the book.

Sturm wrote back to note that his own daimon had told him to apologize for misunderstanding and therefore insinuating an error: "I am to say with regard to Section VI of Book II that as it stands it is literally correct, not merely symbolically, but quite literally and astronomically." He included a diagram to illustrate that

The actual motions of earth & moon, as they exist in nature, are as follows:

(1) The sun is the centre & does not move.
(2) The earth circles round the sun from West to East
(3) The Earth rotates on its own axis from West to East
(4) The Moon circles the earth from West to East (though its apparent daily motion, due to the rotation of the earth is from East to West)

and the explanation that "*rotation, revolution & lunation are all counter clockwise*[.] But the apparent motion of the Sun is from east to west. If therefore it be explained that Section VI of Book II refers to the actual motion of the Moon from West to East, but to the apparent motion of the Sun from East to West, the statement that Solar & Lunar circles move in opposite directions will be as reasonable as it is literally true" (*FPS*, 87–91).

43. The Yeatses received this piece of information on 14 January 1918. To WBY's question "When you are giving a profound philosophy why do you warn me against philosophy," the control Thomas replied,

I warn you against the philosophy that is bred in stagnation—it is a bitter philosophy a philosophy which destroys—I give you one which leads—I give you one which is from outside—a light which you follow not one which will burn you[.]

WBY followed with another question, "Is there a precise significance in burning?" and GY wrote, "A philosophy created from experience burns—one which is created from search leads" (*YVP* 1:252). WBY repeated this bit of explanation in the CF (*YVP* 3:298–99), noting a date of December 1917 and that the advice came after a "warning against 'enforced self realization which creads [creates] philosophy in stagnation.'" GY also copied it into VNB1 as one of several "Definitions" (*YVP* 3:174).

44. For other uses of almost identical phrases, see pp. 108, 138, 183.

45. WBY observed more than once in the AS that the spirits would deceive, even calling one whole class of spirits "Frustrators" (see Book IV, n. 59). See *YVP* 1:27–28 and *MYV* 2:180–85. In a letter of 1 April 1933, Everard Feilding refers to an assertion by WBY (in a lost letter) that "in the unconscious there is a will to cheat *and to be found cheating*" (*LWBY*, 553).

46. On 30 January 1919, the control Thomas gave "the definition of

abstraction": GY drew a diagram of a burning candle and wrote, "Abstraction is that quality in every phase which impedes unity of being" (*YVP* 2:195; reiterated in VNB2 [*YVP* 3:188], and in the CF [*YVP* 3:238]). On 22 November 1919, in the course of a session analyzing the collaboration that was required to receive the system, including relations between the Yeatses' minds and physical desires, the couple learned that its images remained "unquickend & disunited" if "they are in one mind only—they cannot unite unless through a second mind." WBY asked the control Ameritus, "Do you consider the definition that abstraction is anything separated from its opposite covers all forms of abstraction," to which the reply was *Yes* (*YVP* 2:491).

47. The time it takes the "wobble" in the earth's axis to cause the vernal equinox to retrograde one full cycle, about 26,800 years, is called in Western astrology the Precessional or Great Year. See Book II, n. 39 above. WBY explains the Great Year in the introduction (1933) to his play *The Resurrection*, which treats its biblical theme in terms of the historical cones of the system:

> Ptolemy thought the precession of the equinoxes moved at the rate of a degree every hundred years, and that somewhere about the time of Christ and Caesar the equinoctial sun had returned to its original place in the constellations, completing and recommencing the thirty-six thousand years, or three hundred and sixty incarnations of a hundred years apiece, of Plato's man of Ur. Hitherto almost every philosopher had some different measure for the Greatest Year, but this Platonic Year, as it was called, soon displaced all others; it was a Christian heresy in the twelfth century, and in the East, multiplied by twelve as if it were but a month of a still greater year, it became the Manvantra of 432,000 years, until animated by the Indian jungle it generated new noughts and multiplied itself into Kalpas. (*Plays*, 724)

48. With one difference ("describe" rather than "consider"), this sentence was inserted in galley proofs.

49. "Mid Autumn," "Mid Winter," "Mid Spring," "Mid Summer," and "First Lunar Month of Great Year" were inserted in page proofs.

50. In galley proofs, this phrase read: "to get mankind." For an amplification of the meaning, see Book II, n. 42 above.

51. Each of the twelve signs of the zodiac is divided into thirty degrees. "Aries 30," then, is the end of Aries and the beginning of the following sign, Taurus.

52. See Book II, n. 22 above.

53. The idea that an age characterized by one Tincture is followed, after a sudden incarnation of the opposite Tincture, by an age with the other

dispensation is central to "Leda and the Swan" (here called "Leda"), "The Second Coming," *Calvary*, and other works.

54. The term "Fountains" appears in the CF (*YVP* 3:308–9), on a card that summarizes information received in the sleeps of 11 January and 9 February 1921 (*YVP* 3:64–65, 68–69). In the sleeps, the term "Master" is used instead of "Fountain." Masters are born of daimons, the Yeatses learned, and the First Master is Christ.

55. In Plato's *Symposium*, secs. 189ff., Aristophanes explains that originally there were three sexes: male, female, and androgynous; perhaps borrowing from Coleridge, WBY simplifies the myth by stressing this third group. In the DMR-TS, Aherne remarks: "I remember the passage in the Table talk, [Coleridge] said that all great minds are androgynous" (*YVP* 4:43). See also "Among School Children," line 15 (*Poems*, 220). That Coleridge's examples of such minds included Boehme and Swedenborg would certainly have been of interest to WBY.

56. Various sources (e.g., Duhem 1:65–85, 275–96; W. M. Flinders Petrie's *The Revolutions of Civilisation*, 3rd ed. [London and New York: Harper, 1922], 9–10 [O'Shea 1559 and 1559a]) indicate that such ancient philosophers as Plato believed that man developed through a series of cultural stages analogous to the year. Like an individual or like Frazer's year-gods in *The Golden Bough*, each stage developed biologically, and each ultimately fell to a new victor. Modern astronomy eliminated some earlier doubt about the length of time required for the precession of the equinoxes; note WBY's references below to disputed passages in Plato.

57. See Plato's *Timaeus*, secs. 35ff., and *Republic* VIII, secs. 546ff. In *AVB*, WBY changed the number of explanations from seventeen to fourteen (*AVB*, 248).

58. In *Paradise Lost* 10.668–78 (1667), John Milton (1608–74) presents seasonal change following the fall as resulting either from the tilting of the earth's axis from the ecliptic or from a change in the course of the sun. See Milton, 423.

59. This passage refers to the Byzantine chronicler and ecclesiastic Georgius Syncellus (d. 810), whose chronicle preserved fragments of ancient writers and apocryphal books. WBY's copy (O'Shea 1847) of *Milton: Man and Thinker* (London: Jonathan Cape, [1924]) by Denis Saurat has the page turned down on which this information is found:

> In the time of Milton all that was known of this book [the Book of Enoch] was a rather long fragment preserved by the Byzantine historian Georgius Syncellus in his *Chronographia*. This book was published by Goar in Paris in 1657. Professor Hanford, in his article on the 'Chronology of Milton's Private Studies', gives

a list of the Byzantine historians that were in Milton's library in 1658, and Syncellus is in the list under his other name of Georgius Monachus. (254)

60. Here begins a series of passages derived from the *Enc Rel Eth*, which WBY purchased with money from the Nobel Prize in 1923. This passage is based upon Alfred Jeremias, "Ages of the World (Babylonian)," 1:185–86. Castor and Pollux are one set of twins birthed by Leda after her rape by Zeus in swan form; Adam and Eve are the first humans created by God in Genesis 2; Cain and Abel are sons of Adam and Eve in Genesis 4. According to Jeremias, the Age of the Bull followed the Age of the Twins. "Marduk, the god of the city of Babylon," is "symbolized by the bull, which corresponds to the figure of the Bull in the heavens." Furthermore, "Every historical celebrity who, in the Bull age, was distinguished as a ruler of the world, a founder of dynasties, etc., was furnished with the Marduk motive . . ." (*Enc Rel Eth* 1:186).

61. Note Jeremias:

> In the Babylonian conception of the universe, which regards everything earthly as a copy of a heavenly prototype, the zodiac . . . is the broad 'Way' on the heavens, c. 20 degrees, upon which the sun, the moon, Venus and the four other moving stars (planets) known to antiquity, trace out their course; while the other stars, the fixed stars, seem to stand still on the ball of the revolving heavens. The moving stars were regarded as interpreters of the Divine will. The heaven of fixed stars was related to them like a commentary written on the margin of a book of revelation. (*Enc Rel Eth* 1:184)

62. See Franz Cumont, *Astrology and Religion among the Greeks and Romans* (trans. J. B. Baker [New York and London: G. P. Putnam's Sons, 1912]): "the Orientals never had a suspicion of this famous precession before the genius of Hipparchus discovered it" (5). GY owned a copy of this book (O'Shea 455). WBY conceded in *AVB* that written evidence justified Hipparchus's position as discoverer of precession (252).

63. The reference is to Orientalists Alfred Jeremias (1864–1935) and Fritz Hommel (1854–1936). Hommel's entry on the Babylonian calendar states with regard to the "question whether the Chaldaeans had observed the phenomenon of precession, i.e. the advance of the equinoctial point by one zodiacal sign every 2160 (one-twelfth of 25920) years" that it is "undoubtedly to be answered in the affirmative." He further notes that Chaldaea, the area west of the Euphrates, was "the native soil of astrology" and that "it is altogether likely that

the 'Babylonian' calendar has its origin in the same region, and not in Babylonia proper" (*Enc Rel Eth* 3:77). In the section on Babylonia in the multiple entry on "Ages of the World," Jeremias asserts that "The application of the Ages of the World to the periods of the evolution of the aeon of mankind is connected in a special way with the teaching about the calendar, which is based on observation of the *precession of the equinoxes*" (*Enc Rel Eth* 1:185).

64. See Hommel, "Calendar (Babylonian)," *Enc Rel Eth* 3:77.

65. Cicero, Marcus Tullius (106–43 BCE), *De re publica* 6.16. *Somnium Scipionis*, the last section of *De re publica*, was famous on its own throughout the Middle Ages and in the hermetic tradition through the two-volume commentary on it by Ambrosius Theodosius Macrobius, a Latin grammarian and Neoplatonic philosopher (flourished about 400). Cicero's text itself was lost until the nineteenth century, when it was rediscovered on a palimpsest manuscript. In the *Dream of Scipio*, Scipio Africanus Minor relates a dream in which Scipio Africanus Major appears and speaks about the life of the good after their death and the nature of the universe.

The fourth eclogue of Publius Vergilius Maro (Virgil, 70–19 BCE) was often called the "Messianic Eclogue" because of the Christian interpretations of its enigmatic prophetic content that were popular in medieval Europe. The Yeatses owned two translations of the *Eclogues,* one of which is Samuel Palmer's translation and accompanying etchings (O'Shea 2202, 2203). WBY made notes for this passage, mentioning *Timaeus, Republic,* and *Somnium Scipionis,* as well as Seneca's *Naturales Quaestiones* and Stobaeus, in the back flyleaf of his uncle G. T. Pollexfen's copy of *Somnium Scipionis* (trans., with an essay " 'The Vision of Scipio' considered as a fragment of the Mysteries" by L. O.; *The Golden Verses of Pythagoras* [trans., with notes] by A.E.A.; *The Symbols of Pythagoras* [trans., with notes] by S[apere] A[ude], Vol. 5 of W. Wynn Westcott, ed., *Collectanea Hermetica* [London: Theosophical Publishing Society, 1894]; O'Shea 387). Those notes also point to an essay on the fourth eclogue by W. Warde Fowler, first published in *Harvard Classical Studies* for 1903 and reprinted in *Virgil's Messianic Eclogue: Its Meaning, Occasion, & Sources, Three Studies,* by Joseph B. Mayor, W. Warde Fowler, and R. S. Conway, with a text of the eclogue and a verse translation by R. S. Conway (London: John Murray, 1907). See also *Myth1,* 310; *Myth2,* 202; *IDM,* 58; and lines 9–12 of the first of WBY's "Two Songs from a Play" (*Poems,* 217). See also *Myth2,* 422–23n9.

66. See Jeremias in *Enc Rel Eth* 1:186.

67. WBY adds a note with a source for this quotation in *AVB:* Emmeline M. Plunket, *Ancient Calendars and Constellations* (London: John Murray, 1903), 17 (which page is turned down in his copy [O'Shea 1596]).

68. It is unclear which translation is used here. The passage above occurs on p. 12 in the edition in the Yeatses' library, but the translation is slightly different. The copy that the Yeatses had to hand, originally owned by WBY's uncle G. T. Pollexfen, contains much marginalia, especially in sections about the Great Year (O'Shea 387). This passage is also quoted, in French, in Duhem 1:283, an extraordinary scholarly achievement in philosophy and the history of science. WBY had discovered it (or the five of its ten volumes that were completed before Duhem's death in 1916) by the time he was writing later-composed sections of *AVA*, and he used it heavily when revising the book for its second edition. See Thomas L. Dume, "William Butler Yeats: A Survey of His Reading" (Ph.D. thesis, Temple University, 1950), 171. GY could translate both French and Latin.

69. Sturm wrote to WBY on 25 January 1926 to correct his embarrassing error: "Macrobius wrote in Latin a commentary on *Scipio's Dream* at the beginning of the fifth century, but surely *Scipio's Dream* was written in Latin by Cicero & is to be found in his *De Republica*?" WBY thanked him for the correction, noting, "I got Lewis Parsons our chief Dublin Classic to translate Macrobius for me & some other passage & probably muddled up some note on some translation into Latin of (say) the 'Timaeus' with my note of Scipio's Dream" (*FPS*, 93).

70. See Macrobius, *Commentary* 2.11.8–11, 13. See also Duhem 1:288–89 and Book II, n. 73 below.

71. This passage is borrowed directly from Duhem 1:283, which identifies Cicero's lost work as the *Hortensius* and Tacitus's work as *Dialogus de claris oratoribus*, chap. 6.

72. From Virgil, *Eclogue* 4.5–14. Translation probably by GY.

73. See Macrobius, *Commentary* 2.11.5–11. Macrobius's *Commentary on the Dream of Scipio* was translated into English in 1951 by William Harris Stahl (New York: Columbia University Press, 1952); see pp. 220–21 for the passages that WBY used.

74. See Kirby Flower Smith, "Ages of the World (Greek and Roman)," *Enc Rel Eth* 1:200.

75. The most commonly accepted date for the founding of Rome was that of Marcus Terentius Varro, who gave it as 753 BCE. Romulus, the legendary founder of the city, was the twin brother of Remus; they were offspring of the god Mars and Rhea Silvia, a princess in Alba Longa and a Vestal Virgin. They (and she) were thrown into the River Tiber at their birth. She was taken by a river god to be his wife; the infants were discovered and suckled by a she-wolf, then raised by a shepherd, before returning to restore their family to the throne and found a city on the site where they had been saved from the river.

76. See G. Herbig, "Etruscan Religion," *Enc Rel Eth* 5:538; the date should be 967, not 966.

77. See Hommel, "Calendar (Babylonian)," *Enc Rel Eth* 3:77.

78. This seems to be WBY's speculation.

79. See Herbig, *Enc Rel Eth* 5:538:

> The *libri fatales* assigned to human life a duration of twelve hebdomads; but, when life had extended to ten hebdomads, or seventy years, man could no longer delay the incidence of fate by propitiatory rites. From that stage onwards he must ask nothing more from the gods; and even if he should survive for other two hebdomads, yet his soul is really sundered from his body. . . . The doctrine of the periods of human life was adapted also to the life of the Etruscan city-state. . . . [Religious rites could maintain the city] until the tenth *saeculum*, and thereafter fate took its inexorable course.

80. In other words, prophets: in ancient Greece, the term Σίβυλλα ([*sibulla*], "prophetess") was associated with the source for written prophecies but was also a title given to female prophets, usually of Apollo, who were associated with specific holy sites. Some later sibyls were depicted as wandering from place to place; all were possessed by deities, under whose influence they entered ecstatic states and spoke mysterious oracles.

81. The biography of the Roman general and dictator Lucius Cornelius Sulla (138–78 BCE) by Plutarchos, the Greek biographer and author (46–after 119 CE), refers to the first civil war in Rome (88–82 BCE). The fourth-century grammarian and commentator Marius (or Maurus Servius Honoratus) mentions the lost autobiography of Augustus. The third-century grammarian and writer Censorinus, whose treatise *De die natali* (238) contains much astrological and chronological information, also the treatise includes a number of references to the temporal customs of the Etruscans. For these demonstrations, the immediate source is probably Joseph B. Mayor et al., *Virgil's Messianic Eclogue: Its Meaning, Occasion, & Sources, Three Studies* (London: John Murray, 1907), 121–22:

> Servius . . . quotes the Memoirs of Augustus to the effect that the soothsayer Vulcatius had interpreted the appearance of the comet at the funeral games held in honour of Caesar, as denoting the end of the ninth age and the beginning of the tenth. Plutarch (*Vita Sullae* 7), speaking of the signs which foreboded the rise of Sulla, mentions in particular the piercing and terror-striking sound of a trumpet which came from a clear sky, and was understood to announce the end of the eighth stage of the great year. Censorinus (*De Die Natali* 17) adds that the Etruscan soothsayers believed that, when the tenth stage was completed, there would be an end of the Etruscan name. Servius, in his note on this line, says that, according to the Sibyl, the last age is the tenth, the

age of the Sun or Apollo. In the existing Sibylline books . . . the tenth age is also mentioned as the concluding age of the world's history.

The details from Plutarch's life of Sulla may come in part from the translation of the passage in Petrie's *The Revolutions of Civilisation*, 9–10), from which *AVB*, 253, also borrows.

82. The source here is not the article by Reinach in *Revue de l'histoire des religions* (November 1900), but the summary by W. Warde Fowler in "The Child of the Poem," in Mayor et al., *Virgil's Messianic Eclogue*, especially pp. 59–64.

83. In galley proofs, this passage read: "but I, like the Christians of fifteen centuries, find nothing incompatible in believing that Virgil," etc.

84. On sidereal motion, see Book II, n. 39 above.

85. Not the German astronomer Johannes Kepler (1571–1630) but the Danish astronomer Tycho Brahe (1546–1601) made predictions, upon the observation of a new star in Cassiopeia in 1572, that were applied to the life of the Swedish king Gustav II Adolph (or Gustavus Adolphus, 1594–1632), including the year 1632, when Gustav defeated the imperial commander Albrecht von Wallenstein in battle during the Thirty Years' War but was himself killed.

86. WBY confuses the routinely dire prophecies for Rome made by the reformer and preacher Girolamo Savonarola (1452–98) with those he made for Florence during the final days of his life. See Pasquale Villari, *Life and Times of Girolamo Savonarola* (London: T. Fisher Unwin, 1899), 752: "It is said that he also added these words: 'Bear well in mind that these things will come to pass when there shall be a Pope named Clement.' "

87. See p. 123.

88. Duhem quotes from a fragment of Berosius preserved in Seneca's *Natural Questions*, 3.28 and 29, which he believes to be based on the now lost *Meteorology* of Posidonius: "Le globe . . . prendra feu quand tous les astres, qui ont maintenant des cours si divers, se réuniront dans le Cancer et se placeront de telle sorte les uns sous les autres qu'une ligne droite pourrait traverser tous leurs centres" (1:70). See also 2:214.

89. See Macrobius's *Commentary* 2.11.7.

90. This passage roughly summarizes Plato's *Republic* VIII, secs. 544–47.

91. *Republic* VIII, sec. 564.

92. The ultimate source of this passage is Machiavelli's *Discourses*, 1.2.3–13 and 3.1.1–5; but see also H. Butterfield, *The Statecraft of Machiavelli* (London: G. Bell and Sons, 1940), 30–33, 48–49. Machiavelli was usually more optimistic than a cyclical view of history allows, but there are in his works passages that support WBY's statements.

93. In the AS on 27 January and again on 2 June 1918 (*YVP* 1:296–97,

467–68), attempts were indeed made to explain why two-thousand-year cycles were not of precisely the same length and why the cycle preceding the birth of Christ was longer than the next one. WBY summarized some of the reasons, which had to do with avatars and the number of generations required to establish a new religious belief, on two cards in the CF (*YVP* 3:260, 338–39), but he also noted that some of the information may have been false due to "frustration" (see Book IV, n. 59).

94. The AS frequently addresses the coming of an avatar or messiah. For instance, on 27 January 1918, the control Thomas informed the Yeatses that this cycle began "2026 years ago" (*YVP* 1:296); on 17 April and 26 May 1918, the date of the divine birth of the "new Christ" is set at 2100 (*YVP* 1:431, 462). See also Book I, n. 143.

95. The line labeled "Initial Point Grecian Zodiac Fixed by Hipparchus at Equinox 150 B.C." is on the chart facing p. 40 in Plunket's *Ancient Calendars and Constellations.* In the copy in the Yeatses' library, this plate has been annotated: at this line WBY wrote, "No—number understand / that place of equinox / 150 A.D. not initial point."

96. Serapis, a Greco-Egyptian god of the underworld—later of the sun and finally of fertility and healing—was reinvented as a new deity by Ptolemy I Soter (reigned 305–282 BCE) in order to integrate Egyptian with Greek religions during Hellenistic rule. The deity came to be identified with Osiris, and his cult was very popular, surviving until the fourth century CE. See also J. G. Milne, "Graeco-Egyptian Religion," *Enc Rel Eth* 6:376: "As a matter of fact, Serapis came into theological existence at Alexandria in an altogether unusual manner: he was virtually the result of the investigations of a body of philosophers and priests, who collected from all sources and fused together whatever ideas or attributes would be of service for their new conception. . . ." That body came to be called "Ptolemy's committee."

97. See Kirby Flower Smith, "Ages of the World (Greek and Roman)," *Enc Rel Eth* 1:196. Smith explained the Stoic view expressed by Aratus that ideal happiness can only lie in the past and then summarized the underlying principle: "We mean the conclusion stated above, that advance in the arts of civilization is at the expense of the character, health, and happiness of the individual."

98. See Gaston Bonet-Maury, "Ages of the World (Christian)," *Enc Rel Eth* 1:190.

99. See Nathan Söderblom, "Ages of the World (Zoroastrian)," *Enc Rel Eth* 1:206: "The period of mankind being fixed at 6000 years, Zarathrushtra [*sic*], who was born thirty years before the end of the former 3000 years, and whose first intercourse with the celestial beings begins the second trimillennium, makes his appearance in the middle of human history." Söderblom then quotes from the Zoroastrian *Sad Dar,* a passage in which the Creator speaks to Zarathustra:

I have created thee at the present time, in the middle period; for
it is three thousand years from the days of Gayomard till now,
and from now till the resurrection are the three thousand years
that remain. . . . For whatever is in the middle is more precious
and better and more valuable . . . as the heart is in the middle of
the whole body . . . and as the land of Iran is more valuable than
other lands, for the reason that it is in the middle.

100. Revelation 12:14: "And to the woman were given two wings of a
great eagle, that she might fly into the wilderness, into her place,
where she is nourished for a time, and times, and half a time, from the
face of the serpent." See also Daniel 12:7.

101. This sentence was added in galley proofs.

102. Taken from Smith, "Ages of the World (Greek and Roman)," *Enc
Rel Eth* 1:197–98.

103. Taken from Jeremias, "Ages of the World (Babylonian)," *Enc Rel Eth*
1:187.

104. See Bishop George Berkeley, *A Treatise Concerning the Principles of
Human Knowledge*, 1:3 and 1:6; more generally, see Donald T. Torchiana, *W. B. Yeats and Georgian Ireland* (Evanston: Northwestern University Press, 1966), chap. 6 ("God-Appointed Berkeley"). WBY
owned the two-volume *Works of George Berkeley* (Dublin: John
Exshaw, 1784; O'Shea 160).

105. WBY probably knew of French mathematician, theoretical scientist,
and philosopher of science Jules-Henri Poincaré (1854–1912) from
Henry Adams, as a passage in *On the Boiler* (1939) indicates: "The
mathematician Poincaré, according to Henry Adams, described space
as the creation of our ancestors, meaning, I conclude, that mind split
itself into mind and space" (*LE*, 237). WBY owned a copy of *The Education of Henry Adams* (Boston: Houghton Mifflin, 1916; O'Shea
17); see chap. 31, pp. 454–55; see also *LE*, 98.

106. For the origin of this distinction, see the AS of 31 March 1918 (*YVP*
1:407).

107. One typescript (NLI, 36,263/24/1) uses this title for a much longer section, including discussion of the Four Principles of Section XIII.

108. This passage borrows from Blake's *A Descriptive Catalogue*, Number
V (Erdman, 543; *WWB* 2:374). Blake's word was "generation" instead
of "generations."

109. See Kirsopp Lake, "Christmas," *Enc Rel Eth* 3:606. The unnamed
writer of *De pascha computus* "first establishes the fact that the first day
of creation was at the vernal equinox, when everything breaks into life,
and the day and night are equal, for God divided them equally
(chap. 3). Moreover, the moon (created two days later) was created
full."

110. See James G. Carleton, "Calendar (Christian)," *Enc Rel Eth* 3:89:

"As Christians made their Paschal anniversaries coincide in season with the Passover, so, for a long period, they were satisfied to accept the Jewish computation of the time of that festival, which should fall on the first full moon after the vernal equinox." For "the Sunday nearest," see *Enc Rel Eth* 3:88, where the wording is not as similar to WBY's.

111. Most likely from Lake, "Christmas," *Enc Rel Eth* 3:601-5.

112. The reference seems to be to the complicated argument of *De pascha computus*, presented by Lake in "Christmas," *Enc Rel Eth* 3:606.

113. See Lake, "Christmas," *Enc Rel Eth* 3:607: for Ephraim Syrus, "not the equinox, but the solstice, is the important point, and he regards Jan. 6 as representing 12 days after the winter solstice, Dec. 25; and these days refer on the one hand to the twelve Apostles, and on the other to the twelve months."

114. See Lake, "Epiphany," *Enc Rel Eth* 5:332. Demonstrating pagan bases for the Christian choice of 6 January as Epiphany, he writes of

> a story in Epiphanius . . . as to the feast which used to be held in Alexandria in the Koreion, or Temple of Kore, on Jan. 6. He says that on the eve of that day it was the custom to spend the night in singing and attending to the images of the gods. At dawn a descent was made to a crypt, and a wooden image was brought up, which had the sign of a cross, and a star of gold, marked on hands, knees, and head. This was carried round in procession, then taken back to the crypt; and it was said that this was done because 'the Maiden' had given birth to 'the Aeon'.

115. See H. J. Rose, "Calendar (Greek)," *Enc Rel Eth* 3:107: "The Greek year of 12 lunar months contained, as has been said, 354 days, the months having alternately 30 days . . . and 29 days. . . ."

116. Slightly misquoted from Edward FitzGerald's *Rubáiyát of Omar Khayyam*, 2.15-16.

117. By the mid-nineteenth century, explanations abounded for the overlap between traditional calendar customs in the British Isles (including those in the "Celtic" societies in Ireland, Scotland, and Wales) and the Christian liturgical year. One set of such ideas asserted that Christmas and Easter, in particular, were timed to enable the early church to replace older celebrations at winter solstice and spring equinox with equally popular festivals. Pre-Christian solar celebrations have been elicited also to explain such holidays as Mayday (Beltane), Midsummer, Lammastide (Lughnasa), Michaelmas (Wakes Time), and All Saints (Samhain). WBY was well acquainted with such thinkers as John Rhys and James Frazer, among others, whose theories elaborated such ideas.

118. Christ was crucified at Calvary, Julius Caesar assassinated in the Roman Senate, and Socrates put to death in Athens for refusing to recognize the gods of the state and for corrupting youth.

119. Referring to the fifteenth of that month, a soothsayer gives this warning to Caesar in Shakespeare's *Julius Caesar*, 1.2.18.

120. See John Burnet, "Socrates," *Enc Rel Eth* 11:665: "As, however, Socrates was condemned at the beginning of the Delian festival, which appears to have fallen in March. . . ." Plato's *Phaedo*, sec. 59, explains that Socrates' execution was postponed because his sentencing came during a religious festival celebrating Theseus's salvation of Athens from the requirement of sacrifice to the Minotaur. The festival involved the crowning of a sacred ship and its pilgrimage to Delos, and custom dictated that no public executions could take place from the crowning of the ship until after its return from Delos.

121. Loosely based on Lake, "Christmas," *Enc Rel Eth* 3:607. Saint John Chrysostom (347–407) was a notable Christian bishop and preacher from the fourth and fifth centuries in Syria and Constantinople, known for ascetic sensibilities and denunciation of abuse of authority in the church and Roman Empire. His name, which comes from the Greek "golden-mouthed," was added after his death. See also *Mem*, 101; *Au*, 290; and *JSD*, 55.

122. *AVB*, 212, contains more explicit references. According to F. A. C. Wilson, WBY was indebted to Coventry Patmore's essay "The Precursor" and "saw St John as the precursor and necessary antithesis of Christ, natural love where Christ was supernatural, 'a midsummer child' where Christ was 'a midwinter' " (*W. B. Yeats and Tradition* [New York: Macmillan, 1958], 67–68). See the image of John the Baptist with attributes of Bacchus, painted between 1513 and 1516 by Leonardo da Vinci (1452–1519), in the Louvre Museum, Paris.

123. A footnote for this page was deleted in galley proofs: "In one or two diagrams, not given here, the phases of the Millenium [*sic*] are divided into ten divisions or cones, and this may come from comparison with the Ten Epochs of Sybilline prophecy. See also tables on page—."

124. WBY inserted this sentence in galley proofs.

125. In the course of over a week of intense AS about historical cones in early June 1918, WBY asked, "Are these dates exact or approximate?" and received the answer "approximate but within a few years" (7 June 1918; *YVP* 1:485).

126. The Yeatses kept a residence at Oxford from January to March 1918, and again from October 1919 to March 1922. There WBY gained much information for *A Vision* from research and scholars, and there he wrote "All Souls' Night." The distinguished scholar is Eleanor Frances Jourdain (1863–1924), principal of St. Hugh's College, Oxford, from 1915 to 1924; WBY's first question of the evening in the AS for 5 March 1918 asks "Can you explain Miss Jourdains [*sic*] case of seeming shade of Constantine?" to which the control Aymor, writing through GY, replies, "Certain great people remain as spirits for centuries" (*YVP* 1:376). With Charlotte Anne Elizabeth Moberly

(1846–1937), principal of St. Hugh's from 1886 to 1915, Jourdain wrote *An Adventure*, published pseudonymously in 1911 by "Elizabeth Morison and Frances Lamont," describing their visionary apprehension of Marie Antoinette and the gardens of Versailles as they were laid out in her time. Moberly's and Jourdain's papers concerning their experience are held in Oxford's Bodleian Library. See *AVB*, 227n2; *Plays*, 722; *LE*, 115, 270, 272, 354; *MYV* 1:179, 224–25; and *Proceedings of the Society for Psychical Research* 25 (1911), 353–60. *An Adventure* and its authors appear numerous times in the AS. On 30 January 1918, a month after moving to Oxford, WBY observed a great psychic "disturbance which might have resulted in stopping this work." He asks, "Do you wish us to find certain mystic associates here in Oxford," and received the reply, "Yes but only the orderly and philosophic." Several questions later, WBY asks, "Do you wish us to seek out the authors of 'The Adventure'?" receiving the response, "Yes she expects you both" (*YVP* 1:306–7). *An Adventure* and its authors are discussed again on 31 January (*YVP* 1:319), 5 March (*YVP* 1:376), and 15 June (*YVP* 1:507). WBY wrote to Miss Moberly to ask her opinion concerning the appearance of the spirit of her dead father, Bishop George Moberly, to Elizabeth Radcliffe in 1912 (see WBY's essay about Radcliffe's automatic script, *YO*, 141–71). Despite her own "psychical experience," Miss Moberly's reply of 20 March 1918 was cautious: "For the sake of science, I would willingly listen to any so called 'communication' from my Father, but I should try not to surrender my best judgment for any marvel. . . ." She noted that her letter was prompted "by your word to us expressing your great anxiety to unravel all the truth," and added that "pure poetical genius and deep thought are as necessary factors in that work as scientific accuracy of observation" (*LWBY*, 347–48).

127. The note refers to Sir William Crookes, a distinguished scientist and president of the Society for Psychical Research (1896–99), who remained active in the society until his death in 1919. Since WBY was an associate member from 1913 to 1928, he must have known Crookes personally, and he likely read Crookes's articles and his *Researches in the Phenomena of Spiritualism* (London: J. Burns, 1874; O'Shea 449; cited by an incorrect title in *Plays*, 726).

128. See Book II, n. 54 above.

129. This passage is likely based on Smith, "Ages of the World (Greek and Roman)," *Enc Rel Eth* 1:196: "The five ages of Hesiod are reduced [by Aratus] to three—An Age of Gold, of Silver, and of Bronze." Smith finds five ages in Hesiod (vs. WBY's four), referring to a bronze (instead of copper) age in Aratus; either WBY was understandably confused or worked from additional sources. Ovid, for example, finds four ages (*Metamorphoses*, 1.89–162).

130. The AS includes much discussion of the alternation of sexes as the soul moves through the cycles.

131. Covens are discussed in the *Vision* documents, especially in a series of sleeps from 19 to 29 November 1920 (*YVP* 3:53–58, summarized in CF, *YVP* 3:262–63). The four covens mentioned in this passage, along with additional information about the relation between covens and history, appear in the record of a sleep of 9 December 1920 (*YVP* 3:59–60). A later sleep of 26 October 1923 mentions "a statement about covens now incorporated in chapter on covens in 'A Vision' " (that is, Book IV below, where covens are treated in relation to life after death; *YVP* 3:185). See Book II, n. 132 below; Book IV, n. 31; Dedication and Introduction, n. 45.

   Walter Kelly Hood notes that in WBY's copy of Gustav Theodor Fechner's *On Life After Death* (3rd ed. [Chicago and London: Open Court, 1914]; O'Shea 665), WBY wrote "covens" beside this sentence: "All the persons who have any spiritual fellowship between them, belong to the body of one spirit, and as co-ordinate members of it work out the ideas which they have received from that spirit" (Fechner, 53). Hood notes that "As in Fechner, the covens appear to be more than individual humans but capable of acting as individual humans do; each coven has a Daimon to whom the men and women of the group become his body" (" 'Read Fechner,' the Spirit Said: W. B. Yeats and Gustav Theodor Fechner," *YAACTS* 7 [1989]: 94). WBY had argued for the existence of a group mind in the essay "Is the Order of R.R. & A.C. to remain a Magical Order?" (*YGD*, appendix K, pp. 259–68); he also used the term "coven" in *Per Amica Silentia Lunae* (*LE*, 25).

132. See Book II, n. 131 above; Book IV, n. 31; Dedication and Introduction, n. 45. WBY had read several books linking witchcraft with psychic phenomena. See, for example, his two essays and notes for Lady Gregory's *Visions and Beliefs in the West of Ireland* (*LE*, 47–83, 258–88). Much of this information may have come from Robert Kirk's *The Secret Commonwealth of Elves, Fauns, and Fairies* (1691), edited with "comment by Andrew Lang" (London: David Nutt, 1893; O'Shea 1068); see *LE*, 258–61, and *YO*, 87. Kirk wrote that daimons "are said to be of a midle Nature betuixt Man and Angel" (5). *AVB*, 209, also connects the daimons with angels. WBY's conception of "reality as a congeries of beings" is mentioned briefly in "Pages from a Diary in 1930" (*Ex*, 305, 309–10) and summarized succinctly in "Seven Propositions" (Richard Ellmann, *The Identity of Yeats* [New York: Oxford University Press, 1954], 236–37). See also Virginia Moore, *The Unicorn: William Butler Yeats' Search for Reality* (New York: Macmillan, 1954), 378–79; and *FPS*, 100–101.

133. In Shakespeare's *Hamlet* III.iv, Hamlet murders Polonius.

134. The AS of 20 March to 5 April 1919 is the primary source for this section (*YVP* 2:200–235). See Barbara J. Frieling, "The 'Moments of Crisis' in Yeats's *Vision* Papers," *YAACTS* 10 (1992): 281–95.

   WBY does indeed write "little of sexual love" (p. lv): the section seems to introduce terms needed to make the system complete but does not adequately explain them (see *L*, 715, about a reader's response).

The term "Beatific Vision" appears in his note to "The Second Coming" published in *Michael Robartes and the Dancer* (Dundrum, Ireland: Cuala, 1921; *Poems*, 658–60), but he dropped it from *AVB*. This section is omitted in *AVB* (see Janis Tedesco Haswell, "The Sexual Dynamic of Yeats's *A Vision*," *YAACTS* 12 (1994): 114–15).

135. These terms are examined at length in the AS, the CF, and the Sleeps. They may not be explained here because they refer to deeply personal events in the Yeatses' lives. The AS suggests several fairly specific dates that may be linked to known biographical events. For a discussion of this concept in the AS, see Barbara J. Frieling, " 'Moments of Crisis' in Yeats's *Vision* Papers," 281–95.

136. In the rich AS of 7 January 1919, the unnamed control informed the Yeatses of the origin of the complementary dream: "In nervous states you are more closely linked psychically—the nightmare of one runs along this link—creates a shock to the other & then reacts on the dreamer / That form gave the dream." A further explanation, earlier in the same session, illuminates WBY's creative process: the control said, "I gave you dream each—now I give you two more in one—at Castle." The eight lines following record the basic imagery of "Towards Break of Day" (originally called "A Double Dream," *Poems*, 187), the first stanza of which is quoted on p. 141. From the same session, WBY received imagery, in a diagram and broken sentences, for "Another Song of a Fool" and "The Double Vision of Michael Robartes" (*YVP* 2:162–64). See also WBY's experiments with Tattwa cards to evoke "complementary dreams, or reveries" (*Au*, 208).

137. From WBY's "Towards Break of Day," lines 1–4 (*Poems*, 187), and see previous note.

138. In 1924, WBY read and began to cite from *Origin of Christian Church Art* (trans. O. M. Dalton and H. J. Braunholtz [Oxford: Clarendon, 1923]; O'Shea 2026) by the eminent Austrian art critic Josef Strzygowski (1862–1941); see *VPl*, 805; *Au*, 525. From *Orient oder Rom* (Leipzig, 1901) onward, Strzygowski's work emphasized the influence of non-Roman (especially Persian) art upon early Christian and Byzantine work. The book is difficult, and in *AVB*, 257–58, WBY becomes both more specific in his references to Strzygowski's theories but also less confident about their connections to his own. The first quotation in the sentence is not taken from *Origin*, but compare: "The origin of Southern art, with its representational ideal, is on the contrary to be sought in the subject; from the beginning it pursued the imitation of nature" (104). For the North, see *Origin*, 103: "Non-representational art was born out of handicraft; it was from handicraft that art sprang into being in the North and among the nomadic shepherd peoples." For the East, see *Origin*, 41: In the East "the people were at once to be

instructed in the faith and dazzled by magnificent display"; see also *Origin*, 47, 161–62, and 223. For the West, see *Origin*, 249: "Throughout the centuries before the rise of Gothic art it was the function of Western Europe to act as a kind of mirror for all movements coming from the East. . . ."

139. See Book II, n. 14 above.

140. In a rejected typescript (NLI, 36,263/24/1), this idea, somewhat expanded, followed immediately after the four lines from "Towards Break of Day": "These dreams and meditations are now complementary as when two people dream or meditate, the one of Helen's birth from an egg, and the other the birth from an egg of Castor and Pollux, the creation of beauty and the creation of war, and so, necessary parts of the same story. . . ." See Dedication and Introduction, n. 65.

141. See Nathan Söderblom, "Ages of the World (Zoroastrian)," *Enc Rel Eth* 1:209–10: "The Persian periods do not imply an eternal repetition, as in the developments of Aryan speculation and religion in India and Greece, and sometimes in modern thought (e.g. Nietzsche . . .). [The Persian concept of history as progressive rather than cyclical] has arisen only twice in the history of human thought—in the only two ancient prophetic religions, one Aryan, one Semitic—in Zarathustrianism and in Mosaism." Nietzsche's doctrine of *ewige Wiederkehr* is expressed in *Also sprach Zarathustra: A Book for All and None*, trans. Thomas Common (London: George Allen & Unwin, 1905), chap. 46.

142. For Plotinus, see Book II, n. 35 above. A revised but still hesitant version of this passage appears in *AVB*, 193–95. This comparison is rather strained: "nature" is not a major term in Plotinus, as WBY seems to acknowledge, for Plotinus is trinitarian in a pagan sense; "Soul of the World" is not MacKenna's wording (cf. "All-Soul") but probably derives from WBY's reading of the Cambridge Platonists. If WBY was thinking of specific passages from Plotinus's *Enneads*, he does not specify them.

Book III: Dove or Swan

1. In all draft versions, Book III is titled "History."

2. Written 18 September 1923, the poem was first published in *The Dial* (June 1924) as "Leda and the Swan," which title was also used in its journal publication in *To-morrow* (Dublin, August 1924) and in its book publication in *The Tower* (London and New York: Macmillan, 1928). In a note in *The Dial*, WBY explained that he wrote it "because the editor of a political review asked me for a poem." When his friend the editor (Æ) told WBY that his "conservative readers would misunderstand the poem" (*Poems*, 664), it was withdrawn. Beginning from a request for an appropriately current political work, WBY ended with an overtly anachronistic one; his cyclical theory, however, paral-

lels Greek and modern influxes as "contemporary" in Flinders Petrie's sense (see *The Revolutions of Civilization* [81], a work cited by WBY in *Ex*, 312–16).
   In galley proofs the first half-line reads "The great bird drops." Note that in *AVB*, 51, WBY writes that this rape produced two sets of twins, Helen and Clytemnestra, and Castor and Pollux. In typescript for the end of Book III, however, WBY did not include Clytemnestra, perhaps following the common variant where she is the daughter of Leda and her husband, Tyndareus. See Book III, n. 153 below.

3. When Agamemnon returned home after the Trojan War, bringing along Cassandra as a part of his war booty, his wife, Clytemnestra (herself in the interval seduced by Aegisthus), killed him in his bath as retribution for his sacrificial slaying of their daughter Iphigenia and his unfaithfulness with Cassandra. This story is told in many Greek sources, including Homer, Hesiod, Aeschylus, and Pindar.

4. See *AVB*, 262–63. On 6 June 1918, the instructors Thomas and Arnault made it clear that slight inconsistencies in these dates are not significant: to WBY's question, "2000 means 2000 to 2100," GY wrote their answer by hand, "Yes" (*YVP*1:482).

5. According to myth, Aphrodite (ἀφρός [*aphros*], "sea-foam") was born of the sea foam near Paphos, Cyprus, after Cronus cut off his father Uranus's genitals and the elder god's blood and semen dropped into the sea. Helen's abduction by Paris is said to have caused the Trojan War.

6. See *IDM*, 58: "A civilisation is very like a man or a woman. . . ." In Greek mythology, Niobe had seven sons and seven daughters; for boasting to Leto about the size of her brood, her children were killed by Leto's—Apollo and Artemis. Niobe was transformed into a weeping stone.

7. In Greek myth, the peacock derived from a hundred-eyed man, Argus Panoptes, "the all-seeing"; Hera set him to guard the cow Io (whom Zeus desired), and he was killed by Hermes at Zeus's bidding. Hera put his eyes into the peacock's tail. The idea that the cry of the peacock produces terror comes from the bestiary tradition: see, for example, the *Aberdeen Bestiary*: "The peacock, as Isidore says, gets its name from the sound of its cry. For when it starts, unexpectedly, to give its cry, it produces sudden fear in its hearers. The peacock is called pavo, therefore, from pavor, fear, since its cry produces fear in those who hear it" (fol. 60v., trans. Colin McLaren; http://www.abdn.ac.uk/bestiary). See also "Meditations in Time of Civil War," sec. 3 ("My Table"), lines 31–32 ("it seemed / Juno's peacock screamed").

8. This section had two parts in early versions: (1) 2000 BC to 500 BC; (2) 500 BC to AD 1, with two subheadings: (a) "The Climax of Aesthetic Power" and (b) "The Rise of Secular Power" (NLI, 36,269/4).

9. The worship of Leda's eggs is mentioned in two books that WBY knew well: Pausanias, *The Description of Greece* (Book 3, chap. 16),

and Jacob Bryant, *A New System; or An Analysis of Ancient Mythology* ([London, 1774–76], 2:64–85). WBY wrote in 1901 in Lady Gregory's copy of the first edition a long note about the influence of Bryant on Blake.

10. In *AVB*, WBY clarifies his references for this paragraph in a note: "Toynbee considers Greece the heir of Crete, and that Greek religion inherits from the Minoan monotheistic mother goddess its more mythical conceptions (*A Study of History*, vol. i, p. 92). 'Mathematical Starlight,' Babylonian astrology, is, however, present in the friendships and antipathies of the Olympic gods" (268). He likely read of Babylonian astrology in *Enc Rel Eth* (see p. 122), in Burnet 21–22, and in Cumont's *Astrology and Religion Among the Greeks and Romans* 18 (see Book II, n. 63). Cumont posits that the alliance of learning and belief was unusually strong in "Babylon, where we see a practical polytheism of a rather gross character combined with the application of the exact sciences, and the gods of heaven subjected to the laws of mathematics." Cumont asserts that astrology came to Greece and Rome from Babylon (22–41).

11. For the Jewish thinking about long life, see such biblical passages as Exodus 20:12, 1 Kings 3:11–14, or Psalms 91:16. The Greek sentiment is widely diffused; see Plautus, *Bacchides* 4.7.18: "He whom the gods favour dies in youth." WBY frequently connected the Irish and Greek traditions: "Not only Achilles but our own Cuchulain also, as competent men have thought, coming from that tribal fermentation" (NLI, 36,269/4).

12. The "great Empire" of Minoan culture on Crete (ca. 3000–1200 BCE) was, in this reading, destroyed by invading Greek tribes (2000–1000 BCE), who assimilated elements of Minoan culture, and whose Mycenean and other Bronze Age civilizations were followed by what are sometimes referred to as "dark ages." The system does not exactly match history: while the former would place the Ledean annunciation at roughly 2000 BCE (two millennia before Christ), the latter (to the degree that historians believe that a Trojan War was in fact waged) sets the fall of Troy between 1300 and 1200 (1184 BCE was the traditional date). The system stresses the polytheistic nature of Greek religion in contrast to the subsequent Christian revelation, whose monotheism paradoxically creates individualism, but in accord with the one arriving imminently (see WBY's note to "The Second Coming," *Poems*, 658–60). One of the Sleep notebooks includes discussion of cycles and masters in relation to history:

> First master monotheistic. monotheism breaks up unity. Instead of unifying it characterizes by the importance it gives to the individual.
> Second Master philosophical

Third Master. Polytheistic. Polytheism unifies. It adapts its self to each personality. It unifies races as well as individuals. (11 January 1921, *YVP* 3:65)

Christ was the first master. The second master (a "multitudinous Avatar") will appear at 2100, and the Yeatses were preparing the way for his arrival: "As 2nd Master is at 2, 3, 4 the phases 16, 17, 18 have been of great importance historically & persons belonging to those phases are greatly important as preparation for 2nd Master" (9 February 1921, *YVP* 3:68).

13. The dates for the legendary Greek poet Homer are not known. Herodotus dates him at about 850 BCE while other accounts position him as early as the tenth or eleventh centuries BCE.

14. The classical or Phidian period of Greek art (which falls between the Archaic and Hellenistic periods) is named for the Athenian sculptor Phidias (active ca. 465–425 BCE), celebrated especially for his magnificent gold and ivory statues of *Athena Parthenos* (completed 438 BCE) and *Zeus Olympios*. Both were approximately 12.75 meters (42 feet) tall, and the latter was one of the seven wonders of the ancient world. See the mention of "Phidias' famous ivories" in "Nineteen Hundred and Nineteen," line 7 (*Poems*, 210).

15. The Ashmolean Museum of Art and Archaeology at the University of Oxford has in its collection a fifth-century *lekythos* (a container for oil), with a red-figure image of a Nike suspended in air and plucking a cithara (AN 1888.1401 [V. 312]), which Michael Vickers suggests as the one to which WBY refers (*Ancient Greek Pottery* [Oxford, Ashmolean Museum, 1999], 43). The museum also houses an extensive collection of black-figure pottery, including a number of "certain pots" with images of horses; this technique was used in Greek pottery painting from about 700 BCE until the early fifth century. In page proofs, WBY changed "of Botticelli" to "before Raphael." WBY was much influenced by the Pre-Raphaelites (see Elizabeth Bergmann Loizeaux, *Yeats and the Visual Arts* [New Brunswick and London: Rutgers University Press, 1986], 5–33).

16. Greek sculptor Anaxagoras of Aigina (first quarter of fifth century BCE) was given credit by Pausanias for a statue of Zeus at Olympia standing near the Bouleuterion. The Athenian tragic playwrights Aeschylus (ca. 525–455 BCE) and Sophocles (ca. 496–406 BCE) were also fifth century and thus "Phidian."

17. "Under the Round Tower" (*Poems*, 137–38) is a direct outgrowth of an AS (20 March 1918) at Glendalough, the site of a ruined monastic center containing one of Ireland's famous round towers. On the day before, WBY learned that the tower was "your thought" (*YVP* 1:391); on 20 March, the instructors for the session, Arnauld and Aymor, informed him that "The medium must meditate on the image of shut-

tle spiral & funnell." He asked if the tower was a symbol of the Passionate Body and received an affirmative response, that it was a symbol of the "abundant flowing life." "Did you bring us here because of round tower," he asked a little later, and received an ambiguous reply: "To put in *your mind* for a purpose" (*YVP* 1:394–95). The round tower at Glendalough came to be connected with Ballylee, and the abundant life there was a joint one. See, for example, the session of 28 October 1918 with the control Thomas, in which GY wrote three lines in the mirror writing used when the AS was to be kept from her conscious mind: WBY was told that "the tower is for the medium alone—not for you—it is a symbol of the human arm & the human heart—arm and human heart" (*YVP* 2:102). The AS of a few days later makes plain that the sun and moon (as well as their corollaries, king and queen) were WBY and GY. At the start of the session the control Thomas announced that he could answer "a few questions but build the tower & gild the sun" but that (in mirror writing) "the moon is cold and worried and nervous and needs plenty of sun and quiet" (*YVP* 2:108). GY, heavily pregnant, would be stricken with a life-threatening case of influenza two weeks later.

18. The distinction between "Ionic elegance" and "Doric vigour" was a standard feature of art history: the 1911 *Encyclopaedia Britannica*, for example, mentions that "Ionian painting is unrestrained in character, characterized by a license not foreign to the nature of the race, and wants the self-control and moderation which belong to Doric art" (11th ed., s.v. "Greek Art," 476). Ionian art was also associated with the East; the *Encyclopaedia Britannica* calls the spread of its style to the mainland "orientalizing" (477). The Persian wars, in which Greece repulsed attacks by Darius and Xerxes, empowered the Greeks and created the conditions for what has sometimes been termed its Golden Age in the fifth century BCE.

19. Book 3 of Plato's *Republic* suggests the necessity of casting out poets who tell immoral tales.

20. The destruction of Ionia resulted from the Ionian revolt against the Persian empire (499–494 BCE); mainland Greek forces aided the Ionians, thus provoking the Persian Wars between Greece and Persia (ca. 498–448 BCE).

21. Tiziano Vecellio (1488/90–1576) was the greatest Italian painter of the Venetian school, a virtuoso known both for daring in color and design and for elegance and simplicity in perception and mood.

22. That is, this is like the life that the round tower symbolizes. See similar remarks on Phidias and Callimachus in "Certain Noble Plays of Japan" (*EE*, 166) and *Au*, 351. At this point, one version adds: "But Greece has an intellect so keen and a population so small, and is so essentially of the phases near to the Full Moon, that it runs rapidly through the more *primary* phases of its stream and what takes centuries in a nation

fundamentally *primary,* takes but a few generations" (NLI, 36,269/5).

23. The Greek sculptor Callimachus (fifth century BCE) presumably designed the Corinthian capital based on acanthus leaves growing around a basket on a girl's tomb. Adolf Furtwängler had much to say about Callimachus in *Masterpieces of Greek Sculpture* (trans. Eugénie Sellers [Strong] [New York: Scribner's, 1895]); see, for instance: "In any case, the artist [Callimachus] belonged to the same Ionicizing school, which tended to a wide divergence from the Pheidian style . . ." (450–51). Furtwängler describes the "armchair found in front of the Pronaos of the Parthenon" (441), but he neither says that the chair was marble nor refers to the Persian. Note that in "Lapis Lazuli" (lines 29ff., *Poems,* 301), WBY seems to accept the more usual scholarly view that the chair should not be attributed to Callimachus. Pausanias, the second-century Greek traveler and geographer, describes the bronze lamp in *Description of Greece,* 1.26.6–7. The lamp also appears in "Lapis Lazuli" (lines 33–34, *Poems,* 301). Also see Furtwängler, *Masterpieces,* 437.

24. Furtwängler frequently uses the term "archaistic" in references to Callimachus (438–39). Here WBY seems to refer to Nikias, described by Furtwängler as "the head of the conservative party, and personally a man of strictly orthodox belief and timid piety" (432). Furtwängler also asserts that Nikias preferred building the Erechtheion (as representing the "old religion") to the Parthenon; Nikias commissioned a Palladion from Callimachus (438).

25. A passage from Longinus is quoted in Gibbon 1:58 and by H. G. Wells in *The Outline of History* (1940–41 ed. [New York: Triangle Books, 1940], 2:495), although Longinus is a bit late (ca. 213–73 CE). See also J. P. Mahaffy, *Social Life in Greece from Homer to Menander* (7th ed. [London: Macmillan, 1907], 433–34), citing Cicero's *De natura deorum* (i.28) and the twenty-first oration of Dion Chrysostom.

26. The Greek comic dramatist Aristophanes (ca. 448–380 BCE), known for biting satire and bold wit, raised comedy to the highest levels of artistic expression.

27. The ancient Greek philosophers Aristotle (384–322 BCE) and his teacher Plato (427–ca. 347 BCE), the founders of the two most influential schools of ancient philosophy, emblematize the creative and intellectual origins of most later Western thought. Cf. "The Coming of Wisdom with Time" (line 4, *Poems,* 93): "Now I may wither into the truth."

28. Platonic dualism, which distinguishes between a world of unchanging forms or ideas and the perceptual world, and which privileges the former, is here interpreted as promoting a kind of asceticism, in that devaluing the physical world presumably leads to profound dismissals like Stoicism and the practices of Christian hermits in the Egyptian deserts. Suicide was permitted in Stoicism, a Greek philosophical

school widely practiced in Rome that taught detachment from emotions and indifference to all elements of external circumstance. In the third century, the Egyptian Desert Fathers developed forms of spirituality that encouraged physical privation; their ways of life led to Christian monasticism (see Book III, n. 39 below). This sentence was added in galley proofs.

29. Alexander (356–323 BCE) conquered the Persian Empire, including Anatolia, Syria, Phoenicia, Gaza, Egypt, Bactria, and Mesopotamia, and extended the boundaries of his own empire (which had originally included only the unified city-states of ancient Greece) as far as the Punjab. Following the Asian campaign, Alexander turned back westward, possibly intending to conquer Arabia and then perhaps Carthage, Sicily, and Italy (although his intentions have long been disputed). After his death, his empire was divided among his officers, marking the beginning of the Hellenistic period, when Greek culture spread among and was changed by the non-Greek peoples conquered by Alexander.

30. "Adore" is used here in the religious sense; the source for emperor-worship may be W. G. Holmes (*The Age of Justinian and Theodora: A History of the Sixth Century AD,* 2nd ed., 2 vols. [London: G. Bell, 1912]; O'Shea 903), who uses the phrase "adoration of the Emperor" (1:95).

31. The taurobolium, or ritual bull sacrifice, has sources in Frazer, *The Golden Bough,* 5:274–75; Grant Showerman, "Taurobolium," *Encyclopaedia Britannica,* 11th ed. (1910–11), 26:455; *The Oriental Religions in Roman Paganism* (trans. Grant Showerman [Chicago: Open Court, 1911]) by Franz Cumont, who, like WBY, twice uses the metaphor of the shower bath (on pp. 71–72 and 208); see also Wells, *The Outline of History,* 2:543.

32. A typescript reads: "Yet even before Plato that collective image of man created by Stoic and Epicurean alike, the moral equivalent of the Hellenic statues, soon to become their antithesis, had been evoked by Anaxagoras when he declares that thought and not the warring opposites created the world" (NLI, 36,269/5). Stoicism and Epicureanism have often been pitted against each other in popular thinking, the former associated with the denial of pleasure and the latter with hedonism. The schools of thought founded by Epicurus (341–270 BCE), an atomist and materialist, emphasized simple pleasure and friendship. The reference to the Greek philosopher Anaxagoras (ca. 500–ca. 428 BCE) may derive from translated passages about his theory of *Nous* ("mind" or "reason") in Burnet 282–85; Burnet also quotes from Plato's *Phaedo* (sec. 97) in which Socrates remarks, "I once heard a man reading a book, as he said, of Anaxagoras', and saying that it was Mind that ordered the world and was the cause of all things" (292).

33. Eugénie Sellers Strong, in *Apotheosis and After Life: Three Lectures on*

Certain Phases of Art and Religion in the Roman Empire (London: Constable, 1915), addresses the "apocalyptic-messianic character that centred about Alexander looked upon as the 'Prince of Peace' who was to return and unite all mankind under his rule in a brotherhood of love" and the influence of "his portraiture, idealised into a type" upon "the plastic conception of the Christian God" (280–81). She does not, however, mention "the first" sculptured image. GY purchased a copy of this book in early 1916 (Saddlemyer, 83; O'Shea 2015). On Strong's influence on WBY, see Murphy, " 'Old Rocky Face, look forth': W. B. Yeats, the Christ Pantokrator, and the Soul's History (The Photographic Record)," *YAACTS* 14 (1996): 82–85.

34. For an almost identical passage written in 1902, see *Myth1*, 43; *Myth2*, 28.

35. WBY refers here to the story of John the Baptist's death at the behest of Salome as told in Mark 6:14–29.

36. See *Ex*, 291: "Where did I pick up that story of the Byzantine bishop and the singer of Antioch, where learn that to anoint your body with the fat of a lion ensured the favour of a king?" Concerning the depiction of Roman emperors, see Strong's *Apotheosis and After Life*, which is particularly concerned with their deification and the relationship between their depiction and artistic portraits of Christ. She mentions a lead medallion with images of "Diocletian and his colleague, who, with their solar nimbi, resemble two enthroned apostles" (96–97, also 103; see also YVP 3:89). See also Cumont, *Astrology and Religion Among the Greeks and Romans*, 53–56.

37. In manuscript, this section closed with a longer passage concerning "myth or talismanic image": "I am not concerned with historical uncertainty as to what Christ really thought or said or did, for only that which has created Christendom is Christianity, & remains that miraculous or creative force" (NLI, 36,269/1). See also *Au*, 346: "In Christianity what was philosophy in Eastern Asia became life, biography and drama."

38. These dates comprise a complete cycle: 1,050 years is also half the larger cycle, to end in 2100 with the coming of the New Messiah. In a nearly complete manuscript as well as a much-revised typescript derived directly from it, the period was divided into smaller units and related to phases; the first section was headed "Phase 1. AD 1 to AD 100" (NLI, 36,269/1 and 36,269/4).

39. A region in ancient Egypt named for its proximity to the ancient capital of Thebes, the Thebaid is associated with early Christian monasticism, such as that of Saint Anthony. WBY's sources include James O. Hannay's *The Spirit and Origin of Christian Monasticism* (London: Methuen, 1903) and *The Wisdom of the Desert* (London: Methuen, 1904), Gustave Flaubert's *The Temptation of St Anthony* (trans. D. F. Hannigan [London: H. S. Nichols, 1895]), and Gibbon (chap. 37).

WBY mentions the Thebaid in the poem "Demon and Beast," especially in lines 43–50 (*Poems*, 188–89); see also *Ex*, 301, and *Au*, 238, 242. Scopas (fl. 4th c BCE) was a major Greek sculptor.

40. See O. M. Dalton, *Byzantine Art and Archaeology* (Oxford: Clarendon, 1911; O'Shea 461): "The Emperor Marcus Aurelius expressed one truth when he said that everything which is beautiful is beautiful in itself and terminates in itself. But to the artists of the Middle Ages, whether in East or West, this was false doctrine. To them the individual was nothing, the immanent idea or *eidos* was both a type and an ensample" (37). WBY purchased this book in August 1924.

41. Duhem and Burnet outline Greek discoveries. See Burnet's account of Diogenes of Apollonia: "The earth itself is round, that is to say, it is a disc: for the language of the doxographers does not point to the spherical form" (365). The theory of the plurality of worlds also appears in accounts of Anaximander (64), Anaximenes (82), Anaxagoras (295), and Leukippos (358). Duhem notes that Aristarchus of Samothrace endorsed the heliocentric theory (1:418–23).

42. See *LE*, 136–37: "Our moral indignation, our uniform law, perhaps even our public spirit, may come from the Christian conviction that the soul has but one life to find or lose salvation in: the Asiatic courtesy from the conviction that there are many lives."

43. Greek daimons, or spirits, were intermediaries between the gods and humans, like the Christian angel (from Greek ἄγγελος [*angelos*], "messenger"); however, unlike later angels, Greek daimons could be spirits of human beings, especially heroes. See p. 162 for a further reference to angels.

44. The AS frequently contrasts love (antithetical) and pity (primary). The distinction is most forceful in a discussion of Judas and Christ (26 Jan 1918, *YVP* 1:290–92). The contrast is also important to the play *Calvary*: Christ's pity is "an objective realisation of a collective despair"; Judas, "the C[reative] G[enius] only," does not pity (*YVP* 1:291; see *Plays*, 695–97). See also *AVB*, 41; *L*, 876; and Book I, n. 232.

45. Jesus' parable of the Good Samaritan appears in Luke 10:29–37.

46. This date is close to Gibbon's (248 CE) as the turning point for the worse in Roman history (Gibbon, chap. 7). The manuscript begins a new section at this point, with the subtitle "Phases 2 to 7 / AD. 100 to AD 300" (NLI, 36,269/1).

47. Eugénie Strong writes that Roman art "only becomes of paramount importance in the historic chain in the second century after Christ" (*Roman Sculpture from Augustus to Constantine* [London: Duckworth, 1907], 10). A long entry in SDNB8 from 6 April [1921] cites Strong's book. Concerning phase 27 ("always the union with external strength"), WBY observed: "I do not feel that my old people were creative—I have seen something like them though less kindness in roman faces in the procession, perhaps of the altar of peace in Mrs Strongs

book—but their culture is subjective. Will the second master (from 16, 17 or 18) find among such his deciples?, & use their objective method as christ when he personified himself in Judas used the subjective classical method" (*YVP* 3:87–88). On the "altar of peace," see Strong, *Roman Sculpture*, 39–58.

48. Cf. "The Statues," lines 20–22, for a repetition of this idea (*Poems*, 345); see Strong, *Roman Sculpture*, 347–76.

49. WBY references "the young horsemen on the Parthenon" in "Discoveries" (*EE*, 212). And he had surely read Walter Pater's comment in the "Winckelmann" essay in *The Renaissance*: "If a single product only of Hellenic art were to be saved in the wreck of all beside, one might choose perhaps from the 'beautiful multitude' of the Panathenaic frieze, that line of youths on horseback, with their level glances, their proud, patient lips, their chastened reins, their whole bodies in exquisite service" ([New York: Modern Library, n.d.], 181).

50. See Élie Fauré, *Ancient Art*, the first of his five-volume *History of Art* (trans. Walter Pach [London: John Lane; New York: Harper, 1921–30]; O'Shea 664): "Sarcophagi and statues were made in advance: the orator dressed in his toga, the general in his cuirass, the tribune, the quaestor, the consul, the senator, or the imperator, could be supplied at any time. The body was interchangeable. The head was screwed on to the shoulders" (284–85).

51. This passage continues the motif of eyes (see p. 156); see also "Lapis Lazuli," lines 55–56 (*Poems*, 301).

52. Before this sentence, the manuscript has a header, "Phases 8 & 9. AD 300 to 450." In the typescript derived from it, the subtitle reads "Phase 8. A D 325 to 395."

53. Blake, "The Mental Traveller," line 95 (Erdman, 486; *WWB* 2:33). See also p. 35, where WBY quotes this line slightly differently.

54. The Yeatses were more interested in the mental than the physical phenomena of spiritualism, but they had both attended a number of seances where the medium communicated with the dead using methods including trance or "direct voice" speaking and rapping on or tipping tables; both had also read some of the many books written about spiritualism, by both believers and skeptics (see Book IV, n. 72).

55. See Holmes, *The Age of Justinian and Theodora*, concerning the Roman Empire under Anastasius:

> In earlier times a Roman proconsul in his spacious province was almost an independent potentate during his term of office, the head alike of the civil and military power. But in the new dispensation no man was intrusted with such plenary authority, and each contracted province was ruled by a purely civil administrator, whilst the local army obeyed a different master. For fuller security, each of these in turn was dependent on a higher civil or

military officer, to whom was delegated the collective control of a number of his subordinates. Again a shift of authority was made, and the reins of government were delivered into fewer hands, until, at the head of the system, the source of all power, stood the Emperor himself. (1:332)

The Yeatses owned a copy of the first volume of this two-volume work, and their copy is marked with marginal notes up to page 119 (O'Shea 903). "Romanised Gods": it is widely accepted that the Romans adapted their own deities to coalesce with those of Greece.

56. See Gibbon:

Since the time of the Peloponnesian and Punic wars, the sphere of action had not been enlarged; and the science of naval architecture appears to have declined. . . . The principles of maritime tactics had not undergone any change since the time of Thucydides; a squadron of galleys still advanced in a crescent. . . . Steel and iron were still the common instruments of destruction and safety; and the helmets, cuirasses, and shields of the tenth century did not, either in form or substance, essentially differ from those which had covered the companions of Alexander or Achilles. (6:92–94)

57. On the figure of the athlete, see also pp. 152–54.
58. Ammonius Saccas (first half of the third century CE), Alexandrian self-taught philosopher and teacher of Plotinus and Origen, is usually considered the founder of Neoplatonism, although he left no writings; his second name literally indicates that he had been a sack carrier in his youth.
59. Origen (Oregenes Adamantius, ca. 185–ca. 254) was the most learned theologian and biblical scholar of the early Greek church. He studied with Clement of Alexandria, and Porphyry attests to his having attended lectures given by Ammonius Saccas. His deep knowledge of Neoplatonism made him suspect to late Church Fathers, but it probably explains his attractiveness to WBY and GY. GY studied Origen in 1913 (Saddlemyer, 48); in 1928, WBY wrote that Origen was the only "Father of the Church . . . I have read or rather dipped into" (*L*, 734).
60. Constantine I (Gaius Flavius Valerius Aurelius Constantinus, 272–337 CE) defeated Maximian, one of his many rivals for the imperial throne, at the battle of the Milvian Bridge near Rome (312 CE); shortly before this battle, Constantine supposedly had his vision of the flaming cross in the sky ("*In hoc signo vinces*"). According to Socrates Scholasticus's *Ecclesiastical History*, Saint Helena, Constantine's mother, recovered the True Cross and nails of Christ's crucifixion from the Holy Sepulchre in Jerusalem and had them sent to Constantine. Having placed his cap-

ital at Constantinople, Constantine established Christianity as the state religion in 324. For use of the cross, see Gibbon 2:299. According to Saint Gregory of Tours, two of the nails were used to make a bit for the bridle of Constantine's horse, while a third adorned his statue.

61. Although Constantine turned the empire toward Christianity earlier in his life, he did not experience a full conversion until his death (see Gibbon 2:289). Gibbon also stresses that the conversion was both genuine and political: "In an age of religious fervour, the most artful statesmen are observed to feel some part of the enthusiasm which they inspire" (2:305–6).

62. Richard Ellmann (*The Identity of Yeats*, 262) and A. Norman Jeffares offer that this phrase comes from Proclus, "whom [WBY] read in Thomas Taylor's translation" of *The Six Books of Proclus . . . on the Theology of Plato* (1816) (Jeffares, *A New Commentary on the Collected Poems of W. B. Yeats* [London: Macmillan, 1984], 243). Alternately, E. R. Dodds suggests that the Greek idea of the church as "a fabulous and formless darkness mastering the loveliness of the world" comes from Eunapius's *Vita maximi* (see *Select Passages Illustrating Neoplatonism* [London: Society for Promoting Christian Knowledge, 1923], 8). The phrase also appears in WBY's note to *Fighting the Waves* (*Plays*, 706) and is alluded to in the opening song from *The Resurrection* (*Plays*, 482), also published as one of "Two Songs from a Play" (line 16, *Poems*, 217). The text follows the wording in Dodds.

63. The manuscript here has a heading for phases 10 through 16, "AD 450 to 600"; in the revised typescript, the heading is changed to embrace phases 9 to 21, "AD 395 to 830." Despite WBY's claim of ignorance, he and possibly GY as well had studied Byzantine history in Holmes, *The Age of Justinian and Theodora* (O'Shea 903); Dalton, *Byzantine Art and Archaeology* (O'Shea 461); Strong, *Apotheosis and After Life* (O'Shea 2015); Gibbon; the *Encyclopaedia Britannica*; and the *Cambridge Mediaeval History* (see Jeffares, *New Commentary on the Collected Poems*, 212). A number of strongly anti-Christian passages from the manuscript and revised typescript were softened or omitted from *AVA*.

64. This passage suggests both the Yeatses' genuine belief in their instructors and the occasional imprecision of their data. The AS records frequent comments on, questions about, and investigations into the accuracy of information. In general, the system was meant to be symbolic and general rather than empirical and specific. For example, in a discussion of historical and spiritual cones, the control Thomas, with support from the guide Rose, answered "No I do not" to this question about dates: "Do you mean that the method will be a rigorous scientific method discovered by experiment?" (*YVP* 2:169; recorded in CF, *VVP* 3:347).

65. In Revelations (sometimes called the Apocalypse after its Greek title),

the writer, John of Patmos, offers a prophetic vision of the new Jerusalem (21.1–22.5).

66. Justinian I (Flavius Petrus Sabbatius Justinianus, 483–565 CE) was emperor of Byzantium from 527 until his death. He closed the Academy of Plato at Athens in 529 and opened the domed basilica of Hagia Sophia, rebuilt under his direction into the greatest cathedral of its time, in 537. See also Book III, n. 70 below.

67. This idea echoes a famous passage from Gregory Nyssen's "Oratio de deitate Filii et Spiritus Sancti":

> This city [Constantinople] . . . is full of mechanics and slaves, who are all of them profound theologians, and preach in the shops and in the streets. If you desire a man to change a piece of silver, he informs you wherein the Son differs from the Father; if you ask the price of a loaf, you are told, by way of reply, that the Son is inferior to the Father; and if you inquire whether the bath is ready, the answer is, that the Son was made out of nothing.

This passage is quoted in Gibbon (3:142–43), in Holmes (1:280n), and in G. W. F. Hegel's *The Philosophy of History* (3.3.3; trans. J. Sibree [1858; rpt., New York: Dover, 1956], 339).

68. As articles on asceticism in the *Encyclopaedia Britannica* or the *Enc Rel Eth* explain, the word "ascetic" derives from the Greek ἄσκησις (*askesis*), meaning practice or exercise, and once referred to the discipline of the Greek athlete. An exact reference to the ascetic as "God's athlete" in Alexandria has not been found, but WBY read James O. Hannay's *The Spirit and Origin of Christian Monasticism*, which notes: [in Eusebius] "there is mention of Apphianus, an 'athlete of piety' . . . , that is to say, an ascetic. This metaphorical use of the word athlete to denote an ascetic striver after perfection probably had its origin in St Paul's writings. It is common in the accounts of the fourth-century Egyptian hermits" (81). See also Hannay, *The Wisdom of the Desert*, 21 and 143.

69. In *A Packet for Ezra Pound*, WBY writes that he discovered, upon reading Oswald Spengler's *The Decline of the West* (trans. Charles Francis Atkinson, 2 vols. [London: George Allen & Unwin, 1926–29]; O'Shea 1975), that both Spengler and he "had found the same meaning in the round bird-like eyes of Byzantine sculpture, though he or his translator had preferred 'staring at infinity' to my 'staring at miracle' " (*AVB*, 18). WBY did find Spengler just as *AVA* had been finished: on 13 May 1925, he wrote to Dulac, "A German called Oswald Spengler has hit on a number of the same ideas as those in my book. The American *Dial* has just published a long essay by him—the introduction to his work now being translated—which might have been a chapter of 'A Vision.'

He applies the fundamental thought to things outside my knowledge, but his thought and mine differ in nothing. It seems that the thought came to him suddenly and with great excitement" (Hobby 175).

70. The Greek ἅγιος (*hagios*) means both "holy" as an adjective and "saint" as a noun, and σοφία (*sophia*) means "wisdom"; the cathedral in Constantinople, Hagia Sophia, is literally both Saint Sophia and "holy wisdom" (see also *LE*, 133). See also Book III, n. 66 above.

71. Rephrased in *AVB*, 280, to "Ravenna or in Sicily." In January and February 1925, the Yeatses traveled in Italy, visiting Sicily, Naples, Capri, and Rome. WBY's interest in Byzantine mosaics may have begun with his visit to Ravenna and Venice in 1907 (Foster 2:279, 1:367–69). Although Ravenna may be better known for its mosaics—"with their little glimmering cubes of blue and green and gold"—WBY also attended to those in Rome, collecting Alinari photographs of mosaics in the churches and basilicas of Sta Prassede, San Giovanni in Laterano, San Marco, Sant'Agnese fuori le Mura, Santa Constanza, Santa Maria in Trastevere, Santa Pudenziana, Santi Cosma e Damiano, and San Clemente. On the details of WBY's visual encounters with Byzantine mosaics, see Murphy, " 'Old Rocky Face, look forth'," 69–117; and Melchiori, *The Whole Mystery of Art*. See "Sailing to Byzantium" (*Poems*, 197–98).

72. See Josef Strzygowski's *Origin of Christian Church Art* and the summary of Strzygowski's views in Dalton's *Byzantine Art and Archaeology* (pp. 14–15, chaps. 12–13, and pp. 700–703). Roughly, Strzygowski makes a contrast between representational (Western) art and nonrepresentational or merely decorative (Eastern) art. On the influence of Strzygowski's ideas on WBY, see Murphy, " 'Old Rocky Face, look forth'," 82–85.

73. See Strzygowski's *Origin of Christian Church Art*, chap. 6, "Non-Representational Church Art, and the Subsequent Anti-Representational Movement," especially p. 149. The discussion in question deals with the nature(s) of Christ and with artistic representations of him (culminating in the Byzantine problem of Iconoclasm, mentioned below). WBY presented these differing views of Christ's nature in *The Resurrection*, begun in 1925.

74. The opening of Hagia Sophia in 537 (see Book III, n. 66 above) precedes the date 560 for the "climax" that is the midpoint phase 15 on the diagram "The Historical Cones" (see fig. 21, p. 147).

75. This is a reminder that in the Yeatses' system, the Age of Phidias, the Age of Justinian, and the Renaissance are parallel as fifteenth phases of millennial eras. Because alternate eras are parallel in Tincture, however, those after Phidias and after the Renaissance—though parallel to one another—are both antithetical and therefore not parallel to the era after Justinian (a primary cycle).

76. The passage does not refer to a particular part of Strzygowski's *Origins*

of Christian Church Art, but see chapter 6. The contrast is again between Greek, Western, and representational, and Persian, Eastern, and nonrepresentational.

77. Leo III (ca. 680–741), emperor from 717 to his death, issued a series of edicts in 726–29 prohibiting the worship of images. Monophysitism holds that Christ has but a single, divine nature, rather than two, both divine and human, the view promulgated by the Council of Chalcedon in 451. Modern monophysite churches include the Armenian Apostolic, Coptic Orthodox, Ethiopian Orthodox, and Syrian Orthodox. The source for the rather obscure Xenaias, or Philoxenus, is unknown (though he is mentioned in chapter 47 of Gibbon). He was bishop (late fifth century–523) of Maburg (Arabic مَنبِج, *Manbij*) or Hierapolis Bambyce in what is now eastern Turkey and one of the most outspoken advocates of monophysitism. At this point, the manuscript has the heading "Phases 16 to 25. AD 600 to 900"; in the revised typescript it was changed to "Phase 22. AD 630 to 900."

78. Born and educated in Ireland, Erigena or Eriugena (ca. 815–77) went to the court of Charlemagne about 847, translated Dionysius the Areopagite from Greek into Latin, and wrote, as WBY put it in the manuscript, "an exposition of the orders of the angels according to the vision of Dionysius" (i.e., *The Celestial Hierarchy*). The manuscript asks,

> Am I right . . . in considering Johannes Scotus Erigena not as the first schoolman but the last Christianized Greek philosopher, & so a necessary part of the final abstraction & synthesis before submission to fate. My friend Larminie, an Irish poet & folklorist translated him & has left the manuscript in a Dublin library where now one friend & now another turns its pages & perhaps tells me what he finds. (NLI, 36,269/1)

One such "friend" was GY; WBY wrote to T. W. Lyster, the director of the National Library in Kildare Street, or W. K. Magee, asking if his wife could consult the manuscript of Larminie's translation (NLI, 21,749; probable date 1919). Michael III (839–67) was the "last iconoclastic Emperor," but his grandfather Michael II (770–829, ruled 820–29) was most responsible for spreading the Neoplatonic doctrines of Dionysius (Duhem 3:44–47).

79. Phase 22 occurs in one cycle around 323 BCE, with the death of Alexander and the dissolution of his empire, and between roughly 830 to 900 CE, a period that saw the Carolingian empire divided at the death of Charlemagne and contested thereafter; the various wars over succession ended in 843 with the Treaty of Verdun (see also p. 153).

80. The manuscript here has the heading "Phases 26, 27, 28. AD 900 to AD 1000," with "or 1100" crossed out.

81. Sydenham chorea (also known as Saint Vitus' dance) is a neurological

disorder characterized by brief, irregular contractions that appear to flow from one muscle to the next.

82. This passage may be influenced by Strzygowski's discussion of Northern and Eastern influence on Romanesque design. Strzygowski traces East Iranian motifs on one church—"the vinescroll with enclosed animals"—and suggests that comparison "reveals that fusion of Iranian and Greek art which succeeded the displacement of the latter in late Roman times, and led gradually to the development of Byzantine art on the Mediterranean, of 'Romanesque' in the West, and to the complete triumph of Iranian art in the world of Islam (*Origins of Christian Church Art*, 112–14). Romanesque art, sculpture, painting, and manuscript illumination flourished in France, Italy, Britain, and German lands from about 1000 until about 1150; the Romanesque period was succeeded by the Gothic.

83. Although cardinal directions do not remain on the published diagram of "The Historical Cones," they are explained in Book II (pp. 113–16) and occur on the drafted diagram in VNB1 (*YVP* 3:172). At this point, near the year 1050, the spiritual or religious life is near phase 15 and lunar south in the two-thousand-year cycle, but secular history is at the same time near phases 28 and 1, the location of lunar north.

84. See Gibbon:

> The influence of two sister prostitutes, Marozia and Theodora, was founded on their wealth and beauty, their political and amorous intrigues: the most strenuous of their lovers were rewarded with the Roman mitre, and their reign may have suggested to the darker ages the fable of a female pope. The bastard son, the grandson, and the great-grandson of Marozia, a rare genealogy, were seated in the chair of St Peter; and it was at the age of nineteen years that the second of these became the head of the Latin Church.

Gibbon's editor J. B. Bury adds that "John XI was the legitimate, not the bastard, son of Marozia; and it is not true that her great-grandson was Pope" (5:297–98 and n. 140a).

85. "Sequence" is most often paired with "allusion" in the AS and other documents. See, for example, the AS of 4 June 1919 (*YVP* 2:295) and 8 November 1919 (*YVP* 2:476), which establish that sequence is associated with image and desire, allusion with "picture" and "cessation of desire" (this information was summarized in the CF, *YVP* 3:398). In VNB1, GY noted the links between sequence and time, allusion and space (*YVP* 3:169). However, a late AS (1 February 1920; *YVP* 2:532) contrasted "recurrence" and "fixity," and the term "sequence" was later added to the discussion. GY recorded the findings of sleeps in September 1920 in which the Yeatses "Discussed Recurrence, & got cor-

rection of Script on the subject" (*YVP* 3:46, illustration, *YVP* 3:47, 3:49).

"Plato's perfect and imperfect numbers" are sometimes raised in esoteric discussions of the Great Year or the ages of humanity; see Plato, *Republic*, 8.546.

86. Christ's predecessor, two thousand years earlier, had been antithetical. Because he had been concerned with the individual and the beauty of sensuous experience, he had "mourned over the shortness of time," as will the New Messiah, Christ's successor.

87. This passage suggests that the Norman cathedrals at Cefalù (begun 1131) and Monreale (founded 1174) in Sicily reflect the old, transhuman religion through their Byzantine aesthetic: the Greek image now reborn as humanism, though borrowed from a very humanistic outlook, gradually again transcends religious monotheism. See *Ex*, 317, and Dalton, *Byzantine Art and Archaeology*, 410–12. The Yeatses visited both Cefalù and Monreale in early 1925 during their travels in southern Italy with the Pounds. See Murphy, " 'Old Rocky Face, look forth'," 69–117.

88. Here a typescript is headed "Phases 1–8. AD 1000 to 1220" (NLI, 36,269/10). In galley proofs, WBY changed 1000 to 1050.

89. The source is "The Life of St Pelagia the Harlot." The tale is widespread, found in such collections as the *Legenda Aurea*; WBY demonstrated familiarity with a similar tale in *The Celtic Twilight* (*Myth*1, 49; *Myth*2, 32). See also *Ex*, 291.

90. From "The Tale of the Girl Heart's-Miracle, Lieutenant of the Birds" in *The Book of the Thousand Nights and One Night; Rendered into English from the Literal and Complete French Translation of Dr. J. C. Madrus by Powys Mathers* (4 vols., 2nd ed. [London: George Routledge, 1937]), 4:440: "The Khalifāh rose from his throne and, going down to the girl, very gently returned the little silk veil to her face, as a sign that she belonged to his harīm, and that the fairness of her had already retreated into the mystery of our Faith." See Dedication and Introduction, n. 27.

91. This passage draws from William Wells Newell's *King Arthur and the Round Table* (2 vols. [London: A. P. Watt, 1897]):

> Merlin told the story, how a prince of that land had loved a damsel, and had wrought a chamber in the rock . . . where with great joy their lives had been spent; and how both had died on the same day, and had been laid in the chamber, where they had received their delight'. Merlin showed Niniene a cavern 'adorned with mosaic of gold'. Only Merlin could raise the rock, and beneath it lay the lovers, 'wrapped in winding sheets of white samite'. Niniene said Merlin was truly enchanted: 'Thus speak-

ing, she bade her attendants take him by the hand and feet, lay
him in the tomb, and replace the stone. This with pains they
accomplished; and the damsel by her spells, sealed the slab, so
that it might never be removed; from that hour, none beheld
Merlin, dead or alive. (2:137–39)

See also *LE,* 163.

92. See Wolfram von Eschenbach, *Parzival: A Knightly Epic* (trans. Jessie
Weston, 2 vols., [1894; rpt., New York: G. E. Stechert, 1912]), which
WBY knew well. Weston's notes suggest,

> It is very curious that, constantly as Baptism is insisted upon as
> essential to salvation, the equal necessity for the Second Great
> Sacrament of the Faith is passed over. It is perfectly true that
> Wolfram's knights attend Mass, and that Mass is apparently
> celebrated with regularity, but here their obligation seems to
> end; never once do we hear of one of his knights communicating,
> even Gamuret, when dying, though he receives absolution, does
> not receive the viaticum. . . . (2:196–97)

At one point, Kunneware's squire comes on Parzival and sees "A hel-
met all battle-dinted, and a shield which yet traces bore / Of many a
bitter conflict that was foughten for lady fair" (1:161, lines 70–71). See
also *IDM,* 30, 103; *Au,* 138.

93. The *locus classicus* of Gothic freedom is "The Nature of Gothic" in
John Ruskin's *The Stones of Venice.* Blake (in many places) and
William Morris (in *Gothic Architecture*) similarly suggest that Gothic
architecture allowed the workmen to work together yet express their
individual views freely; this is similar to the system's image of Byzantium (pp. 158–59). WBY made the next division in the manuscript
approximately here: "AD 1220 to 1300" (NLI, 36,269/1). Saint
Bernard of Clairvaux expresses his opposition to the aesthetic tenden-
cies of the Clunaic monks and town bishops in chapter 12 of *Apologia
ad Gulielmum sancti Theodorici abbatem*; he describes Romanesque
sculpture as unworthy of monks.

94. Thirteenth-century French architect Villard de Honnecourt's book of
drawings (published Paris, 1858) contains sketches of machines, architecture, monuments, human figures, animals, and important Gothic
churches in process; sometimes geometrical figures are superimposed
on humans, animals, etc. WBY visited Maud Gonne in Normandy in
May 1910, and together they saw Mont-Saint-Michel, home to the
unusual Benedictine abbey and steepled church (built between the
eleventh and sixteenth centuries); see *Mem,* 249–50; *EE,* 245–46; and
Foster 1:421. About Mont-Saint-Michel he wrote,

> Yet at Mont-Saint-Michel I have been seeing a different art, a
> marvellous powerful living thing created by a community work-
> ing for hundreds of years and allowing only a very little place for
> the individual. Are there not groups which obtain, through pow-
> erful emotion, organic vitality? How do they differ from the mob
> of casual men who are the enemies of all that has fineness? Why
> is it that the general thought is our enemy in the towns of Ire-
> land, and would be our friend in the country if we had the same
> symbols? (*Mem*, 250)

He had also read Henry Adams's *Mont-Saint-Michel and Chartres*
(1904; Boston: Houghton Mifflin, 1913; O'Shea 19): "I have read all
Adams and find an exact agreement even to dates with my own 'law of
history' " (*L*, 666).

95. The Dominican order was founded by Saint Dominic in 1216. Dominic
    wanted to bring the dedication and systematic education of the older
    monastic orders (like the Benedictines) to bear on the religious prob-
    lems of the burgeoning city populations.

96. A chronology at the end of SDNB6 shows that WBY's source was
    Adams: for the years 1180 to 1250, WBY wrote "(5.6.7) 1150 to
    1250 given by Henry Adams as time when man most felt his unity in a
    unified world. He seeks its expression in 'Amiens Cathedral & the
    Works of Thomas Aquinas[']" (*YVP* 3:70). See *The Education of
    Henry Adams: An Autobiography* (Boston: Houghton Mifflin, 1918),
    435.

97. This passage is also indebted to Adams. In the same note in SDNB6,
    WBY wrote: "325 to 400 AD (8) Constantine (Constantinople founded
    324 (Gibbon) Henry Adams takes 310 as significant date 'Cross took
    the place of the Legions' (? coming of unification by Church)" (*YVP*
    3:70). Compare with Adams: ". . . the nearest approach to the revolu-
    tion of 1900 was that of 310, when Constantine set up the Cross"
    (*Education*, 383).

98. See p. 18 and Book I, n. 46, and especially WBY's essay "A People's
    Theatre" (1919):

> Dante in that passage in the *Convito* which is, I think, the first
> passage of poignant autobiography in literary history, for there
> is nothing in S. Augustine not formal and abstract beside it, in
> describing his poverty and his exile counts as his chief misfortune
> that he has had to show himself to all Italy and so publish his
> human frailties that men who honoured him unknown honour
> him no more. Lacking means he had lacked seclusion, and he
> explains that men such as he should have but few and intimate
> friends. (*IDM*, 128)

The first treatise of the *Convito* laments the poet's exile and the consequent need to explain his work; see 1.3 and 4 (pp. 14–21). The figure of Dante recurs through the AS, sometimes connected with WBY, a fellow poet of phase 17 who also, in *A Vision*, "imposes his own personality upon a system," sometimes connected with GY, whose True Creative Mind of "Emotional Philosophy" (p. 66) raises the personal to the universal, as did Dante in the *Comedy* and especially the *Convito*. For example, see the discussion of "consciousness of phantasy" or "phantastikon" from 12 and 13 October 1919, when the Yeatses were urged to "read the whole of Dante's Convito"; this session elaborates how a phantasmagoria or personal "dream world" (*YVP* 4:67) may be created in waking life rather than sleep (*YVP* 2:444–45).

99. This division is headed "AD 1300 to 1450" in the manuscript (NLI, 36,269/1).

100. This period is typified by Italian painting from the time of Giotto di Bondone (1267–1337) to that of Il Beato Fra Giovanni Angelico da Fiesole (1395–1455), together with the French chronicler Jean Froissart (ca. 1337–ca. 1405).

101. References here are to Italian painter Masaccio (Tommaso di Ser Giovanni di Monte Cassai, 1401–28), English poet Geoffrey Chaucer (ca. 1343–1400), and French poet François Villon (ca. 1431–ca. 1474).

102. Masaccio is usually said to have lived one more year than he is here allowed; WBY's friend Beardsley, an influential illustrator, author, and artist, lived from 1872 to 1898. In the manuscript, WBY reminded himself with a note to "Bring in Masaccio, Donatello, Villon, Chaucer. Compare them together & contrast with Giotto & Dante & his school which like the art of the Cathedrals still celebrates Christendom mainly. We lost ourselves in Christendom when we share their thoughts, but from Masaccio on it is Christendom & ourselves—then Christendom goes" (NLI, 36,269/1). Another section of the chronology in SDNB6 is pertinent: "1250 to 1300. Aparently [*sic*] struggles to establish Kingly Powers. Note C[haucer]'[s] allusion to King Arthur" (*YVP* 3:70). According to an entry for 20 December 1920 in SDNB6, WBY had confirmation of his theory about this period from one of his controls: "Was looking through some books of history to find why 1250 is the start of 50 years attributed to phase 8 & wondered if St Clovis consolidation of his power was typical of period when GY heard a voice say 'Percys Reliques Vol III poem 5' This proved to be a ballad about Arthurs struggle with his barons & so confirmed the opinion" (*YVP* 3:64). The poem cited is "The Legend of King Arthur" in Thomas Percy's *Reliques of Ancient English Poetry* (1765). This notebook contains several entries about, and diagrams of, the cones. On 9 December 1920, "George began diagram" and that night " 'Carmichael' [the control] gave confirmation of classification of devisions [*sic*] of historical

cone being devided among phases as covens are devided [*sic*]" (*YVP* 3:60). GY's illustration is reproduced in *YVP* 3:61.

103. This passage refers to three of Masaccio's paintings in the Brancacci Chapel (Florence): *The Baptism of the Neophytes, The Rendering of the Tribute Money,* and *The Expulsion of Adam and Eve.*

104. After a life of crime and several narrow escapes from death sentences, François Villon disappeared, leaving his partly serious, partly humorous *Testament,* or will. See *L,* 583, and *Au,* 217, 240.

105. Casts of sculpture and architectural features from classical Greek and Rome and also from later periods in European art were part of the collection of the Victoria and Albert Museum from its establishment in 1852. Acquisitions from the 1860s to the 1880s especially emphasized medieval and Renaissance periods, and after the Architectural or Cast courts opened in 1873, the large exhibit space allowed for considerable expansion of an already extensive collection. In 1916, the cast collection of the Architectural Museum, which was particularly strong in examples of Gothic architectural ornament, was brought permanently to the museum. The collection of casts of postclassical European statuary at the V&A is still perhaps the most comprehensive in the world.

106. Just before the words "man descends the hill," in the much-revised typescript, WBY crossed out a sentence about the importance of gyres to Irish art: "The work of the iconoclasts and of those unknown artists who covered the books of Durrow and of Kells with whirling gyres and forms that represent no living thing is reversed."

107. The sculptor Donatello (ca. 1386–1466); painter, sculptor, and architect Michelangelo Buonarroti (1475–1564); sculptor Jacopo della Quercia (ca. 1374–1438); and painter, draftsman, and architect Raphael (Raffaello Sanzio, 1483–1520) were all associated with the Italian Renaissance. Greek sculptor Myron of Eleutherae (ca. 470–ca. 440 BCE) was a leading early classical bronze sculptor of the Attic school. There may be an echo here of Furtwängler's *Masterpieces of Greek Sculpture,* 181; Furtwängler later observes that "the ancient orators name him among the last masters of the severe style" (182).

108. With reference to two eras of two thousand years each, there were "renaissances," turnings from religious to secular values, at phase 22 of the earlier (500 BCE) and the later (1500 CE). Parallels also exist between Plato (in the earlier cycle) and the Platonic Academy of Cosimo de' Medici headed by Marsilio Ficino (in the later). See p. 151, where Greek art is considered in Pre-Raphaelite terms, Phidias equated with Raphael, and the earlier art found preferable.

109. The phrase "vestibule of Christianity" was a fairly common expression for the periods leading into the Christian era. See, for instance, the title of Johann Joseph Ignaz von Döllinger's *Heidenthum und Judenthum, Vorhalle zur Geschichte des Christenthums* [*Heathenism and Judaism, the Vestibule of Christianity*] (Regensburg: Verlag von G. Joseph Manz,

1857). Perhaps based on Blake's assertion that "All Religions are One" (Erdman, 1–2; in *WWB* 3:n.p., called "There Is No Natural Religion") and Thomas Taylor's claim that the Greeks had taught the Christians, the system aims at "the reconciliation of Paganism and Christianity," and it draws on many sources. See in particular F. X. Kraus in "Medicean Rome" (in vol. 2 of *The Cambridge Modern History,* ed. A. W. Ward et al. [Cambridge: Cambridge University Press, 1902–11], 2:61; O'Shea 14). After describing the work of Julius II (1443–1513; pope from 1503 to 1513), Kraus adds: "Not only Judaism, but also Graeco-Roman paganism, is an antechamber to Christianity . . ." (2:61). Like Kraus, the heavily revised typescript attributes "this fusion . . . of Christian emotionalism and Pagan intellect" to the Florentine Academy: "Ficino, before old age brings caution, speaks of Christianity as a development of Greek Philosophy."

German painter, draftsman, and printmaker Albrecht Dürer (1471–1528) made two trips to Venice, in 1494–95 and 1505–7, during which he secured the commission for an altarpiece in San Bartolommeo, the church of the German community. The finished piece paid tribute to the aesthetics of Venetian painting of the time.

On the "perfectly proportioned human body," see Book I, n. 46.

110. See Book III, n. 68 above, as well as "Long-legged Fly" (*Poems,* 347, lines 21–22). While the preceding pagan cycle had the athlete as its emblem of the Unity of Being, the Renaissance (part of a distinctively Christian two-thousand-year cycle) has the Edenic, prelapsarian Adam. Artistically, this epoch takes its distinctive image from the roof of the Sistine Chapel: see also "Under Ben Bulben" (*Poems,* 333–36, lines 45–52).

111. WBY knew the *De antro nympharum* by the Neoplatonist Porphyry (ca. 234–ca. 305 CE) in Thomas Taylor's translation, *On the Cave of the Nymphs* (reprinted by the Theosophical Society in 1895), as early as 1901, when part 2 of "The Philosophy of Shelley's Poetry" was written (*EE,* 63). WBY attributed the book to Proclus in both manuscript and revised typescript of *AVA.*

112. See the *Mystic Nativity* (1500) of Sandro Botticelli. *The National Gallery Illustrated General Catalogue* (London, 1973) translates the inscription discussed in WBY's note: "I, Sandro painted this picture at the end of the year 1500 (?) in the troubles of Italy in the half time according to the 11th chapter of S. John in the second woe of the Apocalypse in the loosing of the devil for three and a half years then he will be chained in the 12th chapter and we shall see clearly (?) [damage] as in this picture" (62; insertions are from the *Catalogue*).

The Yeatses visited Capri in 1925, and as Murphy notes, WBY is in the note referring to the natural Grotta di Matermania, transformed during Roman times into a nymphaeum, which has frequently, as in WBY's Baedeker (1912), been wrongly associated with Mithra. See

Karl Baedeker, *Handbook for Travellers: Southern Italy and Sicily*
(17th rev. ed. [Leipzig: Karl Baedeker, 1912], 187) and Murphy,
" 'Old Rocky Face, look forth'," 70.
On the linking of the Mithraic cave with the Christian manger, see
Murphy, " 'Old Rocky Face, look forth'," 104–6.

113. Both manuscript and typescript here have the heading: "AD 1450 to
1500." Carlo Crivelli (1435–95) was an important Venetian Renaissance painter who worked largely in Ancona and Ascoli. Although born
near Vicenza, painter Andrea Mantegna (ca. 1431–1506) was strongly
influenced by the aesthetics of Florentine painters. All the painters
listed in this sentence are of the generation following Masaccio.

114. The quotation is from Baldassare Castiglione, *The Book of the
Courtier*, trans. Sir Thomas Hoby (London: David Nutt, 1900; O'Shea
351): "Therefore Beautie is the true monument and spoile of the victory of the soule, when she with heavenly influence beareth rule over
martiall and grosse nature, and with her light overcometh the darke-
nesse of the bodie" (311). See *Mem*, 157.

115. "[T]he Fifteenth Phase of the Moon" lacks historical comment because,
as WBY explains in the manuscript and working typescript, it "is
supernatural"; "and so when we would represent it by natural form we
are lured to a calculated perfection, to measurements to an almost scientific creation, contemplation's barren child." Roughly here in the
manuscript, WBY marked the next division, then crossed out the following: "1500 to—Phases 16, 17, & 18." The terminal date was to
have been 1640.

116. A new generation of artists exemplifies the waning moon that begins
after the phase of "complete beauty" that "knows nothing of desire,
for desire implies effort" (p. 59). See "Under Ben Bulben" (*Poems*,
333–36, lines 45–52). See also the theory of eugenics WBY developed
in *On the Boiler* (*LE*, 220–51).

117. Pope Julius II directed the decoration of these rooms in the Vatican
palace. From 1508 to 1512, Michelangelo decorated the ceiling of
the Sistine Chapel—the pope's private chapel and the site of conclaves
for the election of popes—alternating Hebrew prophets and pagan
sibyls in seated positions around the lower curved part of the barrel-
vaulted room. Raphael painted the Stanza della Segnatura (1508–11),
where the pope signed bulls and briefs. The long wall opposite the
entry to the Stanza holds the *Disputa*, or "Disputation of the Holy
Sacrament," a discussion about the Eucharist but also a glorification of
Catholicism. Opposite it is the *School of Athens*, showing the triumph
of philosophy and a balance to the triumph of theology.

118. John Milton's "On the Morning of Christ's Nativity" (1629) stresses
that the coming of Christ silenced the pagan oracles (Milton, 42–50).
Milton was learned in classical mythology, but he ultimately condemned it (see *Paradise Lost* 7.1–39; Milton, 345–47).

119. On the diagram of historical cones, phases 16–18 are dated 1550, and the next gyre (phases 19–21) has a date of 1680. In 1603, Elizabeth I died, and James I assumed the throne of England. English poets Abraham Cowley (1618–67) and John Dryden (1631–1700) wrote during the English civil wars (1642–51) and Restoration (1660–85).

120. Flemish painter Sir Anthony van Dyck (1599–1641) became an important portrait painter in the English court of Charles I. See also *Au*, 227–28.

121. A break marked "1640 to 1880" (for phases 19, 20, 21) came here in a rejected section of the manuscript. The changed version begins: "I find among my 'documents' the statement that the nineteenth lunar phase 'did all the harm'."

122. English astrologer, philosopher, statesman, and essayist Sir Francis Bacon (1561–1626) is known for establishing an inductive methodology for scientific inquiry. Despite the mention of the "big Altar in St Peter's," the passage seems not to refer to Bernini's baldacchino (1633), whose figures are rather staid, but rather to the Cathedra of St Peter in Glory (1658–66), an enormous reliquary surrounding the episcopal chair attributed to Saint Peter and positioned in the tribune of the cathedral.

123. The reference is to eighteenth-century writers Alexander Pope (1688–1744), Thomas Gray (1716–71), Samuel Johnson (1709–84), and Jean-Jacques Rousseau (1712–78).

124. In *Religio Medici* (1643), Browne (1605–82) declares his belief in witches: "I could believe that Spirits use with man the act of carnality, and that in both sexes; I conceive they may assume, steal, or contrive a body, wherein there may be action enough to content decrepit lust, or passion to satisfie more active veneries . . ." (I.xxx). WBY quotes the same passage in *LE*, 72; see also *Myth1*, 267; *Myth2*, 177. He owned copies of three editions of this work (O'Shea 289–91).

125. The quotation is from the instructors of the AS. In an AS from 22 December 1918, the control Thomas defined the term: "The emotion of sanctity is the link with the afterlife state—sanctity is the voluntary descent into the world when the aridity of the abstract has been passed & the emotion of sanctity attained" (*YVP* 2:147). This passage is also quoted in the CF (*YVP* 3:366, 372, 403). VersB may clarify the meaning: "Before the self passes from 22 it is said to attain what is called 'the emotion of sanctity' & this emotion is described as contact with the life beyond death; . . . sanctity is described as the 'renunciation of personal salvation' " (*YVP* 4:233).

126. The quotation is a paraphrase from the second stanza of "Claire de lune" by French poet Paul Verlaine (1844–96): "Ils n'ont pas l'air de croire à leur bonheur. . . ." This poem and its collection, *Fêtes galantes*, are indebted to the painting of French rococo painter Jean-Antoine Watteau (1684–1721). WBY had met Verlaine: see *Au*, 261–62; *EE*,

197; and *UP*1:397–99. Thomas Gainsborough (1727–88) was a land-scape and portrait painter; as his career advanced, he adopted a formal manner for portraits of his sophisticated clientele. Egyptian sculptors worked in wood but often in more durable materials; the most famous face of an Egyptian princess is the beautifully preserved polychrome limestone bust of Nefertiti, wife of the Egyptian pharaoh Akhenaton (Amenhotep IV), now in the Altes Museum, Berlin.

127. By tradition, WBY would have been prepared to dislike the work of painter Sir Joshua Reynolds (1723–92), whose stay in Rome (1749–52) emphasized study of Raphael and Michelangelo; like Blake, who made adverse marginal comments on Reynolds's *Discourses,* WBY rejected Reynolds's aesthetic and epistemological theories.

128. The reference is probably to Reynolds's portrait of Henrietta Frances, Viscountess Duncannon and Countess of Bessborough, reproduced in Granville Leveson Gower, *Private Correspondence, 1781–1821* (ed. Castalia, Countess Granville, 2 vols. [London: John Murray, 1916]), vol. 1, facing p. 88 (see *L,* 678–79).

129. The "village providence" apparently refers to the eighteenth-century idea of benevolence. Compare *LE,* 44: "To Balzac indeed it [the solution of the social question] was but personal charity, the village providence of the eighteenth century. . . ." See also *L,* 233, and *EAR,* 247.

   The claim here is that the Faust of part 2 (written in Goethe's elder years) expresses a good-hearted eighteenth-century desire, as did the hero of Samuel Richardson's novel *Sir Charles Grandison* (1753). Similarly, in his later years, Voltaire (pen name of François-Marie Arouet, 1694–1778) defended religious freedom. Compare *Mem,* 158: "Faust in the end was only able to reclaim land like some officer of the Agricultural Board."

130. WBY told Lady Gregory that he had enjoyed reading the novels of English novelist Jane Austen (1775–1817) in the American tour that he and GY took in the spring of 1920 (Foster 2:168).

131. English writers Blake and Arnold are compared with Belgian poet Émile Verhaeren (1855–1916).

132. French painter Louis-Gustave Ricard (1823–73) was best known for his still lifes and portraits in the classical manner. See *EE,* 174. According to the *Grove Dictionary of Art,* Ricard, a "reclusive, studious aesthete," "worked for long periods of time on his portraits without his sitters being present. When his task seemed almost complete, he would recall them and was quoted as saying that he took pleasure in seeing how they resembled the portraits he had made of them" (s.v. "Ricard, [Louis-]Gustave").

133. English painter and writer Charles Ricketts (1866–1931) founded the Vale Press and, with English painter and lithographer Charles Shannon (1863–1937), edited *The Dial* (1897–99). His effect on WBY is clear from letters of WBY's and from *Self-Portrait Taken from the Letters*

and Journals of Charles Ricketts, R. A., collected and compiled by T. Sturge Moore, ed. Cecil Lewis (London: Peter Davies, 1939). WBY owned a number of Ricketts's books (O'Shea 1727, 1745–49). Ricketts illustrated the first edition of Oscar Wilde's poem "The Sphinx" (1894). WBY included "the Charles Ricketts of *The Danaides,* and of the earlier illustrations of *The Sphinx,*" among "the great myth-makers and mask-makers" (*Au,* 403–4). Ricketts created three wood engravings for Sturge Moore's *Danae: A Poem* (London: Hacon and Ricketts, 1903).

134. Charles Dickens's (1812–70) first major novel was *The Posthumous Papers of the Pickwick Club,* better known as *The Pickwick Papers* (1836), the main character of which was the founder of the Pickwick Club. See WBY's essay on "The Modern Novel" (*Irish Times,* 9 November 1923), quoted in Donald Torchiana, *W. B. Yeats and Georgian Ireland:*

> Sometime in the middle of the eighteenth century there came into the faces of women, as painted by the great painters, an exquisite subtlety which they called a mark of high breeding. They got it in Gainsborough and one or two painters before him, and they got it in the first volume of 'Sir Charles Grandison'. Then he found the same thing in the novels of Jane Austen. These novels were simply a description, an elaboration, of the pursuit of good breeding—that was to say, a quality which only a few happily nurtured people ever found. Then he did not find that pursuit again until they got to the writings of Henry James.
>
> He discovered, about five years ago, the particular devil that spoiled that celebrated quality in literature. 'Pickwick' was the devil. In 'Pickwick' the qualities celebrated were qualities any man could possess: good humour, a certain amount of openness of heart, kindness—qualities which everyman might hope to possess; they were democratic qualities. It gave them the kind of sculpture they saw in Dublin, like Tom Moore and the statue in Leinster Lawn. That smile of vacuous benevolence came out of 'Pickwick'. (212)

In the AS for 24 Jan 1918, the communicators for the evening, the control Thomas with the guide Fish, suggest that Dickens's art, like that of Keats, Wordsworth, and Tennyson, is "incomplete" because of "love of world"—that is, "material good" (*YVP* 1:287–88).

135. In addition to the already mentioned Blake, Nietzsche (see Book I, n. 129), and Herbert Spencer (see Book I, n. 188), this list includes English poet and critic Coventry Patmore (1823–96), English novelist Samuel Richardson (1689–1761), Russian novelist Leo Tolstoy (1828–1910), English political philosopher Thomas Hobbes

(1588–1679), and English philosopher and political economist John
Stuart Mill (1806–73).

136. See pp. 169–70.

137. See Book I, n. 129. In 1902, WBY wrote excitedly to Lady Gregory
about his discovery of Nietzsche, "that strong enchanter": "I have read
him so much that I have made my eyes bad again. . . . Nietzsche completes Blake and has the same roots" (*L*, 379).

138. WBY seems to have wrestled with this section, which is originally
headed "Phases 22 to 28" in the manuscript, then changed to "Phase
22" in the much-revised typescript. He wrote that "Phases 8 and 22 are
themselves phases of abstraction and are preceded and followed by
abstraction; phase 8 was preceded by the Schoolmen, followed and
accompanied by legalists and inquisitors, and phase 22 was preceded
by the popularisation of physical, social and economic science and has
been accompanied and will be followed by economic and social movements, movements of applied science in some sense or other of an
abstract and probably violent kind."

139. Book 3 of *The Trembling of the Veil* (1921) is so called; see Dedication
and Introduction, n. 15. A rejected sentence clarifies this passage:
"The 22 phase . . . is that of our own epoch—Hodos Chameliontos—
as I called it in 'The Trembling of the Veil'—and when it has passed
away it will be recognized as that wherein broke all that concerns the
common thought."

140. The references are to Leo Tolstoy's *War and Peace* (1865–69) and to *La
Tentation de Saint Antoine* (*The Temptation of Saint Anthony,* 1874)
by Gustave Flaubert.

141. The "recent mathematical research" recalls *The Education of Henry
Adams,* chap. 31, in which the work of various modern scientists and
mathematicians ("since Bacon and Newton") suggested to Adams that
"Chaos was the law of nature; Order was the dream of man" (451);
the older scientific view had transitioned to a scientific relativism
where—as Poincaré had said—Euclidean geometry is not more true but
more convenient than non-Euclidean types (455). From this point to
the end of the paragraph, WBY made numerous revisions in the much-
revised typescript. One surprising rejection is the following sentence:
"Then, as in the novels, the painting, the philosophy, nature suddenly
appears in all her violence and terror returns, so to the individual
comes the sense of fate which Dostoievsky calls 'Gods Love' a knowledge that the world cannot be changed, a doubt of general progress."

In the reference to "a new dimension," there may be an echo of
Lyndon Bolton's *Introduction to the Theory of Relativity* with regard
to "The Limited Universe" (London: Methuen, 1921): "The curvature
of space, or of the aether, leads to the conclusion that any region, if sufficiently extended, may eventually bend round into itself, and thus

that the universe of experience may be limited" (170–71). The new dimension is time.

142. At this point in *AVB*, "Dove or Swan" breaks off, perhaps because what followed was too personal and conjectural.

143. Although the parallel to Alexander the Great (see Book III, n. 29 above) must be expected, that parallel is not clarified. At phase 22 always occurs a defeat: some unidentified hero should now be conquered. A revision in the heavily revised typescript reads: "We have in our great war repeated the wars of Alexander."

144. At this point in both manuscript and revised typescript appears the heading: "Phases 23-24-25." WBY omitted about seven hundred words and dramatically revised the rest of Book III. A few lines will illustrate:

> Hitherto I have described the past or but the near future, but now I must plunge beyond the reach of the senses. . . . Though I think that I too can describe the mind of the future, I must, if I am not to make the description so abstract that it is unintelligible, imagine circumstance which will be at least as unlike the actual future as the water clock [of Alexandria] is unlike my watch. Then too I am *Antithetical* in nature, and find it impossible to see the joy that belongs to *Primary* Phases. . . . Men will come to eat and house and travel in much the same way and in one another's company, . . . as difference of wealth lessens, all grows uniform and rigid, leisure for that aimless brooding which is the manure at the tree's root will cease, and . . . men's minds grow barren through hatred. . . . I find in my documents a statement that population will decline through pestilence and famine and accidents of nature, and I interpret these words as said of what a follower of Heraclitus said of Epochs, and I understand that to mean that man's desire for truth and for the good, as we call his desire to be fated, has now been fulfilled according to the measure of his capacity, and that change must come from without . . . , and it will be in all things the opposite of that which founded Christianity. . . . I see it rise among all those who have resisted or suffered defeat in the defence of some rank, physiological or intellectual, which has sought its own expression, and as satisfying all who thirst for whatever if hierarchical or distinguished. . . . Young and confident they must be, because what we symbolise as the Tower inherits all that once belonged to the Catacombs, and violent because those spiritual energies that have come down from the Sermon on the Mount, through the impersonality of our empirical sciences are now exhausted.

145. Cf. Richard Aldington's review of Wyndham Lewis's *"Timon of Athens"*. *A Portfolio of Drawings*: "One youthful person assured me that Mr Lewis' work was a 'cacophony of sardine-tins' " (*The Egoist* 1.1 [January 1914], 11). See also *L*, 608.

GY was more appreciative of the work of Romanian-French sculptor Constantin Brancusi (1876–1957) than WBY (see Saddlemyer, 250, 368). This passage may draw from Ezra Pound's "Brancusi" (1921; *Literary Essays of Ezra Pound*, ed. T. S. Eliot [Norfolk, CT: New Directions, 1954]):

> Brancusi has set out on the maddeningly more difficult exploration toward getting all the forms into one form. . . . Plate No. 5 shows what looks like an egg. . . . I don't know by what metaphorical periphrase I am to convey the relation of these ovoids to Brancusi's other sculpture. As an interim label, one might consider them as master-keys to the world of form—not 'his' world of form, but as much as he has found of 'the' world of form. (442–43)

The Yugoslav sculptor Ivan Meštrović (1883–1962) was condemned by Wyndham Lewis in *Blast* 2; see William C. Wees, *Vorticism and the English Avant-Garde* (Toronto: University of Toronto Press, 1972), 203. In 1928, when WBY reported to the Irish senate on the work of his committee to choose coins for the Free State, he noted that Meštrović and Swedish sculptor Carl Milles (1875–1955) "have expressed in their work a violent rhythmical energy unknown to past ages, and seem to many the foremost sculptors of our day" (*The Senate Speeches of W. B. Yeats*, ed. Donald R. Pearce [London: Faber and Faber, 1961], 163).

146. From about 1880 until 1910, Auguste Rodin worked on commissioned bronze doors for a planned museum, a project he called *Porte de l'Enfer*. For Rodin's remark to Arthur Symons (1865–1945), see Symons's *Studies in Seven Arts* (London: Constable, 1906): "Every figure that Rodin has created is in the act of striving towards something: a passion, an idea, a state of being, quiescence itself. His 'Gates of Hell' are a headlong flight and falling, in which all the agonies of a place of torment, which is Baudelaire's rather than Dante's, swarm in actual movement" (15).

147. Ezra Pound (see Dedication and Introduction, n. 55), American-British poet T. S. Eliot (1888–1965), Irish novelist James Joyce (1882–1941), and Italian playwright Luigi Pirandello (1867–1936) represent this moment, as do three of their works published in 1922: the lunatic suffering from delirium is the protagonist of Pirandello's *Henry IV*; the Fisher King and the man fishing behind the gas works figure in Eliot's *The Waste Land*; the single Dublin day of Ulysses's wandering is that of Leopold Bloom in Joyce's *Ulysses*. GY, who was closer in age to what

would be termed "modernism" than WBY, owned a number of copies of plays by Pirandello and essays by Eliot, and regarded Pound's work highly. She also appreciated Joyce, even smuggling a copy of *Ulysses* into Ireland (although she also reported in a letter to Lady Ottoline Morrell that "Joyce lingers too much over all the indignities of the flesh. . . . I think a great deal is very fine but I want a large hot bath after each reading & that's a bore!" (quoted in Saddlemyer, 294). In 1937, she gave her sister-in-law Lolly Yeats an unusual gift: a copy of *The Tales of Shem and Shaun* from the "Work in Progress" that would be published as *Finnegans Wake*. See O'Shea 356a, 621, 624, 1045–46, 1570–82, 1616–17, 1619a–20, 1622–23, 1626, 1630a.

148. French patriot, publisher, poet, and devoted Roman Catholic Charles Péguy (1873–1914) wrote the play *Le Mystère de la charité de Jeanne d'Arc* (Paris: Cahiers de la quinzaine, [1910]; O'Shea 1551), read to WBY by Iseult Gonne (see *LE*, 33 and 35). In a letter to T. Sturge Moore, WBY admitted that he found Péguy unappealing unless he imagined himself a peasant (Bridge, *Yeats and Moore*, 26).

In 1913, both WBY and his future wife, George Hyde Lees, probably read the work of French Roman Catholic poet, essayist, and dramatist Paul Claudel (1868–1955) (Saddlemyer, 48). Iseult Gonne helped WBY to read Claudel carefully in 1917 (*LE*, 33). Also in 1917, WBY had seen Claudel's modern miracle play *L'Annonce faite à Marie* in English translation (*L*, 626); he also owned a copy in French (O'Shea 393). Though WBY noted that Péguy's "Christianity is of course for us impossible" (Bridge, *Yeats and Moore*, 26), he thought that "these men in whom an intellectual patriotism is not distinct from religion" might provide valuable examples for the young (*LE*, 36), and he used his connections to find productions for the dramatic works of Claudel and Péguy.

149. This is a translation of the passage from chapter 48 of Petronius Arbiter's *Satyricon* (ca. 60 CE), used as the epigraph to T. S. Eliot's *The Waste Land* (1922).

150. From "The Double Vision of Michael Robartes" (*Poems*, 172–74, lines 9–12). Galley proofs also included lines 13–16, "Obedient to some hidden magical breath. / They do not even feel, so abstract are they, / So dead beyond our death, / Triumph that we obey." The poem grew out of a session of AS on 7 January 1919. Directed by the unnamed control (who was probably Thomas), for script marked "Personal Only," GY drew a symbolic sketch of the rock of Cashel and the ruined church in County Tipperary. WBY asked, "Why have you made this drawing?" and the control said that he should study "a historical & spiritual past" suggesting Cashel through broken phrases about the church, the castle on the hill, and Cormac (*YVP* 2:162–64).

151. See Book III, n. 10 above.

152. See Blake's "The Divine Image" from *Songs of Innocence* (Erdman,

12–13; *WWB* 3:42) and "A Divine Image" from *Songs of Experience* (Erdman, 32; *WWB* 3:59). See also Erdman, 131, 173, and 522. Dürer and Milton were not included in the typescript, which read: " 'The human form Divine' as Blake understood those words . . .' (NLI, 36,269/6). On Nietzsche, see p. 4; Book I, n. 129; and the description of phase 12. Nietzsche had a place in the system from an early date. In the AS of 1 January 1918, WBY was told through the guide Fish that Nietzsche and his most famous superman, Zarathustra, appear in phases 12 and 18. Informed also that the person at phase 12 has the "wisdom of intellect" rather than instinct, WBY asked, "Why wisdom of head at 12?" The instructor responded that "it is generally a propaganda a will to change forms of existing thought—a metaphysician is a nihilist not a creator" (*YVP* 1:182–84), a line which would be quoted as a tag for phase 12 in VNB1 (*YVP* 3:156).

The phrase "a tongue that's dead" is incorrectly quoted from the last line of Coventry Patmore's "Dead Language." WBY had read Patmore as early as 1909 (*IDM*, 92; *Mem*, 190; *L*, 526); see also Book III, n. 135 above.

153. In the heavily marked typescript, Book III closes with a sentence about Leda hearkening back to the poem: "I remember that from the eggs of Leda, which symbolise perhaps the birth of the Greek civilisation, were born not only Helen, but Castor and Pollux." See also Book II, n. 140, and *AVB, 268.* At the coming of Christ, "the myth becomes a biography" (see also p. 154).

154. In galley proofs, this sentence was substituted for a much stronger one, which read, "Victory bringing control of the world's surface must come to those who have made life a preparation for war and so established life in the terror and sweetness of solitude that every act of war is an act of creation and the solitude of each the tribal solitude."

155. Porphyry famously stated that Plotinus had achieved "conjunction" with deity four times and had composed his books from the contemplation and intuition of divinity (see, for instance, Thomas Taylor's translation of *The Philosophical and Mathematical Commentaries of Proclus* [London, 1788–89], 2:235). In a rejected epilogue "To Vestigia," WBY suggested that he and his fellow students in the Golden Dawn "came to think that nothing mattered but to return to the one," an experience "so rare" that "it came . . . to Plotinus but once" (NLI, 36,364/2).

156. In *The Iliad* 1.197, Athena grabs Achilles by the hair and then urges him to curb his passion, rather than battle Agamemnon. WBY uses the same image in "The Wheel and the Phases of the Moon" (p. 4), in *The Resurrection* (*Plays,* 487), and in the rejected epilogue: "& think it is best to be like Plotinus, it may be better to see ghosts than to chop logic. What else did Achilles when Athena came behind & took him by the yellow hair."

157. This sentence was added in galley proofs.
158. See pp. 171–72 and Book III, n. 126 above.
159. See Dedication and Introduction, n. 30.

Book IV: The Gates of Pluto

1. In *AVB*, 23, WBY called this section "the most unfinished of my five books." Its goal is to explain "the way of the soul"—the primary concern of *AVA*.

2. This poem was part (lines 18–29) of a larger poem in *Seven Poems and a Fragment* (Dundrum, Ireland: Cuala, 1922) entitled "Cuchulain the Girl and the Fool"—later retitled "The Hero, the Girl, and the Fool" in *The Tower* (London and New York: Macmillan, 1928). In these longer versions, the Fool's remarks follow seventeen lines of discussion between Hero and Girl, who are poetic versions of WBY and Iseult Gonne (see Jeffares, *A Commentary on the Collected Poems of W. B. Yeats* [Stanford: Stanford University Press, 307], and Foster 2:362).

3. In collected editions, this line reads: "When all works that have" (*Poems*, 223; *VP*, 449).

4. See the AS for 11 November 1917, where Thomas, through GY, mentions that spirits "dream backwards remember" and "when they reach the prenatal they have returned to the condition of being able to go forward" (*YVP* 1:75).

5. This section was called "Death, the Soul, and the Life after Death" in the early typescript that begins with the narrative of "Michael Robartes and the Judwali Doctor" (NLI, 36,263/24/1).

6. WBY frequently quoted from the work of the Renaissance Cabalist and astrologer Heinrich Cornelius Agrippa von Nettesheim (1486–1535), whose *Three Books of Occult Philosophy or Magic* WBY must have read in the 1651 translation because it is the only one that includes book 3 (Dume, "William Butler Yeats: A Survey of His Reading," 119–20). In "Swedenborg, Mediums, and the Desolate Places," WBY quoted the sentence from Orpheus in a longer passage (from chapter 61) suggesting that, after death, spirits atone for their sins in dreams (See *LE*, 68; also *AVB*, 23). GY studied Agrippa seriously beginning in 1913; the copy of Agrippa's *Opera* in the Yeatses' library is marked with her marginalia as well as carefully executed colored diagrams, pasted into the book, of "The Thirty Two Parts of the Sepher Yetzivah," "The Tree of Life. The outward and visible Sign of an inward and Spiritual grace," and "The 22 Tarot Trumps" (*Opera, in duos tomos concinne digesta* . . . [Lyon: Per Beringos Fratres, n.d.]; O'Shea 24; Saddlemyer, 60 and 679n113; NLI, 40,568/2).

7. For daimons, see Book I, n. 62. "Complementary Dream" replaced "correspondence and symbol" in page proofs. For complementary dream, see Book II, n. 136.

8. On 13 August 1920, GY recorded the information Dionertes had given: "All Daimons are in 13th Cone; but there are also perfected men there from whom they differ in form & colour. He [Dionertes] would not however at the time go into these forms & colours, as he did not want to get into symbolism" (*YVP* 3:32). The symbolism of colors had been explained to the Yeatses on 30 May 1920: "Purple—Signifies for the living the Anima Mundi & for the spirits, the 13th cycle which is their anima Mundi. Our anima mundi seems to include the thought & emotion of the world. Everything that is *not Fate*—We inquire in purple about interdependence of Spirits & Guides—Spirits and angels—" (*YVP* 3:21). The session also explains the symbolism of blue, yellow, and rose.

9. On 13 August 1920, Dionertes explained: "The Daimons were more powerful than the men, but had only one man each (human being—) in their charge though they might interest many in carrying out that charge, while the perfected men were in relation each with many men" (*YVP* 3:32).

10. The portion of this sentence following the semicolon was inserted in galley proofs.

11. The CF reads: "G.S. [Ghostly Self] Does not incarnate but has a correspondential relation with Spirit which does" (*YVP* 3:310). From the Ghostly Self " 'issues either the illumination or the slow spiritual vision.' The knowledge 'is always there' " (*YVP* 3:309).

12. See pp. 108, 114, 138 for other uses of this phrase.

13. In a note to "The Second Coming" (written January 1919), WBY comments that, according to the Judwalis, subjective man "has a moment of revelation immediately after death, a revelation which they describe as his being carried into the presence of all his dead kindred" (*Poems*, 659). From this point on, the remainder of *AVA* relies greatly on the experimental techniques and publications of the Society for Psychical Research; WBY was acquainted with many of the society's participants. Perhaps most important was Frederic W. H. Myers, a founding member, whose monumental two-volume *Human Personality and Its Survival of Bodily Death* (1903; rpt., New York: Longmans, Green, 1954) WBY surely read with interest—especially "Introduction" (chap. 1), "Phantasms of the Dead" (chap. 7), "Trance, Possession, and Ecstasy" (chap. 9), and "Epilogue" (chap. 10).

Walter Kelly Hood notes that in WBY's copy of Fechner's *On Life After Death*, WBY wrote "? Vision of the Blood Kindred" beside this passage:

> In the moment of death every one will realize the fact that what his mind received from those who died before him, never ceased to belong to their minds as well, and thus he will enter the third world not like a strange visitor, but like a long expected member

of the family, who is welcomed home by all those with whom he was here united in the community of faith, of knowledge, or of love. (Fechner, 66–67; " 'Read Fechner,' " 95)

14. This entire section rephrases a sleep for 31 May 1920, a dramatization "Dictated by Dionertes." "I am dead," GY wrote, referring perhaps to herself, WBY, Dionertes as dreamer, or a generalized self; "Then I am aware of brilliant light and I see all those of blood relationship in past lives." GY's hand describes, with illustrations, "the separation": "When I recognize myself, I leave the grave, rising up from my body but horizontally for that is the position of complete subjectivity—When I have regained all knowledge of self necessary I shall separate into the four particles thus" (*YVP* 3:22).

The illustration that follows is reproduced on *YVP* 3:23 and well described in *AVA*. The horizontal form of the "husk" with "head" and "feet" marked is at the base. Floating horizontally above it, the "PB rises from generation." At the head of the husk, the "celestial body rises from feet," and at the feet of the husk the "spirit rises from head." Above the Passionate Body is a sketch of a star to suggest "light so brilliant that the eye looking upon it sees radiating lines issuing from it." Calling this explanation "all the dull preliminary," Dionertes promised to "go on tomorrow" (*YVP* 3:22–23). In the description of the horizontally floating spirit, WBY may be recalling one of Blake's striking illustrations from 1808 to Robert Blair's *The Grave* entitled *The Soul hovering over the Body reluctantly parting with Life* (available at *The William Blake Archive*, ed. Morris Eaves, Robert N. Essick, and Joseph Viscomi, http://www.blakearchive.org). Note that "Principles" are called "Particles" at this date (also on 19 June 1920, *YVP* 3:23). See also the AS for 1 February 1918 (*YVP* 1:321–28).

15. See Book IV, n. 92 below.
16. GY's hand wrote this phrase in the AS of 31 January 1918 (*YVP* 1:313).
17. In the same record of the sleep of 31 May 1920, which is the source for this section, Dionertes dictates the first-person account of a dead soul's engagement with both "a ritual of burial" and flowers: "The ritual is a discipline of thought, and intensifies thought. The flowers set on my grave are the only light I see. It is through these flowers that I am first able to enter into the thoughts of the living to discover my own identity—until I have found that I may not leave my body" (*YVP* 3:22). For "The *Spirit* is somewhere said," see *YVP* 1:323 and cf. 3:395.
18. See W. H. Davies's "Body and Spirit" (lines 13–24). WBY printed seven of Davies's poems in *The Oxford Book of Modern Verse* (Oxford: Clarendon, 1936), perhaps after consultation with Dorothy Wellesley (*L*, 859).
19. The record of a sleep dated 18 October 1921 explains this and related terms succinctly: "In the Teachings the spirit is prepared for the other

world; in the Return he studies his past life in relation to that world; in the Shiftings he gets rid of all memory of that life though not necessarily of other earlier lives" (*YVP* 3:101). The Yeatses had explored the subject in the AS on 10 June 1918 (*YVP* 1:490) and in a sleep for 20 April 1921 (*YVP* 3:92). Walter Kelly Hood notes that in WBY's copy of Fechner's *On Life After Death*, WBY wrote "Dreaming Back and Return" beside this sentence: "after separation from the body in death, a person will become aware of all the ideas and effects which, produced by his manifold actions in life, will continue living and working in this world, and will form, as an organic offspring of an individual stem, an organic individuality which only then becomes alive, self-conscious" (Fechner, 36; " 'Read Fechner,' " 95). See also Book IV, n. 13 above.

20. On sage and victim, see Book I, n. 111. VNB2 contains considerable discussion of "Waking State" and "Sleeping State." It also contains a list of the characteristics of "Teacher & Victim" in two parallel columns: "Thin Man" v. "Fat Man," "Frail soul" v. "Strong soul," "Vision is emotion" v. "vision is intellectual," and others (*YVP* 3:193). This note was inserted in galley proofs on 28 September 1925.

21. This description summarizes the Nō play *Motomezuka*, which WBY read in Marie C. Stopes, *Plays of Old Japan: The Nō* (London: Heinemann, 1913), in its first English translation, by Stopes and Joji Sakurai, on pages 39–52. WBY was introduced to the Nō by Ezra Pound in the winter of 1913–14 while the two poets stayed at Stone Cottage, in Coleman's Hatch, Sussex; cf. James Longenbach, *Stone Cottage: Pound, Yeats, and Modernism* (Oxford and New York: Oxford University Press, 1988), p. 203. WBY also mentions the work in a note to *The Dreaming of the Bones* (*Plays*, 692) and "Swedenborg, Mediums, and the Desolate Places" (*LE*, 69–70). An entry in VNB2 refers to this play (*YVP* 3:187, quoted in next note).

22. Seldom used in *AVA*, the term "phantasmagoria" appealed to WBY and became more important in later writing. It first appears in the unpublished essay "The Poet and the Actress," written in 1916 (David R. Clark, " 'The Poet and the Actress': An Unpublished Dialogue by W. B. Yeats," in *YA* 8 [1991]: 135; cf. Foster 2:71). A VNB2 entry for 27 November [1923] records a definition received in a sleep: "Phantasmagoria is result of Principles foreseeing the future in shiftings Phantasmagoria antithesis of dreamed event as shiftings is of the life. We are not solitary in phantasmagoria—see Japanese story of two lovers, but only meet those who are in dreamed event" (*YVP* 3:187). See also references to phantasmagoria on p. 165, in the AS 27 June 1918 (*YVP* 2:2); *Poems*, 604 and 649; and *Au*, 237.

23. On the possible importance of Fechner to this concept, see Book IV, n. 19 above. WBY also wrote "Dreaming Back" beside Fechner's declaration that in the next world an evildoer will not find "rest and peace until his least and last offence be repented and atoned for,"

adding that these men's spirits will wander restlessly and even "infect other men with error and superstition" (*On Life After Death*, 43; see Hood, "'Read Fechner,'" 95).

24. This concept arrived in the AS for 31 January 1918 (*YVP* 1:316).

25. In *Human Personality and Its Survival of Bodily Death*, Myers describes visitations of this kind as "visions of consolation" (2:374). His appendix to chapter 7, made up mostly of extracts from the *Proceedings of the Society for Psychical Research*, categorizes visions.

26. This phrase echoes the famous close of Plotinus's *Enneads* 6.9.11, although this translation closely corresponds to two lines of "The Dark Angel" by Lionel Johnson: "Lonely, unto the Lone, I go; / Divine, to the Divinity" (see *YGD*, 183n20). When WBY used the famous image as an epigraph to his brief introduction to the Cuala Press edition of Synge's *Poems and Translations* (1909), he either forgot that Plotinus was the source or did not know: "'The Lonely returns to the Lonely; the Divine to the Divinity.' *Proclus*" (*EE*, 222). The primary typescript of Book IV, entitled "II. THE SOUL BETWEEN DEATH AND BIRTH," also mistakenly cites Proclus (NLI, 36,270/14–15).

27. In an AS of 22 November 1917, the word "knot" functioned as a synonym for "complex." Thinking largely of Iseult Gonne's mental unrest, WBY asked for a definition of "complex," and the control Thomas responded that "A complex is any knot of hidden thought lying in the subconscious that originates in some passion or violent emotion," and continued to explain that "the complex is formed by a single event or epoch of an event." WBY asked for "Freudian analogies," making explicit that both he and GY had psychoanalysis in mind as they explored the topic. Knots were also spiritual terms: Thomas further explained that "Knots are action impressed forcibly on man from outside . . . , the effect of Karma as implied in each incarnation" (*YVP* 1:105). That is, as recorded in the CF, "'Knots' are part of astral body, that is of P.A.M. [personal *Anima Mundi*]" (*YVP* 3:302; see also *YVP* 2:454). In the record of a sleep dated 3 November [1923], WBY wrote: "In dreaming back after period of dreaming back, comes waking state & in this those who have been part of events that brought about 'knot' now dreamed back display in a kind of 'marionette show' the causes of that knot & event" (*YVP* 3:186).

28. It is a commonplace in the history of spiritualistic experiment that a spirit may direct a person to books and records. WBY and Lady Gregory sought a codicil to Hugh Lane's will by this method. During the sleeps of 1920 and later, the control directed WBY to several literary works: Morris's *The Sundering Flood* (on 6 October; *YVP* 3:50), Blake's "The Mental Traveller" (on 26 November; *YVP* 3:57), Percy's *Reliques* (on 20 December; *YVP* 3:64), and Robert Browning's *Poems* (on 22 August 1923; *YVP* 3:185).

29. During the sleep of 30 August 1920, after "speaking for some time,"

the control Dionertes was interrupted first by "a bird's cry" and then by a clock striking twelve; he said that "Sounds like that are sometimes a great pleasure to us" (*YVP* 3:41).

30. Joseph Glanvill writes in *Saducismus Triumphatus: Or, Full and Plain Evidence Concerning Witches and Apparitions* (1681; rpt., Gainesville, FL: Scholars' Facsimiles and Reprints, 1966), "But I attempt something more particularly, in order to which I must premise, that the *Devil* is a name for a *Body Politick*, in which there are very different *Orders* and *Degrees of Spirits*" (89). WBY uses the same phrase in "Witches and Wizards and Irish Folk-Lore" (*LE*, 76) and cites Glanvill's book in the notes (*LE*, 261).

31. This concept is related to WBY's theory of the *Anima Mundi*, and it runs throughout the *AVA* documents. A series of sleeps (19–29 November 1920) centered primarily on what the unnamed communicator called the "Group Mind" (*YVP* 3:54–58). The information was also summarized in the CF (*YVP* 3:262–63). See also Dedication and Introduction, n. 45; Book II, nn. 131, 132.

32. Many spiritualists found convincing the idea, derived from Swedenborg, that spirits progress after death through a series of spheres rather than moving directly and irrevocably to a single heaven or hell. Theosophists similarly taught that after death a person passed through a series of purgatorial planes. Both WBY and GY were familiar with the concept of the seven planes described, for instance, in A. P. Sinnett's *Growth of the Soul* ([London]: Theosophical Publishing Company, 1896), which includes a chapter on "The Seven Principles," saying: "Each plane of Nature, as we ascend through the refinements of the Cosmos, is constituted of different orders of matter, each order being subject to modifications on its own plane" (156). Sinnett's *Esoteric Buddhism* (1883) and *The Occult World* (1881) are other well-known theosophical sources, as is Madame Blavatsky's *Key to Theosophy*, which discusses the "upper *Triad*" and "lower *Quaternity*" of the seven planes ([London]: Theosophical Publishing Company, 1889, pp. 88–93). Seven planes are listed in the AS (31 January 1918; *YVP* 1:318) and summarized in both the CF (*YVP* 3:370) and VNB2 (*YVP* 3:209); see also *YVP* 1:535n11.

33. WBY had studied Irish folklore during much of his mature creative life, as his two essays in Lady Gregory's *Visions and Beliefs in the West of Ireland* (1920) suggest. At least three times in the AS, he tried to relate this knowledge to the system. On 6 January 1918, he asked, "To what extent is soul at 15 analogous to man or woman of faery?" to which Thomas, the control for the evening (assisted by Leaf and Fish), answered: "The people of fairy the souls at one & fifteen and all other legendary states are but parts of one truth—The truth is in all but in some more concealed by fable & dream than in others—" (*YVP* 1:214). See also *YVP* 1:350 and *YVP* 1:424–25; Book IV, n. 58 below.

34. On 12 June 1918, WBY asked the control Thomas, "Why do you use

the word shiftings in the plural" and was answered, "Because it may be one spiral movement or two" (*YVP* 1:501). Three days later, WBY again asked about the term, and Thomas explained that "shift means to take from one place to another—sift means to pass through a sieve"; referring to the way that "Soul is taken from CB [Celestial Body]" and then "goes out of funnel" (*YVP* 1:503). The shiftings was the first of the afterlife stages to be developed: it was introduced a month into the AS, on 6 December 1917, although there was a little difficulty clarifying it (see *YVP* 1:147–49). See also Book IV, n. 19 above.

35. The passages that follow repeat almost exactly but combine two or three answers from the AS for 10 June 1918 (*YVP* 1:490–95). Long and important (fifty-two questions by WBY), this session addresses the Return, Shiftings, Teachings, and Dreaming Back, as well as the system's explanation of good and evil. See also notes in the CF, *YVP* 3:383–86). See Book I, n. 166. The AS emphasizes personal responsibility and awareness as ethical positions: as Thomas had explained on 21 November 1917, less than a month after the sessions began, "The reliance absolute reliance on the supernatural and the consequent abandonment of personal judgment is as great a temptation as any other—Artistic Genius & moral Genius are the two works of man and in these he has to develop his own powers" (*YVP* 1:99).

36. In the AS for 12 June 1918, WBY asked, "Is there then no place of punishment," and was told: "No . . . The punishment is during the funnell dreaming back." That is, all souls *are equal*" (*YVP* 1:499–500). The AS of 10 June 1918 addresses the lack of emotion or sensation in states of equilibrium, and Thomas remarks that "The soul has been brought to a state of comprehension of good & evil—therefore the most evil & the most good do not either of them force the sense or the emotion" (*YVP* 1:491).

37. Evil is manifested in abstraction (cf. pp. 191, 193). "Abstraction," WBY wrote in VNB2, quoting from the AS of 30 January 1919, is "that quality in every phase which impedes unity of being (& ? of world)" (*YVP* 3:188).

38. The following discussion of the role of the Celestial Body in the soul's progress through the shiftings is related to the discussion in the AS of 11 and 12 June 1918. With Thomas, the Yeatses discussed the shiftings as the afterlife state in which "the accentuating of the individuality of the soul" occurs, as opposed to "the return [which] is the destruction of the individuality of the ego" (see *YVP* 1:495–99 and statements in the CF, *YVP* 3:244, 350, 388). See also definitions of the Celestial Body in the CF (*YVP* 3:369) and compare the early discussion of the shiftings on 7 December 1917 (*YVP* 1:153–59).

39. In the SDNBs, especially SDNB8, there are numerous accounts of such spiritual manifestations (see *YVP* 3:49, 84–85, 95–99). By means of smells and sounds, the Yeatses also received warnings of the machi-

nations of various frustrators (see Book IV, n. 59 below). In May 1922, the Yeatses learned that scents were sometimes associated with symbols, such as violets for the tower and incense for the "voyage myth" (*YVP* 3:104–5).

40. Quoted from the CF (*YVP* 3:410), which repeats information received in the AS on 10 January 1918 (*YVP* 1:237).

41. The typescript reads, "In all great passions there is said in our documents to be 'cruelty and deceit' which require expiation." See *YVP* 3:113 and cf. *YVP* 2:511–12 for a related equation.

42. Several sleeps received in New York during May 1920 explored the topic of expiation. GY recorded a "*Correction about after death state*" dated "May 23 night" that includes this information: "A. has wronged B. A incarnates first[.] A. expiates by going through that which he has inflicted in action. B is in spiritual life & there expiates deception. When we allow a person to wrong us we have been deceived, this not being an action but intellectual is spiritually expiated. If we hit back there is action & that is naturally expiated i.e. in life. The spirit cannot incarnate until both expiations are complete" (*YVP* 3:19; the passage is also summarized in the CF, *YVP* 3:297–98 and 3:388).

43. Recording a sleep of 17 August 1920, GY wrote that

> Victimage for the Dead is connected with the Daimon. Where one has injured some person & that person is between lives, the act of atonement is really made to one's own Daimon & the Daimon does not know good or evil, it is only capable of one course & it is beneficent. When the wrong was done it was seeking contact with another Daimon. The wrong was an interference with it & the atonement corrects this. When that is done the Daimon becomes connected with Daimon of person between lives. It may be a prolonged connexion or merely a momentary recognition as it were, but it is always mutual. (*YVP* 3:34–35)

44. Before this sentence, the typescript adds: "The documents give examples."

45. The theme of victimage as it was discussed in the AS of 26–27 July 1919 included the information that someone may be a victim of a living person, a dead person, or the ghostly self. A "victim for the dead" does not know "that it is for the dead he is victim"; rather, he is aware of "The bitterness of his destiny." WBY supposed, "He is pursued by ill luck" and was informed that it is rather "By inhibition of positive qualities." As the discussion continued the next evening, WBY asked, "When you say 'victim for' do you mean sufferer instead of," to which the control Ameritus replied, "No I mean a definite physical emotional & spiritual—*not moral*—purgation & process undergone by living person for another *not* in place of that other" (*YVP* 2:338–40).

See also the passage on the expiation for the ghostly self (pp. 199–201).

46. During the extended discussion of knots in the AS of 22 November 1917, the two kinds of knots are defined. WBY asked whether knots are "taken over from one life to next" and was told by Thomas, "They are of 2 kinds—of fate which are result of action of others—of destiny which are actions of individual—these pass on to next incarnation as knots of fate." To WBY's request, "Please give illustration of resolution of complex," GY's hand wrote, "A man injures another in one life—That man undergoes the knot of fate—The first man in his next incarnation is injured in some way & suffers the knot of fate & undergoes knot of destiny" (*YVP* 1:105).

47. The AS of 22 November 1917 includes a question by WBY, "Why does luck follow conquest of Knots," and this answer: "Because it is the destruction of Karma the rising above fate & destiny" (*YVP* 1:106).

48. The discussion of 12 June 1918 also focused on the Beatitude. It established that this state is "outside funnell" and "Beyond time" (*YVP* 1:501, reproduced in CF 3:243 and 3:388), that "Souls are gathered into societies 'during the Beatitude' " (*YVP* 3:245 and 248, summarizing from 1:499), and that while Dreaming Back "Is the longest state," "Beatitude is shortest" (*YVP* 3:290, also 3:245, from 1:500). It is described as "beatitude and exultation" (*YVP* 1:499 and in CF 3:248).

49. At this point in the typescript a passage is marked through: "I quote the documents without claiming to understand except vaguely that it [the Spirit] is free from limitation to any one place and to that which decides life, cause, operation and effect past present and future. . . ."

50. This clause—"which is indeed . . . all cycles end"—was added in galley proofs. The phrase "when all cycles end" first read "at the consummation of time" and then was changed to "end of all our cycles" before the final form was adopted.

51. This quotation is a condensation of four questions and answers in the AS of 1 February 1918 (*YVP* 1:326).

52. Bardesanes, or Bar Daisan (154–222) was a Syrian Gnostic, scientist, scholar, and poet. In 1926, WBY wrote to Sturm: "I wonder if you know the works of Bardeasan [*sic*]. He described—they say—a monthly re-creation of all things by a configuration of the [sun symbol] & [moon symbol]. And that excites me especially as he had my doctrine of Mask & Celestial Body—see his Hymn of the Soul—" (*FPS*, 90). See also *Plays*, 700. The source is F. C. Burkitt's *Early Eastern Christianity* (1904); see *Au*, 284–85.

53. This parenthetical paragraph was added to a much-revised page of the typescript.

54. Note inserted in galley proofs on 26 September 1925.

55. See WBY's note to "Among School Children" (*Poems*, 606).

56. This phrase appears in SDNB1 (*YVP* 3:12) and was copied into VNB2 (*YVP* 3:184) and onto two cards in the CF (*YVP* 3:409 and 425).

57. On "frustrators," see Book IV, n. 59 below.

58. The typescript, which demonstrates WBY's familiarity with such spiritualistic folklore as that in the account of the two Arab women, suggests that he was well acquainted with the "two girls," "one of a family where is second sight, and the other second sighted herself." "May I not discover in those mice the shape-changers approaching birth and mastered by the thought of feebleness and littleness," the typescript asks, then adds: "Legend is full of such apparitions before a child is born."

59. This parenthetical paragraph was inserted after the typescript, which contains part of the material in a different form. The most important addition is the term *frustrators*. Although frustrators (Leo Africanus appeared most frequently) occasionally interfered with the AS, they do not become important topics until the period of the sleeps, especially in 1921. The accounts of five sleeps (7, 14, 16, 18, 19 October 1921; *YVP* 3:99–102) are devoted primarily to a discussion between the control (Dionertes) and WBY (recorded by GY) of the nature and danger of two kinds of frustrators. The first "are connected with what we have called the Covins" (99); they "are from those phases" opposite to 14, 15, and 16—that is, 28, 1, and 2 (100). The second are "personal frustrators" and "may come from any phase because [they] may act upon any emotion." Since "[t]he personal frustrators never make their presence known by evil odours," it is clear that this passage is primarily concerned with the other kind—"[t]he frustrators of System" (100). When WBY pressed the control "as to their motive he said that to go into that was to explore the origin of evil which he could not do till conditions were better." The Yeatses were told that "[o]ld age & sickness & death are not the result of frustration" (100). Dionertes also noted that "the Frustrators are the antithesis to all that lives," and that prayer "would help against Frustration" (102). Frustrators led the Yeatses to numerous incorrect conclusions (often simply marked "wrong") in the AS, and they deceived them into failing to record sleeps for an extended period (15 January–2 May 1922) (*YVP* 3:104). Fortunately, as recorded several times, they announced their presence by foul odors (see Book IV, n. 39 above, and *AVB*, 16). But the Yeatses were familiar with the phenomenon of odors as concomitants of seances long before the experiences recorded in the AS and sleeps, as a note in *Visions and Beliefs in the West of Ireland* makes clear: "The sudden filling of the air by a sweet odour is a common event of the séance room. It is mentioned several times in the 'Diary' of Stainton Moses" (*LE*, 288).

60. The words following "womb" in this sentence, as printed, replaced the following in galley proofs: "which is to birth what the *Vision of the Blood Kindred* is to death, and a foreknowledge of the future life, and a knowledge that such a life is the desire of the soul."

61. Slightly misquoted ("but" substituted for "yet") from lines 43–44 of WBY's own "The Double Vision of Michael Robartes" (*Poems*, 173). See WBY's discussion of "COMPLEMENTARY DREAMS" (pp. 140–41).

62. "Going forth" and "return" may echo the end of Blake's *Jerusalem*:

> All Human Forms identified even Tree Metal Earth & Stone. all Human Forms identified, living going forth & returning wearied Into the Planetary lives of Years Months Days & Hours reposing And then Awaking into his Bosom in the Life of Immortality.
> (Erdman, 258; the plate [no. 99] is reproduced in facsimile in volume 3 of *WWB*)

    "Going and returning are the typical eternal motions," WBY explained; "they characterize the visionary forms of eternal life" (*WWB* 1:401).

63. Although this section is not in the typescript, WBY preserved a manuscript draft including some material not in the final version (NLI, 36,270/10).

64. WBY tells this story in 1888, in his edition of *Fairy and Folk Tales of the Irish Peasantry* (*P&I*, 17) and in "Swedenborg, Mediums, and the Desolate Places" (*LE*, 63–64).

65. Also related in *Per Amica Silentia Lunae* (*LE*, 24).

66. Also mentioned in "Swedenborg, Mediums, and the Desolate Places" (*LE*, 72).

67. The king in Herodotus's *Histories* is Periander of Corinth (5.92). The manuscript notes, "I cannot find the exact reference." See *LE*, 333n101; *Myth1*, 98; and *Myth2*, 65.

68. In the manuscript of this section, WBY wrote, "A man once told a society I belong to . . ." and then revised to "A man read a paper to a society," probably referring to the Society for Psychical Research, of which he was a member at this time.

69. Mazdaism is another term for Zoroastrianism.

70. In *Origin of Christian Church Art*, Strzygowski writes that the concept of Hvarenah "is connected with the cult of the dead, representing the might and majesty of departed spirits. Hvarenah is the power that makes running water gush from springs, plants sprout from the soil, winds blow the clouds, and men come to birth. It governs the courses of sun, moon, and stars" (118). Strzygowski does not address the first landscape.

71. WBY recalls two articles by R. H. Saunders: "Story of a Christmas Tree; Children of Both Worlds" (*Light* 43.2191 [6 January 1923]: 7) and "A Christmas Tree in the Spheres" (*Light* 44.2243 [5 January 1924]: 5). See also WBY's note on p. 198.

72. Sir Oliver Lodge's *Raymond* is named for the author's son, killed in battle on 14 September 1915. The book records Lodge's communication with his dead son; part 3, called "Life and Death," relates Lodge's

argument for "belief in continued existence," communication of minds, and such subjects. The discussion of the "synthetic cigars" occurs in the record of a sitting with a famous medium, Mrs. Gladys O. Leonard, on 3 December 1915. Feda, her control, explained the spirit world to Sir Oliver: "A chap came over the other day who *would* have a cigar. 'That's finished them,' he thought. He means he thought they would never be able to provide that. But there are laboratories over here, and they manufacture all sorts of things in them. . . . It's not the same as on the earth plane, but they were able to manufacture what looked like a cigar." Someone smoked four of the synthetic cigars and disliked them, "and now he doesn't look at one." Sir Oliver pointed out that "some of this Feda talk is at least humorous" (197). As the manuscript first read, the cigars had "caused much amusement to readers of 'Raymond.' " On the Yeatses' interest in seances, see Book III, n. 54.

At this point in the manuscript of this section, a sentence refers to the kind of folk traditions recorded in *Visions and Beliefs in the West of Ireland*: "They [synthetic cigars] remind me of a Connemara grave yard where it is or was till lately the custom to lay full pipes upon the graves."

73. In WBY's note, the sentence beginning "I may be mistaken . . ." was added in galley proofs.

In March 1926, WBY wrote in a journal, "I see now that section XII Book IV in 'A Vision' should have been the most important in the book & it is the slightest & worst"; the system should be "symbolized in a study of the relation of man and woman" (NLI, 13,576, p. 278, quoted in Connie K. Hood, "The Remaking of *A Vision*," YAACTS 1 [1983]: 37).

74. Writing years later (in 1934) to Olivia Shakespear about his poem "He and She," WBY observed: "When George spoke of Michael's preoccupation with Life as Anne's with death she may have subconsciously remembered that her spirits once spoke of the centric movement of phase 1 as the kiss of Life and the centric movement of phase 15 (full moon) as the kiss of Death" (*L*, 829). See also YVP 2:9, 2:118, 3:403, 3:386–87.

75. A possible source is one definition of "Archon" given by the OED: "A power subordinate to the Deity, held by Gnostics to have made the world." On 27 November 1920, WBY asked the unnamed communicator "if I might modify teminology & he accepted the following Instead of avatars—Arcons" (YVP 3:58). WBY added "Such *Arcons* deal with form not wisdom" in galley proofs.

76. With two minor alterations, WBY quotes from *The Only Jealousy of Emer* (lines 213–17) as it appeared in *Plays and Controversies* (1923; see also *Plays*, 324). During much of the period of the AS and sleeps, and with significant automatic help from GY, WBY worked on *The Only Jealousy of Emer*, in which WBY, GY, Maud Gonne, and Iseult

Gonne are symbolized in the four main characters. In the AS of 20 November 1917, the control Thomas revealed, "There is a symbolism of the growth of the soul" in the Cuchulain plays (*YVP* 1:91). On 21 December, WBY learned that his "own sins exactly correspond to those of C[uchulain]" and that GY (Emer), Iseult (Eithne), and Maud (Woman of the Sidhe) represent race, passion, and love, respectively (*YVP* 1:166–67). On 7 January 1918, WBY asked, "Who will C[uchulain] love?" and the guide Leaf replied, "I cannot tell you till you know yourself and you do know I think perhaps unconsciously." When he asked if it were Emer, he received no reply (*YVP* 1:219). WBY had thought (on 6 January) that *The Only Jealousy* belonged to phase 12, the heroic phase, although Thomas, with Leaf and Fish assisting, responded, "Perhaps I ought to have said 12 to 22" (*YVP* 1:209). The lines from the play were inserted after the typescript.

77. This ambiguous passage (beginning at the start of the paragraph) seems to refer indirectly to Maud Gonne's refusal of WBY's invitation to marriage. Although veiled, the corresponding passage in the typescript is clearer:

> There is the means of equilibrium, but not as yet equilibrium, marriage. The first denial of experience was the work of the spirit at Fifteen that imposed an image or fixed idea, and if this is to be marriage other spiritual beings must intervene, instruments of the *Ghostly Self,* for unlike the equilibrium which follows expiation for the dead man cannot will it.

A related sentence was added after the typescript and then crossed out in galley proofs: "Upon the other hand, a man out of phase may receive through some Spirit at Phase 1, not the 'Kiss of Life' but a fixed idea, a perversion as it were of the 'Kiss of Death,' a cold obsession." In both these passages about the rejection of experience (exchanging the "Kiss of Life" for a "fixed idea"), the system explains both spiritual abstractions and personal issues of import to both WBY and GY. In the AS of 6 September 1919, the control Ameritus describes Gonne as a "tall woman" of "fixed ideas" (*YVP* 2:407), and the CF notes that "Killing PB makes spirits stronger (Hence MG's fixed idea)" (*YVP* 3:383; see also *YVP* 3:290). Directly related, of course, is the fact that Gonne appears in *The Only Jealousy of Emer* as the Woman of the Sidhe, strongly criticized by Emer (GY) (*Plays,* 324, lines 212–17; see previous note). Also pertinent is the sentence in galley proofs that was replaced by the sentence ending "time-less infinity": "The *Ghostly Self* upon the other hand, having desired experience in vain, ceases to expend itself, becomes as it were full and stationary." Compare also "A Prayer for My Daughter" (*Poems,* 190–92, lines 57–64).

78. This phrase is likely an allusion to Plato's myth in *Symposium*, secs.

202–5, and to Plotinus's commentary in *Enneads* 3.5.7–9: Love's parents are Plenty and Poverty (variously translated); love is thus the desire of deprived mortals for the plenitude of the transcendent.

79. See Book III, n. 39.

80. See *Deirdre* (*Plays*, 189–91). The final versions of *The Hour-Glass* are concurrent with the AS, and note that the hour-glass is a geometric figure with symbolic importance often discussed in the AS.

81. This play by Swedish writer August Strindberg (1849–1912) was first produced in 1899 and was performed at the Abbey Theatre on 6 March 1913.

82. Christ appears frequently in the AS, CF, and sleeps as the great initiate, the First Master, or the Avatar. In the AS of 1 and 2 January 1918, the Yeatses learned through the guide Fish that "time is God—space is Christ—eternity Holy Ghost" and how to "place events of Christs [*sic*] history on diagram of lunar phases" (*YVP* 1:184, 187). See also *YVP* 3:68, 3:252, 3:253–54, and see Book I, n. 143). The combination of primary and antithetical characteristics of Christ varies at different points on the wheel (*YVP* 3:62).

83. The phrasing and content of this first paragraph are very close to those of the note published in 1921 to "An Image from a Past Life" (*Poems*, 655). Although the note contains deliberately misleading dates (12 and 15 May 1917), it is based directly upon the AS.

   At the end of this paragraph in galley proofs, WBY crossed out an extension of his sentence: "or as it is sometimes called in the Rhythmical Body" (a term that was not used).

84. This parenthetical insert attributed to Owen Aherne has a complicated history. At one point, a much longer version (four typed pages), called "Michael Robartes and the Judwali Doctor," was intended for the first section of Book IV (NLI, 36,263/24/1–2). The Yeatses had themselves conducted the experiments described. As the doctor in the typescript said, "I was always told Kusta-ben-Luka or his wife [i.e., WBY and GY] would come if we could find the right sleeper." The doctor observed also that "the sleeper, if it was the sleeper, had strange gifts of abstraction and arrangement, as though the mind had been purged of some gross element." "It was these conversations with a sleeping man," according to Aherne, "that enabled Robartes to adapt the thought of Kusta ben-Luka to modern necessities, and to find a European expression for the Arabian Law of history." With slight variations, GY had actually experienced the sensations of the lapping cat, the mouth full of feathers, and others described in several sleeps of 1920 (*YVP* 3:40, 42, 49–50). On the substitution of "Arab boy" for GY as sleeper, see Margaret Mills Harper, *Wisdom of Two*, 265–71.

85. The automatic faculty was discussed at some length in the AS and "codified" onto several cards in the CF. See, for example, the discussion on 18 September 1918, which began with WBY asking, "What is the

purpose or mission of the automatic faculty in making pictures that have no aparent relation to the activities of the ego?" Thomas replied, "The automatic faculty does not so much make pictures as present a surface on which pictures can be reflected & only those pictures which have a correspondance to some portion of the egos experience can be seen by the ego—" (*YVP* 2:59, summarized in CF, *YVP* 3:229). It is described elsewhere in terms of personal *Anima Mundi* (*YVP* 2:40–41), as a "mirror" and astral light, a term from theosophy for a substance that forms images (*YVP* 2:70), as the origin of dream images and "machinery" (*YVP* 2:175–76), and with reference to sequence and allusion (*YVP* 3:294, summarized from *YVP* 2:38–39).

86. This parenthetical paragraph is an extension of the previous one. The typescript gives an excellent general description of the Yeatses' method:

> He brought his suggestions to the sleeper that they might be rejected, accepted, or modified. When the voice itself took the initiative the method of exposition was always that adopted according to legend by Kusta-ben-Luka's wife. A series of statements would be made that could not be reconciled with the system as a whole until that particular subject was exhausted.

87. See WBY's "Preliminary Examination of the Script of E[lizabeth] R[adcliffe]" (1913): "I had already made the experiment of getting Miss R. to draw an object with her eyes open and then a complex mathematical form with her eyes closed. She drew badly with her eyes open but the complicated [complex] mental image was well drawn, the bounding line returning into itself exactly." When WBY tried to draw a similar but simpler form with closed eyes, he "got the proportions wrong" and "did not join the line" (*YO*, 156).

88. In lines 155–61 of Percy Bysshe Shelley's *Hellas*, Hassan speaks of the wandering Jew Ahasuerus, saying,

> The sage, in truth, by dreadful abstinence
> And conquering penance of the mutinous flesh,
> Deep contemplation, and unwearied study,
> In years outstretched beyond the date of man,
> May have attained to sovereignty and science
> Over those strong and secret things and thoughts
> Which others fear and know not. (Shelley, 456)

WBY also quotes this passage in *Au*, 152, and in a rejected version of the dedication of *AVA* (NLI, 36,264/3).

89. Probably the most famous of the Greek and Roman sibyls, or prophetesses of Apollo, was the Cumaean Sibyl, Aeneas's guide to the underworld in *Aeneid* 6. Diotima (Diotime) was the prophetess of Mantineia

from whom Socrates supposedly learned the nature of love (Plato, *Symposium*, secs. 201–12; see Book II, n. 80). The magician and scryer probably refer to John Dee and Edward Kelly (see Dedication and Introduction, n. 40).

90. See *EE*, 43–44; *LE*, 120 and 198; *L*, 846; and "The Old Age of Queen Maeve" (line 27; *Poems*, 396). WBY refers to Ralph's lucky eyes in *The Well at the World's End*: "thou seemest to me to have a lucky look in thy eyes" (Morris, *Collected Works* 18:29; see also 18:306 and 19:14). For the second part of his comment, WBY seems to recall the father's remarks to the passive Ralph, "O son . . . whatsoever thou dost, that thou dost full well" (19:215). Perhaps WBY added "unwitting" in unintended imitation of Morris's frequent alliteration. In a meditation of 3 October 1920, WBY discussed the significance of another of Morris's quest romances, *The Sundering Flood* (YVP 3:50). See also Book I, n. 87.

91. The *"Four Daimons"* in one sense, at least, are the daimons of WBY, GY, Anne, and Michael (see Book I, n. 72), representing wisdom, love, beauty, and truth, respectively. On 13 August 1920, Dionertes "explained the correspondence between the 4 Daimons & the Four Faculties" and said, "The coming epoch will have a 3rd Daimon character though 4th Daimon's will be working in it as well as 3rd" (YVP 3:32). On 17 August, GY recorded the further information that "The 4th Daimon is not the Daimon of an individual but of an idea & it is connected with a group. . . . Though much of this philosophy comes through 3rd Daimon it is ultimately through the Fourth" (YVP 3:35).

92. Discovered as a term late in the psychical research for *AVA*, "Record" virtually replaces "Anima Mundi," the focal concept of the first recorded questions in the AS (see, for instance, 8 November 1917, YVP 1:65); it occurs most often in the sleeps. A long discussion on 28 March 1920, near the end of the AS, distinguishes the record from memory by a hair-splitting distinction: "nothing but sight of natural objects & fragrance pass into record"—not thought or sound, which is "intellectual perception," like thought. A last question on the last day of AS before the "other methods—sleeps" began does allow for one other category of sensation in the record: to WBY's question "Does not touch also pass into record," Dionertes replied, "Yes quite easily obvious goodnight" (YVP 2:539–40). The "personal Record" may be compared to the "Personal Anima Mundi," which is more consistently discussed than the generalized *Anima Mundi*.

93. A canceled phrase in the much-corrected typescript explains where the statement was found: "in my documents."

94. In galley proofs, WBY cut the following sentence here: "nor is there any form characteristic of a life we can only know by symbol and correspondence."

95. The Society for Psychical Research experimented extensively with

clairvoyants and mediums who spoke and wrote, usually in broken sentences, languages about which they presumably had no knowledge. For WBY's account of such experiments, see the essay on Elizabeth Radcliffe's script (*YO*, 130–71).

96. See *Mem*, 104.
97. This section was inserted in galley proofs on a typed sheet, and so not part of the book when it was "Finished at Syracuse, January, 1925."
98. This idea is much expanded in WBY's introduction to Joseph M. Hone and Mario M. Rossi's *Bishop Berkeley: His Life, Writings, and Philosophy* (London: Faber and Faber, 1931), especially in this passage from sec. 11:

> 'God', 'Heaven', 'Immortality', those words and their associated myths define that contemplation [of a pure activity]. . . . Giambattista Vico has said that we should reject all philosophy that does not begin in myth, and it is impossible to pronounce those three words without becoming as simple as a camel-driver or a pilgrim. (*LE*, 111)

On Diotime, see Book IV, n. 89 above. Cf. the reference to Berkeley on p. 128.
99. See Dedication and Introduction, n. 30, and Foster 2:279.
100. Written in November 1920 and published in March 1921 (in *The New Republic* and *The London Mercury*), the poem would later appear as the close of *The Tower* (London and New York: Macmillan, 1928). Here it was substituted for a prose epilogue addressed "To Vestigia," which may have been rejected because WBY decided to dedicate the book to Moina Mathers rather than William Thomas Horton, to the living rather than the dead (see p. liv). Horton (first identified as H, then as X, in line 21) remained anonymous until the publication of *The Collected Poems* (1933). Horton, Florence Farr Emery, and MacGregor Mathers, the three recent dead friends whose ghosts are summoned, had been "old fellow students" in the Golden Dawn. Thinking of them as well as Moina Mathers, Allan Bennett, and others, WBY wrote in the rejected version of the dedication, "I find that I write my poetry too more often than not for people who are dead, or estranged."
    In the Roman Catholic Church, All Souls' Day (usually 2 November) is the feast on which the earthly church prays for the souls of the faithful departed suffering in purgatory. It is also "the night before the Irish *Samhain*," which "was the proper time for prophecy and the unveiling of mysteries" (John Rhys, *Lectures on the Origin and Growth of Religion as Illustrated by Celtic Heathendom*, 2nd ed. [London: Williams and Norgate, 1892], 514). WBY had most likely read a chapter devoted primarily to the Feast of All Souls in Frazer's *The Golden Bough* (6:51–83; see also 10:224, and *IDM*, 10).

101. One of the Oxford University colleges.

102. Horton's beloved was Amy Audrey Locke; see Dedication and Introduction, n. 10.

103. For Florence Farr Emery, see Dedication and Introduction, n. 7.

104. In 1912, Emery left England to teach in India.

105. Richard Finneran tentatively identifies this person as Sir Ponnambalam Ramanathan (1851–1930), founder of the school at which Emery taught (*Poems*, 666).

106. In *AVB*, this line reads, "I call MacGregor Mathers from his grave" (*Poems*, 233). WBY met the English occultist and founder of the Golden Dawn (Samuel Liddell) MacGregor Mathers (1854–1918) between 1887 and 1890.

107. The Yeatses had been apart in the summer of 1920, he in Ireland, she in Oxford, and their lives had been eventful. Iseult Gonne's impulsive marriage to Francis Stuart had disintegrated because of his abuse, and she was also pregnant; the Yeatses worked on solutions to her difficult problems. GY had a miscarriage. WBY had tonsillitis and would soon undergo the "operation of my throat & consequent slow recovery" mentioned in a sleep of 19 November 1920 (*YVP* 3:53). Anne Yeats was nearing her second birthday. The friends of WBY mentioned in the poem, who had all died relatively recently, share poetic space with the "marvellous thing to say" made possible by the AS and the sleeps, begun some six months before.

APPENDICES

Corrections to the Yeatses' Copies of A Vision (1925)

Note: The Yeatses kept four copies of *AVA* in their library: (1) number 83 of the six hundred copies printed (O'Shea 2433); (2) number 385 (O'Shea 2433b); (3) number 366 (O'Shea 2433a); and (4) number 498 (O'Shea 2433c). As Richard J. Finneran notes in his essay "On Editing Yeats: The Text of *A Vision* (1937)" (*Texas Studies in Literature and Language* 19 [1977]: 121–22), the last three of these copies have postproduction corrections made by WBY and GY. The three tables that follow present the changes made to these three copies, with indications of the changes, who made them (when it is possible to distinguish whether the marking was made by WBY or GY, or in a few instances by Macmillan editor Thomas Mark), whether the change appears in one or more of the other copies, and if the correction was carried over into the 1937 edition. Page numbers are given for the original book (in parentheses) and this edition.

Table 1. *A Vision* (1925), W. B. Yeats, copy 2
number 385, O'Shea 2433b.

Page.Line	Change	By	Copy	1937
flyleaf	bookplate of GY with name canceled; at top, note pasted in and then torn out			
(ii.2) l.2	under portrait of Giraldus: correction of "Homenorum" to "Hominum"	WBY	4	✓(p. 39)
(36.27–30) 33.10–13	directs to "transpose" columns in table of "Elemental Attributions"	WBY		
(36) 33	add a new table of "Where the Four Faculties predominate": First quarter Creative Mind Second quarter Mask Third quarter Will Fourth quarter Body of Fate	WBY		
(202.7) 167.23	correction of "great traditional faith" to "Greek traditional faith"	GY?	3, 4	✓
(206.7) 170.28	correction of "1650" to "1680"	GY?	3	

Table 2. *A Vision* (1925), W. B. Yeats, copy 3
number 366, O'Shea 2433a.

Page.Line	Change	By	Copy	1937
flyleaf	bookplate of GY and inscription: "To Dobbs in memory of all tribulation / when we were making this book / W. B. Yeats"			
(ii.2) l.2	entire line, "from the Speculum Angelorum et Homenorum," marked to delete			

Page.Line	Change	By	Copy	1937
(xiv) lviii	diagram of the Great Wheel; upper left corner triangle is changed from pointing up, △, to pointing down; the symbol ♋ at the top left just beyond the inner circle is marked ♑, and the ♑ opposite it is marked ♋; the triangle at the lower right is marked "reverse" and redrawn to point up	GY	4 (in part)	✓ (in part)
(13.illustration) 14.illustration	"♑" symbol under "Heart" (top right) changed to "♋"; "♋" under "Loins" (bottom left) changed to "♑"	GY	4	✓ (see p. 81)
(20.19) 19.32	section "V" is changed first to "VIII" (crossed out) and then "VII" (blue ink)	WBY	4	
(22.1) 21.1	section "VI" to "IX" (crossed out) then "VIII"	WBY	4	
(23.16) 22.5	section "VII" to "X"	WBY	4	
(23.25) 22.12	section "VIII" to "XI" (crossed out) then "X"	WBY	4	
(24.20) 23.1	section "IX" to "XII"	WBY		
(26.1) 24.3	section "X" has had added to it "II" (to make "XII"); this is crossed out and "XIII" is added	WBY	4	
(26.26) 24.24	section "XI" to "X"	WBY		
(33.4) 29.26–27	Body of Fate for Phase 22 is changed: "versus" to "through" ("Temptation through strength")	GY		
(33.13) 29.34–35	Body of Fate for Phase 24 is changed: "in" to "of" ("Enforced success of action")			✓
(38.1) 34.1	"EMBODIMENTS" to "Incarnations" in title (blue ink)	WBY	4	✓

Page.Line	Change	By	Copy	1937
(59.23–24) 51.3	"some," "not recorded in his biography," marked deleted (pencil); "a" added in margin ("one divines a quarrel, with the thought")	WBY		
(93.16–19) 76.30–31	"At Phase 8 there is a similar interchange, but it does not display its significance" to "At Phase 8 there may or may not be a similar interchange; nothing is clear" (light black ink)	WBY		(see p. 159.22 –23)
(184.8–9) 153.20–21	"some dominant" marked to delete; "in what intellect cannot analyse" added after "belief" (light black ink)	WBY		
(202.7) 167.23	correction of "great traditional faith" to "Greek traditional faith"	GY	2, 4	✓
(206.7) 170.28	"1650" to "1680" (light black ink)	WBY	2	

Table 3. *A Vision* (1925), W. B. Yeats, copy 4 number 498, O'Shea 2433c.

Page.Line	Change	By	Copy	1937
cover	"KEEP CLEAN" and "W. B. Yeats 'A Vision' Book A" written on rough brown paper, cover pasted over cover			
flyleaf	inscription: "This copy must not be given to any body on any excuse however plausible / W B Yeats / George Yeats"	WBY		
next recto	"Extracts for new *Vision* to be taken from the book & as corrected here / W.B.Y." (pencil)	WBY		

Page.Line	Change	By	Copy	1937
(ii.2) l.2	under Dulac's portrait of Giraldus: correction of "Homenorum" to "Hominum"	GY	2	✓(p. 39)
(xiv) lviii	the symbol "☾" at the top left just beyond the inner circle is replaced with a small cutout of white paper with the symbol "☽," and the "☽" opposite it with a similar cutout "☾"		3	✓
(xvii.26) lix.28–29	"Hominorum" changed to "Hominum" and a line to a possible revision: "? in the ungrammatical dog Latin of the time" to be inserted after "had been written"	WBY		✓(in part)
(3.2) 3.1	title of poem changed: "I. THE WHEEL AND" marked to delete (thin black ink)	GY		✓
(13.illustration) 14.illustration	"☽" symbol under "Heart" (top right) changed to "☾"; "☾" under "Loins" (bottom left) changed to "☽," in thin black ink	GY	3	(see p. 81)
(14.28–29) 15.30	in footnote: "Creative" and "Genius" capitalized	GY?		
(16.1–17.9) 16.14–17.8	whole page and first four lines of next page canceled in blue ink; lines 5 through 9 on p. 17 canceled in thin black ink	WBY, GY		
(17.10–14) 17.13–16	"Between Phase 12 and Phase 13, and between Phase 4 and Phase 5" revised to "At Phase 11 and Phase 12"; in line 13, "and between Phase 4 and Phase 5 what is called" marked to delete	GY		

Page.Line	Change	By	Copy	1937
(17.10–19) 17.13–23	the first seven lines of this paragraph (10–16), expanded to include the first 10 lines (10–19), is marked to be moved to follow the end of this paragraph (line 24)	GY?		
(17.25–27) 17.25–26	last paragraph of the section is also marked to delete in thin black ink (GY); it is then reinserted in another ink and marked "stet" in the margin (WBY)	GY, WBY		
(18.1) 17.33	"a" from "a scenario" deleted to be replaced in three tries: "~~inherited from the~~," "~~partly remembered~~," "an inherited"	WBY		✓
(18.1–4) 17.33–35	"which offers to his *Creative Mind* . . . a rôle" marked to delete; "wear" deleted; "or rôle" marked to insert after "*Mask*" (to read "an inherited scenario and a *Mask* or rôle as unlike as possible")	WBY		✓
(18.9–13) 18.5–8	all after first word ("active") marked to delete (that is, "and for that reason . . . Convito.")	WBY		✓
(18.20) 18.13–14	after "of topical allusions" the numeral III is marked to insert, and a line is drawn before "In the *primary* phases Man must" and in the margin is noted N P	GY		
(20.6–7) 19.23	"up to four" is replaced with "several" (to read "the being may return several times before it can pass on."	WBY		

Page.Line	Change	By	Copy	1937
(20.7–9) 19.23–24	sentence ("It is claimed . . . the utmost possible") is marked to delete	WBY		
(20.9–12) 19.24–27	sentence "By being is understood that which divides into *Four Faculties* . . ." changed to "The automatic script ~~understands~~ defines being as that which divides into *Four Faculties*, the individual as the *Will* analysed in relation to itself, the personality as the *Will* analysed in relation to the *Mask*" (black ink)	WBY		
(20.12–16) 19.27–30	sentence ("It is because . . . are called *primary*.") marked to delete (blue ink)	WBY		
(20.19) 19.32	Section numbers from pages 20 through 58 are marked to be changed (see O'Shea). Although they are authorized by WBY, who marked the changes in copy 3, they are not listed here because they are probably not in either his hand or GY's. See Connie Hood, "A Search for Authority: Prolegomena to a Definitive Critical Edition of W. B. Yeats's *A Vision* (1937)" (diss. University of Tennessee, Knoxville, 1983), 176–77.		3	
(25.22–25) 23.31–32	"and it will be seen later that" marked to delete; "used as a technical term" marked to delete; "is a technical term of my teachers" marked to add in blue ink: thus, with changes, the sentence would read "Without this continual	WBY		✓

Page.Line	Change	By	Copy	1937
(25.22–25) 23.31–32 (*cont.*)	*discord* through *deception* there would be no conscience, no activity; *deception* is a technical term of my teachers and may be substituted for 'desire.' "			
(26.26 –30.16) 24.24–27.22	whole of section XI marked to delete	WBY		✓
(33.36) 30.13	deletion of line: "At P. 16, P. 17, P. 18 Unity of Being"	WBY		
(34.3–4) 30.17–18	the circled words "Intellect" and "Heart" in the grouping "Four Types of Wisdom" marked "transpose"	WBY		(see p. 100)
(34.29–31) 31.29–31	last sentence of the note ("The relation of . . . in their minds.") is marked through; in left margin are three attempts: "~~at first my ins~~"; followed by: "~~at first the Great Year was divided into ten divisions~~"; followed by: "At first my instructors divided the Great Year also into ten divisions"	WBY		✓
(37) 33	Three sections added in bottom margin:	WBY		✓

Enforced & ~~uninforced~~ free Faculties
In Primary Phases the *Mask* & *Will* are enforced
the *Creative Mind* & *Body of Fate* free
In Antithetical Phases the *Creative Mind* & *Body of Fate*
are enforced & the *Mask* & *Will* free

The Two Conditions
Primary means democratic
Antithetical means aristocratic

Relations
Those between *Will* and *Mask, Creative Mind* & *Body of Fate*
are oppositions or contrasts
Those between *Will* & *Creative Mind, Mask* & *Body of*
Fate discords

Page.Line	Change	By	Copy	1937
(38.1) 34.1	in title, "4." marked to delete; "EMBODIMENTS" changed to "Incarnations"	WBY	3	✓
(38) after 34.19	addition at bottom of page: "None of those phases where the tinctures are closed, except phase 27, produce characteristics of sufficient distinctiveness to become historical"	WBY		✓
(59.11) 50.29–30	"would have forced" marked to be changed to "would force"	WBY		✓
(59.30–32 to 60.1–2) 51.8–11 after 52.4	First sentence of the section (last three lines of p. 59 into second line on p. 60) marked for deletion. In bottom margin: "Just ~~before the place or the~~ phase for the splitting or opening of each," also marked to delete.	WBY		
(60.3) 51.12	"is said to open" marked to delete	WBY		
(60.10) 51.18	added and crossed through at end of paragraph "~~This I do not understand~~"	WBY		
(65.20–21) 55.24–25	first sentence in new paragraph revised to read: "From now, if not from Phase 12, and until Phase 17 or Phase 18 has passed, happy love . . ."	WBY?		✓
(84.13) 69.29	"reverse" corrected to "reveres"; this correction is in larger letters (pencil)	GY		✓
(112.18–21) 91.9–11	"and we shall discover . . . hypnogogic vision" marked to delete, as well as the associated note in bottom margin	WBY		✓

Page.Line	Change	By	Copy	1937
(125.28) 101.20	"wondering vegetative dream" corrected to "wandering vegetative dream"	WBY		
(132.16) 106.25	"Birkett" corrected to "Burnet"	WBY		
(135.24 to 136.1–3) 109.21–23	"A" to "C," "B" to "D," "C" to "A," and "D" to "B"; the corrected passage reads: "we can express to the eye the unalterable relation between C which is the energy, and D which is its *Destiny* or beauty, and that between A, which is mind, and B which is its *Fate* or Truth."	WBY		
(136) 110	note in margin: "cones are transposed shadow cone is that of Mind etc."	WBY		
(136.7–9) 110.1–3	changed to: "That is to say when B is three quarter antithetical and one quarter primary A is three quarter primary and one quarter antithetical, and so on;" the terms are added in margin and not italicized	WBY		
(140.18 to 141.1–6) 114.10–15	changed to: "We may represent the two qualities of life by two circles one within the other which move in opposite directions, the Lunar from West to East according to the Moon's phasal movement, the Solar from East to West according to the Sun's apparent daily movement, or we may call the first the moons zodiacal movement and the second that of the precessional sun."	WBY		

Page.Line	Change	By	Copy	1937
(143) 116	diagram revised: opposite to "♋" at the wide end of the diamond in the middle is to be the symbol "♑" (just above line dividing cone at "♓" and "♐")	WBY		
(152.2) 123.16	"translated Cicero's Greek into Latin" and the "and" of "and said" omitted; "at the end of the fifth century" marked to move; text is to read "Macrobius said in his commentary at the end of the fifth century that Cicero")	WBY		
(159) after 129.30	note at bottom of page: "I think there is an error or rather clumsy statement in this chapter. The Four Principles are I now think better placed in one whole cone whereas the Faculties are a half cone. See MSS notebook (vellum)"	WBY		
(178.5) 147.5	"~~May Feb~~ May 1925" to be added after "the present moment"	WBY		✓
(180.1–2) 150.1–2	"2. THE GREAT WHEEL AND HISTORY" marked to delete, to be changed to "Book V: DOVE OR SWAN" in pencil	GY?		✓
(183.7–14) 152.27–33	the paragraph from "Each age unwinds . . . living each other's death." is marked for deletion, but it is also marked "stet"	WBY		
(194.35) 161.33	"the South" marked for deletion, "Full Moon" to replace it	WBY		✓

Page.Line	Change	By	Copy	1937
(195.1) 161.35	"South" marked to delete, "Full Moon" in margin	WBY		✓
(196.2) 162.29–30	"of *recurrence**" marked to delete	WBY		✓
(196.20) 163.13	"God" marked through to be replaced with "Faith"	WBY		✓
(196) after 163.18	note at bottom: "~~The documents~~" marked through and "My instructors" written in margin to replace it; then: "~~If I understand rightly Plato's perfect and imperfect numbers they have much the same meaning.~~" all struck through; then whole note marked to delete, as well as the "My instructors" in the margin	WBY		✓
(202.7) 167.23	correction of "great traditional faith" to "Greek traditional faith"	WBY or GY	2, 3	✓
(207.35–36) 172.4	"Lady Bessborough's rises before me" marked to delete with large mark (pencil)	WBY		✓
(214.3) 176.31	comma at "groups, *covens*" crossed out and marked to delete	WBY		
(214.16) 177.5–6	"Second Fountain" crossed out and "new revelation" written in margin to replace it	WBY		
(221.28–29) 183.17	"*Body*" crossed out and "Creative Mind" written to replace it	WBY		
(253.top) 208.top	Thomas Mark has written in top margin: "As in latest text: Coll. Poems". Two pencils and one pen have made corrections to the poem throughout; all but two corrections appear in *AVB*. See also Hood, "A Search for Authority," 185–86.	Thomas Mark, GY, and/or WBY		✓

Page.Line	Change	By	Copy	1937
(253.2 [line 1 of poem]) 208.2	"bell" at end of line marked to be capitalized, comma at end of line marked to delete			✓ (comma only)
(253.3) 208.3	comma between "bell" and "sound" marked to delete			✓
(253.4) 208.4	comma added at end of line after "Soul's Night"			
(253.18) 208.18	semicolon at end of line after "mock" replaced with comma	GY or Mark		✓
(253.22) 208.22	"X——'s" marked to delete: WBY has written "Horton is to replace X——'s" (ink); the words in ink are written over the same words in pencil, and this penciled line is written above another penciled line with "Horton's" (marked through in pencil); above WBY's correction is the printer's cleaner hand: "Horton's"	WBY, Mark, perhaps GY		✓
(254.9) 209.9	comma added at end of line after "ghost" (pencil)	GY or Mark		✓
(254.12) 209.12	comma at end of line after "house" marked to delete	WBY		✓
(254.21) 209.21	comma added at end of line after "friend" (pencil)	GY or Mark		✓
(254.23–24) 209.23	comma at end of line after "wear" marked to delete	WBY		✓
(254.24) 209.24	comma in "from eyesight, to the" marked to delete			✓
(254.30) 209.30	comma at end of line after "sun" marked to change to semicolon (pencil)	GY or Mark		✓
(254.31) 209.31	dash after "there" marked to replace with comma (pencil)	GY or Mark		✓
(254.32) 209.32	dash after "Choice" marked to replace with comma (pencil)	GY or Mark		✓

Page.Line	Change	By	Copy	1937
(255.1) 210.1	"And I call up MacGregor from the grave," "And" marked through (pencil), "up" marked through (pencil and pen), "the" marked through and replaced with "his" (pen); "Mathers" added in margin (pencil), marked over (pen), and written neatly by printer below WBY's notation, to create the changed line "I call MacGregor Mathers from his grave,"	WBY, Mark, or GY		✓
(255.5) 210.5	semicolon after "so" marked to replace with comma, comma at end of line after "ends" marked to replace with semicolon	GY or Mark		✓
(255.10) 210.10	period at end of line after "blind" replaced with exclamation point	GY or Mark		✓
(255.27) 210.27	semicolon at end of line after "mock" replaced with comma			✓
(255.28) 210.28	comma added at end of line after "ear"			✓
(255.30) 210.30	"weep and laugh" marked through (pencil), "laugh and weep" written in margin (pencil)	Mark		✓
(256.6) 211.4	comma at end of line after "wandering" marked to delete	WBY		✓

Emendations to the Copy-Text

Original Page.ln	Current Page.ln	As Printed	As Corrected	Authority for Correction
xiii.3	lvi.4	"Arabian Nights"	*Arabian Nights*	title of book
xvii.26	lix.28–29	'Speculum Angelorum et Hominorum,'	*Speculum Angelorum et Hominorum,*	title of book
xviii.22	lx.16	"Speculum"	*Speculum*	title of book
xix.11–12	lx.37–38	"The Way of the Soul between the Sun and the Moon"	*The Way of the Soul between the Sun and the Moon*	title of book
xix.30–31	lxi.14–15	"Speculum Angelorum et Hominorum."	*Speculum Angelorum et Hominorum.*	title of book
xxi	lxii.25–26	Passivalli	Passavalli	spelling of proper name
1.2	1.2	BOOK I *WHAT THE CALIPH PARTLY LEARNED*	BOOK I WHAT THE CALIPH PARTLY LEARNED	typographical consistency
4.30	4.27	cat-o'-nine-tales	cat-o'-nine-tails	misspelling
16.18	16.28	four faculties	*Four Faculties*	terminology
17.12	17.14	of the tinctures,	of the *Tinctures,*	terminology
17.15	17.17	each Tincture divides	each *Tincture* divides	terminology
17.17	17.19	the Tinctures become	the *Tinctures* become	terminology
17.31	17.30–31	Commedia del Arte	*Commedia dell' Arte*	spelling of term
18.13	18.8	the Convito.	the *Convito.*	title of book
18.14	18.9	*Primary* Man	*primary* Man	terminology

Original Page.ln	Current Page.ln	As Printed	As Corrected	Authority for Correction
18.15	18.9–10	*Commedia del Arte*	*Commedia dell' Arte*	spelling of term
18.25–26	18.18–19	"The Imitation of Christ"	The Imitation Christ	title of book
18.30	18.21–22	enforced mask	enforced *Mask*	terminology
19.21–22	19.6	*Antithetical Man*	*antithetical Man*	terminology
21.3–4	20.11	*Primary Tincture*	*primary Tincture*	terminology
21.20	20.23	*Primary,*	*primary,*	terminology
22.31	21.28	*Creative Mind Phase*	*Creative Mind phase*	terminology
22.7, 32	21.7, 28	*of that Phase.*	*of that phase.*	terminology
22.10, 23.2	21.10, 30–31	that Phase is modified	that phase is modified	terminology
22.18	21.16	*Primary and so*	*primary and so*	terminology
22.28	21.25	*in Primary Phases*	*in primary phases*	terminology
23.6	21.32	false *Creative Mind*	False *Creative Mind*	terminology
23.6	21.33–34	that Phase which	that phase which	terminology
23.26–27	22.15	(*Phases 8, 22, 15, 1,*)	(*Phases 8, 22, 15, 1*)	terminology & extra comma
24.21	23.2	DISCORDS, OPPOSI-TIONS AND CONTRASTS.	DISCORDS, OPPOSI-TIONS AND CONTRASTS	typographical consistency
26.8	24.10	in *antithetical* phases	in *antithetical* phases	terminology
26.11	24.12	in *primary* phases	in *primary* phases	terminology
26.28	24.26	AND SUPER-NATURAL UNITY.	AND SUPER-NATURAL UNITY	typographical consistency

Original Page.ln	Current Page.ln	As Printed	As Corrected	Authority for Correction
32.12	28.42–43	None except monotony	None except monotony.	consistency within table
34.19	31.4	Affecting 28, 1, 2,	Affecting 28, 1, 2	consistency within table
35.1	31.9	Affecting 14, 15 16	Affecting 14, 15, 16	consistency within table
35.10	31.18	[Affecting] 3, 4, 5, 6,	[Affecting] 3, 4, 5, 6	consistency within table
36.12	32.20	Intensity (affecting Third Quarter)	Intensity (affecting Third Quarter).	consistency within table
36.23	33.7	In *primary* Phases	In *primary* phases	terminology
39.4	34.22	*Mask* (from P. *16*).	*Mask* (from Phase 16).	consistency of phase headings
39.6	35.1	*Creative Mind* (from P. *28*).	*Creative Mind* (from Phase 28).	consistency of phase headings
39.8	35.3	*Body of Fate* (from P. *14*)	*Body of Fate* (from Phase 14)	consistency of phase headings
41.4	36.23	*Mask* (from P. *17*).	*Mask* (from Phase 17).	consistency of phase headings
41.5	36.24	*Creative Mind* (from P. *27*).	*Creative Mind* (from Phase 27).	consistency of phase headings
41.7	36.26	*Body of Fate* (from P. *13*)	*Body of Fate* (from Phase 13)	consistency of phase headings
42.6–7	37.17–18	"Water of the Wondrous Isles",	*Water of the Wondrous Isles,*	title of book
42.17	37.27	*Mask* (from P. *18*).	*Mask* (from Phase 18).	consistency of phase headings
42.18	37.28	C.M. (from P. *26*).	*Creative Mind* (from Phase 26).	consistency of phase headings
42.20	37.30	B.F. (from P. *12*)	*Body of Fate* (from Phase 12)	consistency of phase headings
44.3	39.6	*Primary Tincture*	*primary Tincture*	terminology

Original Page.ln	Current Page.ln	As Printed	As Corrected	Authority for Correction
44.10	39.11–12	'The Water of the Wondrous Isles'	*The Water of the Wondrous Isles*	title of book
45.9	40.4	*Mask* (from *P. 19*).	*Mask* (from Phase 19).	consistency of phase headings
45.11	40.5	*Creative Mind* (from *P. 25*).	*Creative Mind* (from Phase 25).	consistency of phase headings
45.13	40.7	*Body of Fate* (from *P. 11*)	*Body of Fate* (from Phase 11)	consistency of phase headings
46.19	41.4	*Mask* (from *Phase* 20).	*Mask* (from Phase 20).	consistency of phase headings
46.21	41.5	*Creative Mind* (from *Phase* 24).	*Creative Mind* (from Phase 24).	consistency of phase headings
46.23	41.7	*Body of Fate* (from *Phase 10*)	*Body of Fate* (from Phase 10)	consistency of phase headings
48.4	42.7	*Mask* (from phase 21).	*Mask* (from Phase 21).	consistency of phase headings
48.6	42.8	*Creative Mind* (from phase 23).	*Creative Mind* (from Phase 23).	consistency of phase headings
48.8	42.10	*Body of Fate* (from phase 9)	*Body of Fate* (from Phase 9)	consistency of phase headings
49.14	42.12	Alexander Dumas	Alexandre Dumas	Yeats's own usage in list of phasal examples and spelling of proper name
50.9	43.30	Dostoieffsky	Dostoyevsky	standard Anglicization
51.12, 13	44.24–25	Dostoieffsky's Idiot	Dostoyevsky's Idiot	standard Anglicization
52.12	45.15	true *Mask*	True *Mask*	terminology
52.13	45.16	true *Creative Mind*	True *Creative Mind*	terminology

Original Page.ln	Current Page.ln	As Printed	As Corrected	Authority for Correction
57.19	49.12–13	of the Phase,	of the phase,	terminology
60.15	51.22–23	all *phases* before	all phases before	terminology
62.8	53.2	are equisdistant.	are equidistant.	misspelling
62.32	53.21	antithetically	*antithetically*	terminology
69.16	58.16–17	Condor [twice]	Conder	*Au,* spelling of proper name
69.18	58.19	antithetical phases	*antithetical* phases	terminology
71.9	59.34	Celestial Body	*Celestial Body*	terminology
71.11	59.35	*antithetical phases*	*antithetical* phases	terminology
75.7	62.35	*False—* Dispersal	*False—* Dispersal.	consistency of phase headings
75.9	63.2	antithetical emotion.	*antithetical* emotion.	consistency
75.10	63.2–3	self-realization	self-realisation	consistency of spelling
76.8	63.26	The Divine Comedy	the *Divine Comedy*	title of long poem
76.18	63.34	as Phase	as phase	terminology
77.33	64.38	"The Cenci"	*The Cenci*	title of play
79.17	66.10	*antithetical tincture*	*antithetical Tincture*	terminology
79.18	66.11	old antithetical life	old *antithetical* life	terminology
80.17	66.32	a *phase* where	a phase where	terminology
82.1–2	68.1–2	XX Phase Nineteen	XXI Phase Nineteen	the Roman number XX has already been used as a header; must also renumber following sections

Original Page.ln	Current Page.ln	As Printed	As Corrected	Authority for Correction
82.12	68.10	This Phase is	This phase is	terminology
84.13	69.29	and reverse them	and reveres them	misspelling
85.7–8	70.17–18	XXI Phase Twenty	XXII Phase Twenty	see page 82.1
85.13	70.21	Dramatisation of Mask.	Dramatisation of *Mask*.	terminology
88.16–17	73.1–2	XXII Phase Twenty-one	XXIII Phase Twenty-one	see page 82.1
88.18	73.3	*Will*. The acquisitive Man.	*Will*—The acquisitive Man.	consistency of phase headings
90.15	74.18	in Dostoieffsky's "Idiot,"	in Dostoyevsky's *Idiot*,	standard Anglicization, title of book
91.13–14	75.7–8	XXIII Phase Twenty-two	XXIV Phase Twenty-two	see page 82.1
91.22	75.15	Herbert Spenser,	Herbert Spencer,	spelling of proper name
93.31–32	77.8	his "Temptation of St Anthony" and his "Bouvard and Pécuchet" are	his *Temptation of St Anthony* and his *Bouvard and Pécuchet* are	titles of books
94.21	77.26	in Dostoieffsky the	in Dostoyevsky the	standard Anglicization
94.26–27	77.31	of "Bouvard and Pécuchet"	of *Bouvard and Pécuchet*,	title of book
94.27	77.32	the "Temptation" even,	the *Temptation* even,	title of book
96.14	79.3	Dostoieffsky, to	Dostoyevsky, to	standard Anglicization
97.9–10	79.30–31	XXIV Phase Twenty-Three	XXV Phase Twenty-Three	see page 82.1, consistency in titles

Original Page.ln	Current Page.ln	As Printed	As Corrected	Authority for Correction
98.27	80.32–33	a primary mirror	a *primary* mirror	terminology
102.15–16	83.28–29	XXV Phase Twenty-four	XXVI Phase Twenty-four	see page 82.1
106.1–2	86.10–11	XXVI Phase Twenty-five	XXVII Phase Twenty-five	see page 82.1
106.15–16	86.23–24	some organized belief	some organised belief	consistency of spelling
110.3–4	89.16–17	XXVII Phase Twenty-six	XXVIII Phase Twenty-six	see page 82.1
113.1–2	91.22–23	XXVIII Phase Twenty-seven	XXIX Phase Twenty-seven	see page 82.1
115.1–2	93.4–5	XXIX Phase Twenty-eight	XXX Phase Twenty-eight	see page 82.1
125.28	101.20	wondering	wandering	typographical error corrected by WBY (see table 3 above)
128.13	103.11–12	"Spiritual Diary," and in "The Principia"	*Spiritual Diary,* and in *The Principia*	titles of books
129.6	104.2	EXPANDING AND CONTRASTING GYRES	EXPANDING AND CONTRACTING GYRES	section elsewhere speaks of contracting, but never of contrasting
133.17	107.18	the Mental Traveller	"The Mental Traveller"	title of poem
134.35–36	108.30	"The Spiritual Diary"	*The Spiritual Diary*	title of book
139.5	112.10	*Great Wheel*	Great Wheel	terminology
139.18–19	113.1–2	*Primary Tincture* and the *Antithetical Tincture*	*primary Tincture* and the *antithetical Tincture*	terminology

Original Page.ln	Current Page.ln	As Printed	As Corrected	Authority for Correction
142.10	115.15	that on page 140	that on page 113	current pagination
146.9	119.4	The Four Principles are	The *Four Principles* are	terminology
147.4–5	119.18	between phase 18 and phase 19.	between Phase 18 and Phase 19.	terminology
147.11–12	120.3	*Head, Heart, Loins and Fall*	*Head, Heart, Loins* and *Fall*	stylistic consistency
149.30	121.27–28	tenth book of Paradise Lost to	tenth book of *Paradise Lost* to	title of long poem
150.25	122.13–14	Dr Fritz Homell,	Dr Fritz Hommel,	spelling of proper name
150.27–28	122.15–16	"The Encyclopaedia of Religion and Ethics,"	*The Encyclopaedia of Religion and Ethics,*	title of book
150.29	122.17	Dr Homell fixes	Dr Hommel fixes	spelling of proper name
151.11–12	122.32	Dr Fritz Hommell	Dr Fritz Hommel	spelling of proper name
151.15	122.35	Dream of Scipio	*Dream of Scipio*	title of book
152.18	123.29	in ¹fifteen	in *fifteen	standardization of reference marks for WBY's notes
152.35	123.35	1. The Greek	*The Greek	standardization of reference marks for WBY's notes
153.12	124.18	Homell's Aries	Hommel's Aries	spelling of proper name
153.15	124.21	4 B.C.¹	4 B.C.*	standardization of reference marks for WBY's notes

Original Page.ln	Current Page.ln	As Printed	As Corrected	Authority for Correction
153.35	124.35	1. Some one gave	*Some one gave	standardization of reference marks for WBY's notes
154.16	125.16	the *Spiritual* and the *Physical Primary*	the *Spiritual* and the *Physical primary*	terminology
154.19	125.19	sideral	sidereal	consistency of spelling
155.10	126.3	the Republic	the *Republic*	title of book
155.21	126.12	Macchiavelli	Machiavelli	spelling of proper name
156.18	127.1–2	E. M. Plunkett's "Ancient Calendars"	E. M. Plunket's *Ancient Calendars*	spelling of proper name, title of book
157.10	127.24	millenium	millennium	misspelling
159.6	129.4	always antithetical	always *antithetical*	terminology
159.18	129.14	(Phase 8) birth	(Phase 8) at birth	printer error?
164.17	133.17	Tinctures	*Tinctures*	terminology
165.11	134.6	symbolize	symbolise	consistency of spelling
165.14	134.8	the Divine Comedy	the *Divine Comedy*	title of long poem
166.1	134.16	at A.D.1 travels	at A.D. 1 travels	regular spacing
166.21	135.10	previous Millenium	previous Millennium	misspelling
167.2	135.11	a millenium each	a millennium each	misspelling
167.3	135.12	Head, Heart, Loins and Fall	*Head, Heart, Loins* and *Fall*	terminology
167.15, 35	135.21–22, 136.15	facing page 180	on page 147	current pagination

Original Page.ln	Current Page.ln	As Printed	As Corrected	Authority for Correction
169.10	137.19	three Phases	three phases	terminology
171.4	138.31	the great year	the Great Year	terminology
171.11	139.1	round the wheel	round the Wheel	terminology
172.28, 30, 173.1, 10, 11	140.8, 9, 11–12, 19, 19–20	harmonization	harmonisation	consistency of spelling
176.2	142.24	Nietsche's	Nietzsche's	spelling of proper name
180.9	150.9	each millenium,	each millennium,	misspelling
180.16	150.15	A millenium is	A millennium is	misspelling
182.34	152.20	Furtwingler	Furtwängler	spelling of proper name
189.30	157.34	Ammonius Sacca	Ammonius Saccas	spelling of proper name
190.17	158.15–16	civilization	civilisation	consistency of spelling
196.15	163.9	Cefalu	Cefalù	spelling of proper name
197.18	163.32–33	Cretien de Troyes	Chrétien de Troyes	spelling of proper name
197.32	164.9	"Parsifal"	*Parzival*	title of book, spelling of book title
197.35, 198.4	164.12, 15–16	Parsifal	Parzival	spelling of proper name
198.9	164.20	millenium	millennium	misspelling
198.29–30	164.36	Villars de Honecourt	Villard de Honnecourt	spelling of proper name
199.31	165.29	"Convito"	*Convito*	title of book
199.33–34	165.31	the Divine Comedy	the *Divine Comedy*	title of long poem
201.30	167.12	Michaelangelo	Michelangelo	spelling of proper name

Original Page.ln	Current Page.ln	As Printed	As Corrected	Authority for Correction
201.32	167.14	Jacopo della Guercia	Jacopo della Quercia	spelling of proper name
203.28 204.3–4, 7, 18	169.2, 5, 8, 17	Michaelangelo	Michelangelo	spelling of proper name
204.7	169.8	Camera della Segnatura	Stanza della Segnatura	incorrect name
205.5	169.35	16th phase	16th Phase	terminology
205.12	170.3	Camera Segnatura	Stanza della Segnatura	incorrect name
205.31	170.18	Vandyke's	van Dyck's	spelling of proper name
207.1	171.15	heterogenous	heterogeneous	misspelling
207.8–9	171.21	*Antithetical* structure *Primary* material	*antithetical* structure *primary* material	terminology
207.12–13	171.24	*Antithetical*	*antithetical*	terminology
207.18–19	171.28–29	*Spiritual Primary*	*Spiritual primary*	terminology
208.34	172.33	Pickwick	*Pickwick*	title of book
209.9, 33	173.4, 23	Tolstoi	Tolstoy	standard Anglicization
209.33–34	173.23	"War and Peace"	*War and Peace*	title of book
211.11	174.26	Brancussi	Brancusi	spelling of proper name
211.34	175.7	"Henry IV," "The Waste Land," "Ulysses,"	*Henry IV, The Waste Land, Ulysses*	titles of play and books
212.25	175.28	Peguy	Péguy	spelling of proper name
212.27	175.30	24th phase	24th Phase	terminology
212.28	175.31	"L'Otage"	*L'Otage*	title of play
213.9	176.7	Sibyll	Sibyl	misspelling

Original Page.ln	Current Page.ln	As Printed	As Corrected	Authority for Correction
213.33–34	176.28	*Physical Primary*	*Physical primary*	terminology
214.7	176.35	Daimon	*Daimon*	terminology
220.5	182.5	"De Occulta Philosophia"	*De Occulta Philosophia*	title of book
228.14–15	188.22–23	the dreaming back or the waking state,	the *Dreaming Back* or the *Waking State,*	terminology
228.27	188.33	*Dreaming back*	*Dreaming Back*	terminology
229.18	189.19	phases 23, 24 and 25,	Phases 23, 24 and 25,	terminology
231.14	190.37	*Waking State of The Shiftings*	*Waking State of the Shiftings*	terminology
239.27	197.26	Heroditus	Herodotus	spelling of proper name
241.33	198.36	Sec. XIV	Sec. XX	incorrect number in cross reference
243.18	200.23	"Hour Glass"	*Hour-Glass*	title of play
245.20	202.12	Bagdad	Baghdad	standard spelling
251.24–25	207.6–7	"Principles of Human Knowledge"	*Principles of Human Knowledge*	title of book

The reference marks used for the footnotes in *AVA* are not consistent. On pages xxii, 14, 27, 34, 87, 112, 168, 196, 202, 224, 236, 240, 241, and 244, an asterisk (*) is used. On pages 93, 152, and 153, a superscript numeral 1 is used. While adhering to the original placement of the annotation marker (sometimes preceding the annotated word), we have used an asterisk throughout the text, to limit confusion between WBY's footnotes and our explanatory endnotes.

End-of-Line Word Division in the Copy-Text

Page.Line this edition   Reading in this edition]   Reading in copy-text
  Page.Line in copy-text (*A Vision* [London: T. Werner Laurie, 1926]).

liii.15 seventy-two] seventy-/ two ix.15
lvii.6 fellow-students] fellow-/ students xv.6
lvii.13 sun-/ darkened xv.13
lix.1 fellow-students] fellow-/ students xvi.28
11.30 elsewhere] else-/ where 11.7
13.26 metaphysical] meta-/ physical 13.4
18.16 self-expression] self-/expression 18.21
21.12 self-realisation] self-/ realisation 22.11
27.table Supersensi-tive] Super-/ sensitive 30.table
28.table Self-analysis] Self-/ analysis 31.table
28.table Self-adaptation] Self-/ adaptation 31.table
28.table Self-driven] Self-/ driven 31.table
28.table Self-assurance] Self-/ assurance 31.table
28.table Self-reliance] Self-/ reliance 31.table
28.table Self-desecration] Self-/ desecration 31.table
28.table Forerunner] Fore-/ runner 31.table
28.table Self-realization] Self-/ realization 31.table
28.table Self-abandonment] Self-/ abandonment 31.table
29.table Self-dramatization] Self-/ dramatization 32.table
36.3 good-humour] good-/ humour 40.16
37.16 overhanging] over-/ hanging 42.4
44.26 twenty-eight] twenty-/ eight 51.14
52.30 Forerunner] Fore-/ runner 61.31
53.1 self-hatred] self-/ hatred 62.6
55.8 self-denial] self-/ denial 65.1
55.35 Self-distrust] Self-/ distrust 66.2
69.5 watercourse] water-/ course 83.19
74.3 self-analysing] self-/ analysing 89.32
74.10 self-adaption] self-/ adaption 90.4
79.33 Self-pity] Self-/ pity 97.12
82.23 self-regarding] self-/ regarding 100.35
89.18 Hunchback] Hunch-/ back 110.5
89.30 self-expression] self-/ expression 110.19
90.24 self-regarding] self-/ regarding 111.25
112.14 twenty-eight] twenty-/ eight 139.9
115.12 Twenty-five] Twenty-/ five 142.5
115.13 Twenty-eight] Twenty-/ eight 142.7
120.8 twenty-six] twenty-/ six 147.17
155.22 Neo-Pythagorean] Neo-/ Pythagorean 186.29

INDEX

Abbey Theatre, 334
Academy of Plato, 158, 302
Adam and Eve, 121, 122, 127, 166, 167, 278, 311
Adams, Henry, 284, 308, 316; *Education of Henry Adams, The,* 308; *Mont-Saint-Michel and Chartres,* 308
Adolphus, Gustavus, 125, 282
Æ. *See* George William Russell
Aeschylus, 152, 256, 291, 293
After Life States: Beatitude, 130, 193–197, 220, 329; Dreaming Back, 130, 187–190, 192, 193, 195–198, 324, 325, 327, 329; Meditation (Awakening of the Spirits), 184–185, 186; Return, 185, 186, 189, 191, 197, 198, 324, 327; Shiftings, 130, 189–193, 195, 324, 327; Sleeping State, 185, 187, 324; Waking State, 185, 186, 188, 190, 191, 193, 198, 202, 203, 324. *See also* States before Birth
Agrippa von Nettesheim, Heinrich Cornelius, xxix, 182, 239, 321; *Three Books of Occult Philosophy or Magic,* 182, 321
Aherne, Owen, xxii, xxiii, xxx, xxxii, xxxv, xxxviii, lviii, 3–8, 10, 142, 194, 196, 202, 204, 216, 221–223, 227–231, 233, 234, 252, 266, 277, 334
Alastor; or the Spirit of Solitude (Shelley), 243, 262
Alexander the Great, 71, 153, 154, 161, 174, 296, 297, 300, 304, 317
Alexandria, 132, 159, 226, 227, 283, 285, 300, 302, 317

An Introduction to the Theory of Relativity (Bolton), 268, 316
Anatomy Lesson of Dr. Nicholas Tulp, The (Rembrandt), 261
Anaxagoras, 151, 154, 293, 296, 298
Anaximander, 298
Anaximenes, 298
Ancient Calendars and Constellations (Plunket), 127, 279, 283
Anima Hominis, xlviii, 104, 106, 107, 252
Anima Mundi, xlviii, 104, 106, 107, 142, 143, 184, 202, 239, 251, 270, 322, 325, 326, 335, 336
Anthony, Saint, 173, 259, 297
Antioch, 163, 297
Apocalypse of Saint John (Book of Revelation), 158
Apotheosis and After Life (Strong), 296, 297
Aquinas. *See* Thomas Aquinas, Saint
Arabian Nights [The Book of the Thousand Nights and One Night] (tr. Mathers, E. P.), lvi, 163, 226, 306
Aran Islands, 81, 82, 88, 261
Arcon, 199–201, 204, 332
Aretino, Pietro, 60, 61, 169, 253
Aristarchus of Samothrace, 298
Aristophanes, 153, 277, 295
Aristotle, 108, 153, 273, 295
Arnold, Matthew, 66, 172, 256, 314; "Strayed Reveller, The," 243; "The Scholar-Gypsy," 225
Art and Life (Moore), 260, 268
As You Like It (Shakespeare), 244
Ascoli, 312
Asia, 89, 141, 152, 153, 228, 297
astrology, xxvi, 250, 273, 274, 276, 278, 281, 292
Athens, 117, 285, 286, 302, 312
"Auguries of Innocence" (Blake), 238

367

Augustus (Gaius Julius Caesar Octavianus), lvi, 221, 281
Aurelius (Caesar Marcus Aurelius Antoninus Augustus), 298
Austen, Jane, 172, 314, 315
Autobiography of Alice B. Toklas, The (Stein), 217
automatic faculty, 203–205, 334, 335
automatic writing, xxii, xxviii, 29, 218, 219, 259
Automatonisms, Four, 24, 32, 65
Avatar, 225, 252, 263, 283, 293, 334
Avicenna (Abu 'Ali al-Husayn ibn 'Abd Allah ibn Sina or Ebn e-Sina), 113, 273
Axël (Villiers de l'Isle Adam), 253

Babylon, 122, 128, 151, 176, 278, 279, 292
Bacon, Sir Francis, 170, 313, 316
Baghdad, xxxi, 11, 202, 226, 233
Ballylee (tower), xxxvi, lxii, 94, 124, 227, 230, 266, 294
Balzac, Honoré de, 70, 72, 78, 258, 260, 261, 314
Baptist, John the, 133, 286, 297
Bardesanes (Bar Daisan), 329; "Hymn of the Soul," 194, 329
Baudelaire, Charles, 54, 174, 251, 318
Beardsley, Aubrey, 54, 166, 218, 251, 253, 309
Beatific Vision, xliii, lv, 140, 220, 289. *See also* Moments of Crisis
Beatitude, 130, 193–197, 220, 329. *See also* After Life States
Beatrice Portinari, 26, 240
beauty, 6, 8, 25, 29, 35, 37, 48, 52–54, 56, 58, 59, 62, 63, 66, 67, 78, 83, 102, 105, 108, 109, 113, 138, 140, 151, 155, 163, 165, 168, 170, 172, 185, 194, 209, 225, 228, 231, 242, 243, 252–254, 273, 290, 305, 306, 312, 336
Beddoes, Thomas Lovell, 67, 256
Bedouin, 268
Bembo, Pietro, 37, 243, 244
Benedict XVI (pope), 228
Bennett, Allan, 217, 337

Berkeley, George (bishop), 104, 128, 269; *Treatise Concerning the Principles of Human Knowledge, A*, 207, 284
Bernard of Clairvaux, Saint, 164, 307
Bernini, Giovanni Lorenzo, 170, 313
Berosius, 282
Bessborough, Viscountess Duncannon and Countess of (Henrietta Frances), 172, 314
Between Sun and Moon (French), 226
Biographia Literaria (Coleridge), 231, 232, 235
Birkett, F. C. *See* Burkitt, F. C.
Blair, Robert, 323
Blake, James, 272
Blake, William, 219, 314; as historical example, 172–173, 176; as phasal example, 60–61, 251–253, 315; as precursor, xxv, xxix, lvi, 235, 236, 239, 269, 271–273, 292, 311, 316; ideas, images, or style, 15, 109, 112–113, 218, 229, 230, 307, 323; quoted, 107–108, 238, 240, 242–243, 253, 260–262, 284, 299, 320; "Auguries of Innocence," 238; "Descriptive Catalogue, A," 243, 253, 284; "Divine Image, The," 319; "Eternity," 243; *Europe*, 262; *Jerusalem*, 260, 261, 331; *Marriage of Heaven and Hell, The*, 265, 269; "Mental Traveller, The," 107, 242, 271, 272, 325; "Several Questions Answered," 243; *Songs of Experience*, 320; *Songs of Innocence*, 319; *Visions of the Daughters of Albion*, 260
Blavatsky, H. P. (Helena Petrovna), xxix, 239, 240; *Isis Unveiled*, 240; *Key to Theosophy*, 326; *Secret Doctrine, The*, 239, 240
Bloomsbury, lxi, lxiii
Boccaccio, Giovanni, lv, 219, 222, 256; *Decameron, The*, 219, 222
"Body and Spirit" (Davies), 323

Body of Fate. *See* Four Faculties
Boehme, Jacob, xxix, 103, 253, 265, 269, 277
Bolton, Lyndon, 268, 269; *Introduction to the Theory of Relativity, An*, 268, 316
Bonaparte, Napoleon, 70–74, 78, 171, 173, 258, 259
Book of the Courtier, The (Castiglione), 244, 312
Book of the Thousand Nights and One Night, The [*Arabian Nights*] (tr. Mathers, E. P.), lvi, 163, 226, 306
Borrow, George, 42, 43, 246
Botticelli, Sandro (Alessandro di Mariano di Vanni Filipepi), 57, 168, 169, 251, 254, 293, 311
Bouvard and Pécuchet (Flaubert), 77, 78, 260
Brahe, Tycho, 282
"Brancusi" (Pound), 318
Brancusi, Constantin, 174, 318
Brontë, Patrick Branwell, 44, 247
"Brooklyn Bridge" (Whitman), 245
Browne, Sir Thomas, 171, 313
Browning, Robert, 38, 244, 258, 325; *Pippa Passes*, 244; "Paracelsus," 244; "Pauline," 244; *Poetical Works of Robert Browning, The*, 244; *Sordello*, 244
Bryant, Jacob, 292
Buddha, 252
Burkitt, F. C. (Francis Crawford), 106, 270
Burne-Jones, Sir Edward, 57, 69, 222, 251, 252, 254, 258; *Golden Stair, The*, 57, 251, 252; *Sleep of King Arthur in Avalon, The*, 57, 251
Burnet, John, 239, 270, 271, 296, 298
"Burning Babe, The" (Southwell), 62, 253
Byron, Lord (George Gordon), 65, 68, 245, 257, 264; *Deformed Transformed, The*, 264; *Don Juan*, 40, 245; *Giaour, The*, 40, 245

Byzantine Art and Archaeology (Dalton), 298, 303, 306
Byzantium. *See also* Constantinople: 97, 152, 158, 160, 164–166, 302, 307

Cæsar, Gaius Julius, 90, 125, 132, 238, 264, 276, 285, 286
Cain and Abel, 122, 278
Callimachus, 152, 172, 294, 295
Calvin, John, 86, 263
Cambrensis, Giraldus (Gerald of Wales), 215
Campbell, Mrs. Patrick (*née* Beatrice Stella Tanner), 257, 258
Canterbury Tales, The (Chaucer), 222
Capri, xxxix, xlii, lvi, 178, 221, 303, 311
Carlyle, Thomas, 42, 43, 46, 229, 246, 258
Cashel, 319
Castiglione, Baldassare, 168, 244; *Book of the Courtier, The*, 244, 312
Cavalcanti, Guido, 26, 241
Cefalù, Sicily, 163, 306
Celestial Body. *See* Four Principles
Cenci, Beatrice, 64, 256
Cenci, Francesco, 256
Cenci, The (Shelley), 64, 256
Censorinus, 281; *De die natali*, 281
Cervantes, Miguel de, 253
Cézanne, Paul, 252
Charlemagne, 161, 304
Chaucer, Geoffrey, 166, 234, 258, 309; *Canterbury Tales, The*, 222; "Clerk's Tale, The," 222; "Franklin's Tale, The," 234
Chrétien de Troyes, 163
Christ, 120, 194, 218, 221, 252, 255, 265, 266, 277, 286, 297, 304, 320; and pity, 59, 264, 298; and the Great Year, 126, 127, 131–134, 137, 138, 276, 283, 312, 334; as phase example, 247, 264; crucifixion of, xlii, 25, 132, 240, 247, 285, 300; image of, 81, 154, 160, 168, 261, 297, 303; second coming of, 283, 293, 306
Chrysostom, Saint John, 133, 286

Cicero, Marcus Tullius, xlvii, 122, 123, 125, 132, 279, 280; *De re publica,* 279, 280; *Somnium Scipionis,* 122, 279, 280
Claudel, Paul, 175, 319; *L'annonce faite à Marie,* 319; *L'Otage,* 175
Claudius (Tiberius Claudius Drusus Nero Germanicus), 264
Clement of Alexandria (Titus Flavius Clemens), lxii, 227, 300
"Clerk's Tale, The" (Chaucer), 222
Coleridge, Hartley, 44, 247
Coleridge, Samuel Taylor, 232, 247, 277; *Biographia Literaria,* 231, 232, 235
Collected Works of William Morris, The (Morris), 240
commedia dell'arte, 17, 18, 236, 245
Commentary on Somnium Scipionis (Macrobius), 279, 280
communicators, xxii, xxiii, xxvi, xxvii, xlv, 76, 206, 218, 219, 315; Alastor, 243; Ameritus, xxvii, 228, 237, 276, 328, 333; Apple, xxvii; Arnauld, 293; Arnault, 291; Aymor, xxxii, 286, 293; Carmichael, 309; Dionertes, xxvii, xxviii, xxxiv, 272, 322, 323, 326, 330, 336; Fish, xxvii, 236, 315, 320, 326, 333, 334; Leaf, 326, 333; Thomas of Dorlowicz, xxvii, xxxiv, 218, 224, 228, 235–237, 250, 256, 257, 264, 270, 275, 283, 291, 294, 301, 313, 315, 319, 321, 325–327, 329, 333, 335
complementary dreams, 140, 141, 182, 192, 195, 200, 289, 321
Conder, Charles, 58, 252
cone, xxiv, xxxv, xliii, lvii, 104–113, 115–121, 128, 129, 131, 133–142, 152, 161, 167, 171, 183, 224, 242, 272, 273, 286, 301, 309, 310, 322; historical, xxi, 134, 147, 173, 267, 276, 286, 313, 315
Connemara, 3, 230, 332
Constantine (Gaius Flavius Valerius Aurelius Constantinus), 136,

157, 158, 165, 286, 300, 301, 308
Constantinople. *See also* Byzantium: 267, 286, 301–303, 308
Convito (Dante), xxix, 18, 26, 165, 236, 237, 240, 308, 309
Coole Park, 227
Count of Monte Cristo, The (Dumas), 246
covens, xl, xliv, 45, 138, 139, 176, 189, 288, 310
Cowley, Abraham, 170, 313
Cracow, Poland, lix, 224
Creative Genius, xlv, 235, 241, 242, 264, 298. *See also* Four Faculties
Creative Mind. *See* Four Faculties
Critical Moment, 140, 220, 247. *See also* Moments of Crisis
Crivelli, Carlo, 168, 312
Crookes, Sir William, 136, 287
Crowley, Aleister, 217
Cuala Press, xxxiv–xxxvi, xli–xliii
Cuchulain, xxix, xxxii, 292, 333
Cumont, Franz, 122, 278, 292, 296

d'Annunzio, Gabriele, 68, 257
Daimon, xliv, xlv, xlviii, 15, 24–27, 29, 55, 62, 63, 105, 106, 118, 128, 129, 139, 151, 176, 182–184, 190–193, 196, 204, 205, 225, 227, 233, 235, 239, 240, 242, 247, 274, 277, 288, 298, 321, 322, 328, 336
Dalton, O. M., 289; *Byzantine Art and Archaeology,* 298, 303, 306
Damascus, lx, 225, 226
Danae: A Poem (Moore), 315
Dance of the Four Royal Persons, 11, 109, 111, 233
Dante Alighieri, xxix, lv, 18, 26, 63, 65, 165–167, 171, 174, 200, 219, 237, 240, 241, 245, 254, 255, 308, 309, 318; *Convito,* xxix, 18, 26, 165, 236, 237, 240, 308, 309; *Divine Comedy,* 63, 134, 165, 240, 241, 255, 309; *Paradiso,* 63, 245, 255; *Vita Nuova,* 241
"Dark Angel, The" (Johnson), 325
Darwin, Charles, 76, 259

David, Jacques-Louis, 262
Davies, W. H. (William Henry), 185,
 323; "Body and Spirit," 323
De claris oratoribus dialogus
 (Tacitus), 280
De die natali (Censorinus), 281
De re publica (Cicero), 279, 280
Decameron, The (Boccaccio), 219,
 222
Dee, John, lix, 223, 224, 336
Deformed Transformed, The (Byron),
 264
Deirdre of the Sorrows (Synge), 261
Demon est Deus Inversus, 25, 240
Descartes (Mahaffy), 268
Descartes, René, 103, 268
Descent from the Cross (Rembrandt),
 261
"Descriptive Catalogue, A" (Blake),
 243, 253, 284
Destiny, 16, 39, 59, 105, 109, 111,
 126
Devil, 64, 74, 139, 154, 170, 188,
 240, 256, 311, 315, 326. *See
 also* Satan
Diane de Poitiers, 254
Dickens, Charles, 172, 258, 259,
 315; *Pickwick Papers, The,*
 172, 315
Dionysius the Areopagite, 304
discords, xlv, 17, 23, 53
Discourses (Machiavelli), 282
Discourses (Reynolds), 314
Divine Comedy (Dante), 63, 134,
 165, 240, 241, 255, 309
"Divine Image, The" (Blake), 319
*Doctrine and Discipline of Divorce,
 The* (Milton), 231
Dodds, E. R. (Eric Robertson), 301
Dominic, Saint, 308
Don Juan (Byron), 40, 245
Donatello (Donato di Niccolo di
 Betto Bardi), 167, 309, 310
Dostoyevsky, Fyodor, 43, 44, 75–77,
 79, 246, 259; Idiot of, 43, 44;
 Idiot, The, 74, 246, 247, 259;
 Possessed, The, 246; Prince
 Lyov Nikolaievich Myshkin
 43, 44, 246
Dowden, Edward, 252
Dowson, Ernest, 54, 251
Dreaming Back, 130, 187–190, 192,
 193, 195–198, 324, 325, 327,
 329. *See also* After Life States
Dryden, John, 170, 313
Dublin, Ireland, lxii, 175, 222, 244,
 261, 266, 280, 304, 315, 318
Duhem, Pierre Maurice Marie, 280,
 282, 298
Dulac, Edmund, portrait of Giraldus,
 xxiv, xxxix, 215–216; wood-
 cuts for *AVA,* xxi, 223, 224,
 225, 232; correspondence with
 WBY, xxxi–xxxii, xxxiv,
 xxxvii, xxxviii, xl, xlii, 222,
 302; as phasal example, 256
Dumas, Alexandre, 42, 43, 246;
 Count of Monte Cristo, The,
 246; *Three Musketeers, The,*
 246
Dürer, Albrecht, 167, 176, 216, 256,
 311, 320
Durrow, Book of, 310

Education of Henry Adams, The
 (Adams), 308
egg, lxiv, 43, 142, 151, 174, 229,
 291, 320
Ego, 236, 241, 242. *See also* Will;
 Four Faculties
Egypt, 169, 194, 296, 297
Eliot, T. S. (Thomas Stearns), xliv,
 175, 318, 319; *Waste Land,
 The,* 175, 318, 319
Ellis, Edwin John, 108, 236
Ellmann, Richard, xxv, 301
Emerson, Ralph Waldo, 245, 256
Empedocles, 106, 109, 239, 271, 272
Encyclopædia Britannica, 254, 294,
 302
Endymion (Keats), 243
England, liv, 169, 170, 217, 313, 338
Enneads (Plotinus), 273, 290, 325,
 334
Epicureanism, 154, 296
Epicurus, 296
Epitome Astrologiae (Hispalensis),
 234
Erigena, Johannes Scotus, 161, 304
Eternal Idol, The (Rodin), 57
"Eternity" (Blake), 243
Eunapius, 301
Europe (Blake), 262
Eusebius of Caesarea, 240, 302

evil, 25, 26, 59, 65, 73, 74, 84, 91,
94, 121, 130, 143, 176, 182,
186, 188–191, 200, 238, 240,
241, 256, 324, 327, 328, 330

Faculties. *See* Four Faculties
fairies and fairylore, xxvii, 60, 219,
240, 265, 288, 326
Fall, xlviii, 235, 236, 277. *See also*
Head, Heart, Loins, and Fall
Fallon, Gabriel, 246
Farr Emery, Florence, liii, 197, 209,
217, 264, 337, 338
Fate, 39, 45, 54, 59, 60, 103,
105–107, 109, 111, 126, 128,
186, 236, 322
Faust (Goethe), 248, 314
Fauvelet de Bourrienne, Louis
Antoine, 258
Fechner, Gustav Theodor, 288,
323–325; *On Life after Death*,
288, 322, 324, 325
Felkin, Robert, 233
Ficino, Marsilio, 310, 311
Fielding, Joseph, 258
Finnegans Wake (Joyce), 319
Finneran, Richard J., xlvii, 338
Fisher King, 175, 318
Flaubert, Gustave, 75–77, 79, 103,
106, 173, 259, 260, 268;
Bouvard and Pécuchet, 77, 78,
260; *Temptation of Saint
Anthony, The*, 77, 259, 316;
"La Spirale," 103
Flaxman, John, 108, 272
Fletcher, John, 255
Florence, 167, 236, 250, 282
Fool, 8, 29, 30, 57, 60, 93, 266, 321
Foreknowing, 131, 195. *See also*
States before Birth
Foster, R. F., xxv
four dancers, 10, 11, 109, 111, 233
Four Faculties, xlix, 11, 15, 16, 19,
23, 25, 27, 51, 53, 111, 135,
140, 194, 235, 241, 242, 274,
336
Body of Fate, 15–17, 19–31, 33,
35, 36, 39–46, 48–53, 55–64,
67, 69, 71–75, 78–81, 83, 84,
86, 88–90, 93, 94, 111,
116–119, 128–130, 133, 134,
137, 139, 140, 142, 152, 183,

196, 235, 241. *See also*
Personality of Fate
Creative Mind, xlviii, xlix, 15–31,
33, 35, 36, 38, 44, 51, 53–56,
58–60, 64, 67–69, 72–75,
78–80, 83, 87, 94, 111, 112,
116–119, 128, 129, 131, 133,
134, 136, 139, 140, 142, 172,
235, 241, 309. *See also*
Creative Genius
Mask, 15–20, 22–30, 32, 33, 35,
37, 41, 43–51, 53–76, 78–90,
92–94, 111, 116–119,
128–130, 134, 137, 140, 142,
172, 175, 194, 235, 238,
240–242, 254, 255, 329
Will, 15–25, 27–30, 32, 37, 39–42,
44–46, 48, 49, 51, 53, 54,
58–61, 63, 66, 67, 69, 73, 75,
76, 78, 79, 81–83, 86, 90, 92,
94, 105, 106, 109, 111, 112,
116–119, 129, 130, 133–136,
139, 140, 142, 235, 241, 246,
250, 254, 298. *See also* Ego
Four Principles, xlviii, 27, 119, 235,
284; Celestial Body, xlviii, 59,
119, 129–131, 133, 142, 143,
172, 183, 185–187, 191, 193,
194, 202, 242, 272, 327, 329;
Husk, xlviii, 119, 129–131,
143, 184, 188, 194, 195, 206;
Passionate Body, xlviii, 119,
129–131, 143, 184, 185, 187,
188, 194, 202, 272, 294, 323;
Spirit, xlviii, 119, 129–131,
133, 142, 183–185, 187–189,
193–195, 197–199, 202,
333
Fourth Eclogue ("*Messianic
Eclogue*") (Virgil), 122, 123,
125, 279
Fra Angelico (Giovanni da Fiesole),
165, 309
France, lxii, 170, 202, 305
France, Anatole, 79, 258, 260
"Franklin's Tale, The" (Chaucer),
234
Frazer, Sir James George, 249, 285;
Golden Bough, The, 249, 277,
296, 337
French, Cecil; *Between Sun and
Moon*, 226

Froude, J. A. (James Anthony), 246
Frustrators, 196, 275, 330
Furtwängler, Adolf, 152, 295, 310

Gainsborough, Thomas, 171, 177, 314, 315
Galsworthy, John, 83, 262
George, Saint, 61, 253
Georgius Syncellus, 121, 122, 277, 278
Gerard of Cremona, 215
Germany, 229, 263, 305
Ghostly Self, 183, 194, 195, 200, 205, 322, 328, 329, 333
Giaour, The (Byron), 40, 245
Gibbon, Edward, 267; *History of the Decline and Fall of the Roman Empire, The,* 226, 295, 298, 301, 305
Giorgione (Giorgio Barbarelli da Castelfranco), 56, 251
Giotto di Bondone, 165, 309
Giraldus, xi, xxiv, xxx, xxxi, xxxiv, xxxix, xlvii, lxi, lxiii, 10, 215, 216, 223, 232, 233, 248; *Speculum Angelorum et Hominum,* xxiv, xxxi, xxxii, xxxiv, xxxv, lix–lxi, 61, 213, 216, 224
Giraldus of Ferrara, Lilio Gregorio, 215
Gitanjali (Tagore), 265
Gladstone, William, 249
Glanvill, Joseph, 225, 326; *Vanity of Dogmatizing, The,* 225
Glendalough, Co. Wicklow, Ireland, 293, 294
Goethe, Johann Wolfgang von, 66, 67, 172, 220, 248, 256, 257, 314; *Faust,* 248, 314
Going Forth, 131, 197. *See also* States before Birth
Golden Bough, The (Frazer), 249, 277, 296, 337
Golden Dawn, Hermetic Order of the, xxix, xl, 217–219, 223, 224, 233–235, 239, 240, 249, 259, 266, 274, 320, 337, 338
Golden Stair, The (Burne-Jones), 57, 251, 252
Goncourt, Edmond and Jules, 79, 260

Gonne, Iseult, 214, 251, 319, 321, 325, 332, 333, 338
Gonne, Maud, xxvii, 233, 253, 254, 307, 332, 333
good, 7, 25, 26, 46, 65, 70, 73, 85, 87, 91, 94, 130, 143, 176, 177, 182, 186, 189–191, 193, 206, 238, 240, 241, 256, 264, 279, 327, 328
Gosse, Edmund, 257
Gould, Warwick, xlix, 273
Gourmont, Rémy de, 260
Grandison, Sir Charles, 172, 315
Gray, Thomas, 171, 313
Great Wheel, xlviii, 10, 11, 13, 16, 22, 25, 31, 45, 51, 76, 78, 111–113, 119, 120, 130, 133, 135–137, 139, 140, 142, 178, 215, 216, 223, 225, 232, 233
Great Year, xlviii, lxiv, 31, 114, 117–127, 131, 132, 137, 138, 273, 276, 280, 306
Greece, 151–153, 156, 157, 159, 165, 281, 290, 292, 294–296, 300
Gregory, Augusta, Lady, xxx–xxxii, 83, 225, 227, 246, 262, 292, 314, 316, 325; *Visions and Beliefs in the West of Ireland,* xxx, 239, 266, 288, 326, 330, 332
Gregory of Tours, Saint, 301
gyre, xxiv, xxxv, lv, lvii, lix, 102–112, 114, 117, 118, 120, 121, 129, 133, 136, 137, 140, 142, 152, 155, 159, 160, 164–167, 169–171, 173, 176, 177, 189, 193, 195, 219, 224, 245, 246, 268, 269, 271, 310, 313

"Hamadryad, The" (Landor), 243
Hamlet (Shakespeare), 139, 197, 288
Harper, George Mills, xxiv, xlix, 218, 220
Harris, Frank, 246
Harris, Thomas Lake, 72, 258, 259
Hawthorne, Nathaniel; *Marble Faun, The,* 243
Head, 51, 67, 220. *See also* Head, Heart, Loins, and Fall
Head, Heart, Loins, and Fall, xlviii, 16, 119, 120, 135, 236, 238, 241

Heald, Edith Shackleton, 228
Heart, 51, 220. *See also* Head, Heart,
    Loins, and Fall
Helen of Troy, 48, 56, 113, 150, 248,
    251, 273, 290, 291, 320
Hellas (Shelley), 243, 254, 255,
    335
Hellenics (Landor), 243
Henry II of France, 254
Henry IV (Pirandello), 175, 318
Heraclitus, 103, 106, 239, 270, 271,
    317
Herbert, George, 86, 88, 263
Hermes Trismegistus, xxix, 123, 230,
    291
Herod, 154
Herodotus, 197, 293, 331
Hesiod, 137, 287, 291
Hipparchus, 122, 123, 278, 283
Hispalensis, Johannes; *Epitome
    Astrologiae*, 234
historical cones. *See* cone
*History of the Decline and Fall of the
    Roman Empire, The* (Gibbon),
    226, 295, 298, 301, 305
Hobbes, Thomas, 173, 315
Hodos Chamelionis (Chameliontos),
    liv, 218
Hodos Chameliontos (*See also* Yeats,
    W. B., *The Trembling of the
    Veil*), xxxvi, 173, 316
Holy Sepulchre, lx, 225, 300
Homer, 113, 151, 254, 291, 293;
    Iliad, The, 273; *Odyssey, The*,
    273
Hommel, Fritz, 122, 124, 278
Honnecourt, Villard de, 164, 307
Hood, Connie, 332
Hood, Walter Kelly, xlix, 288, 322,
    324
Horace (Quintus Horatius Flaccus),
    259; *Odes*, 262
horoscope, 71, 88, 89, 94, 233, 254,
    274
Horton, W. T. (William Thomas),
    xxx, 214, 218, 259, 337,
    338; *Way of the Soul, The*,
    226
"Hugh Selwyn Mauberley" (Pound),
    258
Hugo, Victor, 249, 264; *Toilers of the
    Sea, The*, 248

Hunchback, 8, 29, 53, 89, 90, 93,
    251
Husk. *See* Four Principles
"Hymn of the Soul" (Bardesanes),
    194, 329

Iconoclasm, 160–161, 303–304
Idiot, The (Dostoyevsky), 74, 246,
    247, 259
"Il Penseroso" (Milton), 230
Iliad, The (Homer), 273
Image, 15, 16, 18, 23, 24, 27, 36, 37,
    41, 46, 47, 49, 52, 54, 58, 60,
    63, 64, 67, 69, 71, 72, 166
Imaginary Conversations (Landor),
    238, 243
Imitation of Christ, The, 18, 237
India, 157, 217, 290, 338
Initiatory Moment, 140, 220. *See
    also* Moments of Crisis
Ireland, xxviii, lxii, 215, 223, 230,
    248, 285, 293, 304, 308, 319,
    338
Isis Unveiled (Blavatsky), 240
Italy, xxxix, xliv, 17, 124, 171, 221,
    243, 296, 303, 305, 306, 308,
    311

Jacquiot, Ponce, 254
Jaffer (vizir), 98, 268
Jeffares, A. Norman, 221, 238, 301
Jeremias, Alfred, 122, 278, 279
Jerusalem, 77, 225, 300, 302
Jerusalem (Blake), 260, 261, 331
Joan of Arc, 175
John, Augustus, 248
John, Saint, 133, 286
Johnson, Lionel, 222, 263; "Dark
    Angel, The," 325
Johnson, Samuel, 171, 246, 259, 313
Jonson, Ben, 72, 258
Jourdain, Eleanor Frances, 286, 287
Joyce, James, xliv, 175, 318, 319;
    Finnegans Wake, 319; *Ulysses*,
    175, 217, 318, 319
Judas, 90, 247, 264, 265, 298, 299
Judwalis, xxxi, xliii, lx, 11, 61, 202,
    233, 268, 322
Julius Caesar (Shakespeare), 286
Julius II (pope), 167, 311, 312
Justinian (Flavius Petrus Sabbatius Jus-
    tinianus), 158, 160, 302, 303

Kabbalah Unveiled, The (Mathers, M.), 217
Kant, Immanuel, 269
Keats, John, 56, 58, 222, 250, 251, 315; *Endymion,* 243; "Ode to a Nightingale," 251
Kells, Book of, 310
Kelly, Edward, lix, 223, 224, 336
Kepler, Johannes, 125, 282
Key to Theosophy (Blavatsky), 326
King Lear (Shakespeare), 266
Kircher, Athanasius, 234
Kirk, Robert, 288
Kiss of Death, 199, 333
Kiss of Life, 199, 332, 333
Knot of Destiny, 193
Knot of Fate, 193
Kusta ben Luka (Qusta ibn Luqa), xi, xxxi, xlvii, lxi, 10, 97, 196, 215, 226, 227, 233, 252, 266, 334; wife of, 11, 233, 267, 268, 334, 335
Kyd, Thomas; *Spanish Tragedy, The,* 257

L'annonce faite à Marie (Claudel), 319
L'Otage (Claudel), 175
"La Spirale" (Flaubert), 103
Lamarck, Jean-Baptiste, 73, 76, 259
Landor, Walter Savage, xxxii, 18, 37, 65, 78, 238, 254, 256, 260; "Hamadryad, The," 243; *Hellenics,* 243; *Imaginary Conversations,* 238, 243
Lane, Hugh, 325
Lane, John, 216
Laurie, Joan Werner, 217
Laurie, T. Werner, xxi, xxii, xxiv, xxxvi–xxxix, xli, xlii, xlvii, xlix, 213, 216, 217, 229
Law, William, 269
Lazarus, 155, 156
Leaves of Grass (Whitman), 245
Leo Africanus (Al Hassan Ibn-Muhammed al-Wezar Al-Fasi), xxx, 330
Leonardo da Vinci, 133, 168, 169, 286
Lévi, Eliphas, xxix
Lewis, Wyndham, 174, 247, 248, 318

Lives of Alchemystical Philosophers (Waite), 273
Locke, Amy Audrey, lv, 218, 338
Lodge, Sir Oliver, 331, 332; *Raymond,* 198, 331, 332
Loins, 149. *See also* Head, Heart, Loins, and Fall
London, England, xl, liii, lxii, lxiv, 214, 217, 222, 227
Lonely Tower, The (Palmer), 230
"Love's Nocturne" (Rossetti), 66, 256
Loyola, Ignatius, 263
lunar months, lxiv, 114, 115, 117, 120, 132, 138, 276, 285
Luther, Martin, 86, 88, 263
Lyster, T. W. (Thomas W.), 304
Lyttelton, Lady Edith, xxx

Macbeth (Shakespeare), 262
Machiavelli, Niccolò, 126, 282; *Discourses,* 282
MacKenna, Stephen, 273, 290
MacLeod, Fiona [William Sharp], xxix
Macpherson, James, xxix, 42, 43, 246
Macrobius, Ambrosius Theodosius, 123–125, 132, 280; *Commentary on* Somnium Scipionis, 279, 280
"Maeterlinck as a Mystic" (Symons), 265
Magee, W. K. (William Kirkpatrick) [John Eglinton], 304
Mahabharata, 265
Mahaffy, J. P. (John Pentland); *Descartes,* 268
Mannin, Ethel, 240, 250
Mantegna, Andrea, 168, 312
Marble Faun, The (Hawthorne), 243
Marius the Epicurean (Pater), 231
Marlowe, Christopher, 248
Marriage of Heaven and Hell, The (Blake), 265, 269
Marx, Karl, 79, 260
Masaccio (Tommaso di Ser Giovanni di Mone Cassai), 166, 168, 309, 310, 312
Mask. *See* Four Faculties
Mathers, Edward Powys, 249; *Book of the Thousand Nights and One Night, The (Arabian Nights),* lvi, 163, 226, 306

Mathers, Moina Bergson ("Vestigia"), xl–xlii, liii, 41, 217, 320, 337
Mathers, S. L. (formerly Samuel Liddell) MacGregor, xxix, 210, 217, 219, 222, 266, 337, 338; *Kabbalah Unveiled, The,* 217
Mayor, Joseph B., et al., 281; *Virgil's Messianic Eclogue: Its Meaning, Occasion, & Sources,* 281
Mead, G. R. S., xxix
Mecca, lx, 225
Meditation (Awakening of the Spirits), 184–185, 186. See also After Life States
Memoirs of Augustus, 125, 281
"Mental Traveller, The" (Blake), 107, 242, 271, 272, 325
Meredith, George, 258
Mesopotamia, xxxv, lxiii, 223, 228, 296
Messiah, 252, 283, 297, 306. See also Avatar
Meštrović, Ivan, 174, 318
Michelangelo Buonarroti, 167, 169, 261, 310, 312, 314
Middleton, Thomas, 255
Milbank, Ralph, Earl of Lovelace, 257
Mill, John Stuart, 173, 316
Millais, Sir John Everett, 222
Milles, Carl, 174, 318
Milton, John, 3, 121, 170, 171, 176, 207, 230, 259, 277, 278, 312, 320; *Doctrine and Discipline of Divorce, The,* 231; "Il Penseroso," 230; "On the Morning of Christ's Nativity," 170, 312; *Paradise Lost,* 121, 277; *Shorter Poems of John Milton, The,* 230
Milton: Man and Thinker (Saurat), 277
Mirandola, Pico della, xxix, 215
Moberly, Charlotte Anne Elizabeth, 286, 287
Moments of Crisis: Critical Moment, 140, 220, 247; Beatific Vision, xliii, lv, 140, 220, 289; Initiatory Moment, 140, 220; OM, 220

monophysitism, 160, 304
Monreale, Sicily, 163, 306
Mont-Saint-Michel and Chartres (Adams), 308
Mont-Saint-Michel, France, 307, 308
Montaigne, Michel de, 256
Monticelli, Adolphe Joseph Thomas, 58, 252
Moore, George, 73, 216, 259
Moore, T. Sturge, 319; *Art and Life,* 260, 268; *Danae: A Poem,* 315
Moreau, Gustave, 88, 263
Morley, John, 49, 249
Morris, William, 78, 205, 222, 240, 243, 244, 260, 307, 336; *Collected Works of William Morris, The,* 240; *Sundering Flood, The,* 325, 336; *Water of the Wondrous Isles, The,* 37, 39, 243, 244; *Well at the World's End, The,* 336
Moses, 49, 132, 231, 249
Moses, William Stainton, xxix, 214, 330
Muhammad, 225, 233
Muqtadir, al- (caliph), 232, 233
Murray, Sir James Augustus Henry, 13, 14, 234
Mussolini, Benito, xliv
Myers, Frederic W. H., 259, 322, 325
Myron of Eleutherai, 167, 310
Mystère de la charité de Jeanne d'Arc, Le (Péguy), 319

Naturales Quaestiones (Seneca), 279, 282
Neoplatonism, xxix, 239, 273, 279, 300, 304, 311
Nero, Claudius Caesar Augustus Germanicus, 90, 264
Newman, John Henry Cardinal, 86–88, 263
Newton, Sir Isaac, 173, 268, 316
Nietzsche, Friedrich, 4, 52, 142, 173, 176, 221, 231, 250, 290, 315, 316, 320
Nō drama (Japan), xl, 236, 324

O'Connell, Daniel, 261
O'Shea, Katherine (Mrs. Charles Stewart Parnell), 49, 248, 249, 263

objective man, 239
Objectivity, 13, 29, 83
"Ode to a Nightingale" (Keats),
    251
"Ode to the West Wind" (Shelley),
    66, 256
Odes (Horace), 262
Odyssey, The (Homer), 273
On Life after Death (Fechner), 288,
    322, 324, 325
On the Cave of Nymphs (Taylor),
    311
"On the Genius of Socrates"
    (Plutarch), 239
"On the Morning of Christ's Nativ-
    ity" (Milton), 170, 312
Origen (Oregenes Adamantius),
    157, 300
Outline of History, The (Wells),
    295
Oxford, England, xxxv, 136, 211,
    219, 263, 286, 287, 338

Palmer, Samuel, 3, 230, 279; *Lonely
    Tower, The,* 230
Paracelsus (Browning), 244
Paracelsus (Theophrastus Bombastus
    von Hohenheim), 60, 244,
    253, 269
Paradise Lost (Milton), 121, 277
Paradiso (Dante), 63, 245, 255
Paris, France, liii, lix, 152, 176, 217,
    251, 277, 286, 291
Parmenides (Plato), 267, 268
Parmenides of Elea, 97, 102,
    106–108, 267, 271, 272
Parnell, Charles Stewart, 47, 49, 85,
    248, 249, 263
Parnell, Mrs. Charles Stewart (*née*
    Katherine O'Shea), 49, 248,
    249, 263
Pascal, Blaise, 91, 265
Passionate Body. *See* Four Principles
Passivalli, Capuchin Archbishop
    (Capuchin Luigi Puecher-
    Passivalli), lxii, 227, 228
Pater, Walter, 4, 230, 231, 249, 299;
    Marius the Epicurean, 231;
    Renaissance, The, 230, 299;
    "Romanticism," 249
Patmore, Coventry, 173, 176, 286,
    315, 320

Pattinson, Thomas Henry, 218
"Pauline" (Browning), 244
Pausanias, 152, 291, 293, 295
Péguy, Charles, 175, 319; *Mystère de
    la charité de Jeanne d'Arc, Le,*
    319
Percy, Thomas, 309; *Reliques of
    Ancient English Poetry,* 309,
    325
Pericles, 157
Persia, 97, 127, 128, 142, 152, 160,
    228, 233, 273, 289, 290,
    294–296, 304
Personality of Fate, 238. *See also*
    Body of Fate; Four Faculties
Peter, Saint, 25, 157, 160, 166, 170,
    240, 305, 313
Petrie, W. M. Flinders, 291;
    *Revolutions of Civilisation,
    The,* 282
Phaedo (Plato), 239, 286, 296
phantasmagoria, xxii, xxiii, xxxiv,
    35, 165, 187, 223, 309, 324.
    See also After Life States
Phidias, 152, 154, 160, 167, 293,
    294, 298, 303, 310
Phœnix, lxiv, 229
Pickwick Papers, The (Dickens), 172,
    315
Pippa Passes (Browning), 244
Pirandello, Luigi, xliv, 175, 318, 319;
    Henry IV, 175, 318
Plato, xxix, 30, 121, 123, 125,
    126, 153, 154, 162, 230,
    231, 239, 258, 265, 268,
    276, 277, 295, 296, 306,
    310; *Parmenides,* 267, 268;
    Phaedo, 239, 286, 296;
    Republic, 121, 122, 126,
    152, 239, 277, 279, 294;
    Symposium, 239, 255, 272,
    277, 333; *Timaeus,* 121, 122,
    239, 277, 279, 280
Platonism, xxxviii, liii, 3, 54, 121,
    128, 168, 188, 208, 230, 239,
    276, 295, 310
Playboy of the Western World, The
    (Synge), 261
Plotinus, xxix, 109, 142, 143, 157,
    158, 177, 187, 239, 273, 290,
    300, 320, 325; *Enneads,* 273,
    290, 325, 334

Plunket, Emmeline M.; *Ancient Calendars and Constellations*, 127, 279, 283
Plutarch (Lucius Mestrius Plutarchus), 124, 239, 256, 281, 282; "On the Genius of Socrates," 239
Poetical Works of Robert Browning, The (Browning), 244
Poincaré, Jules Henri, 128, 284, 316
Pollexfen, G. T., 279, 280
Pollio, 124
Pope, Alexander, 171, 313
Porphyry, 168, 300, 311, 320
Porte de l'enfer (Rodin), 318
Possessed, The (Dostoyevsky), 246
Pound, Dorothy (*née* Shakespear), xxxix, 221, 306
Pound, Ezra, xxxiii, xxxix, xliv, 174, 175, 221, 227, 230, 241, 250, 306, 318, 324; "Brancusi," 318; "Hugh Selwyn Mauberley," 258
Pre-Raphaelitism, lvii, 222, 251, 293, 310
"Prince Athanase: A Fragment" (Shelley), 230, 254, 255
Principia, The (Swedenborg), 103, 268
Principles. *See* Four Principles
Prometheus Unbound (Shelley), 65, 256
Ptolemy (Claudius Ptolemaeus), xxix, 276
Punch-and-Judy Shows, 97, 245
Pusey, Edward Bouverie, 87, 263

Queen Mab; A Philosophical Poem (Shelley), 254, 262
Quercia, Jacopo della, 167, 310
Quinn, John, xxxii, 230

Rabelais, François, 60, 61, 169, 253
Radcliffe, Elizabeth [ER], xxix, 287, 335
Raftery, Anthony (Antoine Ó Raifteiri), 85, 262
Rape of Lucrece, The (Shakespeare), 257
Raphael Sanzio, 151, 167, 169, 222, 293, 310, 312, 314

Rashid, Harun al- (caliph), lxi, 10, 97, 163, 226, 233, 268
Raymond (Lodge), 198, 331, 332
Record, xxviii, 183–185, 188, 189, 191, 202, 205, 206, 336
Recurrence, 173, 305
Regardie, Israel, 218, 269
Reinach, Salomon, 125, 282
Reliques of Ancient English Poetry (Percy), 309, 325
Rembrandt van Rijn, 62, 80–83, 88, 248, 261; *Descent from the Cross*, 261; *Anatomy Lesson of Dr. Nicholas Tulp, The*, 261
Renaissance, 152, 160, 167, 171, 172, 175, 230, 251, 303, 310–312, 321
Renaissance, The (Pater), 230, 299
Republic (Plato), 121, 122, 126, 152, 239, 277, 279, 294
Return, 185, 186, 189, 191, 197, 198, 324, 327. *See also* After Life States
Revolutions of Civilisation, The (Petrie), 282
Reynolds, Sir Joshua, 172, 314; *Discourses*, 314
Rhymers Club, 216–217, 251
Rhys, Sir John, 234, 285, 337
Ricard, Louis Gustave, 172, 314
Richard III (Shakespeare), 248, 264
Richardson, Samuel, 173, 314, 315
Ricketts, Charles, 172, 314, 315
Robartes, Michael xxiii, xxx, xxxii, xxxv, xxxviii, lvii, lviii, lxiii, 3–8, 10, 64, 194, 196, 202, 203, 216, 221–224, 226, 227, 229, 231, 233, 248, 250–253, 258, 259, 268, 334
Roberts, Captain, 222
Robespierre, Maximilien François Marie Isidore de, 18, 238, 250
Rodin, Auguste, 57, 174, 251, 318; *Eternal Idol, The*, 57; *Porte de l'enfer*, 318
Roman Sculpture from Augustus to Constantine (Strong), 299
"Romanticism" (Pater), 249
Rome, Italy, lix, 117, 122, 124, 125, 127, 152, 153, 156, 157, 159, 169, 170, 172, 221, 241, 242,

258, 264, 280–282, 292, 296, 300, 303, 310, 314
Romulus, 123, 124, 280
Rosicrucianism, xxix, 218, 221, 255, 269, 274
Ross, Sir Edward Denison, xxxi, 32, 57, 214, 225, 226
Rossetti, Dante Gabriel, 57, 222, 251, 254; "Love's Nocturne," 66, 256
Rousseau, Jean Jacques, 171, 313
Russell, George William [Æ], xxi, 86, 88, 221, 222, 225, 263, 290

Saccas, Ammonius, 157, 300
Saddlemyer, Ann, xxv, 230
Sage, 37, 45, 76, 120, 137, 154, 169, 185, 253, 263. See also Teacher; Victim
Saint, 8, 20, 21, 27, 30, 55, 91, 159, 162, 177, 265
Salome, 154, 297
sanctity, lx, 30, 55, 92, 163, 171, 264, 265, 313
Sappho, 97, 267
Satan, 159, 253. See also Devil
Saurat, Denis; Milton: Man and Thinker, 277
Savonarola, Girolamo, 50, 125, 168, 250, 282
"Scholar-Gypsy, The" (Arnold), 225
Schopenhauer, Arthur, 250
Scopas, 154, 298
Secret Commonwealth of Elves, Fauna, and Fairies (Kirk), 288
Secret Doctrine, The (Blavatsky), 239, 240
Seneca, Lucius Annaeus (Seneca the Younger); Naturales Quaestiones, 279, 282
Sequence, 162, 305, 335
Servius (Maurus Servius Honoratus), 125, 281
"Several Questions Answered" (Blake), 243
sexual love, lv, 25, 52, 139, 288
Shakespear, Olivia, xxi, xxxvi, 37, 220, 236, 246, 332
Shakespeare, William, 70, 72, 74, 81, 93, 169, 207, 222, 238, 244, 257, 258, 262; As You Like It,

244; Hamlet, 139, 197, 288; Julius Caesar, 286; King Lear, 266; Macbeth, 262; Rape of Lucrece, The, 257; Richard III, 248, 264
Shakespere, Dorothy (Pound), 306
Sharp, William [Fiona MacLeod], xxix
Shaw, George Bernard, 73, 76, 257, 259
Shelley, Percy Bysshe, 3, 37, 63–65, 82, 204, 220, 230, 243, 251, 254–256, 262; Alastor; or the Spirit of Solitude, 243, 262; Cenci, The, 64, 256; Hellas, 243, 254, 255, 335; "Ode to the West Wind," 66, 256; "Prince Athanase: A Fragment," 230, 254, 255; Prometheus Unbound, 65, 256; Queen Mab; A Philosophical Poem, 254, 262
Shiftings, 130, 189–193, 195, 324, 327. See also After Life States
Shorter Poems of John Milton, The (Milton), 230
Sicily, 159, 163, 221, 243, 296, 303, 306
Sinai, Mount, 5, 231, 249
Sinbad the Sailor and Other Stories, 215
Sinnett, A. P. (Alfred Percy), 326
Sitwell, Edith, 228
Sleep of King Arthur in Avalon, The (Burne-Jones), 57, 251
Sleeping Spirit, 205
Sleeping State, 185, 187, 324. See also After Life States
Smith, Kirby Flower, 124, 283
Society for Psychical Research, xxix, 259, 287, 322, 331, 336
Socrates, 91, 132, 133, 204, 265, 267, 268, 285, 286, 296, 300, 336
solar month, lxiv, 115, 117, 119, 124, 126, 127, 137
Somnium Scipionis (Cicero), 122, 279, 280
"Song of Myself" (Whitman), 245
Songs of Experience (Blake), 320
Songs of Innocence (Blake), 319
Sophia, Saint, 158, 160, 303

Sophocles, 152, 169, 293
Sordello (Browning), 244
Soter, Ptolemy I, 127, 283
Southwell, Robert, 253; "Burning Babe, The," 62, 253
Spain, Nancy Brooker, 373
Spanish Tragedy, The (Kyd), 257
Speculum Angelorum et Hominum (Giraldus), xxiv, xxxi, xxxii, xxxiv, xxxv, lix–lxi, 61, 213, 216, 224
Spencer, Herbert, 75, 79, 173, 259, 315
Spengler, Oswald, 302
"Sphinx, The" (Wilde), 315
Spinoza, Baruch de, 50, 249, 250
Spirit. *See* Four Principles
Spiritual Diary, The (Swedenborg), 103, 108, 219, 268, 272
States before Birth: Foreknowing, 131, 195; Going Forth, 131, 197. *See also* After Life States
Stein, Gertrude: *Autobiography of Alice B. Toklas, The*, 217
Stendhal, Henri Beyle, 77, 260
Stephens, James, 253
Stobaeus, Joannes, 279
Stoicism, 153–155, 283, 296
Stothhard, Thomas, 61
"Strayed Reveller, The" (Arnold), 243
Strindberg, August, 200, 334; *There are Crimes and Crimes*, 200
Strong, Eugénie Sellers, 298; *Apotheosis and After Life*, 296, 297; *Roman Sculpture from Augustus to Constantine*, 299
Strzygowski, Josef, 141, 160, 198, 289, 303, 305, 331
Stuart, Francis, 338
Sturm, Frank Pearce, xxiv, xlvii, 216, 224, 226, 235, 245, 272, 274, 280, 329
subjective man, 13, 322
Subjectivity, 13, 29, 52, 54
Sulla, Lucius Cornelius, 125, 281, 282
Summum Bonum, liv, 218
Sundering Flood, The (Morris), 325, 336
swan, xxii, 238, 278

Swedenborg, Emanuel, xxix, lv, 75, 76, 77, 103, 108, 142, 219, 259, 260, 268, 269, 277, 326; *Principia, The*, 103, 268; *Spiritual Diary, The*, 103, 108, 219, 268, 272
Symbolist Movement in Literature, The (Symons), 93
Symons, Arthur, 174, 257, 265, 318; "Maeterlinck as a Mystic," 265; *Symbolist Movement in Literature, The*, 93
Symposium (Plato), 239, 255, 272, 277, 333
Synge, John Millington, 80–83, 88, 261; *Deirdre of the Sorrows*, 261; *Playboy of the Western World, The*, 261
Syracuse, xli, 207, 337

Tacitus, Publius (Gaius) Cornelius, 123, 280; *De claris oratoribus dialogus*, 280
Tagore, Rabindranath, 265; *Gitanjali*, 265
Tarot, xxix, 225, 233, 240, 266, 321
Taylor, Thomas, 268, 270, 273, 301, 311, 320; *On the Cave of Nymphs*, 311
Teacher, 185, 191, 247, 252, 263, 324. *See also* Sage; Victim
Teaching Spirits, 186, 188, 198
Temptation of Saint Anthony, The (Flaubert), 77, 259, 316
Tennyson, Alfred, Lord, 226, 250, 251, 315
Thebaid, 154, 200, 297, 298
Theocritus, 37, 243
theosophy, xxix, 217, 223, 269, 335
There are Crimes and Crimes (Strindberg), 200
Thirteenth Cycle, 138, 182, 191
Thomas à Kempis; *Imitation of Christ, The*, 18, 237
Thomas Aquinas, Saint, 41, 165, 166, 245, 253
Thomas of Dorlowicz. *See* communicators
Thoreau, Henry David; *Walden*, 245
Three Books of Occult Philosophy or Magic (Agrippa), 182, 321

Three Musketeers, The (Dumas),
246
Tiberius (Tiberius Julius Caesar
Augustus), lvi, 221
Timaeus (Plato), 121, 122, 239, 277,
279, 280
Time, 15, 100, 128
Tinctures, 14–18, 20–22, 34, 35, 39,
44–46, 51, 55, 57, 59, 66, 68,
69, 71, 73, 80, 83, 112, 113,
120, 133, 136, 171, 199, 235,
257, 276, 303
Titian (Tiziano Vecellio), 152, 169,
170, 256, 294
Toilers of the Sea, The (Hugo), 248
Tolstoy, Leo, 173, 315; *War and
Peace,* 173, 316
Toomey, Deirdre, xlix, 273
Toynbee, Arnold J., 292
*Treatise Concerning the Principles
of Human Knowledge, A*
(Berkeley), 207, 284

Ulysses (Joyce), 175, 217, 318,
319
Unicorn, 225, 232
Unity of Being, 24, 26, 30, 51, 52,
54, 63, 65, 68–71, 78, 79,
134, 167, 190, 237, 241, 251,
276, 311, 327
Unity with God, 27, 133
Urbino, Italy, 37, 243, 244

van Dyck, Sir Anthony, 170, 313
Vanity of Dogmatizing, The
(Glanvill), 225
Varro, Marcus Terentius, 280
Velázquez, Diego, 248, 258
Venice, Italy, 167, 169, 243, 303,
311
Verhaeren, Emile, 172, 314
Verlaine, Paul, 171, 251, 313
"Vestigia" [Moina Bergson Mathers],
xl–xlii, liii, 41, 217, 320, 337
Victim, 45, 76, 120, 132, 137, 185,
188, 205, 247, 252, 263, 324,
328. *See also* Sage; Teacher
victimage, 76, 91, 200, 205, 328
Victoria of Great Britain and Ireland
(queen), 83, 85, 86, 262
Villiers de l'Isle Adam, Phillippe-
Auguste, 253; *Axël,* 253

Villon, François, 166, 256, 309, 310
Virgil (Publius Vergilius Maro), 122,
124–127, 250, 281–282;
Fourth Eclogue ("*Messianic
Eclogue*"), 122, 123, 125,
279
*Virgil's Messianic Eclogue: Its
Meaning, Occasion, & Sources*
(Mayor et al.), 281
Vision of Evil, 65, 245
Vision of the Blood Kindred, 183,
184, 196, 322, 330. *See also*
After Life States
*Visions and Beliefs in the West of
Ireland* (Gregory), xxx, 239,
266, 288, 326, 330, 332
Visions of the Daughters of Albion
(Blake), 260
Vita Nuova (Dante), 241
Voltaire (François-Marie Arouet),
172, 314
von Stein, Charlotte, 257

Waite, A. E., xxix, 255; *Lives of
Alchemystical Philosophers,*
273
Waking Spirits, 205
Waking State, 185, 186, 188, 190,
191, 193, 198, 202, 203, 324.
See also After Life States
Walden (Thoreau), 245
Wallenstein, Albrecht von, 282
war, xlv, 5, 28–29, 43, 52, 97, 113,
150, 151, 174, 176, 199, 270,
290, 320; Franco-Prussian
War, 252; Irish Civil War,
xxxvi–vii, xl, 94, 266; Irish
War of Independence, xxviii;
Peasants' War, 263; Roman
Civil War, 125, 281; Thirty
Years' War, 282; Trojan War,
251, 264, 273, 291–292;
World War I, xxviii, 229,
317
War and Peace (Tolstoy), 173, 316
Waste Land, The (Eliot), 175, 318,
319
Water of the Wondrous Isles, The
(Morris), 37, 39, 243, 244
Watkins, Geoffrey N., 223
Watkins, John M., lix, 223
Watson, Sir William, 266

Watt, A. P., xxxix, xlii, 229
Watteau, Jean-Antoine, 171, 313
Watts, George Frederic, 256
Way of the Soul, The (Horton), 226
Way of the Soul between the Sun and the Moon (Kusta ben Luka), lx
Well at the World's End, The (Morris), 336
Wellesley, Dorothy, 323
Wells, H. G. (Herbert George), 73, 76, 83, 259, 262, 295; *Outline of History, The,* 295
Whitman, Walt, 41, 46, 71, 85, 86, 245, 256; "Brooklyn Bridge," 245; *Leaves of Grass,* 245; "Song of Myself," 245
Wicklow, Ireland (county), 82, 261
Wilde, Oscar, 68, 69, 216, 257, 259; "Sphinx, The," 315
Will. *See* Four Faculties
Williams, Charles, 228
Wisdom, Four Types, 30, 113, 140, 241
Wordsworth, William, 57, 58, 251, 252, 315

Xenaias, 160, 304

Yeats, Anne Butler, 332, 338
Yeats, Elizabeth Corbet (Lolly), 224, 319
Yeats, George (*née* Hyde Lees): and automatic writing or other methods, xxii–xxxi, xxxiii, 218–219, 237; as topic, 232–223, 256, 267, 294, 334, 336; as typist, secretary, or editor, xliii, 229, 270, 304; automatic script or other methods quoted, 213, 218, 225, 236, 245, 247–251, 255, 271, 275–276, 286, 291, 294, 301, 305, 309–310, 319, 321–323, 325–330, 332–334; life with WBY, 214, 221, 314, 338; knowledge and reading, xlvi, 234, 237, 239, 241, 244, 273, 278, 280, 297, 300, 318–319
Yeats, John Butler, 264
Yeats, Michael Butler, 332
Yeats, William Butler, xxi–xlvii, xlix, 213, 215–280, 282–304, 306–338; as character, xxxviii, lviii, lix, lxi–lxiv, 11, 64, 194
A Vision (1925): "Dance of the Four Royal Persons, The," xxxviii, 10; "Death, the Soul, and the Life after Death" (draft), xl, 267, 321; "Discoveries of Michael Robertes" (draft), xxxii, xxxiii, 229; "Dedication," xli, xlii, liii, 217, 243, 335; "Dove or Swan," xxxix, xli, xliv, xlv; "Gates of Pluto, The," xl; "Great Wheel, The," xxxiii, lv; "Great Wheel, The," xxxviii; "Introduction by Owen Aherne," xxxvi–xxxviii, xlii, lvii, 216, 229, 230, 322; "Michael Robertes and the Judwali Doctor" (draft), xl, 267, 321, 334; "Twenty-Eight Embodiments, The," xxxiii, xxxviii, xlviii, 231
A Vision (1937): "Dove or Swan," 317; *Packet for Ezra Pound, A,* 302; *Stories of Michael Robertes and his Friends,* 232
edited works: *Fairy and Folk Tales of the Irish Peasantry,* 331; *Works of William Blake, The,* 236, 272
fiction: "Adoration of the Magi, The," xxii, 221–222, 227, 231; "Rosa Alchemica," xxii, lix, 221–223; *Secret Rose, The,* xxii, xxix, 223; "Tables of the Law, The," xxii, lxii, 221, 222, 227
nonfiction prose: "Bishop Berkeley," 244, 337; "Bounty of Sweden, The," xlii, 244, 261; *Celtic Twilight, The,* 306; "Certain Noble Plays of Japan," 294; "Edmund Spenser," 245; "Four Years," xxxiv–xxxvi, 258; "Friends of the People of Faery, The," 219; "Happiest of the Poets, The," 243; "Hodos Chameliontos," xxxvi;

"Ireland after Parnell,"
xxxvi, 245; "Irish Dramatic
Movement, The," xl; "J. M.
Synge and the Ireland of his
Time," 231; "Leo Africanus,"
239; "Magic," 225; "Modern
Poetry: A Broadcast," 228;
"More Memories," xxxvi;
Mythologies, xlix; *On the
Boiler*, 253, 284, 312;
"People's Theatre, A," 237,
308; *Per Amica Silentia Lunae*,
xxx, 214, 219, 231, 239, 247,
251, 253, 255, 258, 270, 288,
331; "Philosophy of Shelley's
Poetry, The," 311; *Plays and
Controversies*, 332; "Poet and
the Actress, The," xxx, 324;
"Preliminary Examination of
the Script of E[lizabeth]
R[adcliffe]," 335;
"Prometheus Unbound," 245;
"Swedenborg, Mediums, and
the Desolate Places," xxx,
239, 253, 321, 324, 331;
*Synge's Poems and
Translations*, 325; "Tragic
Generation, The," xxxvi;
Trembling of the Veil, The,
xxv, xxxiv–xxxvii, xxxix, xli,
173, 216, 218, 219, 316;
"Witches and Wizards and
Irish Folk-Lore," 326
plays: *At the Hawk's Well*, xxxvi;
Calvary, xxv, xxxvi, 225, 238,
247, 264, 277, 298; *Dreaming
of the Bones, The*, xxxiv,
xxxvi, 324; *Four Plays for
Dancers*, xxxv; *Hawk's Well,
The*, xxix; *Hour-Glass, The*,
200, 334; *King's Threshold,
The*, 233; *Only Jealousy of
Emer, The*, xxv, xxxii, xxxiv,
xxxvi, 332, 333; *Player
Queen, The*, xxxvii, 220, 225;
Plays for an Irish Theatre,
238; *Resurrection, The*, xlii,
221, 276, 301, 303, 320; *Two
Plays for Dancers*, xxxiv
poetry: "All Souls' Night," xxiv,
xxxv, xxxvi, lv, 208, 217, 286;
"Among School Children,"

277, 329; "Another Song of
a Fool," xxxiv, 289; "At
Algeciras—a Meditation upon
Death," 221; "Cat and the
Moon, The," xxxiii; *Cat and
the Moon and Certain Poems,
The*, xli, 266; *Collected
Edition of the Works*, xxxvii;
Collected Poems, The, 230,
337; "Coole and Ballylee,
1931," 262; "Demon and
Beast," 298; "Double Vision
of Michael Robartes, The,"
xxxiv, 223, 227, 230, 261,
289, 319, 331; "Easter, 1916,"
228; "Ego Dominus Tuus," lv,
251, 254; "Four Ages of Man,
The," 236; "Gift of Harun Al-
Raschid, The," xl–xli, 11, 12,
266; "He and She," 332;
"Hero, the Girl, and the Fool,
The," 321; "Image from a Past
Life, An," 334; "Lake Isle of
Innisfree, The," 245; "Lapis
Lazuli," 295, 299; *Later
Poems*, xxxvii, 217, 230;
"Leda and the Swan," xxv,
xxxix, 277, 290; "Long-legged
Fly," 311; "Magi, The," 242;
"Meditations in Time of Civil
War," xxxvii, xli, 291; *Michael
Robartes and the Dancer*, xxv,
xxxv, xliii, xlv, 214, 222, 223,
289; "Mohini Chatterjee,"
221; *Nine Poems*, xxxiii,
xxxiv; "Old Age of Queen
Maeve, The," 336; "Phases of
the Moon, The," xxxiv, lv, lxii,
217, 220, 223, 227, 229,
320; "Prayer for My Daughter,
A," 333; "Saint and the
Hunchback, The," xxxiv;
"Second Coming, The," xxv,
xliii, 277, 289, 292, 322;
Seven Poems and a Fragment,
xxxvi, 321; "Solomon and the
Witch," 252; "Solomon to
Sheba," xxxiii; "Statues, The,"
299; "Tom O'Roughley,"
xxxiii; "Towards Break of
Day," 289, 290; *Tower, The*,
xxv, 219, 267, 290, 321, 337;

poetry (*cont.*)
  "Tower, The," 273; "Two Songs
  from a Play," 279, 301; "Two
  Songs of a Fool," xxxiv;
  "Under Ben Bulben," 311,
  312; "Under the Round
  Tower," xxxiii, 293; "Upon a
  House Shaken by the Land

Agitation," 238; *Wild Swans
  at Coole, The,* xxxiv, 217, 222,
  229, 254; *Wind among the
  Reeds, The,* 221

Zeno of Elea, 267, 268
Zodiac, lx, 114, 120–123, 127, 224,
  273, 274, 276, 278, 283